AF371529

19 Key Essays on
**How Internet is
Changing our Lives**

CH@NGE

OpenMind   BBVA   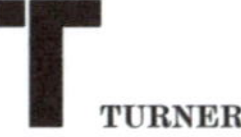 TURNER

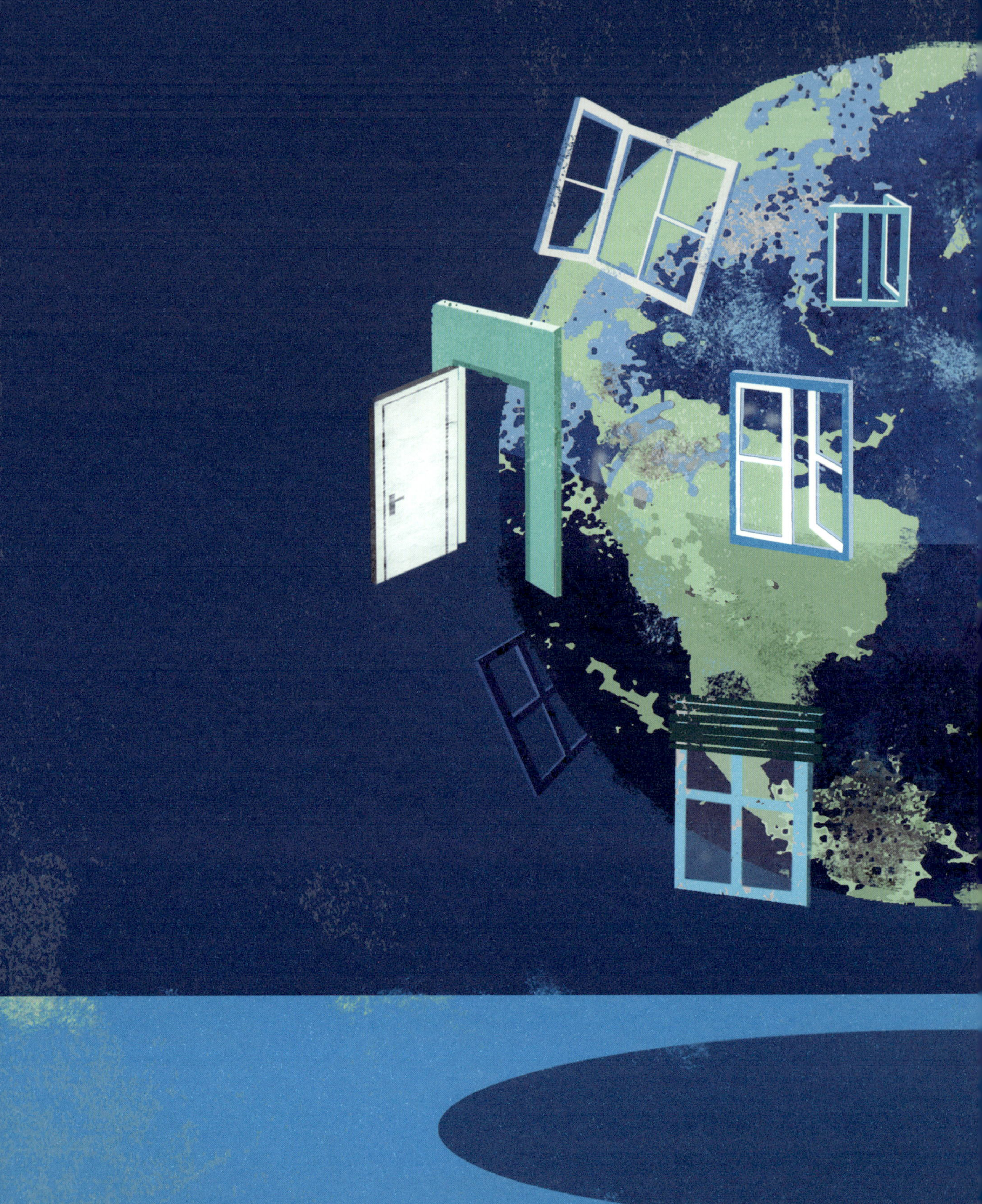

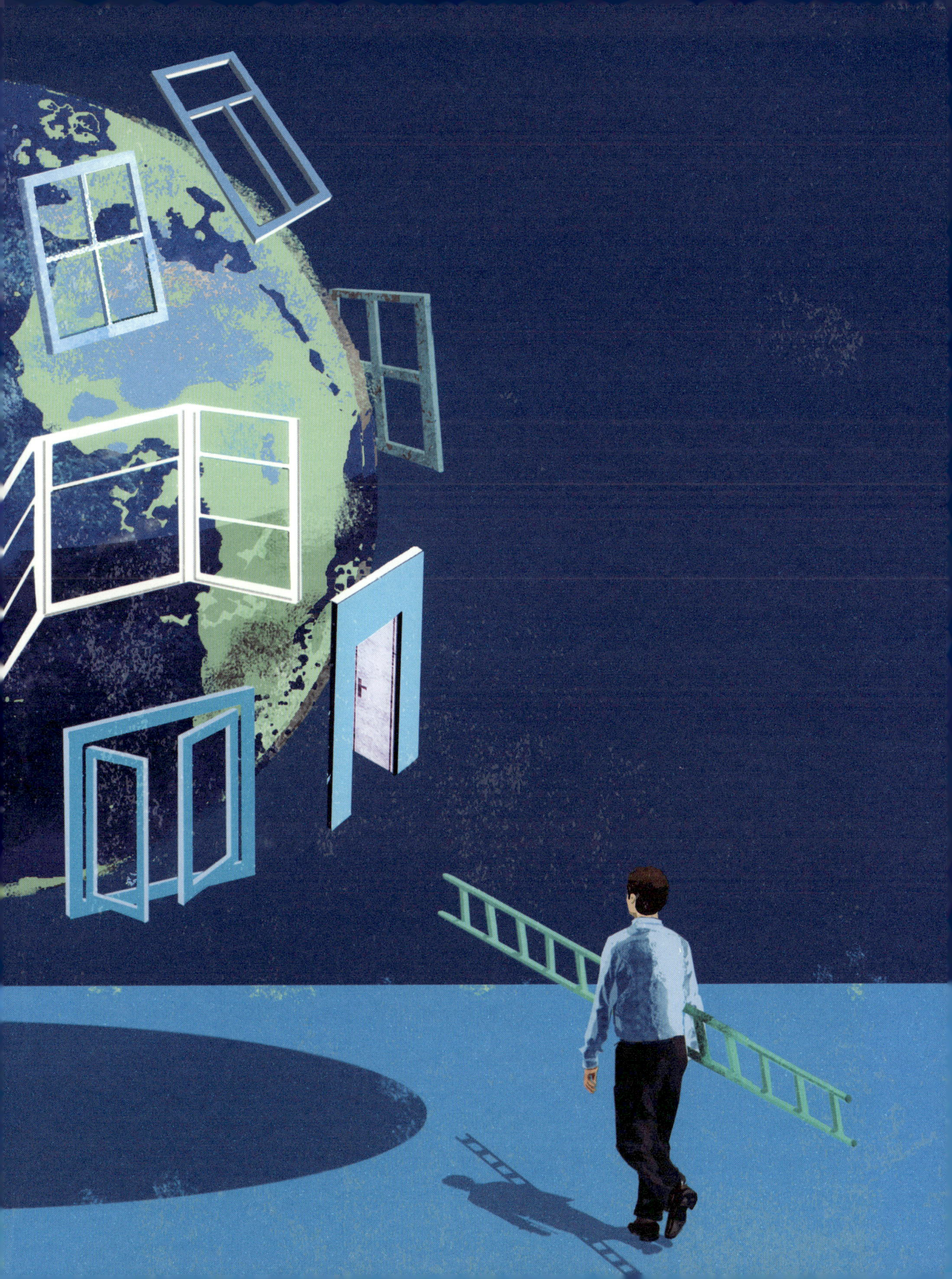

Illustration
Eva Vázquez

Knowledge Banking for a Hyperconnected Society

Francisco González

Chairman and CEO, BBVA

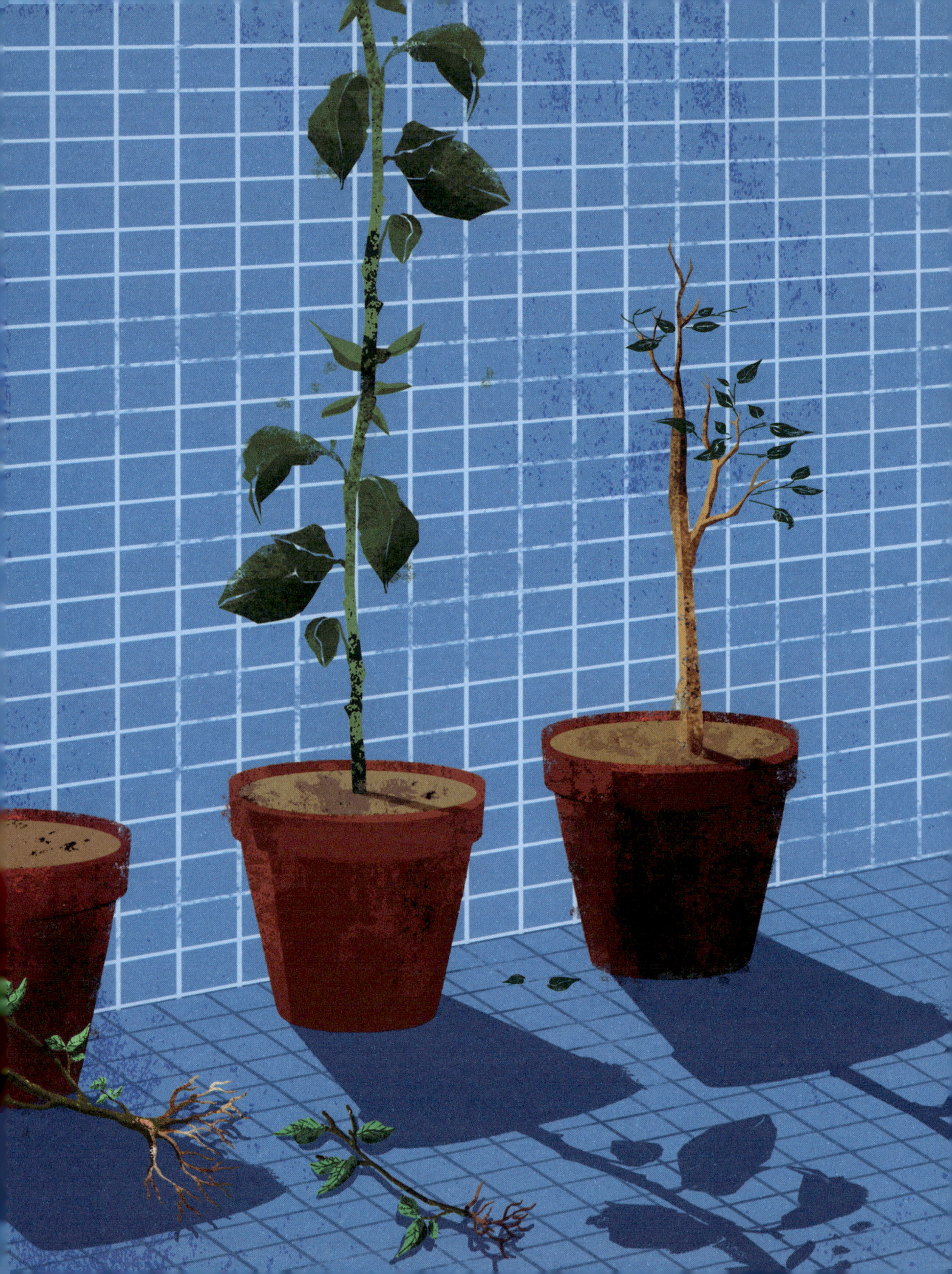

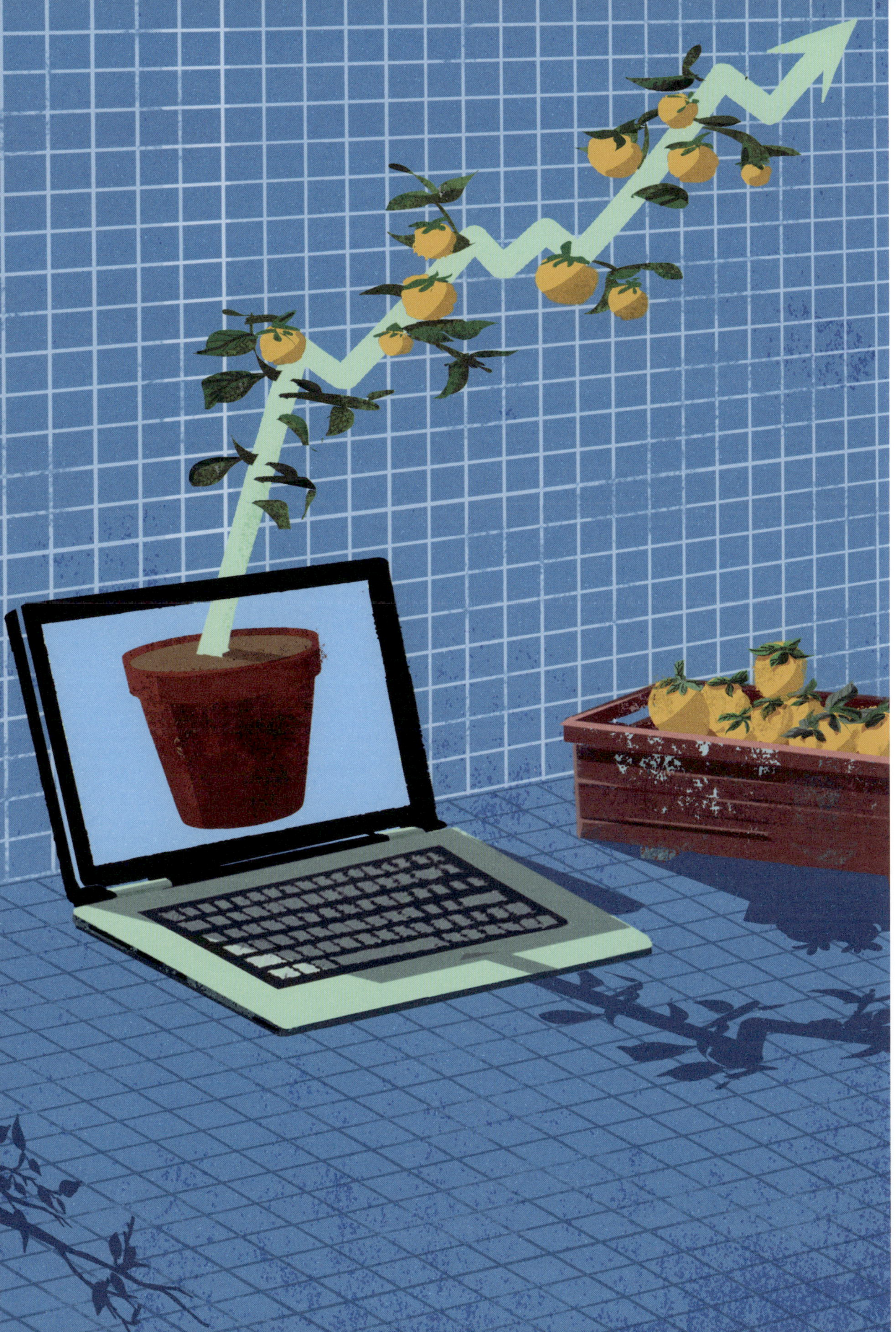

Francisco González

Francisco González
Chairman and CEO, BBVA

Knowledge Banking for a Hyperconnected Society

The Web as I envisaged it, we have not seen it yet. The future is still so much bigger than the past.

Tim Berners-Lee

This book, *Ch@nge: 19 Key Essays on How Internet Is Changing Our Lives*, is the sixth installment in BBVA's annual series devoted to the exploration of the most important issues of our time. We seek out the world's leading experts and ask them to use a straightforward approach and language accessible to laypeople to explore the best and most current knowledge on topics that matter to us all. Over these past few years, we have been incredibly fortunate to have presented the work of more than 130 authors at the forefront of their fields, authors who have enriched us with their contributions; they are the very essence of our project. I would like at this point to acknowledge all of our contributors and, in particular, those authors who in this year's issue are new to our community.

BBVA began this series in 2008 in conjunction with the launch of the Frontiers of Knowledge prizes awarded by the BBVA Foundation. In response to the outstanding reception to the first few books, in 2011 we created OpenMind, an online community dedicated to the dissemination of knowledge. OpenMind—which contains all our books to date—is a space for discovery, discussion, and the sharing of ideas in a multidisciplinary environment. Over the past few years, our community has expanded the content and broadened its audience in keeping with what has been its overriding objective from the outset: the sharing of knowledge to build a better future.

If I had to identify a single guiding principle for our book series, it would be the desire to understand the major forces that are shaping our world. In the course of this quest, we have published five successive essay collections that address the present frontiers of science, globalization, innovation, the ethical challenges of our time, and our vision of the future.

The Internet: The Engine of Change

This year, our chosen theme is the Internet, the single most powerful agent of change in recent history. In the words of Arthur C. Clarke, "Any sufficiently advanced technology is indistinguishable from magic." The rapid pace and reach of the changes wrought by the Internet indeed have a touch of magic about them.

As a tool available to a fairly wide public, the Internet is only twenty years old, but it is already the key catalyst of the most extensive and fastest technological revolution in history. It is the most extensive because over the past two decades its effects have touched practically every citizen in the world. And it is the fastest because its large-scale adoption is quicker than that of any earlier technology. To put this into perspective—it was 70 years after the invention of the airplane that 100 million people had traveled by air; it took 50 years after the invention of the telephone for 100 million people to use this form of communication. The 100-million user mark was achieved by PCs in 14 years, the Internet in 7. The cycles of adoption of Internet-related technologies are even shorter—Facebook reached 100 million users in 2 years.

It is impossible today to imagine the world without the Internet: it enables us to do things that only a few years ago would have been unthinkable, and reaches every facet of our lives.

Yet what makes the Internet even more amazing is that it is such a young technology—still developing, still rapidly changing. Everything we have seen so far is just the beginning. First, because Moore's Law still holds: processing power doubles every 18 months. Any iPhone today has approximately the same capacity as the largest supercomputer of the 1970s. The key difference is that a supercomputer cost $5 million in 1975 dollars, occupied a very large room, was completely disconnected from other devices, and its use was restricted to very few people for very limited purposes. In contrast, an iPhone costs less than $400 in today's money, we can carry it in our pocket, and we can connect it to millions of other devices for any number of purposes.

The increasing capacity of devices will continue, along with an exponential increase in the speed of data transfer. The global average data transfer speed is about 2 megabytes (MB) per second. But speeds of 100 petabytes (in other words, 100 billion MB per second) have already been achieved.

This means that 400 DVDs-worth of data could be transmitted every second. Over time, the cost of creating ultra-fast data transfer networks will gradually decrease. Soon any consumer will be able to download a high-definition movie within the space of a second. In parallel to this, technologies enabling mobile wireless Internet access at speeds comparable to broadband continue to advance.

This ties in with the second multiplier effect of the Internet's influence—increasing connectivity. Internet access has moved from personal computers to mobile phones, on the path toward what has been called *the Internet of Things*, in which myriad everyday objects will become capable of receiving, generating, and sending information. It is estimated that by 2015 there will be more than 200 billion devices connected to the Internet—four times more than in 2010. In only a few years, this will be the most complex structure ever created by humankind. There will be billions of nodes able to measure anything measurable, extracting and communicating any form of information; and this information will be used to monitor every aspect of the *real* world.

This entails the generation of an almost unimaginable volume of data, growing at an exponential rate. Just for us to get an idea, it is estimated that by 2003 humankind had generated 5 exabytes (5 trillion bytes) of information. Today, however, that figure is reached every two days, such that 90 percent of all available data has been generated in the past two years. And the volume of information generated is growing at a rate of 50 percent a year.

This vast wealth of data is potentially highly valuable, but only if the right systems are available to handle it—to capture, store, transfer, analyze, and visualize the information. This is the field of information and communications technology known as *Big Data*, which is fast becoming the vital key for the generation of useful knowledge. Big Data holds immense potential to raise productivity, enhance innovation, and, ultimately, improve the way we live.

Such huge volumes of data call for equally vast processing power. *Cloud computing* essentially consists of services involving a large number of computers connected over a network, such as the Internet, to provide the capacity for cheap, flexible access to powerful data storage, processing, and analysis capabilities.

As a result of the very speed at which the Internet has developed and the rapid pace of the changes it has brought about, we quite possibly still do not understand the most important and far-reaching implications, nor can we possibly anticipate the transformations the future has in store for us.

Eric Schmidt's famous quote—"The Internet is the first thing that humanity has built that humanity doesn't understand, the largest experiment in anarchy that we have ever had"—remains as true today as ever.

The perception of the immense potential of the Internet to change our lives, the difficulty of predicting how it will evolve, and its free, *anarchic*, barely controllable character, combine to produce both great hope and profound apprehension.

This hope and apprehension are visible in all spheres of human activity—society, politics, culture, and the economy. And changes at the aggregate (macro) level simply mirror the changes taking place at a far more granular and profound stratum. Preferences are shifting, as are people's daily habits—the way we work, relate to one another, learn, have fun... in short, the Internet is changing the way we live.

The Internet may even be changing the way our brains work, modifying the substrate of our memories and thoughts. In recent years, Nicholas Carr

(2008, 2010) has argued that the Internet impairs our cognitive abilities, particularly of concentration and abstraction. These claims have been hotly debated in academia. For instance, Steven Pinker (2010), the distinguished experimental psychologist and cognitive scientist, sharply disagrees with Carr. A survey conducted by the Pew Research Center (2010) found that close to 80 percent of experts thought the Internet had in fact increased human intelligence, against 15 percent believing the opposite. Since the human brain is a malleable organ, it may be the case that the Internet enhances certain faculties at the expense of others. It is indisputably true, however, that the Internet helps us store, manage, and retrieve knowledge—and this, whatever the effect may be on each individual mind, collectively makes us far more intelligent as a society, as a species.

Authors in various fields have pointed to the risks, both real and imagined, associated with the Internet. In the economic arena, there are fears that a *digital divide* will lead to increasing inequality between different industries and geographic regions, with some proving capable of taking advantage of the Internet's potential while others are left behind.

Socially, there is an increasing concern about, among other issues, the loss of direct human contact as a result of the overexposure to virtual relationships, with the potential consequence of the impoverishment of people's emotional lives as well as the loss of social cohesion. Moreover, the privacy of the individual will be at the mercy of political and economic groups capable of exercising some degree of control over the Internet.

In the political sphere, some are apprehensive that the issue of control over the network and the data it supports will harm the very fabric of democracy by giving a powerful few the ability to manipulate public opinion; there is also concern that a proper balance be kept between protecting the public against cybercrime and cyber terrorism and respecting individual rights and liberties.

Yet it is perhaps in the field of culture where we hear the most voices alerting us to the dangers of the Internet, probably because culture and communications are the industries that have most been affected by the advent of the online world that has revolutionized paradigms entrenched for centuries—in many respects, since the invention of the printing press.

Over the past two decades, opinion leaders around the globe have heralded the *end of culture*. In the Spanish-speaking world, the ideas of the Nobel prize-winning author Mario Vargas Llosa (2012) have had a particular influence.

Of course, on the other hand there are any number of highly optimistic opinions of how the Internet is affecting us. I already mentioned Steven Pinker and the work being done by the Pew Research Center on the effects of Internet use on human intelligence. And many economists have pointed out the positive effects the Internet has on productivity, as well as its potential to stimulate the development of disadvantaged individuals and geographic regions. Examples include Brynjolfsson and McAfee (2011), Choi and Hoon Yi (2009), and Barro (2003). Yochai Benkler (2006)—a contributor to this book—points out the ways in which the Internet enables us to work together to improve the well-being of society at large. At any rate, the empirical evidence is overwhelming that the strong growth of many of the world's underdeveloped regions has been supported by the paradigm shifts brought about by the Internet's development. In the social and political realm, authorities such as Manuel Castells (2009)—also a contributor to this book—emphasize the opportunities provided by the Internet that allow us to become better informed, and to cooperate and coordinate with one another; in his view, these are factors that help raise the quality of democracy and strengthen bonds across society. And, in the cultural field, there are those—such as Lipovetsky and Serroy (2008)—who argue that we are moving toward a "world culture," which is more democratic, and less elitist, academic, and exclusive.

To form an opinion on these issues we should look at what the Internet can and cannot do for us.

The Internet was first conceived of—and primarily used—as a vast repository of information. But it has proved to be much more than this. It is a collaborative tool within everybody's grasp; and it is collaboration that has breathed life into the Internet's immense potential as a generator of knowledge and a driver of innovation. As Eric Schmidt has said, "None of us is as smart as all of us." The Internet has broadened the horizon of opportunity for billions of people, particularly in the least developed regions of the world, and has become vital to global prosperity and stability.

The Internet involves risks. Like any other powerful tool, it can be misused. And the truth is that the Internet is enormously powerful—we still don't even know what it can do, or how it will evolve. We don't know how to control it. We need to address the tough challenges the Internet poses, particularly in terms of governance, *ownership*, control, and allocation of *responsibilities*. In the words of Clay Shirky, one of the most influential thinkers working in the field of the Internet and social media:

> *The whole, "Is the Internet a good thing or a bad thing?" We're done with that. It's just a thing. How to maximize its civic value, its public good that's the really big challenge.*
>
> (Aitkenhead 2010)

Given the rise of all manner of literature about the Internet and its impact on every last corner of human life, we thought it would be useful to gain some perspective on these issues and the dizzyingly fast changes we are seeing by bringing together a collection of essays by undisputed experts, each in their field and each with their own particular approach.

In truth, the Internet has always had a presence in our books, simply because the Internet is ubiquitous in our times. Contemporary science, economics, society, politics, and culture cannot be understood without the Internet. I would, however, like to expressly cite three key essays—from our earlier books—that specifically concerned the Internet. Having stood the test of time, all three would perfectly complement the articles presented this year: Janet Abbate's "The Internet: Global Evolution and Challenges" (2008), Robert Schultz's "Ethics and the Internet" (2011), and Brian Kahin's "Knowledge Markets in Cyberspace?" (2009).

In this year's book—as in past editions—we are very fortunate to have with us some of the finest minds in their respective fields, to present to us in an accessible manner their thoughts on a wide spectrum of issues raised or prompted by the Internet. With the purpose of somehow ordering such diverse, interlocking, and interrelated contributions, we have classified the essays into four sections:

- The Future of the Internet
- Society, Community, Individuals

- The Economy, Business, and Work
- Communication and Culture

The first section seeks to predict where the Internet is going—or, what is almost the same thing, where it is taking us. In the first essay included in this section, *David Gelernter* argues that, since humans are better at handling information when it is arranged in a time-sequenced narrative, it is plausible that the Internet will evolve toward a system that organizes information not—as so far—on a spatial basis, but over time. This will cause the web as we know it to be replaced by a new form of "Cybersphere," a single data narrative flowing through time ("Worldstream").

The *Internet of Things* has for a long time been a buzzword without much of a real-world correlate. In his essay, *Juan Ignacio Vázquez* explains how hyperconnectivity is finally making the Internet of Things a reality; coupled with Big Data and computing, it will enable everyday objects to improve our lives.

One of the ongoing themes of this book is that Big Data is one of the central nodes in any discussion about the Internet—some have described it as "the database of human purpose." *Michael Nielsen* argues for the critical importance of powerful infrastructure providing freely accessible data, built and managed by nonprofits, as platforms for experiment, discovery, and the creation of new and better ways of life.

One of the crucial aspects of the future of the Internet is security. *Mikko Hypponen* explores scenarios for an increasingly sophisticated Internet that is open to attack; effective oversight by governments is accordingly becoming an urgent and vital need.

The Internet has become an indispensable practical tool that we use for widely diverse purposes in our everyday lives. The second section looks at the ways in which the Internet is influencing society as a whole, different communities and social groups, as well as individuals.

A long-standing authority in this field, *Manuel Castells*, highlights how the Internet is expanding the freedom of and empowering users, and how it is nurturing the creation of online communities that are becoming increasingly influential and playing a significant role in many areas of the *real world*.

In his essay, *Evgeny Morozov* shows how difficult it is to evaluate the meaning and magnitude of the Internet's impact on politics. Internet-centrism is in fact confounding the debate; because the Internet is only a tool and the truly critical question is how the same networks and protocols are being used in different countries and from different positions toward conflicting objectives.

Federico Casalegno points out that one of the main problems with online connectivity is that it may discourage direct human contact. He accordingly presents a number of projects initiated by MIT in which technology is used to transfer knowledge, culture, history, and memory; by linking individuals to a wider community, the Internet becomes a tool that supports—rather than replaces—human interaction.

The next essay discusses the role of the Internet in education. *Neil Selwyn* explains how new learning tools, such as wiki tools, MOOCs, and School in the Cloud initiatives, are revolutionizing the field and testing the boundaries between teacher and student. Many of the difficulties in contemporary education have social and cultural roots, and technological solutions are ineffectual in the short term; however, the Internet is fostering a new *bottom-up* education culture that helps people break free from physical limitations.

Lucien Engelen uses real-life examples to explore the sweeping changes that the Internet is bringing about in healthcare. Patients are playing a far more active role in looking after their health, while Big Data is set to revolutionize clinical research.

The section ends with an article by *Zaryn Dentzel*, who focuses on social communication and underscores how the Internet and social media are changing both the way in which we interact with one another and the very structure of society.

The Internet has completely changed the rules for the whole economy, for industries, and for individual businesses. And the process of change is far from over. In fact, it is just getting started: having sparked a chain of innovations that overlap, combine, and feed off each other to bring about still more change, every time there is an alteration in the rules and the general environment, a fresh wave of innovations washes over us.

Dan Schiller opens the section on the Internet and the economy with an essay exploring how businesses in the United States have contributed to give the Internet its current form and the macroeconomic consequences of this reality. The U.S. captures more than 30 percent of the revenue and more than 40 percent of the net earnings generated by the Internet around the world. The U.S.'s privileged position in cyberspace is becoming a source of inter-governmental conflict centered on the structure and politics of the Internet.

According to *Yochai Benkler*, the Internet has given rise to new forms of production—he calls it "social production"—based on the free and open flow of information over social media. These new models regard innovation and creativity as assets held in common, and stimulate economic and social change alike.

In his essay, *Thomas Malone* claims we are witnessing the first stages of a revolution in the way we organize our work. He thinks that we are moving toward decentralized organizations in which large numbers of individuals take important decisions based upon a wide range of information. This reorganization will demand a radical change in the way that businesses manage their human resources, with a shift from "command and control" to "coordinate and cultivate."

The final section of the book concerns communication and culture, where the Internet has had an especially powerful impact.

David Crystal terms the language we use on the Internet "electronically mediated communication"—an entirely new form of communication unlike both writing and speaking that features innovative possibilities such as "interfering" at any time with the text, giving rise to "panchronic" communication. Crystal predicts the emergence of a new revolution in step with the development of Voice over Internet Protocols (VoIP).

Paul DiMaggio presents a broad perspective on how the Internet has affected the media and cultural industries. In his view, the Internet has brought more culture to more people, and that the magnitude of disruption varies greatly depending upon the cultural industry or sector: music has witnessed the rise of new opportunities, while print media is being driven out of the market.

Peter Hirshberg focuses on how the Internet has revolutionized the ways in which we watch TV and listen to music. No longer is the audience a passive recipient; each individual has become his or her own content producer and distributor. Television used to be a family activity, but now it comes within the autonomous sphere of the individual—although it can later be shared and discussed in social media.

Patrik Wikström analyzes the profound changes in the music industry over the past 15 years. People are listening to more recorded music than ever before in history, yet revenue has collapsed. On the other hand, music licensing and live music have taken on great importance. A growing number of artists are involving the audience in the creative process, thus changing the artist/listener relationship and modifying the audience's interaction with music.

In the closing essay, *Edward Castronova* speaks of the rise of Internet-based games. He maintains that games lie at the core of our society, our economy, and our culture. These complex phenomena are in fact structured as vast tissues of interrelated games whose rules mold our behavior. So the emergence and growing influence of Internet-based games creates subtle, gradual, yet, in the long run, profound changes in our culture.

Banking, Information, and Technology: Toward Knowledge Banking

Several of the essays in this book explain how the Internet is transforming the economy, industrial sectors, and business life. Practically every single business in every part of the world must cope with these changes. They are unavoidable, because the technological underpinnings of the production and distribution of goods and services have shifted. What's more, society and the people it is made up of have themselves changed. They are more informed and more demanding; they have new consumption habits, and in virtually every domain imaginable their decision-making criteria have shifted.

So even large companies that formerly made huge profits and enjoyed universal brand recognition now fade away or are driven out by other, far newer businesses that form part of the online explosion.

The S&P 500 clearly reflects this situation. Kodak and the *New York Times* have dropped off the index; Kodak replaced by a cloud computing firm, and the *New York Times* pushed out by Netflix, a company that rents movies and TV series over the Internet.

This is a chiefly information-driven revolution. Thus the industries undergoing the fastest and most far-reaching changes are those where the informational component is largest: the service sector industry in general, and, more specifically, media, culture, and entertainment.

Banking and the wider financial services industry also carry a very high information load. Their *raw materials* might in fact be said to be money and information. Money is readily dematerialized (converted into electronic form) by being turned into accounting entries; in other words, information.

Banking and finance have of course changed to some extent, but the magnitude of the change has been far less than in other sectors. There are several possible reasons for this: the industry is tightly regulated; users' average age is comparatively high; and the financial sector grew at an amazing rate in the decades leading up to the downturn, which allowed for the sustaining of relatively high levels of inefficiency.

But all this is on the way out. In the aftermath of the financial crisis, we are moving toward an industry guided by far more stringent requirements with respect to transparency and good practice, solvency and control. Margins will inevitably be thinner and profits smaller.

Banks need to restore their reputations while continuing to operate profitably in a far more demanding environment in terms of principles, quality, and service pricing.

In addition, a whole generation of customers has grown up with the Internet—they use social media and have an *online life*. They have never been to a bricks-and-mortar branch office, and never will. Various estimates suggest that by 2016 retail customers will contact their bank once or twice a year at a physical branch office, as against 20 or 30 times a month using their cell phones (see King 2013).

Moreover, a whole new league of competitors is emerging, mostly but not exclusively from the online world. These new players are free of legacies, the structures inherited by the banks: obsolete and inefficient IT systems and costly physical distribution networks.

Today, the use of online payment mechanisms, the execution of money transfers using e-mail, automatic personal finance management with various software apps, or the use of the cell phone as an e-wallet is increasingly possible and widespread. There are even several online currencies.

So far, most of the companies developing these capabilities—such as Paypal, Square, iZettle, SumUp, TransferWise—are niche players targeting a single segment of the financial industry's value chain.

But there increasingly more sectors coming under attack. Even lending, the key area where it is hardest to cut out the middleman, is no longer the exclusive preserve of banks: in the United Kingdom, supermarket chains like Tesco are selling mortgages. You can get a loan on Amazon. Peer-to-peer lending is growing exponentially.

And the emerging competition is increasingly strong. Some bankers and analysts believe that the *Internet giants*—Google, Facebook, and Amazon—are unlikely to fully commit to a business like banking, which is heavily regulated and offers only thin, declining margins. Yet it is unlikely that these companies, with their incredibly strong and well-known brands and billions of users, will stay on the sidelines of a business that generates a large number of recurring contacts and transactions—and thus a wealth of information—and which also facilitates additional sales opportunities.

The good news for banks is that they enjoy a crucial competitive advantage—the huge store of information they already have about their customers. The challenge is to convert this information into knowledge, and use this knowledge to offer customers what they want.

And What Is It That Customers Want?

First, they want a quick, sensibly priced real-time service under transparent terms and conditions, tailored to their own conditions and needs.

Secondly, they want the ability to carry out transactions anywhere, anytime, using mobile devices. This has significant implications. On one hand, the need for a large branch network is fading away; on the other, the potential market is far greater.

Today, there are 4.7 billion cell phone users on the planet, as compared to only 1.2 billion bank customers. Mobile telephony furnishes a powerful infrastructure to access billions of people who have never been bank customers, largely as a result of conventional banking's inability to develop an efficient model capable of catering to low-income individuals, many of them living in geographically remote or dispersed locations. To give one example, in Kenya M-Pesa started to provide basic cell phone banking services in 2007; today, it has almost 20 million users.

Thirdly, customers want a genuine multichannel experience. They expect the same value proposition, the same service, anytime, anywhere, using any channel—a branch office, ATMs, a desktop or laptop, a landline or cell phone, etc.

They also need the ability to switch from one channel to another instantly, seamlessly, without any discontinuity. This seamless experience still lies far beyond the current *multichannel* approaches offered by most banks.

Finally, customers are increasingly looking to their banks for new forms of value—goods and services that meet their needs.

To satisfy all these requirements, banks must develop a new, knowledge-based business model adapted to the online world.

How can we develop this model? According to Peter Weill (see Weill and Vitale 2001; Weill and Ross 2009), every online business model comprises three critical components. First, the content; in other words, whatever is being sold. Second, the customer experience; that is, how the product is presented and consumed. And third, the technology platform, which determines how the product is produced and distributed.

It is probably this third element—the platform—that poses the toughest challenge, because most banking platforms were designed and built in the 1960s and 1970s. It is upon this base that the later retouches, patches, and add-ons are layered, giving rise to what Professor Weill calls "spaghetti" platforms, evoking the complexity that results from the connections among the various applications. Inevitably, these platforms are rigid and inefficient, overly complex, and expensive to maintain. And they certainly do not provide tools capable of competing with the new players in the industry—who are far more agile and flexible—or of creating the experience that today's customers demand.

To compete in the twenty-first-century banking industry, we need a completely different platform concept developed from scratch under the aegis of far more advanced paradigms than those of 50 years ago, so that the system can integrate vast quantities of data with all possible points and channels of contact with all customers, without any cracks or discontinuities.

This new form of platform should consist of three levels. The core system is the platform engine, providing all the basic information-processing and data-analysis capabilities. The middleware level comprises the software that processes and packages the data and functionalities of the core system to make them available to the third level, the *front office* seen by customers, with fully interconnected channels, social media functionalities, high security standards, and the ability to capture all customer data and enable managers to react to it promptly.

With respect to the platform content and customer experience, banks need to completely revise their traditional concepts if they are to meet customers' true needs. Customers are people and businesses whose ultimate goal is to buy a new car, move house, travel, start up a business, build a manufacturing plant, and so forth. Getting a loan is not an end in itself, it is merely the means. Grasping this insight and taking action accordingly is vital to offering attractive content and a distinctive customer experience.

Technology enables us to build new content based on the knowledge generated from the available data. It also offers the customer an improved experience. The bank no longer needs to wait for the customer to request a given service; it can anticipate the customer's decision-making process, offering what he or she needs at the right time and in the most convenient format. To achieve this banks must take their place at the forefront of Big Data analysis and make use of all the information they have amassed about their customers, as well as the wealth of available external data, particularly sourced from social media.

This, in turn, calls for vast data storage and processing capabilities. Cloud computing allows us to access capabilities of almost unlimited size, flexibly and efficiently, while improving the customer's experience.

These steps forward are necessary if a bank is to survive and successfully compete in the new knowledge-banking environment. And this represents a profound transformation of current business models. Not only must technology be radically upgraded but, in addition, operations and processes and organizational structures must all be comprehensively reinvented, and the manner of working and the capacities and skills required must also change. What is called for is a total transformation of the corporate culture.

And all these initiatives must be put to the service of an ongoing effort toward innovation. Open innovation models are critical to overcoming the existing limitations of an organization and attracting the best talent to work on better value propositions—employees, customers, shareholders, and other bank stakeholders can and should contribute to the design of better content.

The shift from offline to online, from analog to digital, "from place to space"—as expressed more than a decade ago by Peter Weill and Michael Vitale (2001)—is for conventional banks an inevitably long and complex process. It entails an *ongoing revolution* at every level of the organization, all while the bank is kept fully operational at all times.

At BBVA, we started work on this process six years ago. We made a conscious decision to start from scratch. We ruled out other options that on the face of it seemed easier, such as slotting in more middleware or enhancing channel applications without addressing the replacement of core systems. These options, which in one way or another have been the solutions of choice for many banks, smooth out intermediate difficulties, come at a lower cost, and produce some results in the short term. But this approach multiplies patches and inefficient interconnections—*adding spaghetti to the plate*—and leads to a dead end when increasing data storage, and processing requirements outstrip the feeble power and flexibility of the core engine.

As a result, today at BBVA we have a state-of-the-art platform that allows us to speed up channels in the rest of our business divisions. What's more, even after achieving genuinely significant progress, after six years the transformation of our business model is still far from complete; it will continue to be our key priority in the coming years.

The fact is that the future of every bank depends on the decisions made about its operational platforms. We are moving toward an entirely new map of the financial services industry. Banks will be fiercely culled by rising competition, falling margins, and declining prices, in step with the shift of products and services to online media—as has already happened in other industries.

The new financial services industry will allow room for more than one viable model, chiefly depending on each company's degree of knowledge of its end customers and of its ability to access them.

There will always be niche players, of course, but most operators will be specialist suppliers: players with a reduced knowledge of and access to customers, and focusing on a strongly productive specialization. These suppliers will have to find their place within the value chain of larger and more powerful businesses, with better customer knowledge and access. The stronger operators will be far fewer in number—perhaps not more than a hundred worldwide—and will act as *knowledge distributors* while exerting control over the value chain. Their control will take the form of *ownership* of the open platform on which suppliers and customers interact, within the framework and under the rules created by the owner, who will in turn be able to integrate all the knowledge generated about the end customer.

This *ecosystem* model provides many small businesses—suppliers—with the opportunity of achieving global reach within their area of expertise. The platform owner can expand its range of products and services and improve the customer's experience. Moreover, cooperation among all players—businesses and customers—will stimulate innovation.

This model is already operational in the online domain. What Amazon is really doing is heading up an ecosystem by opening up its platform to a broad selection of suppliers who offer the customer base a growing range of products and services: books, of course, but also music, software, hardware, and so on.

This phenomenon has yet to reach the banking world—or has done so only in a very incomplete form. But the process is inexorable, driven by digitalization and increasing consumer needs. It is on this terrain that the newly digitized banks will meet the new entrants from the Internet. The banks will generate knowledge based on the financial information at their disposal—supplemented by other sources—to offer financial and, increasingly, non-financial services; and their rivals will in turn use general information about their users to offer them financial services.

For today's banks, the necessary transformation represents a great challenge, but also a wonderful opportunity. Those who fail to react quickly, decisively, and accurately will wither away, as their customers leave them behind and their revenues decline. Those who successfully adapt to the new environment, however, will discover a new field of possibilities. While the market will offer very low prices—digitalization necessarily entails a sharp drop in prices—costs will likewise be far lower. In the words of the economist Erik Brynjolfsson:

> *When goods are digital, they can be replicated with perfect quality at nearly zero cost, and they can be delivered almost instantaneously. Welcome to the economics of abundance.*

What's more, the market will be far larger in at least two ways. First, it will be genuinely universal, bringing in billions of people who currently have no access to financial services. Secondly, banks will be able to extend their offerings beyond the financial domain, embracing a potentially endless range of knowledge-based products and services.

The banks are equipped with a highly significant initial advantage—they have more and better data about their customers. But they need to turn this data into relevant knowledge.

In this new world, the banks have lost their monopoly over banking. Each bank is called upon to prove that it is capable of offering the (financial or non-financial) services that people really need, when they need them, in the way they need them.

Financial authorities, regulators, and supervisory bodies face perhaps even greater challenges. Their main goal should be to keep a level playing field between banks and new entrants to the business. This means that the regulatory and supervisory absence from what has so far been a practically unregulated online realm needs to be addressed, to ensure security, privacy, fair competition, and financial stability.

This is no easy task in the largely unexplored digital domain, which is continuously growing and becoming more complex, and where unfettered freedom is the norm. An even greater challenge will be in addressing these issues while also preserving a high degree of competition and sufficient incentive for innovation, the factors that ultimately benefit customers and drive growth.

The conventional financial services industry is becoming what I call the BIT (Banking, Information, and Technology) industry, a staging post on the road to its growing into Knowledge Banking: an industry able to provide us with far greater value, furnishing more and better solutions for our needs, and effectively supporting economic development at the global level. In this process, banks are merely accompanying the economy at large and the global society as they rapidly evolve toward knowledge-based forms of themselves.

BBVA is committed to collaborating in this effort in order to extract the highest possible benefit from the Internet for the well-being of individuals and for the global society, in keeping with the vision of our business group: "BBVA, working towards a better future for people."

This vision provides the framework for our strategy, which rests on three pillars: principles, people, and innovation.

We first make our vision and our strategy a reality in our day-to-day work. BBVA is determined to offer our customers the best, most efficient, most agile, simplest, and most convenient solutions.

That is why BBVA aims to be one of the leaders in the transformation of the current financial services industry into a new knowledge-based banking establishment powerfully supported by technology.

Our business group has pioneered the creation of a cutting-edge technological platform, which is now practically complete. In addition, we are undertaking a sustained innovation drive that goes far beyond technology, extending into the organizational and cultural spheres.

Our approach to integration is founded on knowledge, because knowledge is our salient competitive advantage. We were among the first in the industry to conduct data mining and construct smart algorithms to anticipate and interpret our clients' needs. Similarly, BBVA has pioneered the use of the cloud to maximize the efficiency and flexibility of its processes.

For the past six years, at BBVA we have moved forward to bring about the change that I believe our industry must urgently address: turning an analog bank—highly efficient and profitable by twentieth-century standards—into an online venture focusing on knowledge services, thus rising to the far more elevated and demanding standards of the twenty-first century.

In addition, BBVA has a strong commitment to corporate responsibility, which we regard as another way of helping people to grow and to improve their lives in the communities where we operate. This work is focused on the areas we believe to be the most powerful levers for extending the horizon of opportunities for individuals: financial inclusion, social entrepreneurship, education—with a particular emphasis on financial education—and the creation and dissemination of knowledge.

Final implementation of these initiatives is chiefly the province of the BBVA Foundation. But the bank itself is also directly involved. One of the results of our participation is this collection of books and its parallel initiative, the OpenMind Knowledge Community, which aims to leverage the power of the Internet as a collaborative tool to create a space in which to share and discuss our knowledge of the key issues set to shape our future. I would like to thank all the authors and contributors, and to express the wish that our readers and visitors will enjoy this book and learn from it as much as we have.

References

Abbate, Janet.
"The Internet: Global Evolution and Challenges." In *Frontiers of Knowledge*. Madrid: BBVA, 2008.

Aitkenhead, Decca.
"Clay Shirky: 'Paywall Will Underperform—The Numbers Don't Add Up'." *Guardian*, July 5, 2010.

Barro, Robert J.
"Determinants of Economic Growth in a Panel of Countries." *Annals of Economics and Finance* 4, no. 2 (2003): 231–74.

Benkler, Yochai.
The Wealth of Networks: How Social Production Transforms Markets and Freedom. New Haven: Yale University Press, 2006.

Benkler, Yochai.
The Penguin and the Leviathan: How Cooperation Triumphs Over Self-Interest. New York: Crown Business, 2011.

Brynjolfsson, Erik, and Andrew McAfee.
Race Against The Machine: How the Digital Revolution is Accelerating Innovation, Driving Productivity, and Irreversibly Transforming Employment and the Economy. Lexington, MA: Digital Frontier Press, 2012.

Carr, Nicholas.
"Is Google Making Us Stupid?" *The Atlantic*, July/August 2008.

Carr, Nicholas.
The Shallows: What the Internet is Doing to Our Brains. New York: W.W. Norton & Company, 2010.

Castells, Manuel.
Rise of the Network Society. Oxford: Wiley-Blackwell, 2009.

Choi, Changkyu, and Myung Hoon Yi.
"The Effect of the Internet on Economic Growth: Evidence from Cross-Country Panel Data." *Economic Letters* 105, no. 1 (2009): 39–41.

Kahin, Brian.
"Knowledge Markets in Cyberspace." In *The Multiple Faces of Globalization*. Madrid: BBVA, 2009.

King, Brett.
Bank 3.0: Why Banking is No Longer Somewhere You Go, But Something You Do. Singapore: John Wiley & Sons, 2013.

Lipovetsky, Gilles, and Jean Serroy.
La culture-monde: Réponse à une société désorientée. Paris: Éditions Odile Jacob, 2008.

Malone, Thomas W.
The Future of Work: How the New Order of Business Will Shape Your Organization, Your Management Style, and Your Life. Boston: Harvard Business School Press, 2004.

Pew Research Center.
"Pew Internet & American Life Project." Future of the Internet IV, February 19, 2010.

Pinker, Steven.
"Mind Over Mass Media." *The New York Times*, June 10, 2010.

Schiller, Dan.
Digital Capitalism: Networking the Global Market System. Cambridge, MA: MIT Press, 1999.

Schultz, Robert A.
"Ethics and the Internet." In *Values and Ethics for the 21st Century*. Madrid: BBVA, 2011.

Vargas Llosa, Mario.
La civilización del espectáculo. Madrid: Alfaguara, 2012.

Weill, Peter, and Jeanne W. Ross.
IT Savvy: What Top Executives Must Know to Go from Pain to Gain. Boston: Harvard University Press, 2009.

Weill, Peter, and Michael Vitale.
Place to Space: Migrating to eBusiness Models. Boston: Harvard Business School Press, 2001.

The Future of
the Internet

Cyberflow

David Gelernter

Professor of Computer Science, Yale University

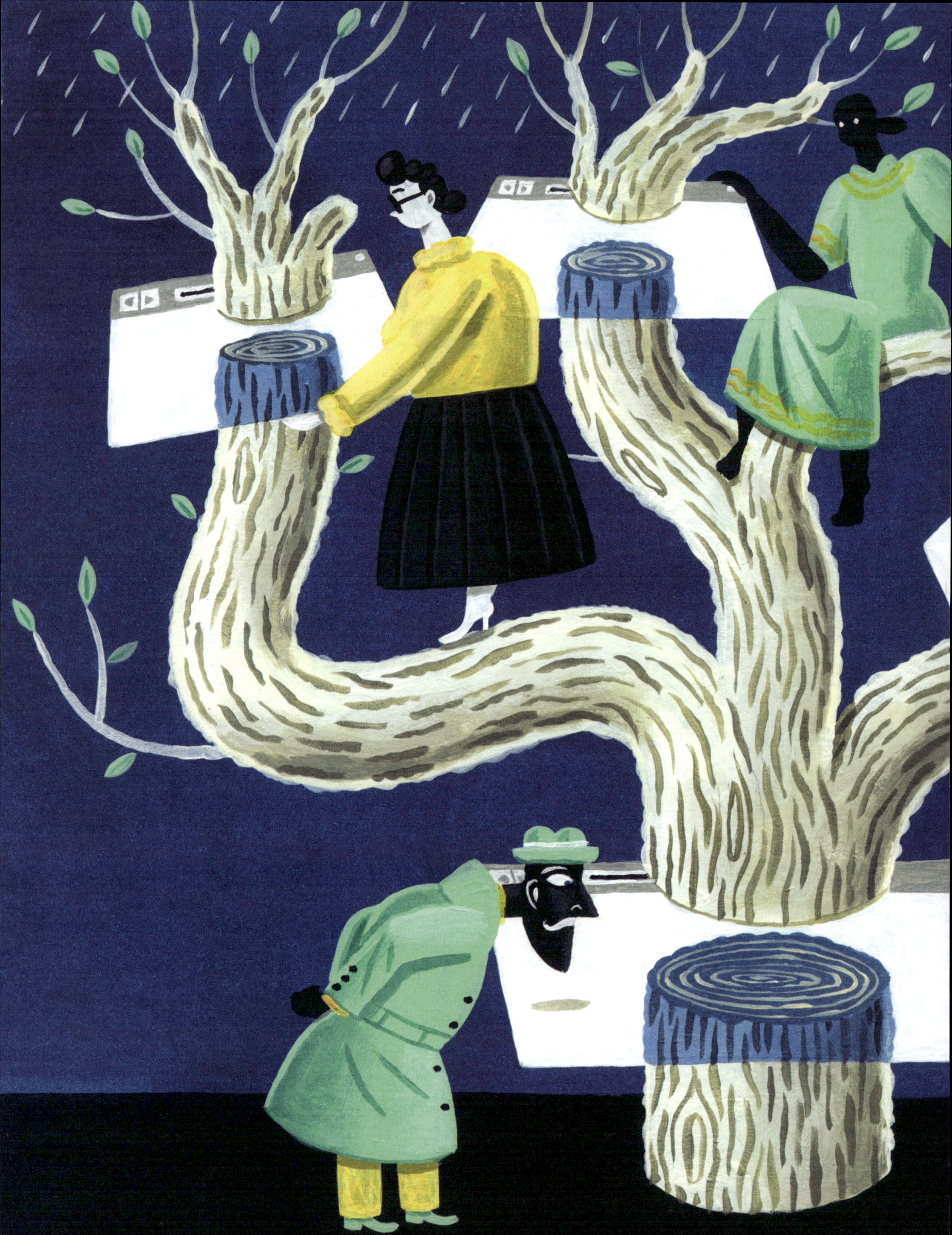

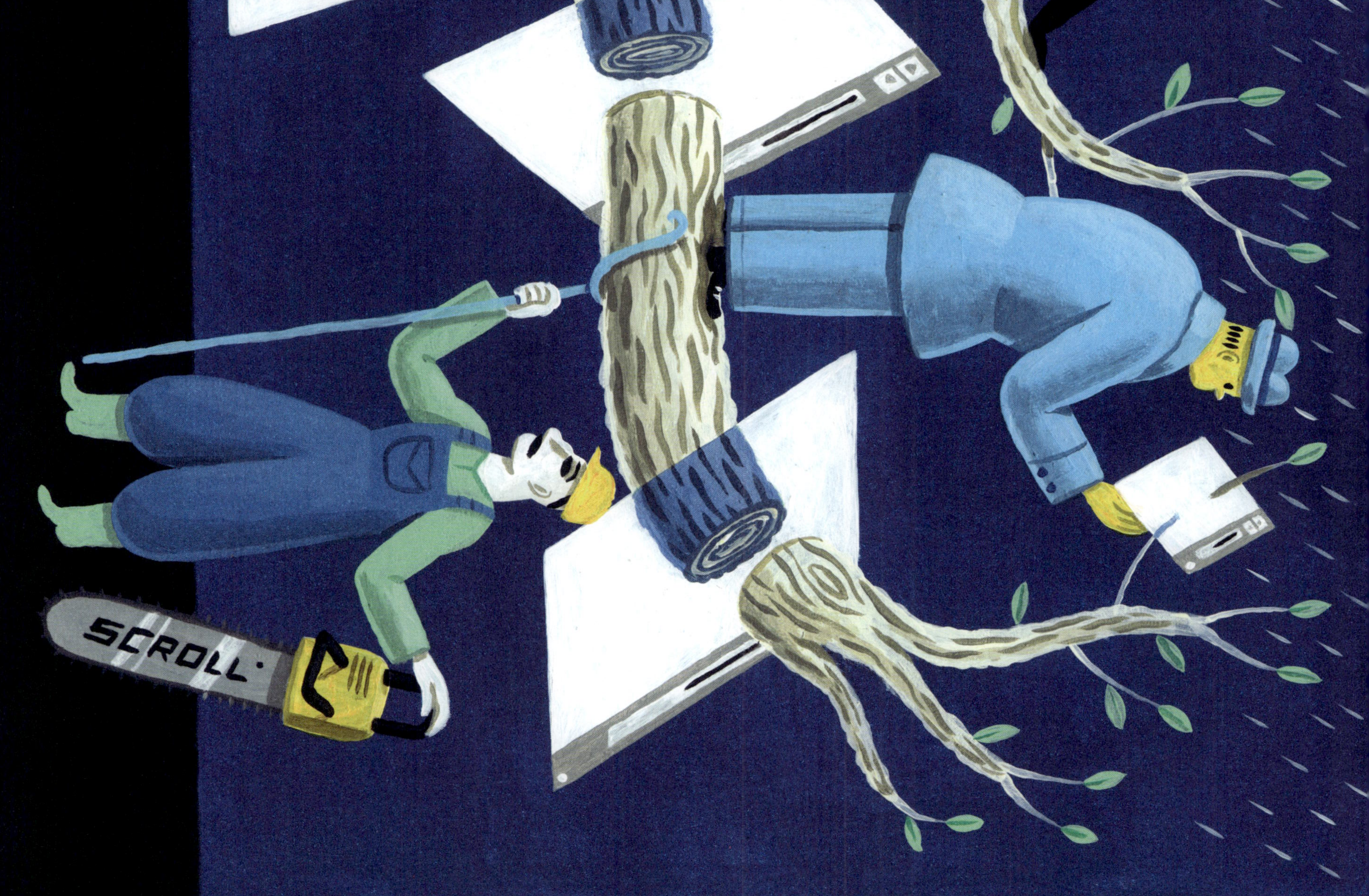SCROLL·

David Gelernter
en.wikipedia.org/wiki/David_Gelernter

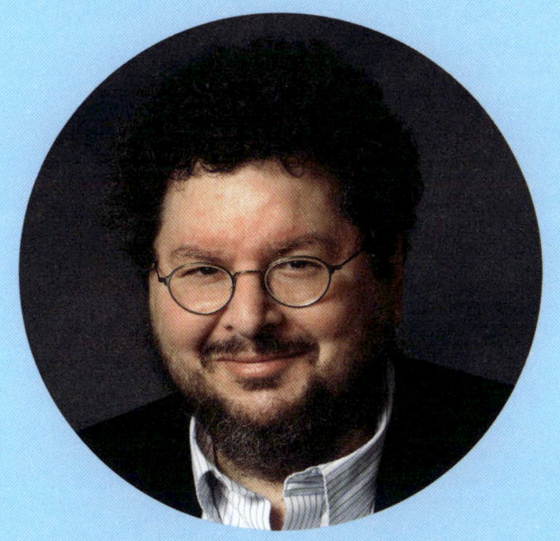

David Gelernter received his BA at Yale University (1976) and his PhD in Computer Science from SUNY Stony Brook (1982). Gelernter's work with Nick Carriero in the 1980s showed how to build software frameworks for expandable, superfast web search engines. His book *Mirror Worlds* (Oxford University Press, 1991) *foresaw* the World Wide Web (Reuters, March 20, 2001, and others), and according to *Technology Review* (July 2007) was "one of the most influential books in computer science." *Mirror Worlds* and Gelernter's earlier work directly influenced the development by Sun Microsystems of the Internet programming language Java. His work with Eric Freeman on the "Lifestreams" system in the 1990s led to the first blog on the Internet (which ran on Lifestreams at Yale) and anticipated today's stream-based tools at the major social-networking sites (chat streams, activity streams, Twitter streams, feeds of all sorts) and much other ongoing work. Gelernter's paintings are in the permanent collections of the Tikvah Foundation and the Yeshiva University Museum, where he had a one-man show last fall, as well as in private collections.

Sites and services that have changed my life
edge.com
drudge.com
abebooks.com

Cyberflow

The web will change dramatically—will disappear, and be replaced by a new form of Cybersphere—because there are only two basic choices when you arrange information, and the web chose wrong. You can arrange information in space or in time. Arranging information in space means distributing it over a surface or through a volume, as in any ordinary data structure; as in any shop selling fruit, where different kinds of fruit are stored in different places (in different crates or heaps or boxes). Arranging information in time requires that it be time-ordered to begin with, as in a diary or journal or on a timeline; we borrow one dimension of space to indicate the flow of time. A fruit shop arranged by time would be a single vector of fruit crates or boxes. The nearest fruit would be the newest, most recently arrived. Moving further back, you would find successively older arrivals.

There are certain advantages to arranging a fruit shop by time. If you want the freshest (newest) oranges, you pick the ones that are closest to the front of the time vector. If you want to make sure to get ripe fruit, you might move away from the front. But on the whole, an ordinary space-arranged fruit shop is more efficient and reasonable.

Information on the Internet is very different, for several reasons. What we most often seek on the Internet is the latest or newest information. The Internet's most important role is to deliver information directly to human users, not to software; and the oldest and most natural way for people to convey and absorb information is *in time*, in the form of a story or narrative. If the matrix and the recursive list are, in a sense, the *basic data structures* of software, the *story* is the basic data structure of human beings. As we will see, information arranged into stories is far more easily handled than space-distributed information: stream algebra is simpler than graph algebra.

It's clear a priori that the web is only a temporary state in the evolution of the Cybersphere (meaning sum of all data available via the Internet). We can tell it's temporary because the web takes the same form as the Internet—both are a set of points or nodes, unsystematically connected.

Both are irregular graphs. Both are chaotic. The first stage in the evolution of software generally works this way: in the beginning, software looks like or strongly reflects the underlying hardware. The web belongs to the same state of Cybersphere evolution that early machine and assembler languages, or the operating systems of the 1950s and 1960s, belong to.

It's therefore not surprising that feeds or time-ordered streams or lifestreams are increasingly dominant on the Internet. By *lifestream* (which I will discuss further), I mean a heterogeneous, content-searchable, real-time narrative (i.e., time-ordered) stream. We invented lifestreams in the early 1990s as a data management system to integrate documents (in file systems and other storage applications) and real-time messages such as e-mail, and make all data objects available to users in narrative order by means of content search and browsing. A lifestream was to be stored in the cloud, so as to be available on all platforms.

Lifestreams, under many different names, are the dominant organizing paradigm for new data on the web today—lifestreams in the form of blogs, Twitter streams, chat streams and activity streams, Facebook wall and time-line and other feeds, RSS feeds, and many others. Before long, I believe, we will think of the Cybersphere as information ordered by time, not scattered in space. We will think of it as an enormous, fast-flowing river of information roaring backwards into the past.

This new view has many important implications. We will understand the Internet not as we do a chaotic graph (or spider's web) but as we think of electronic circuits: in a circuit, the *flow* (or current or amperage) is important. We will think of individual computers as *step-down information transformers*, like the step-down voltage transformers that connect us to electric power networks. Most important, any two streams (or many streams) can be merged into one, automatically. This stream addition and corresponding stream subtraction are the basis of stream algebra, which will allow each user to make easy adjustments to his own view of the Internet and the Cybersphere.

Of course, *flow through time* is (ordinarily) visible only in one particular sense: by watching something grow older, we watch it move through time. Flow through time would be easier to see if we ourselves were moving through time at a faster or slower rate than data in the Cybersphere. But since this is difficult to arrange, it's more convenient to borrow one dimension of space to represent time, and to imagine the Cybersphere as a gigantic river of information flowing backwards into the past.

Along with many other people, I believed at first that a space-based organization was ideal for the Cybersphere. A book called *Mirror Worlds* (1991) pre-dated the web, but did describe a space-based Cybersphere: it imagined the Cybersphere as a perfectly smooth pond, reflecting the image of a village (meaning the world at large) standing right beside it. The Cybersphere (like a smooth pond) would mirror the structures and activities of the real world. The image created by the Cybersphere would be entirely independent of implementation—just as the image on a pond's surface has little to do with the composition or density of the water, or the shape of the basin.

Mirror Worlds opened by saying, "This book describes an event that will happen someday soon. You will look into a computer screen and see reality. Some part of your world ... will hang there in a sharp color image, abstract but recognizable, moving subtly in a thousand places" (Gelernter 1991).

To get information about some school or government agency or hospital or shop or museum, you'd steer or navigate to the part of the *reflected image* that represented the particular organization in which you were interested. "Search for Bargello, Florence" would take you on a quick trip from a whole-world view down to a view of Italy, Tuscany, Florence, and finally the Bargello. You would then go inside to find (in effect) the Bargello's website. (I've described something like a trip within Google maps, but of course the book was written long before Google existed.)

All this information—the *Mirror World*, or *Cybersphere*—would be stored in the sort of *distributed object memory* we had built earlier when we designed the distributed programming system called Linda—a *tuple space*, so called. A tuple space was a *content-addressable cloud*. Reality *mirrored* in a pond, implemented by a globally addressable, content-searchable cloud—that was the original idea. (Notice that, in this view, searching is intrinsic to the structure of the Cybersphere, not layered on top.) We developed the Lifestreams system starting in 1994. Eric Freeman built the first implementation, and he's the co-inventor of Lifestreams. Today (as I have mentioned), the searchable, heterogeneous, time-ordered real-time messaging stream is the dominant paradigm on the web.

Now to the future: today's web is likely to evolve into a single Worldstream, one raging torrent of information. One way to picture it is to start with an old-fashioned well, with a bucket for drawing water. Imagine the bucket plunging deeper and deeper down an infinite shaft, at increasing speed, as the rope unreels.

The unreeling rope is the Worldstream. The bucket is the start of the stream the oldest, earliest document in the stream—plunging deeper and deeper into the past.

The unspooling, unreeling, rushing-downwards rope is a sequence of all kinds of digital documents; whenever anybody anywhere creates a *new* electronic document, either a purely private document or a document to be published, it appears at the top of the rope. The new document is spliced into the rope at that point—and the instant it appears, it goes plunging down into the well as *part* of the downward-plunging rope, into the past, into history, down into the unbounded well of time.

Of course, we are talking about a virtual structure built of software. So consider one more image. (The search for images is made necessary by the fact that we can invent and build virtual structures using software that have no close analogs in the physical world.)

Imagine standing on a bridge over a large, fast river (say the Danube or the Rhine). The source of the river lies behind us. In front of us, we see the great river rushing outward toward the sea. If we think of the Worldstream as this river, we are watching the Worldstream rush into the past.

Of course this global Worldstream is itself a virtual structure. It exists nowhere as a single, centralized data structure, any more than the cloud or the web is one single, centralized structure.

The Worldstream is, like them, a useful and powerful abstraction realized or implemented using many millions of separate streams all over the global Internet.

Today's web is an abstraction too, though a strikingly literal-minded one. It reflects the structure of the underlying hardware—just as machine code reflects the structure of the underlying processor. The Internet consists of many millions of nodes (each a separate network) connected into a chaotic graph. The web likewise is many millions of addressable sites and objects connected into a chaotic graph. When a software structure (such as the web) reflects the shape of the underlying hardware (the Internet), we can assume we are seeing a first-generation software solution.

The Worldstream is a higher-level abstraction, based on a structure (the narrative or story) that makes sense at the user level rather than the hardware level.

The Worldstream begins with each user's and each organization's individual lifestreams. An individual lifestream and the Worldstream are structurally identical: the tools users need to search or browse, publish or consume information in the Worldstream are identical to the ones they will use in dealing with their own individual lifestreams. The web, on the other hand, is an unwieldy structure for local use. Local information management *used* to be a matter (not of an individual web but) of the file system, desktop, and many specialized applications, including the mailer, browser, MP3 stores, photo albums, and so forth. Today it's unclear what the dominant model is. The field is in transition. In the future, the dominant model is apt to be some form of lifestream.

A lifestream has a past and future, divided by the *now line*. New information joins the stream at the now line and flows into the past. The user puts information in the future when it deals with future events (notices of appointments or deadlines), and *moves* information from the past to the future when there is no time to handle it right now. (If an e-mail appears that the user must deal with but has no time for now, he can copy the e-mail into the future.) The future flows toward *now*, then into the past.

Each user's lifestream is the sum of all his own private and public data, in the form of *cards* ordered by time. We first introduced the *card* in our first lifestream implementation in 1996. We faced then a problem that computing still faces today: no user-level data structure corresponds to "data of *any* type that has meaning to the user *as a unit*." A photo or video, a single e-mail, or a large document are all examples of this non-existent (but extremely important) type—henceforth called a *card*. I'll use the word *card* not only as an element of the user Interface but as the user-level "makes sense as a unit" data structure.

The user's private data cards consist of everything he creates or receives, and intends to keep private. Each arriving e-mail takes it place in time order. Photos and video are uploaded to the lifestream. Documents are added, at time of creation or revision, to the stream. When they are next revised, the previous document can be moved forward to its new (and later) time of modification, or the old document can be left in place and a new version copied to *now* for further work. Every card in the stream is fully indexed by contents and metadata. Searching the stream yields another (persistent) substream. The user can maintain many simultaneous substreams (each might flow at a different rate, depending on the frequency at which new cards are added); or he can depend on his single comprehensive lifestream and search whenever he has to find some particular card or group of cards.

Each card in the stream is individually permissioned, marked public, private, or (some version of) *friends*. Private cards are visible only to the owner. Public cards are visible to anyone. This simple mechanism makes my lifestream both a *personal information-management* and a *publication* medium. All public cards in my stream are (in essence) a blog that I publish—or equivalently, they are my stream-structured website. *Friends* covers any combination of individuals and groups; might extend access to one other person or a million others.

Stream algebra is simple, and its simplicity makes it easy to build, specify, and understand lifestream and Worldstream tools. Adding two streams means blending them together in time-order:

$$X + Y = Z$$

where X, Y, and Z are all lifestreams. Subtracting one lifestream from another simply means deleting its cards; and subtraction is the basis of searching.

$$\texttt{Search(Z, Bargello)}$$

yields the stream **Z** minus the stream consisting of all stream elements that do *not* mention *Bargello*.

Lifestreams have been implemented since our very first system using virtual 3D interfaces designed to make browsing easy and give users a feel of *overview*, of *seeing the big picture*. Our first implementation showed a single file of cards seen from the front, and slightly to the side and above. The stream disappeared into the virtual depths of the screen. In the next few years, we switched to the *V-stream* (which we still use today), where the stream has two arms meeting at a point in front. This point—the point that is closest to the user in virtual space—represents *now*. The future, in the right arm, flows forward toward *now*; the past, in the left arm, flows away from *now* into the depths of the screen. The stream has always been intended to flow in real time, although different streams flow at widely different rates.

Notice that our approach is to treat the screen not as a flat, opaque surface (as in most standard UIs, except for those belonging to video games) but as a transparent windshield with an infinitely deep virtual space beyond. The amount of space you can see *through* a pane of glass is much greater than the amount of space that is available *on* the pane of glass when it is treated as a simple surface.

We have found since the beginning of lifestreams development that search together with visual browse is a powerful combination. Users often search the stream to focus on potentially interesting cards, and then browse the result stream directly to find the exact card or group of cards they need.

We have left squish(**Z**), where **Z** is any lifestream, as a user-defined operation; the intent is to map an entire stream **Z** to a single card. (The card is itself a variable-size structure, but it consists of a single part.)

Squish makes it possible to search for all cards dealing with, for example, Matisse cut-outs, and then to compress the whole stream into a single-card summary or overview of all information on Matisse cut-outs in the stream. There are endless variations on this summary or overview function.

Lifestreams were always designed for storage in the cloud. The system was easily implemented in Linda; when a lifestream was built using Linda, the cards it contained would be distributed automatically over the multi-machine *tuple space* in which Linda stores data structures. Cloud storage (or at least Internet server storage) was central to lifestreams from the start, because the system was to be orthogonal not only to all separate type-specific data stores (file systems, desktops, specialized storage applications) but to all of a user's computing platforms. In the 1990s, personal computers, laptops, and *personal digital assistants* (PDAs) were already proliferating. It was crucial that a user have access to his lifestream from any Internet-connected platform.

Users were intended to have access to lifestreams by means of *stream browsers*—like ordinary browsers, but optimized to the display of lifestreams and able to do stream algebra efficiently. A user's lifestream, a stream browser for each platform, and the applications that (collectively) created the content of each card in the stream, constituted a complete personal operating environment. (The applications might be web apps, or platform-native; a card can always be downloaded from the stream to some particular machine, and uploaded from machine to stream.)

Now I'll consider the Worldstream environment from the opposite side, the viewpoint of public streams; and see how the two views come together.

The web will be replaced by the Worldstream; but the Worldstream moves much too fast to be useful to any individual. And most (or much) of the information moving through the Worldstream is private: available only to its owner, or to some limited group.

The user accordingly makes use of the Worldstream in *disaggregated* form, as a huge number of separate streams (which, added together, make the Worldstream). The user deals with these many streams in roughly the way a web user deals with websites. But the Worldstream user, as well as examining as many separate streams as he chooses, can build his own version of the Worldstream, watch it flow past, search, filter, and browse it.

Virtually all public organizations or institutions will have lifestreams (or some equivalent form of time-ordered stream). Any organization tells its story in the public cards of its lifestream. Its own private cards can be mixed into the same stream. The Bargello in Florence (a national museum of sculpture) might announce its public events, gallery openings and closings, publications, and so on by means of cards on its lifestream. Private information for the staff flows through the same lifestream. A lifestream is also a good medium for a catalogue (one card for each artwork, for example); the catalogue cards might be arranged in order of creation or acquisition. In either case, they are searchable and browsable along with the rest of the stream.

Of course the Bargello (or anyone else) can keep its old-style website— filed on one card in the stream. The newest *website* card in any stream contains the latest version of the old-style site.

Now, the Worldstream user has available an endless collection of streams like the Bargello's. Some are organizational or institutional, corresponding roughly to today's conventional websites. But of course every user in the world has a stream also. It might consist only of private or restricted cards and have no public visibility. But any user who chooses can mark any chosen subset of his cards *public*. Those public cards constitute a personal stream that's available to any Worldstream user.

The Worldstream user chooses any set of streams he likes and blends them together—simply adds them. Imagine a gigantic custom coffee machine where you choose any set of bean types or other flavors you like, press a button, and they're all blended together into your ideal cup of coffee. The Worldstream user makes himself an ideal sub-Worldstream in the same way. By watching this blended-together stream, he watches those parts of the Cybersphere (those aspects of the Worldstream) that are of greatest interest. (The resulting stream might flow too fast for convenient watching; we have a family of simple flow-control algorithms we are now testing to deal with over-fast streams. Controlling the flow rate of real-time streams will be one of the most important software challenges over the next decade.)

Of course the user can also focus on specific substreams of his blended sub-Worldstream. Suppose he's interested in David Cameron and African elephants. He can blend together every newspaper stream in the world, then search on Cameron and African elephants; the result is a global stream of all news stories dealing with exactly those two fascinating topics.

A user might add to this stream the blending together of all the streams belonging to his friends. No doubt he has access to many of the restricted *friends* cards in each of these streams, and of course to any *public* cards. By blending together the streams of all my friends, I develop a friends stream which keeps me up to date on all their activities and comments. (This mechanism might well be as flexible and useful as Facebook.)

Of course, users can also search the Worldstream directly—with access restricted to public cards, and others for which they qualify.

The Worldstream is a Cybersphere model based on flowing rather than static data. The Worldstream is fed by many sources—in principle, by every Internet user in the world.

Or we could equally well say that it's fed by exactly one source, a virtual stream called *the future*. Billions of people are each feeding into the grand global Worldstream their *own* streams or sequences of cards, digital things—and all those *not-yet-added* streams of *not-yet-created* digital things, blended together, merged together, are the Worldstream's future. An as-yet-unrealized future.

So we have a single enormous river of data—and after all, in the world at large we generally care about *new* data, we need the *latest* data— that's the particular value of the Internet: it can supply us with *the latest, newest*, most up-to-date information.

And so it's natural to understand Internet information as a flow or current—a constant supply of new information. The Worldstream is like a huge
power network that carries information at enormously high voltage; we all
tap into this high-voltage worldwide cyber-main—connecting of course
not by means of a voltage transformer but of a stream browser. The stream
browser is a kind of cyber-transformer, standing between the user and the
Worldstream—not just the Cybersphere but the Cyber-main, or *Cyberflow*.

The Worldstream carries *flowing* information, new information that creates
value in the Internet economy. It's the motion and momentum of a stream that
turns a waterwheel, the current in an electric circuit, driving a load (or en-
countering a resistance), that makes it possible to do work. In the case of the
stream-structured Internet, an information flow encounters a software load.

And again, we depend not just on information but on the *flow of information*; the trend or direction of information. After all, we care not only about
the state of the world now, but the direction in which the world is moving.

The *flow* of news, of financial information, the flow of e-mail, of Twitter
tweets, of blog posts or Facebook posts—of all sorts of lifestreams—and of
course the flow of text messages, voicemail, phone calls, taking place largely
on a separate physical network but part of the same worldwide *cyberflow*.

Again it's not just cyberspace but *cyberflow* that's important. And in
the cyberflow view of Internet information, what matters is not the URL or
identity of individual documents or conventional websites. What matters
is the identity of particular *streams* of information; you can identify such
a stream—a substream of the Worldstream—by describing the subset to a
stream browser, just as you identify a subset of *websites* by describing the
subset to a search engine.

(One important implementation note: cards I drop into the global stream
are maintained in my own personal partition of the Cybersphere or cloud;
but I make some of those cards visible to *global stream search* by labeling
them *public* of *for friends*. When we consider privacy and security, we only
need to focus our attention on our own private pieces of the Cybersphere.)

In talking about the Worldstream or Cyberflow, and the stream browser, I am, of course, neglecting the sort of relevance-ordered list of search results that's so important today. But of course we're not disabling relevance measures, and if you want to display a stream ordered not by time but by something else—for example relevance—you can do it.

But *time* has the useful characteristic that it's a worldwide total order on everything, all cards, all digital things—everything has a position in the Worldstream. (Same-time objects are arranged in random order; and of course we neglect relativistic simultaneity effects.) In normal web use today, we prefer time order to relevance order whenever we look at a blog, a Twitter stream, any sort of chat stream or activity stream, an e-mail inbox or voicemail box, a timeline profile, a receding stream of saved drafts, or saved states of any kind; whenever we look to the Internet for news of the world or the markets or the weather or any other topic. And my own guess is that traditional relevance-ranked search results will be increasingly replaced by automatic summaries—answers to questions, or one-screen information summaries—of the sort provided by various implementations of the squish() function in lifestreams.

To conclude: there is an *underlying idea or thesis or guess* here. The thesis is that *the* basic human data structure is the story (conversation, narrative).

If I have a digital conversation with one other person, it's usually what we think of as mail or messaging; a conversation that involves myself and a group of friends is the basic function of social networks; a conversation with the public—where I make comments and anyone can respond—yields a blog or, in some cases, a different form of social network. A conversation with *myself* is more of a *story or narrative*. And of course, when I deal with the world at large, I often want to know, *what's the story?* Or—just as often—what's the situation *right now*? And perhaps I also want to know, how did it *get* this way? These are all questions about stories, narratives, time-ordered events.

Equally basic to this thesis: with lots of information sources and types in the world, it's crucial that you be able to take the hundred sources or thousand that are most interesting, most important to you and *add them* or *blend them* into *one* thread, *one* stream of information. It isn't practical to start the day by checking 100 separate websites. It's a nuisance and it doesn't scale; the idea of a bookmark list, or a desktop, is a way of *discouraging* you from discovering interesting new sites.

Information arithmetic will clearly become a fundamental issue in the Cybersphere.

References

Gelernter, David.
Mirror Worlds: or the Day Software Puts the Universe in a Shoebox… How It Will Happen and What It Will Mean. New York: Oxford University Press, 1991.

The Internet of Things:
Outlook and Challenges

Juan Ignacio Vázquez

Professor of Telematics, University of Deusto

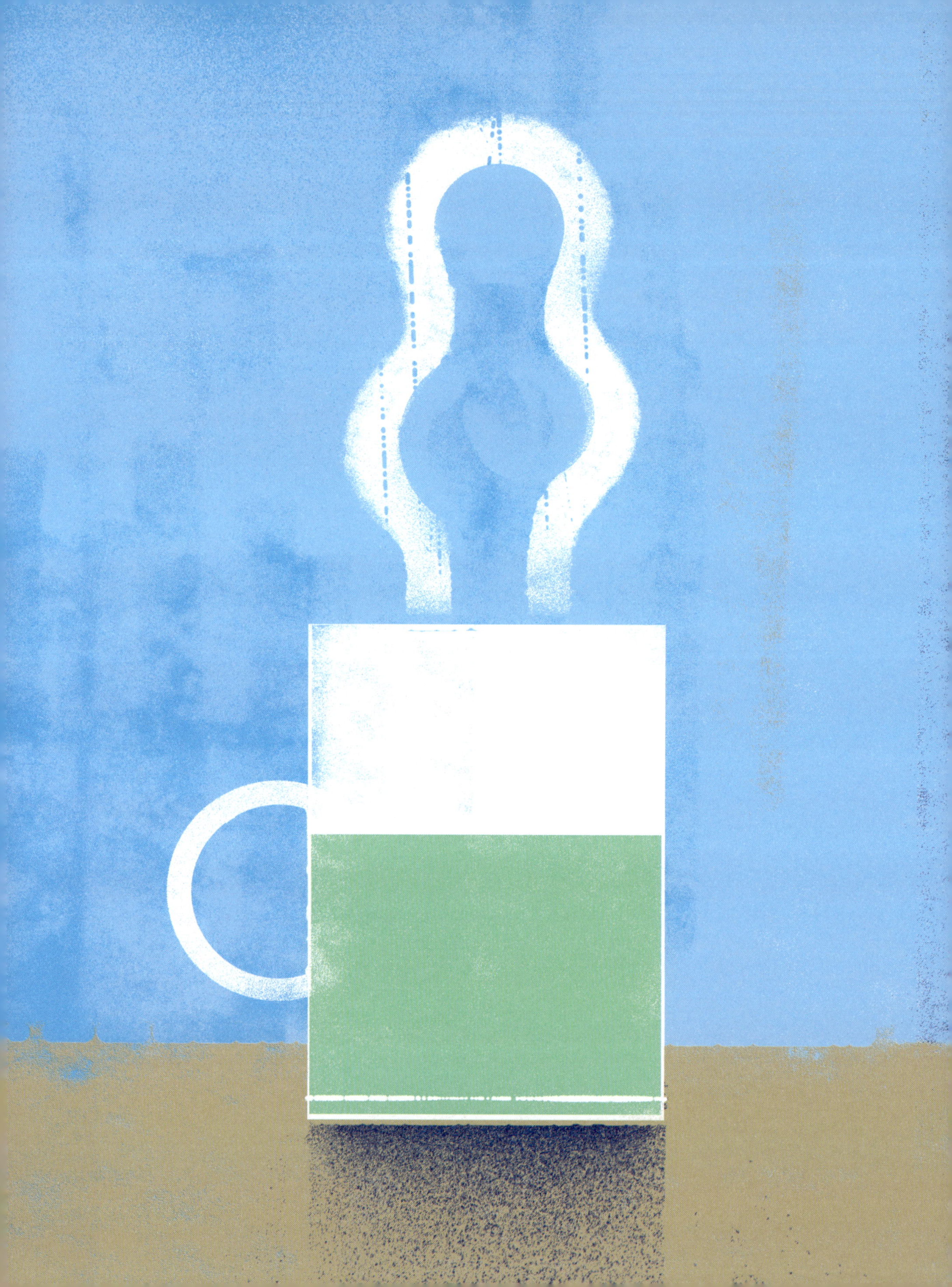

Juan Ignacio Vázquez

The Internet of Things: Outlook and Challenges

Juan Ignacio Vázquez

paginaspersonales.deusto.es/ivazquez

Illustration
Ignacio Molano

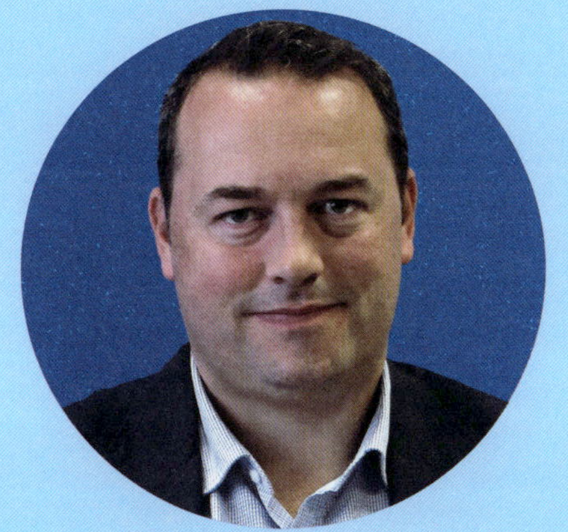

Juan Ignacio ("Iñaki") Vázquez is a Professor of Telematics at the University of Deusto. His main research interest is Smart Objects, and he has been involved in several tech startups in the field of the Internet of Things. He earned his PhD in Computer Science at Deusto in 2007, with the award of a Doctor Europaeus distinction. Until 2010, he was Smart Objects Research Unit Director at DeustoTech, where he headed OpenThingsLab (an Internet of Things competitiveness and innovation center for society and industry). He is currently a member of the Internet of Things Council, and takes part in both public and private initiatives, advising on new business models and creating new value propositions for existing products based on the Internet of Things.

Sites and services that have changed my life
facebook.com
wikipedia.org
virtualtourist.com

The Internet of Things: Outlook and Challenges

As children, we were fascinated by seemingly everyday objects that turned out to be magic. The heroes of fairytales, legends, and myths would routinely surmount the difficulties they faced with the help of some magic item whose hidden powers defied the laws of nature.

In modern popular culture this motif is perhaps best embodied in Disney films where inanimate objects become sentient beings who come to the aid of the main character. The prime exponent might be the brooms in the "Sorcerer's Apprentice" sequence in *Fantasia*, which sweep the floor all on their own; other examples that spring to mind are the magic mirror in *Snow White* or the talking candlesticks, clocks, and teacups in *Beauty and the Beast*.

"Any sufficiently advanced technology is indistinguishable from magic." Arthur C. Clarke's widely quoted proposition seems particularly apt in this context. What in an earlier age we would have culturally construed as *magic* is now a reality—designed, planned, documented, and operated by technologists around the world. Our magic brooms are home-cleaning robots; our magic mirrors are smartphones, equipped with Internet search engines that work much like all-knowing oracles, answering our questions out loud in an ersatz human voice. The value of our home appliances increasingly lies in their embedded electronics and software, enabling them to engage in a rich range of behaviors that earns them the qualifier *smart*.

In fact, the term *magic items*, used above, is echoed in a concept coined by David Rose, one of the most active innovators in this field: "enchanted objects."

The term *Internet of Things* was proposed by Kevin Ashton in 1999 in a presentation in which he argued that by associating physical objects with RFID labels we can give each object an identity enabling it to generate data about itself and its perceptions and publish that information on the

Internet. What was new about this insight was that so far the information available on the Internet had been produced almost exclusively by people (news, articles, commentaries) or by computerized systems (flight information, stock prices), not by actual physical things.

The idea of the Internet of Things is that the things around us—home appliances, vehicles, clothes, soft drink cans, even the street bench where I am now tapping out these words—should become first-class Internet citizens, producing and consuming information generated by other things, by people, or by other systems.

Every technological advance should move humankind forward in some way.

So what can the Internet of Things do for us humans? How can things connected to the Internet make our lives happier, better, or longer?

In this discussion I shall return several times to a simple example targeted by any number of research projects: the smart chair. A smart chair looks like—and is—an ordinary chair, but the back and seat conceal a set of small sensors that continually track the user's posture. Then a wireless module sends the posture data to a set of servers, where the data is stored and analyzed for patterns that tell us whether or not the sitter has good posture, spends too long in the same position, or doesn't take enough breaks. This information can help the user of the smart chair to improve her posture and relieve her back trouble. Some smart chairs vibrate when they detect an unhealthy way of sitting, prompting the user to learn and adopt good posture in an almost unconscious way.

The key take-away of this example is that the value proposition of the chair has crucially shifted: it is no longer just an item of furniture; it is a medical device designed to prevent lower back pain.

And this may be the most promising feature of the Internet of Things— its ability to create a new, different, and enhanced value proposition by providing conventional objects with Internet connectivity and data processing power in the cloud. The Internet of Things makes things smart.

The horizons that open up to us are as wide as they are new and unheard of. When conventional physical objects get Internet access, what kind of hybrids can we expect to see? Entirely new economic flows could emerge. A manufacturer might give away a smart chair for free because it has based its business model on the monthly fees for back health monitoring, shifting from sale of goods to service subscription. How can smart, all-knowing *things* help people?

Why Now?

Although the idea of magic objects has existed in human culture since antiquity, it is no happenstance that it is only now when they are beginning to be real. There are three main reasons for this: electronic parts have become smaller and cheaper; the world is interconnected by communications; and people have adopted a digital lifestyle.

The lower price of the electronics needed to connect an object to the Internet and endow it with a new value proposition has made it profitable to produce such goods, while the smaller size of the components have made it feasible to *hide* them within the product so that the user does not perceive it as bulky. Popular clothing labels now sell products that let you monitor your running performance using a tiny electronic device under the sole of your running shoe—later on, you can view your stats using a smartphone app. But it is cost reduction and miniaturization that have made this possible.

Global connectivity—over the Wi-Fi networks that are now ubiquitous in the developed world, or over 2G, 3G, or 4G mobile networks—allows objects connected to the Internet to keep in touch with the associated services that make them *smart*. For example, Ambient Umbrella, a web-connected umbrella designed in 2007, would connect with weather forecasting servers to find out if it would be useful in the next few hours—if so, it would subtly alert the user by emitting a halo of light.

Finally, the digital lifestyle that wraps around every aspect of our existence enables web-connected things to get past the barrier of human resistance to novelty and change—perhaps the greatest obstacle we humans are apt to pose—and gradually to become a part of everyday life. Because we use Internet-driven services every day (online news, social media, e-commerce), we do not resist the notion that some of the objects in our environment also partake of that ecosystem as a way of making life easier for us.

Let's now discuss some of the ways in which the Internet of Things is already at work in society.

WikiCity and SmartCities

One of the major achievements of humanity—though perhaps not as widely recognized now as it will be eventually—is Wikipedia. This is a repository of information in more than two hundred languages that has brought knowledge closer to millions of people around the world, including regions that would otherwise never have been able to distribute the information among their communities in such a short space of time. Wikipedia content is written and kept up to date by thousands of users around the world on the basis of the openness and freedom embodied in the Wikipedia tagline—"The free encyclopedia that anyone can edit"—to create the largest repository of knowledge ever known.

Let's now try to visualize how the wiki concept could apply to the Internet of Things in a specific location, such as a city. A WikiCity would be a repository of knowledge about the city whereby the physical objects within it—street furniture, pollution sensors, traffic lights, garbage trucks, green area irrigation systems—would create and update content in keeping with the changes perceived over time. So the "daily pollution level" webpage would be updated continually by pollution and particulate matter sensors at given times of day, in given areas; the "weather information" page would be updated by temperature, wind, sunlight, and rainfall sensors deployed in the city's parks and gardens. And then both pages would be referred to by traffic control systems to determine the interrelationships between rising pollution levels in a given area, vehicle traffic in that area tracked by sensors embedded in the road surface, and weather data, so as to take traffic planning decisions that improve the quality of life of the community.

The WikiCity concept is not that different from Wikipedia. The only difference lies in who produces and consumes the information—now it is physical objects connected to the Internet that create a store of knowledge about a given environment to enhance one another's functionality and grow *smarter* when viewed as a conjoined whole. "WikiCity, the free city that anyone can edit."

Some real-life cities have already deployed networks of smart sensors experimentally to create *sentient* cities that are self-aware and adapt accordingly: the Smart Cities trend. Leading examples include Smart Santander (Spain), Amsterdam Smart City (Netherlands), and Songdo IBD (South Korea). Many of these initiatives are backed by big software and equipment corporations that have chosen to make a strategic bid to develop the value-added services that a connected city can offer to its citizens.

Quantified Self

"You can't manage what you don't measure." This quotation—variously attributed to the American statistician William Edwards Deming or to Peter F. Drucker, the founder of modern corporate management philosophy—has become one of the most widely followed management adages today.

When we have figures and other information about a given phenomenon, and we also have the knowledge and techniques to interpret the data correctly, then we can identify the factors influencing that phenomenon and act upon them to get the desired outcome.

Businesses apply this principle all the time, analyzing and cross-referencing the data throughout the value chain—R & D, procurement, manufacturing processes, distribution, and after-sales service—to create products and services that provide the highest possible value at the lowest possible cost. This is made possible by the fact that each of those areas of the value chain has quality management mechanisms in place that collect information continuously for ex post or real-time analysis.

What about individual people—can we do the same thing in our everyday lives? Can we track all the data about our daily activities—sleeping, walking, eating, breathing—to analyze our habits? And how can we use the results of our analysis?

In the past decade these questions have become hot topics in the scientific community. And thanks to all-pervasive connectivity and the diminishing size and price of electronics—which we mentioned above—we can now have small *spy devices* living in our homes or hiding in our clothes to collect data about us which can later be interpreted to provide us with a more accurate picture of the way we live.

The *Quantified Self* trend has emerged in the shape of popular commercial products that exhibit the object/service duality that is the hallmark of the Internet of Things. The trigger is the physical object, which collects data from the user's environment; the object then sends the data to an online platform, the home of the service, which interprets the information, integrates it with other sources to enhance value, and reports it in user-friendly form.

Many recent startups have jumped on the Quantified Self bandwagon to sell wristbands or clips with a built-in accelerometer that you can wear to monitor your level of physical activity. The device detects whether you are standing still, walking, or running. The data captured throughout the day is sent to the related app, which then tells you whether your daily physical activity burns enough calories; in response, you might set yourself goals such as walking to work two days a week or doing more daily exercise to improve your metrics.

One of the key signatures of almost all sensor-based web-connected products—like wellness-tracking wristbands—is that they "make the invisible visible," revealing data which was always there but had never been measured before.

The new generation of wearable sensors can be likened to the invention of the microscope: suddenly, a whole new world of information opens up, a new science, where you are the researcher and your own habits and behavior are the subject matter being researched.

Other consumer goods in the Quantified Self category include web-connected bathroom scales that let you monitor your diet and set weight-loss goals, sleep trackers that help identify sleep disorders, sports shoes that monitor your performance and suggest ways you can improve, and wearable necklace micro-cameras that take snaps at regular intervals as you go about your daily life so that later on you can remember what you were doing.

A particularly good example is a device that displays three of the distinctive features of the Internet of Things. The Air Quality Egg is a personal air-quality sensor that measures pollution levels outside your own home. In addition, you can work together with other Egg users to create maps that track patterns of change in air quality across entire cities.

The Air Quality Egg can be classified equally well to the Quantified Self and Smart Cities categories, but it has a third trait that makes it all the more interesting—it gives users a way to work together as a community, and this makes their information more valuable.

The overlap of the Internet of Things with Big Data (data captured on an ongoing basis in such vast quantities and to such a degree of complexity that it resists conventional analysis techniques) and Open Data (open, public data available for analysis by anyone) is encouraging the rise of a new generation of analytics services capable of finding counterintuitive interrelationships among factors which seemed to have nothing to do with each other.

Designers of web-connected products face a major technological

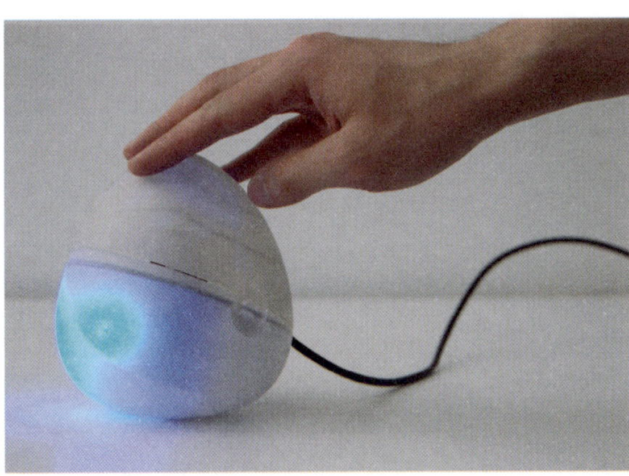

Fig. 1

First prototype of the Air Quality Egg.
Source: Air Quality Egg

challenge, however: how to make the devices self-powering. While you can afford the inconvenience of having to recharge your phone more or less every day, it is too much of a burden to devote the same sort of daily attention to another five or ten devices. The whole point, after all, is that the devices look out for us, not the other way around. Right now, it would strike you as silly to have to think "I need to recharge my smart shoes" or "I should put my umbrella in standby mode."

We are still seeing constant forward movement in technology, but telecommunications and electronic smart devices carry an energy cost, which rises in proportion to how smart and how communicative the given device is—these being the two key benefits of our *enchanted objects*. Electrical cells with higher capacity per unit of volume, low-powered microprocessors, and energy-efficient Wi-Fi modules form the landscape of today's research *battleground* where the question will be answered of which future product line users will adopt.

Some smart devices, particularly wearable and outdoor ones, can *harvest* enough energy in a natural way from their environment to keep functioning self-sufficiently for long periods. The most widespread examples are environmental sensors in cities and wooded areas that generate solar power using photovoltaic cells. More striking, however, are wearable devices— sports shoes and equipment, for instance—that can draw off the energy that accumulates in the materials themselves as a result of movement and flexion while being used. These small quantities of energy can be sufficient to extend the device's energy life to a significant degree; paradoxically, the more you use the product, the less you need to recharge it and the better it works.

The Right to the Silence of the Chips

On June 18, 2009, the European Commission released a document entitled *Internet of Things: An Action Plan for Europe*. This ten-page report contains a brief discussion of the strategic opportunity proffered by connected products to improve the quality of life of European citizens and support industrial development. Yet what caught media attention was that the

Commission set out some interesting and novel ideas about the role of government authorities in a highly sensorized world.

That objects everywhere are connected to the Internet is a fact that should obviously give us pause. Could a cyber terrorist have a field day with web-connected utilities, vehicles, and home appliances? Here, it would not just be information we would lose; physical assets and systems would be destroyed.

Who controls and who is entitled to access all the information about individuals captured by sensors throughout our cities and homes? What should be the new ethical and legal frameworks governing the interrelationships among people, connected objects, and their related services?

In response to these questions, the European Commission recommends ongoing supervision of the privacy and protection of captured personal data, identification of potential risks, and the creation of committees and forums monitoring the Internet of Things paradigm. The commission places particular emphasis on a line of action dubbed "the silence of the chips."

The so-called right to the silence of the chips expresses the idea that an individual is entitled to disconnect, and to have sensor networks stop capturing and monitoring his or her activities. National security naturally demands a certain minimum level of supervision to exist. However, the gist of the commission's paper is that there will come a point when we are monitored by so many objects that we may not even be aware of them in a way which enables us to exercise our rights properly.

Take the example of an apparently harmless product, such as a web-connected television set. It is obviously a good product to have, because we can access virtually unlimited content created in real time anywhere in the world. But what you may not realize is that your TV usage data—what you are watching, in what time frames, how often—is stored on the online platform and can be used to build up a user profile of your behavior patterns, your entertainment preferences, and even your political orientation. All this is very personal information about you.

A kitchen robot that is connected to the Internet to download firmware updates and meal plans can capture usage data capable of supporting inferences about how many people live in your home, what sort of food you like to eat, and the heart disease risk associated with it—which might eventually be used as grounds to raise your life insurance premium.

So we have characterized some of the commercial products within the Internet of Things paradigm as silent spies that track everything we do. The upside is that they can uncover hidden data, "make the invisible visible," and help us acquire knowledge about our environment and ourselves. The downside is that because these devices capture highly personal information—which can be cross-referenced to other data about you already available via social media—it is necessary to take rigorous steps and urgently pass laws to protect individuals' privacy and give them full and effective rights to decide what happens to that information.

Democratization: Open Source and the Maker Movement

Another trend that is driving new concepts and exploration in the Internet of Things framework is a corollary of the rise of highly accessible and easily learned development platforms that do not require technical qualifications or months of training for a layperson to create his or her own *connected objects*.

The most popular such platform is Arduino, created in 2005 by a team headed by Massimo Banzi and David Cuartielles at the Interaction Design Institute Ivrea, Italy. Because it is cheap—the basic version is priced at around 20 euros—and easy to program and use, Arduino quickly attracted interaction designers, artists, and hobbyists, who found that experimenting with this platform was more fun and easier to learn, and led to quicker prototyping cycles.

The effect of open-source platforms in fostering the rise of communities of developers sharing expertise and resources was already well understood and widely applied in the arena of software; but Arduino was the first mass platform to do the same for hardware, inaugurating the movement known as *Open-Source Hardware*. The openness and the specific architecture of Arduino encourage the emergence of new variants of itself, as well as add-ons and accessories—called *shields*—that let you quickly make fully functioning gadget prototypes by just fitting different parts together as if you were playing with a Lego set.

And, as we know, since the Internet is the largest existing source of data and services, it is a natural assumption that many of the available shields are designed to provide Bluetooth, Ethernet, Wi-Fi, 2G, or 3G connectivity for Arduino. So creating a physical object that captures environmental data and uploads it to online servers, or, in the opposite direction, that pulls down data from the net to affect the user's physical environment by means of light halos, sound, or movement, turns out to be quite easy to do even by people with no electronics expertise, including teenagers and children.

Arduino and similar web-connected quick prototyping platforms have proved a special boon for product designers and artists. Now, for the first time, they can cheaply produce a physical embodiment of a concept, whereas before they could only picture it in their minds. Bubblino is a bubble-blowing robot that looks out for a certain keyword on Twitter and blows a bubble every time someone uses that word. GoodNightLamp comprises two or more paired lamps that keep people who live in different places in touch with another by lighting up at the same time, thus strengthening their emotional bond. reaDIYmate consists of connected animated paper figures and sculptures that move in whichever way you have chosen in response to online events, such as incoming e-mail or stock price movements. iSouvenir is a *souvenir 2.0* created by me, the author of this article; it lights up and buzzes every time somebody on social media says they are at the place or heritage site depicted by the souvenir, thus imbuing a traditional object with a sort of global sentience.

The democratizing of technology surrounding the creation of web-connected concepts has been powerfully nurtured by the *maker* movement.

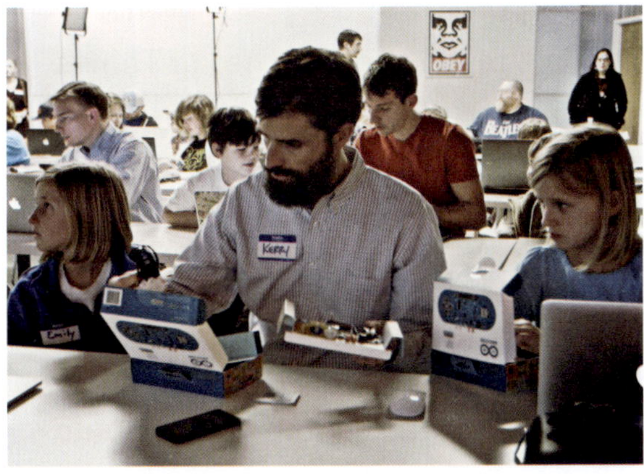

Fig. 2
Schoolchildren learning to prototype using Arduino.
Photograph: Chris Brank.
Source: Arduino Blog (http://blog.arduino.cc)

DIY or do-it-yourself is a decades-old movement that advocates the idea that you should make or repair goods on your own initiative, not just to save money, but also—and mainly—to learn how they work and so acquire the ability to design your own personal variants, with features not provided by commercial versions. The *maker* movement is a DIY variant that adopts technology to create personalized objects boasting electronic smarts and, a lot of the time, Internet connectivity. Low-cost, quick prototyping platforms—like the aforementioned Arduino—are one way of pursuing this hobby. Many users proudly upload to the Internet accounts of the various steps they took to create their home temperature and humidity monitoring system, or their lamp that lights up in different colors depending on weather forecasts provided by an Internet server.

Makers are interesting because their hobby is based on user communities that, again, freely share their expertise, experiment with sharply innovative ideas and product concepts that appeal to specific niches, and even produce commercial variants of their inventions—which benefits the local economy. The *maker* ethic is pretty much the opposite of massive corporate investment in manufacturing spitting out huge series of industrialized goods; what makers do is create personalized, almost hand-crafted technological products for customer niches outside the scope of the conventional market.

Business Models Driven by the Object/Service Duality

As the examples in the earlier sections have shown, the Internet of Things paradigm poses some challenges, but also a world of opportunity, for new enterprises and business models. Beyond RFID and NFC (Near Field Communication) tags —the earliest implementations of the Internet of Things—these opportunities are inherent in the object/service duality that is the hallmark of web-connected products. To return to the example of the smart chair, a smart chair manufacturer could be seen as moving on from "manufacturing and selling chairs" to "selling a lower back wellness monitoring service," the service being triggered by the chair, which could be hired or financed while the user's subscription is active. The shift in the value proposition, in relations with customers, and in the way the offering is communicated is immense—so much so, that the business becomes something completely different.

This strategy has already been used in conventional contexts—mobile phones partly or wholly financed by fixed service contracts, cable TV subscriptions inclusive of converter box rental, and, more recently, arrangements whereby some of the recurring income from mid- and high-end cars comes from monthly fees for vehicle information and monitoring by the manufacturer.

Web-connected devices are an ideal setting for *servification*—the process of shifting the value proposition from the physical object to the online service. The key advantage of this approach is that, although the physical object usually cannot be modified once it is in the consumer's hands, its related online services can be adapted and improved at any time. This extends the lifetime of the product (defined as the whole object/service package) and raises the value perceived by the user, who witnesses how the product is accommodated to his or her needs and accordingly views it as *smarter*.

To return to our earlier example of the smart chair, the manufacturer could offer, with reference to one and the same physical object—the chair—several different service levels of lower back monitoring at different rates: the customer might be a home office user, or a small or medium-sized enterprise, or a large corporation that might want to generate anonymized detailed reports that are sent to the occupational risk prevention department and employees themselves so that they can take corrective action.

By building up a mass of data, the manufacturer—or service provider—can obtain usage metrics for each user type so as to identify where the value is for each customer and adapt its service range and pricing plans accordingly without having to modify the physical chair: only the analytics and reporting services provided from its servers need to be reprogrammed.

The *servification* process involves two key benefits.

First, the provider obtains ongoing metrics characterizing the way that customers use the service. In a conventional setting, once the chair reaches the purchaser, the way it is used is traceable only in the form of customer surveys, or complaints about specific problems with given batches. But now the object is being monitored all the time and the manufacturer has a lot more information to work with. To take another example, a manufacturer of ovens could obtain anonymized data on oven usage—rewarding users for the data with gifts and prize drawings, for instance—and so gain a better understanding of how its products are used by various population groups (young couples, families with children, geographical differences, and so on). This information can then serve as the basis for developing new, specifically targeted ovens with more accurate pricing that reflects the functionalities that contribute value to the given market segment.

Secondly, because most of the product's *smarts* are in the cloud and, like any other Internet-based service, can be readily altered and adapted without need of involving the user directly, the product can be evolved through far quicker iteration cycles. For the smart chair, for instance, new premium reports could be developed for users willing to pay more for specific kinds of data. Iteration cycles for developing new services associated with the product can be rolled out in a matter of weeks or months and entail little cost—they are much quicker and cheaper than development cycles for the physical component.

There is no one market for the Internet of Things; rather, the paradigm is applicable to a wide swath of sectors and markets, embracing logistics and transport management, connected furniture and appliances, agricultural monitoring systems, smart clothes and accessories, toys, entertainment, and art. Predictions range from 20 to 50 billion products being connected to the Internet by the end of this decade. All of them based on the object/service duality. All of them designed to make life easier for us.

Conclusions

In 1874 a team of French engineers built a system of sensors allowing for remote monitoring from Paris of weather and snow depth conditions on Mont Blanc.

In 2013, you can use your smartphone to estimate the calories you burned over the past hour of running or cycling. Next, you get in your car, which will suggest the best route to take based on traffic density and the cheapest service stations on the way. While driving, you can give voice commands to your refrigerator so that it produces an inventory and suggests balanced, healthy recipes you can cook today using the available ingredients. Twenty minutes in advance of your arrival, the central heating in your home is triggered remotely.

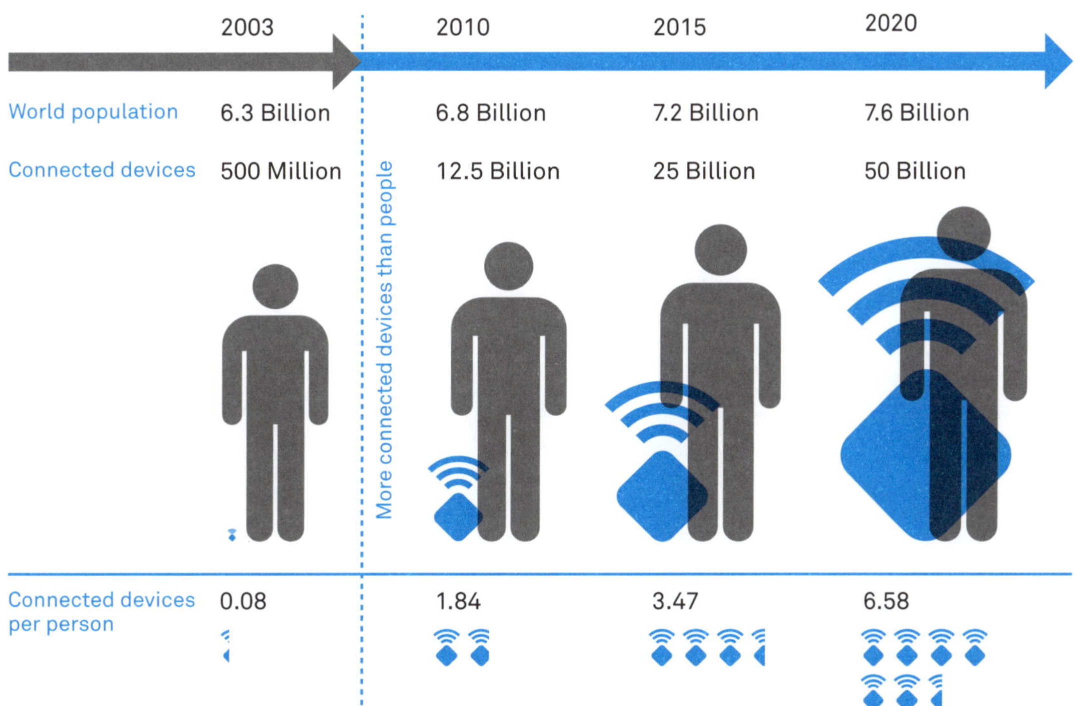

Fig. 3
Forecast change in connected devices per capita for this decade.
Source: Evans 2011

These two scenarios are separated by an interval of more than hundred years and several technological revolutions.

All the products mentioned in this article as examples are, or are about to be, a reality, although many of them have not yet been adopted on a mass scale or integrated with one another. We are witnessing only the early stages in the history of smart web-connected products. Many challenges lie ahead—security and privacy, product energy and maintenance needs, new product/person relationship models leading to product/user/manufacturer relationships, and new business models reflecting the object/service duality.

The magic of *enchanted objects* is finally becoming a reality. Enchanted objects are here. They are here to stay. And they are here to help us, opening up fascinating new horizons.

References

Chui, Michael, Markus Löffler, and Roger Roberts.
"The Internet of Things." *McKinsey Quarterly*, no. 2 (March 2010). http://www.mckinsey.com/insights/high_tech_telecoms_internet/the_internet_of_things

Evans, Dave.
"The Internet of Things: How the Next Evolution of the Internet Is Changing Everything." Cisco White Paper, April 2011. http://www.cisco.com/web/about/ac79/docs/innov/IoT_IBSG_0411FINAL.pdf

Gruman, Galen, Scott Bauer, and Vinod Baya. 2013.
"Using Technology to Help Customers Achieve Their Goals." In "Internet of Things: Evolving Transactions into Relationships," *PWC Technology Forecast*, no. 1 (2013).

Harbor Research.
"Shared Destinies: How The Internet of Things, Social Networks & Creative Collaboration Will Shape Future Market Structure." White Paper, 2009.

Nold, Christian, and Rob van Kranenburg.
The Internet of People for a Post-Oil World. Situated Technologies Pamphlets 8. New York: The Architectural League, 2011. http://www.situatedtechnologies.net/files/ST8_InternetOfPeople_web.pdf

Smith, Ian G, ed.
"The Internet of Things 2012: New Horizons." Halifax, UK: IERC - Internet of Things European Research Cluster, 2012. http://www.internet-of-things-research.eu/pdf/IERC_Cluster_Book_2012_WEB.pdf

Swan, Melanie.
"Sensor Mania! The Internet of Things, Wearable Computing, Objective Metrics, and the Quantified Self 2.0." *Journal of Sensor and Actuator Networks* 1, no 3 (2012): 217–53.

Van Kranenburg, Rob.
The Internet of Things. A Critique of Ambient Technology and the All-Seeing Network of RFID. Network Notebooks 02. Amsterdam: Institute of Network Cultures, 2007. http://www.networkcultures.org/_uploads/notebook2_theinternetofthings.pdf

Vázquez, Juan Ignacio, and Diego López-de-Ipiña.
"Social Devices: Autonomous Artifacts That Communicate on the Internet." In Christian Floerkemeier, Sanjay E. Sarma, Marc Langheinrich, Friedemann Mattern, and Elgar Fleisch, eds. *The Internet of Things: First International Conference, IOT 2008, Zurich, Switzerland, March 26–28, 2008, Proceedings.* Berlin and Heidelberg: Springer Verlag, 2008. 308–24.

Vázquez, Juan Ignacio, Jonathan Ruiz-de-Garibay, Xabier Eguiluz, Iker Doamo, Silvia Rentería, and Ana Ayerbe.
"Communication Architectures and Experiences for Web-Connected Physical Smart Objects." *Pervasive Computing and Communications Workshops (PERCOM Workshops), 8th IEEE International Conference on March 29 – April 2, 2010*. Mannheim, Germany: IEEE Explore, 2010. 684–89.

Vázquez, Juan Ignacio.
"Exploring Business Models for Web-Connected Consumer Products." Presentation, Third Annual Internet of Things Europe 2011: Bridging the Divide between Policy and Reality, Brussels, June 28/29, 2011.

Who Owns Big Data?

Michael Nielsen

Writer, scientist, and programmer

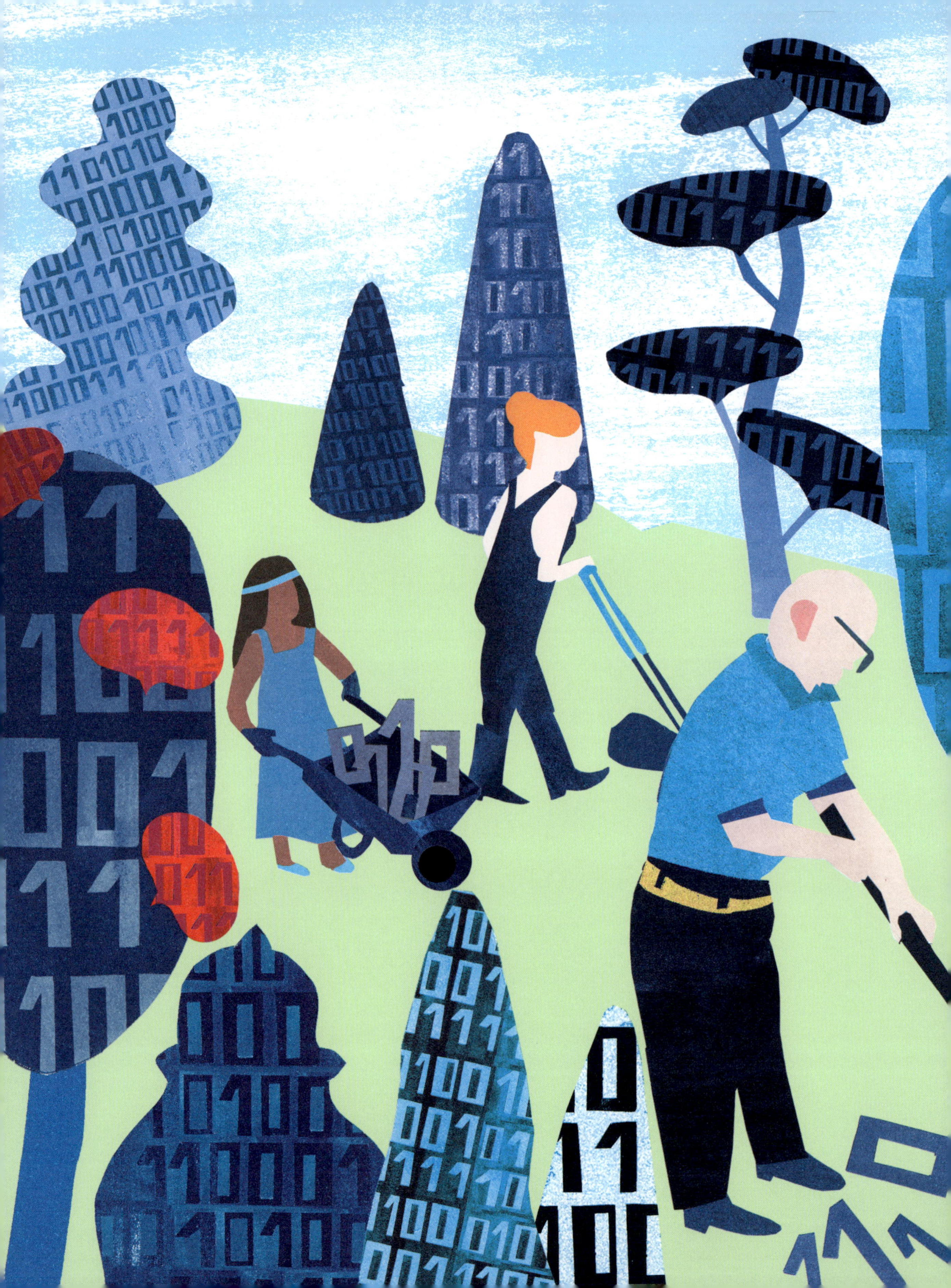

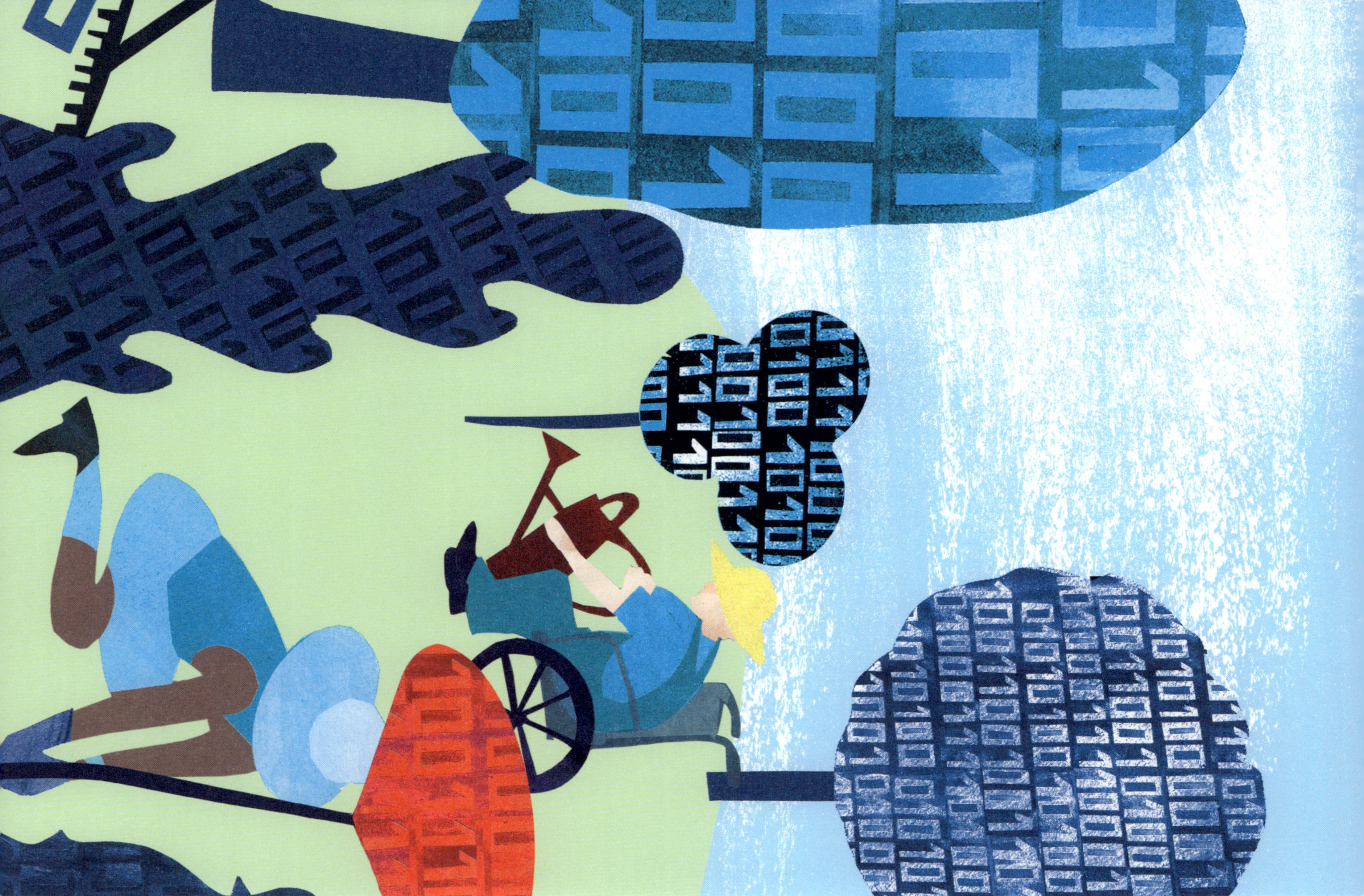

Michael Nielsen

michaelnielsen.org

Illustration
Catell Ronca

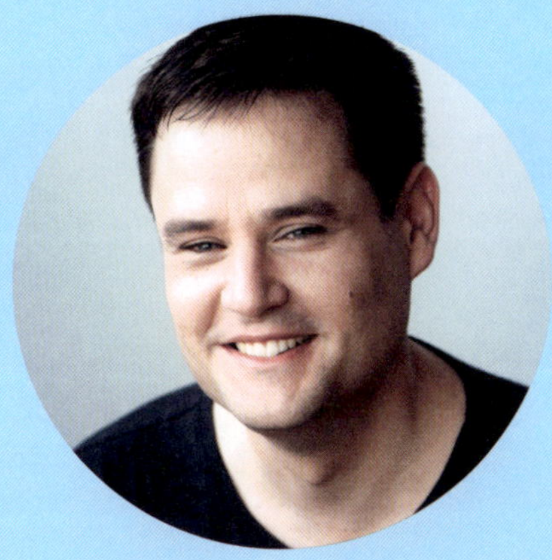

Michael Nielsen is a writer, scientist, and programmer. Originally trained as a theoretical physicist, he worked on quantum computing for 15 years at institutions that include the California Institute of Technology and the Los Alamos National Laboratory. As he pursued that work, Michael became fascinated by the potential of the Internet and collective intelligence to change the way scientific research is done, and in 2008 he left his job as a tenured professor to pursue that interest. He is the author of *Reinventing Discovery* (Princeton University Press, 2011), a book describing how the Internet is changing science. His current major project is a technical book about artificial intelligence and neural networks.

Sites and services that have changed my life
arxiv.org
github.com
scholar.google.com

Who Owns Big Data?

In 2010, the CEO of Google at the time, Eric Schmidt, made a remarkable statement at a media event in Abu Dhabi: "One day we had a conversation where we figured we could just [use Google's data about its users] to predict the stock market. And then we decided it was illegal. So we stopped doing that" (Fortt 2010).

The journalist John Battelle (2010) has described Google as "the database of [human] intentions." Battelle noticed that the search queries entered into Google express human needs and desires. By storing all those queries—more than a trillion a year—Google can build up a database of human intent. That knowledge of intention then makes it possible for Google to predict the movement of the stock market (and much else). Of course, neither Google nor anyone else has a complete database of human intentions. But part of the power of Battelle's phrase is that it suggests that aspiration. Google cofounder Sergey Brin has said that the ultimate future of search is to connect directly to users' brains (Arrington 2009). What could you do if you had a database that truly contained all human intentions?

The database of human intentions is a small part of a much bigger vision: a database containing all the world's knowledge. This idea goes back to the early days of modern computing, and people such as Arthur C. Clarke and H. G. Wells exploring visions of a "world brain" (Wikipedia 2013). What's changed recently is that a small number of technology companies are engaged in serious (albeit early stage) efforts to build databases which really will contain much of human knowledge. Think, for example, of the way Facebook has mapped out the social connections between more than 1 billion people. Or the way Wolfram Research has integrated massive amounts of knowledge about mathematics and the natural and social sciences into Wolfram Alpha. Or Google's efforts to build Google Maps, the most detailed map of the world ever constructed, and Google Books, which aspires to digitize all the books (in all languages) in the world (Taycher 2010). Building a database containing all the world's knowledge has become profitable.

This data gives these companies great power to understand the world. Consider the following examples: Facebook CEO Mark Zuckerberg has used user data to predict which Facebook users will start relationships (O'Neill 2010); researchers have used data from Twitter to forecast box office revenue for movies (Asur and Huberman 2010); and Google has used search data to track influenza outbreaks around the world (Ginsberg et al. 2009). These few examples are merely the tip of a much larger iceberg; with the right infrastructure, data can be converted into knowledge, often in surprising ways.

What's especially striking about examples like these is the ease with which such projects can be carried out. It's possible for a small team of engineers to build a service such as Google Flu Trends, Google's influenza tracking service, in a matter of weeks. However, that ability relies on access to both specialized data and the tools necessary to make sense of that data. This combination of data and tools is a kind of data infrastructure, and a powerful data infrastructure is available only at a very few organizations, such as Google and Facebook. Without access to such data infrastructure, even the most talented programmer would find it extremely challenging to create projects such as Google Flu Trends.

Today, we take it for granted that a powerful data infrastructure is available only at a few big for-profit companies,[1] and to secretive intelligence agencies such as the NSA and GCHQ. But in this essay I explore the possibility of creating a similarly powerful *public* data infrastructure, an infrastructure which could be used by anyone in the world. It would be Big Data for the masses.

Imagine, for example, a 19-year-old intern at a health agency somewhere who has an idea like Google Flu Trends.[2] They could use the public data

1. Many companies (including Google and Facebook) do, in fact, offer outsiders some limited access to their internal data. For example, the Facebook platform (http://en.wikipedia.org/wiki/Facebook_Platform) is a way for outside programmers to integrate applications with Facebook. Google products such as Google Maps offer "open APIs" (application programming interfaces) which allow outside programmers to use Google's maps in their own applications. This kind of openness is valuable, but usually has stringent limitations that make it very different from, and far less powerful than, the direct access to infrastructure available to programmers at these companies.
2. http://www.google.org/flutrends/

infrastructure to quickly test their idea. Or imagine a 21-year-old under-graduate with a new idea for how to rank search engine results. Again, they could use the public data infrastructure to quickly test their idea. Or perhaps a historian of ideas wants to understand how phrases get added to the language over time; or how ideas spread within particular groups, and die out within others; or how particular types of stories get traction within the news, while others don't. Again, this kind of thing could easily be done with a powerful public data infrastructure.

These kinds of experiments won't be free—it costs real money to run computations across clusters containing thousands of computers, and those costs will need to be passed on to the people doing the experiments. But it should be possible for even novice programmers to do amazing experiments for a few tens of dollars, experiments which today would be nearly impossible for even the most talented programmers.

Note, by the way, that when I say *public* data infrastructure, I don't necessarily mean data infrastructure that's run by the government. What's important is that the infrastructure be *usable* by the public, as a platform for discovery and innovation, not that it actually be publicly owned. In principle, it could be run by a not-for-profit organization, or a for-profit company, or perhaps even by a loose network of individuals. Below, I'll argue that there are good reasons such infrastructure should be run by a not-for-profit.

There are many nascent projects to build powerful public data infrastructure. Probably the best known such project is Wikipedia. Consider the vision statement of the Wikimedia Foundation (which runs Wikipedia): "Imagine a world in which every single human being can freely share in the sum of all knowledge. That's our commitment." Wikipedia is impressive in size, with more than 4 million articles in the English language edition. The Wikipedia database contains more than 40 gigabytes of data. But while that sounds enormous, consider that Google routinely works with data at the petabyte scale—a million gigabytes! By comparison, Wikipedia is miniscule. And it's easy to see why there's this difference. What the Wikimedia Foundation considers "the sum of all knowledge" is extremely narrow compared to the range of data about the world that Google finds useful—everything from scans of books to the data being generated by

Google's driverless cars (each car generates nearly a gigabyte per second about its environment! [Gross 2013]) And so Google is creating a far more comprehensive database of knowledge.

Another marvelous public project is OpenStreetMap,[3] a not-for-profit that is working to create a free and openly editable map of the entire world. OpenStreetMap is good enough that their data is used by services such as Wikipedia, Craigslist, and Apple Maps. However, while the data is good, OpenStreetMap does not yet match the comprehensive cover provided by Google Maps, which has 1,000 full-time employees and 6,100 contractors working on the project (Carlson 2012). The OpenStreetMap database contains 400 gigabytes of data. Again, while that is impressive, it's miniscule by comparison to the scale at which companies such as Google and Facebook operate.

More generally, many existing public projects such as Wikipedia and OpenStreetMap are generating data that can be analyzed on a single computer using off-the-shelf software. The for-profit companies have data infrastructure far beyond this scale. Their computer clusters contain hundreds of thousands or millions of computers. They use clever algorithms to run computations distributed across those clusters. This requires not only access to hardware, but also to specialized algorithms and tools, and to large teams of remarkable people with the rare (and expensive!) knowledge required to make all this work. The payoff is that this much larger data infrastructure gives them far more power to understand and to shape the world. If the human race is currently constructing a database of all the world's knowledge, then by far the majority of that work is being done on privately owned databases.

I haven't yet said what I mean by a "database of all the world's knowledge." Of course, it's meant to be an evocative phrase, not (yet!) a literal description of what's being built. Even Google, the organization which has made most progress toward this goal, has for the most part not worked directly toward this goal.[4] Instead, they've focused on practical user needs—search,

3. http://www.openstreetmap. org/#map=5/51.500/-0.100

4. An exception is the Google Knowledge Graph (http:// en.wikipedia.org/wiki/Knowledge_ Graph), which really does seem to be a start on a database of all the world's knowledge.

maps, books, and so on—in each case gathering data to build a useful product. They then leverage and integrate the data sets they already have to create other products. For example, they've combined Android and Google Maps to build up real-time maps of the traffic in cities, which can then be displayed on Android phones. The data behind Google Search has been used to launch products such as Google News, Google Flu Trends, and (the now defunct, but famous) Google Reader. And so while most of Google's effort isn't literally aimed at building a database of all the world's knowledge, it's a useful way of thinking about the eventual end game.

For this reason, from now I'll mostly use the more generic term *public data infrastructure*. In concrete, everyday terms this can be thought of in terms of specific projects. Imagine, for example, a project to build an open infrastructure search engine. As I described above, this would be a platform that enabled anyone in the world to experiment with new ways of ranking search results, and new ways of presenting information. Or imagine a project to build an open infrastructure social network, where anyone in the world could experiment with new ways to connect people. Those projects would, in turn, serve as platforms for other new services. Who knows what people could come up with?

The phrase *a public data infrastructure* perhaps suggests a singular creation by some special organization. But that's not quite what I mean. To build a powerful public data infrastructure will require a vibrant ecology of organizations, each making their own contribution to an overall public data infrastructure. Many of those organizations will be small, looking to innovate in new ways, or to act as niche platforms. And some winners will emerge, larger organizations that integrate and aggregate huge amounts of data in superior ways. And so when I write of creating *a public data infrastructure*, I'm not talking about creating a single organization. Instead, I'm talking about the creation of an entire vibrant ecology of organizations, an ecology of which projects like Wikipedia and OpenStreetMap are just early members.

I'll describe shortly how a powerful public data infrastructure could be created, and what the implications might be. But before doing that, let me make it clear that what I'm proposing is very different from the much-discussed idea of open data.

Many people, including the creator of the web, Tim Berners-Lee, have advocated open, online publication of data. The open data visionaries believe we can transform domains such as government, science, and the law by publishing the crucial data underlying those domains.

If this vision comes to pass then thousands or millions of people and organizations will publish their data online.

While open data will be transformative, it's also different (though complementary) to what I am proposing. The open data vision is about decentralized publication of data. That means it's about small data, for the most part. What I'm talking about is Big Data—aggregating data from many sources inside a powerful centralized data infrastructure, and then making that infrastructure usable by anyone. That's qualitatively different. To put it another way, open publication of data is a good first step. But to get the full benefit, we need to aggregate data from many sources inside a powerful public data infrastructure.

Why a Public Data Infrastructure Should Be Developed by Not-for-Profits

Is it better for public data infrastructure to be built by for-profit companies, or by not-for-profits? Or is some other option even better—say, governments creating it, or perhaps loosely organized networks of contributors, without a traditional institutional structure? In this section I argue that the best option is not-for-profits.

Let's focus first on the case of for-profits versus not-for-profits. In general, I am all for for-profit companies bringing technologies to market. However, in the case of a public data infrastructure, there are special circumstances which make not-for-profits preferable.

To understand those special circumstances, think back to the late 1980s and early 1990s. That was a time of stagnation in computer software, a time of incremental progress, but few major leaps. The reason was Microsoft's stranglehold over computer operating systems. Whenever a company discovered a new market for software, Microsoft would replicate the product and then use their control of the operating system to crush the original innovator. This happened to the spreadsheet Lotus 1-2-3 (crushed by Excel), the word processor Word Perfect (crushed by Word), and many other lesser-known programs. In effect, those other companies were acting as the research and development arms of Microsoft. As this pattern gradually became clear, the result was a reduced incentive to invest in new ideas for software, and a decade or so of stagnation.

That all changed when a new platform for computing emerged—the web browser. Microsoft couldn't use their operating system dominance to destroy companies such as Google, Facebook, and Amazon. The reason is that those companies' products didn't run (directly) on Microsoft's operating system, they ran over the web. Microsoft initially largely ignored the web, a situation that only changed in May 1995, when Bill Gates sent out a company-wide memo entitled "The Internet Tidal Wave" (Letters of Note 2011). But by the time Gates realized the importance of the web, it was too late to stop the tidal wave. Microsoft made many subsequent attempts to get control of web standards, but those efforts were defeated by organizations such as the World Wide Web Consortium, Netscape, Mozilla, and Google. Effectively, the computer industry moved from a proprietary platform (Windows) to an open platform (the web) not owned by anyone in particular. The result was a resurgence of software innovation.

The lesson is that when dominant technology platforms are privately owned, the platform owner can co-opt markets discovered by companies using the platform. I gave the example of Microsoft, but there are many other examples—companies such as Apple, Facebook, and Twitter have all used their ownership of important technology platforms to co-opt new markets in this way. We'd all be better off if dominant technology platforms were operated in the public interest, not as a way of co-opting innovation. Fortunately, that is what's happened with both the Internet and the web, and that's why those platforms have been such a powerful spur to innovation.

Platforms such as the web and the Internet are a little bit special in that they're primarily standards. That is, they're broadly shared agreements on how technologies should operate. Those standards are often stewarded by not-for-profit organizations such as the World Wide Web Consortium and the Internet Engineering Task Force. But it doesn't really make sense to say the standards are *owned* by those not-for-profits, since what matters is really the broad community commitment to the standards. Standards are about owning hearts and minds, not atoms.

By contrast, a public data infrastructure would be a different kind of technology platform. Any piece of such an infrastructure would involve considerable capital costs, associated with owning (or leasing) and operating a large cluster of computers. And because of this capital investment there really is a necessity for an owner. We've already seen that if a public data infrastructure were owned by for-profit companies, those companies would always be tempted to use their ownership to co-opt innovation. The natural alternative solution is for a public data infrastructure to be owned and operated by not-for-profits that are committed to not co-opting innovation, but rather to encouraging it and helping it to flourish.

What about government providing public data infrastructure? In fact, for data related directly to government this is beginning to happen, through initiatives such as data.gov, the U.S. Government's portal for government data in the U.S. But it's difficult to believe that having the government provide a public data infrastructure more broadly would be a good idea. Technological innovation requires many groups of people to try our many different ideas, with most failing, and with the best ideas winning. This isn't a model for development that governments have a long history of using effectively. With that said, initiatives such as data.gov will make a very important contribution to a public data infrastructure. But they will not be the core of a powerful, broad-ranging public data infrastructure.

The final possibility is that a public data infrastructure not be developed by an organization at all, but rather by a loosely organized network of contributors, without a traditional institutional structure. Examples such as OpenStreetMap are in this vein. OpenStreetMap does have a traditional not-for-profit at its core, but it's tiny, with a 2012 budget of less than 100,000 British pounds (OMS 2013). Most of the work is done by a loose network of volunteers. That's a great model for OpenStreetMap, but part of the reason it works is because of the relatively modest scale of the data involved. Big Data involves larger organizations (and larger budgets), due to the scale of the computing power involved, as well as the long-term commitments necessary to providing reliable service, effective documentation, and support. All these things mean building a lasting organization. So while a loosely distributed model may be a great way to start such projects, over time they will need to transition to a more traditional not-for-profit model.

Challenges for Not-for-Profits Developing a Public Data Infrastructure

How could not-for-profits help develop such a public data infrastructure?

At first sight, an encouraging sign is the flourishing ecosystem of open-source software. Ohloh,[5] a site indexing open-source projects, currently lists more than 600,000 projects. Open-source projects such as Linux, Hadoop, and others are often leaders in their areas.

Given this ecosystem of open-source software, it's somewhat puzzling that there is comparatively little public data infrastructure. Why has so much important code been made usable by anyone in the world, and so little data infrastructure?

To answer this question, it helps to think about the origin of open-source software. Open-source projects usually start in one of two ways: (1) as hobby projects (albeit often created by professional programmers in their spare time), such as Linux; or (2) as by-products of the work of for-profit companies. By looking at each of these cases separately, we can understand why open-source software has flourished so much more than public data infrastructure.

Let's first consider the motivations for open-source software created by for-profit companies. An example is the Hadoop project, which was created by Yahoo as a way of making it easier to run programs across

5. http://www.ohloh.net

large clusters of computers. When for-profit companies open source projects in this way, it's because they don't view owning the code as part of their competitive business advantage. While running large cluster-based computations is obviously essential to Yahoo, they're not trying to use that as their edge over other companies. And so it made sense for Yahoo to open-source Hadoop, so other people and organizations can help them improve the code.

By contrast, for many Internet companies owning their own data really *is* a core business advantage, and they are unlikely to open up their data infrastructure. A priori nothing says this necessarily has to be the case. A for-profit could attempt to build a business offering a powerful public data infrastructure, and find some competitive advantage other than owning the data (most likely, an advantage in logistics and supply chain management). But I believe that this hasn't happened because holding data close is an easy and natural way for a company to maintain a competitive advantage. The investor Warren Buffet has described how successful companies need a *moat*—a competitive advantage that is truly difficult for other organizations to duplicate. For Google and Facebook and many other Internet companies their internal data infrastructure is their moat.

What about hobby projects? If projects such Linux can start as a hobby, then why don't we see more public data infrastructure started as part of a hobby project? The problem is that creating data infrastructure requires a much greater commitment than creating open-source code. A hobby open-source project requires a time commitment, but little direct expenditure of money. It can be done on weekends, or in the evenings. As I noted already above, building effective data infrastructure requires time, money, and a long-term commitment to providing reliable service, effective documentation, and support. To do these things requires an organization that will be around for a long time. That's a much bigger barrier to entry than in the case of open source.

What would be needed to create a healthy, vibrant ecology of not-for-profit organizations working on developing a public data infrastructure?

This question is too big to comprehensively answer in a short essay such as this. But I will briefly point out two significant obstacles to this happening through the traditional mechanisms for funding not-for-profits: foundations, grant agencies, and similar philanthropic sources.

To understand the first obstacle, consider the story of the for-profit company Ludicorp. In 2003 Ludicorp released an online game called *Game Neverending*. After releasing the game, Ludicorp added a feature for players to swap photos with one another. The programmers soon noticed that people were logging onto the game just to swap photos, and ignoring the actual gameplay. After observing this, they made a bold decision. They threw out the game, and relaunched a few weeks later as a photo-sharing service, which they named Flickr. Flickr went on to become the first major online photo-sharing application, and was eventually acquired by Yahoo. Although Flickr has faded since the acquisition, in its day it was one of the most beloved websites in the world.

Stories like this are so common in technology circles that there's even a name for this phenomenon. Entrepreneurs talk about *pivoting* when they discover that some key assumption in their business model is wrong, and they need to try something else. Entrepreneur Steve Blank, one of the people who developed the concept of the pivot, has devised an influential definition of a startup as "an organization formed to search for a repeatable and scalable business model" (Blank 2010). When Ludicorp discovered that photo sharing was a scalable business in a way that *Game Neverending* wasn't, they did the right thing: they pivoted hard.

This pattern of pivoting makes sense for entrepreneurs who are trying to create new technologies and new markets for those technologies. True innovators don't start out knowing what will work; they discover what will work. And so their initial plans are almost certain to be wrong, and will need to change, perhaps radically.

The pivot has been understood and accepted by many technology investors. It's expected and even encouraged that companies will change their mission, often radically, as they search for a scalable business model. But in the not-for-profit world this kind of change is verboten. Can you imagine a not-for-profit telling their funders—say, some big foundation—that they've decided to pivot? Perhaps they've decided that they're no longer working with homeless youth, because they've discovered that their technology has a great application to the art scene. Such a change won't look good on the end-of-year report! Yet, as the pivots behind Flickr and similar companies show, that kind of flexibility is an enormous aid (and arguably very nearly essential) in developing new technologies and new markets.

A second obstacle to funding not-for-profits working on a public data infrastructure is the risk-averse nature of much not-for-profit funding. In the for-profit world it's understood that technology startups are extremely risky. Estimates of the risk vary, but typical estimates place the odds of failure for a startup at perhaps 70 to 80 percent (Gompers et al. 2008). Very few foundations or grant agencies would accept 70 to 80 percent odds of failure. It's informative to consider entrepreneur Steve Blank's startup biography. He bluntly states that his startups have made "two deep craters, several 'base hits,' [and] one massive 'dot-com bubble' home run" (Blank 2013). That is, he's had two catastrophic failures, and one genuine success. In the for-profit startup world this can be bragged about; in the not-for-profit world this rate of success would be viewed as disastrous. The situation is compounded by the difficulty in defining what *success* is for a not-for-profit; this makes it tempting (and possible) for mediocre not-for-profits to scrape by, continuing to exist, when it would be healthier if they ceased to operate, and made space for more effective organizations.

One solution I've seen tried is for foundations and grant agencies to exhort applicants to take more risks. The problem is that any applicant considering taking those risks knows failure means they will still have trouble getting grants in the future, exhortation or no exhortation. So it still makes more sense to do low-risk work.

One possible resolution to this problem would be for not-for-profit funders to run *failure audits*. Suppose programs at the big foundations were audited for failures, and had to achieve a failure rate *above* a certain number. If a foundation were serious about taking risks, then they could run a deliberately high-risk grant program, where the program had to meet a target goal of at least 70 percent of projects failing. Doing this well would require careful design to avoid pitfalls. But if implemented well, the outcome would be a not-for-profit culture willing to take risks. At the moment, so far as I am aware, no large funder uses failure audits or any similar idea to encourage genuine risk taking.

I've painted a bleak picture of not-for-profit funding for a public data infrastructure (and for much other technology). But it's not entirely bleak. Projects such as Wikipedia and OpenStreetMap have found ways to be successful, despite not being started with traditional funding. And I am optimistic that examples such as these will help inspire funders to adopt a more experimental and high-risk approach to funding technological innovation, an approach that will speed up the development of a powerful public data infrastructure.

Two Futures for Big Data

We're at a transition moment in history. Many core human activities are changing profoundly: the way we seek information; the way we connect to people; the way we decide where we want to go, and who we want to be with. The way we make such choices is becoming more and more dominated by a few technology companies with powerful data infrastructure. It's fantastic that technology can improve our lives. But I believe that we'd be better off if more people could influence these core decisions about how we live.

In this essay, I've described two possible futures for Big Data. In one future, today's trends continue. The best data infrastructure will be privately owned by a few large companies who see it as a competitive advantage to map out human knowledge. In the other future, the future I hope we will create, the best data infrastructure will be available for use by anyone in the world, a powerful platform for experimentation, discovery, and the creation of new and better ways of living.

Acknowledgments
Thanks to Jen Dodd, Ilya Grigorik, and Hassan Masum for many conversations about these ideas.

References

Arrington, Michael.
"Google CEO Eric Schmidt On The Future Of Search: "Connect It Straight To Your Brain." *Tech Crunch*, September 3, 2009. http://techcrunch.com/2009/09/03/google-ceo-eric-schmidt-on-the-future-of-search-connect-it-straight-to-your-brain/

Asur, Sitaram, and Bernardo A. Huberman.
"Predicting the Future with Social Media." *arXiv*, March 29, 2010. http://arxiv.org/abs/1003.5699

Battelle, John.
"The Database of Intentions Is Far Larger Than I Thought." *John Battelle's Searchblog* (blog), March 5, 2010. http://battellemedia.com/archives/2010/03/the_database_of_intentions_is_far_larger_than_i_thought.php

Blank, Steve.
"What's a Startup? First Principles." Steve Blank.com, January 25, 2010. http://steveblank.com/2010/01/25/whats-a-startup-first-principles/

Blank, Steve.
"About Steve." Steve Blank.com. http://steveblank.com/about/ (accessed September 9, 2013).

Carlson, Nicholas.
"To Do What Google Does In Maps, Apple Would Have To Hire 7,000 People." *Business Insider*, June 26, 2012. http://www.businessinsider.com/to-do-what-google-does-in-maps-apple-would-have-to-hire-7000-people-2012-6

Fortt, Jon.
"Top 5 Moments from Eric Schmidt's Talk in Abu Dhabi." *CNN Money*, March 11, 2010. http://tech.fortune.cnn.com/2010/03/11/top-five-moments-from-eric-schmidts-talk-in-abu-dhabi/

Ginsberg, Jeremy, Matthew H. Mohebbi, Rajan S. Patel, Lynnette Brammer, Mark S. Smolinski, and Larry Brilliant.
"Detecting Influenza Epidemics Using Search Engine Query Data" (Letter). *Nature* 457 (February 19, 2009). http://www.nature.com/nature/journal/v457/n7232/full/nature07634.html

Gompers, Paul A., Anna Kovner, Josh Lerner, and David S. Scharfstein.
"Performance Persistence in Entrepreneurship." Harvard Business School. Working Paper 09-028. Cambridge, MA: Harvard University, 2008. http://www.hbs.edu/faculty/Publication%20Files/09-028.pdf

Gross, Bill.
"Google's Self-Driving Car gathers almost 1 GB per SECOND." Twitter, April 13, 2013. https://twitter.com/Bill_Gross/statuses/329069954911580160

Letters of Note.
"The Internet Tidal Wave." Letters of Note: Correspondence Deserving of a Wider Audience, July 22, 2011. http://www.lettersofnote.com/2011/07/internet-tidal-wave.html

O'Neill, Nick.
"Facebook Knows That Your Relationship Will End in a Week." *AllFacebook* (blog), May 17, 2010. http://allfacebook.com/facebook-knows-that-your-relationship-will-end-in-a-week_b14374

OMS (OpenStreetMap Foundation).
"Finances/Income 2012." Open Street Map Foundation, June 4, 2013. http://www.osmfoundation.org/wiki/Finances/Income_2012

Taycher, Leonid.
"Books of the World, Stand Up and Be Counted! All 129,864,880 of You." *Google Books Search* (blog), August 5, 2010. http://booksearch.blogspot.ca/2010/08/books-of-world-stand-up-and-be-counted.html

Wikipedia contributors.
"World Brain." *Wikipedia, The Free Encyclopedia*. http://en.wikipedia.org/w/index.php?title=World_Brain&oldid=571755421 (accessed September 17, 2013).

Cyber Attacks

Mikko Hypponen
Chief Research Officer of F-Secure

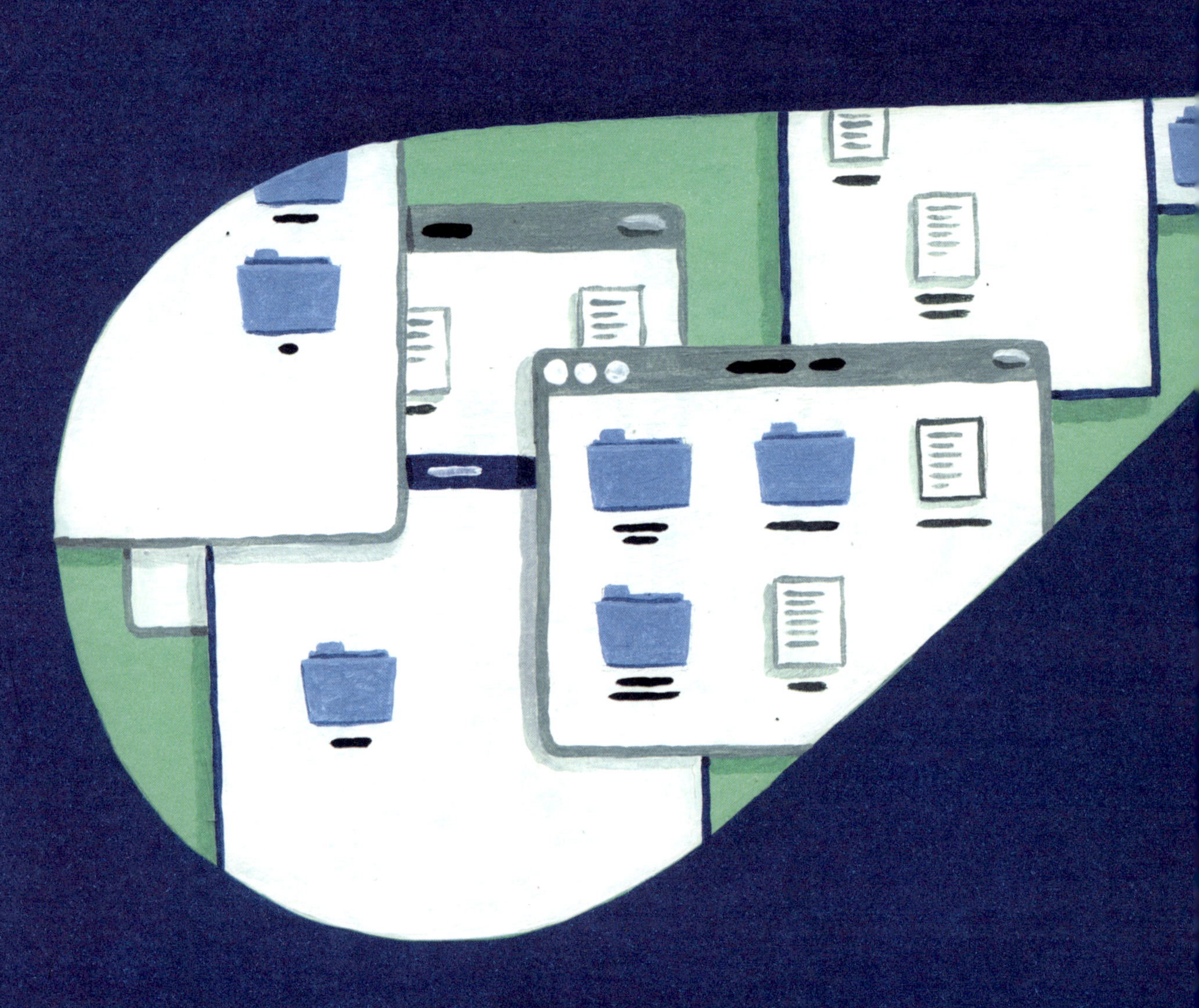

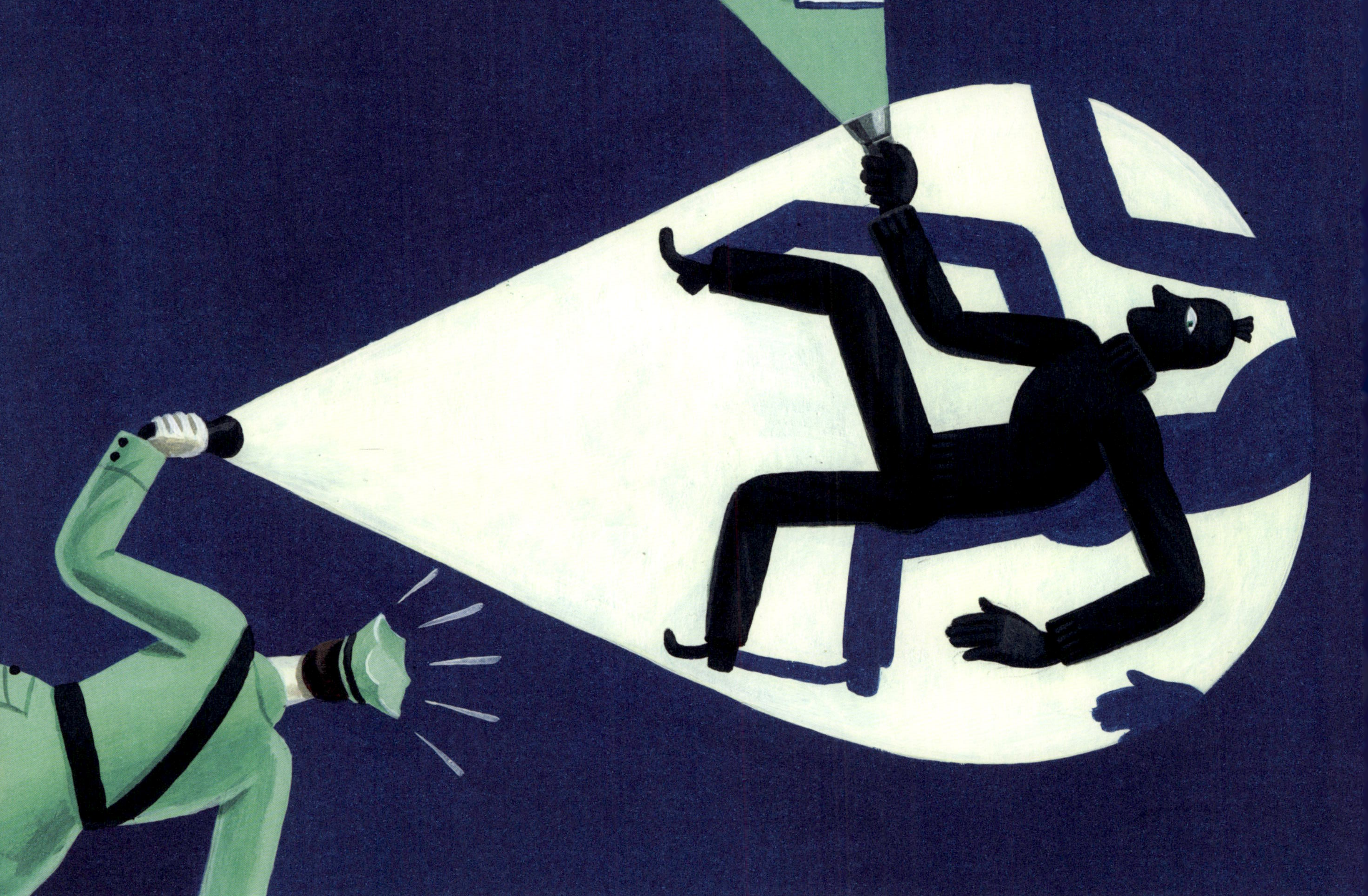

Mikko Hypponen

mikko.hypponen.com

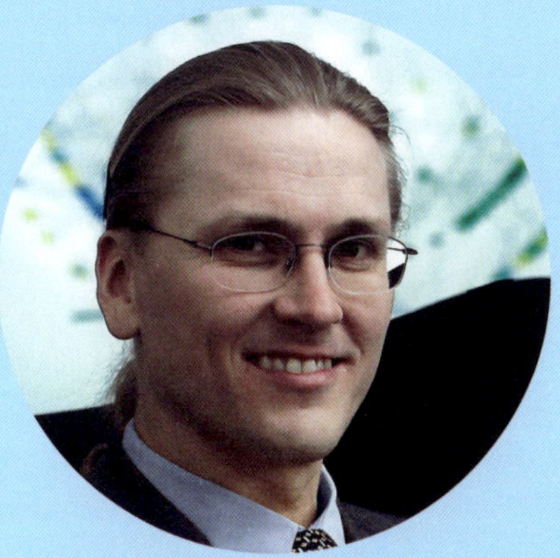

Mikko Hypponen is the Chief Research Officer of F-Secure in Finland. He has been working with computer security for over 20 years and has fought the biggest virus outbreaks in the net, including LoveLetter, Conficker, and Stuxnet. His TED Talk on computer security has been seen by almost a million people and has been translated into over 35 languages. His columns have been published in the *New York Times*, *Wired*, CNN, and the BBC. Mr. Hypponen was selected among the 50 most important people on the web by *PC World* magazine. *Foreign Policy* magazine included him on the list of "Top 100 Global Thinkers." Mr. Hypponen sits on the advisory boards of the ISF and the Lifeboat Foundation.

Cyber Attacks

The Future of the Internet

Sites and services that have changed my life
reddit.com
hxkcd.com
news.ycombinator.com

Cyber Attacks

Preface

The real world isn't like the online world.

In the real world, you only have to worry about the criminals who live in your city. But in the online world, you have to worry about criminals who could be on the other side of the planet. Online crime is always international because the Internet has no borders.

Today computer viruses and other malicious software are no longer written by hobbyist hackers seeking fame and glory among their peers. Most of them are written by professional criminals who are making millions with their attacks. These criminals want access to your computer, your PayPal passwords, and your credit card numbers.

I spend a big part of my life on the road, and I've visited many of the locations that are considered to be hotspots of online criminal activity. I've been to Moscow, São Paulo, Tartu, Vilnius, St. Petersburg, Beijing, and Bucharest.

I've met the underground and I've met the cops. And I've learned that things are never as simple as they seem from the surface. One would think that the epicenter for banking attacks, for example, would prioritize fighting them, right?

Right, but dig deeper and complications emerge. A good example is a discussion I had with a cybercrime investigator in Brazil. We spoke about the problems in Brazil and how São Paulo has become one of the largest sources of banking trojans in the world.

The investigator looked at me and said, "Yes. I understand that. But what you need to understand is that São Paulo is also one of the murder capitals of the world. People are regularly gunned down on the streets. So where exactly should we put our resources? To fight cybercrime? Or to fight crimes where people die?"

It's all a matter of balancing. When you balance the damage done by cybercrime and compare it to a loss of life, it's pretty obvious what's more important.

National police forces and legal systems are finding it extremely difficult to keep up with the rapid growth of online crime. They have limited resources and expertise to investigate online criminal activity. The victims, police, prosecutors, and judges rarely uncover the full scope of the crimes that often take place across international boundaries. Action against the criminals is too slow, the arrests are few and far between, and too often the penalties are very light, especially compared with those attached to real-world crimes.

Because of the low prioritization for prosecuting cybercriminals and the delays in launching effective cybercrime penalties, we are thereby sending the wrong message to the criminals and that's why online crime is growing so fast. Right now would-be online criminals can see that the likelihood of their getting caught and punished is vanishingly small, yet the profits are great.

The reality for those in positions like the São Paulo investigator is that they must balance both fiscal constraints and resource limitations. They simply cannot, organizationally, respond to every type of threat. If we are to keep up with the cybercriminals, the key is cooperation. The good news is that the computer security industry is quite unique in the way direct competitors help each other.

The Turning Point

If you were running Windows on your computer 10 years ago, you were running Windows XP. In fact, you were most likely running Windows XP SP1 (Service Pack 1). This is important, as Windows XP SP1 did not have a firewall enabled by default and did not feature automatic updates. So, if you were running Windows, you weren't running a firewall and you had to patch your system manually—by downloading the patches with Internet Explorer 6, which itself was ridden with security vulnerabilities.

No wonder, then, that worms and viruses were rampant in 2003. In fact, we saw some of the worst outbreaks in history in 2003: Slammer, Sasser, Blaster, Mydoom, Sobig, and so on. They went on to do some spectacular damage. Slammer infected a nuclear power plant in Ohio and shut down Bank of America's ATM systems. Blaster stopped trains in their tracks outside Washington, D.C., and shut down Air Canada check-in systems at Canadian airports. Sasser thoroughly infected several hospitals in Europe.

The problems with Windows security were so bad that Microsoft had to do something. And they did. In hindsight, they did a spectacular turn-around in their security processes. They started Trustworthy Computing. They stopped all new development for a while to go back and find and fix old vulnerabilities. Today, the difference in the default security level of 64-bit Windows 8 is so much ahead of Windows XP you can't even compare them.

We've seen other companies do similar turnarounds. When the Microsoft ship started to become tighter and harder to attack, the attackers started looking for easier targets. One favorite was Adobe Reader and Adobe Flash. For several years, one vulnerability after another was found in Adobe products, and most users were running badly outdated products as updating wasn't straightforward. Eventually Adobe got their act together. Today, the security level of, say, Adobe Reader, is so much ahead of older readers you can't even compare them.

The battle at hand right now is with Java and Oracle. It seems that Oracle hasn't gotten their act together yet. And maybe don't even have to: users are voting with their feet and Java is already disappearing from the web.

The overall security level of end-user systems is now better than ever before. The last decade has brought us great improvements. Unfortunately, the last decade has also completely changed who were fighting.

In 2003, all the malware was still being written by hobbyists, for fun. The hobbyists have been replaced by new attackers: not just organized criminals, but also hacktivists and governments. Criminals and especially governments can afford to invest in their attacks. As an end result, we're still not safe with our computers, even with all the great improvements.

But at least we don't see flights grounded and trains stopped by malware every other week, like we did in 2003.

Crypto Currencies

In 2008, a mathematician called Satoshi Nakamoto submitted a technical paper for a cryptography conference. The paper described a peer-to-peer network where participating systems would do complicated mathematical calculations on something called a *blockchain*. This system was designed to create a completely new currency: a crypto currency. In short, a currency that is based on math. The paper was titled "Bitcoin: A Peer-to-Peer Electronic Cash System."

Since Bitcoin is not linked to any existing currency, its value is purely based on the value people believe it's worth. And since it can be used to do instant transactions globally, it does have value. Sending Bitcoins around is very much like sending e-mail. If I have your address, I can send you money. I can send it to you instantly, anywhere, bypassing exchanges, banks, and the tax man. In fact, crypto currencies make banks unnecessary for moving money around—which is why banks hate the whole idea.

The beauty of the algorithm behind Bitcoin is solving two main problems of crypto currencies by joining them: how do you confirm transactions and how do you inject new units of currency into the system without causing inflation. Since there is no central bank in the system, the transactions need to be confirmed somehow—otherwise one could fabricate fake money. In Bitcoin, the confirmations are done by other members of the peer-to-peer network. At least six members of the peer-to-peer network have to confirm the transactions before they go through. But why would anybody confirm transactions for others? Because they get rewarded for it: the algorithm issues new Bitcoins as reward to users who have been participating in confirmations. This is called *mining*.

When Bitcoin was young, mining was easy and you could easily make dozens of Bitcoins on a home computer. However, as Bitcoin value grew, mining became harder since there were more people interested in doing it. Even though the dollar-to-BTC exchange rate has fluctuated, fact remains that in the beginning of 2013, the exchange rate for the U.S. dollar to a Bitcoin was $8 and by the fall it was $130. So Bitcoins now have very real real-world value.

When Bitcoins became valuable, people were more and more interested in Satoshi Nakamoto. He gave a few e-mail interviews, but eventually stopped correspondence altogether. Then he disappeared. When people went looking for him, they realized Satoshi Nakamoto didn't exist. Even today, nobody knows who invented Bitcoin. Indeed, however, Bitcoin fans have been spotted wearing T-shirts saying "Satoshi Nakamoto Died for Our Sins."

Today, there are massively large networks of computers mining Bitcoins and other competing crypto currencies (such as Litecoin). The basic idea behind mining is easy enough: if you have powerful computers, you can make money. Unfortunately, those computers don't have to be your own computers. Some of the largest botnets run by online criminals today are monetized by mining. So, you'd have an infected home computer of a grandmother in, say, Barcelona, running Windows XP at 100 percent utilization around the clock as it is mining coins worth tens of thousands of dollars a day for a Russian cybercrime gang. It's easy to see that such mining botnets will become very popular for online criminals in the future.

Even more importantly, such an attack does not require a user for the computers in order to make money. Most traditional botnet monetization mechanisms required a user's presence. For example, credit card key-loggers needed a user at the keyboard to type in his payment details or ransom trojans needed a user to pay a ransom in order to regain access to his computer or his data. Mining botnets just need processing power and a network connection.

Some of the upcoming crypto currencies do not need high-end GPUs to do the mining: a regular CPU will do. When you combine that with the fact that home automation and embedded devices are becoming more and more common, we can make an interesting forecast: there will be botnets that will be making money by mining on botnets created out of embedded devices. Think botnets of infected printers or set-top boxes or microwave ovens. Or toasters.

Whether it makes sense or not, toasters with embedded computers and Internet connectivity will be reality one day. Before crypto currencies existed, it would have been hard to come up with a sensible reason for why anybody would want to write malware to infect toasters. However, mining botnets of thousands of infected toasters could actually make enough money to justify such an operation. Sooner or later, this will happen.

Espionage

Spying is about collecting information. When information was still written on pieces of paper, a spy had to physically go and steal it. These days information is data on computers and networks, so modern spying is often carried out with the help of malware. The cyber spies use trojans and backdoors to infect their targets' computers, giving them access to the data even from the other side of the world.

Who spends money on spying? Companies and countries do. When companies do it, it's called industrial espionage. When countries do it, it's just espionage.

In the most typical case, the attack is made through e-mail to a few carefully selected people or even a single person in the organization. The target receives what seems like an ordinary e-mail with an attached document, often from a familiar person. In reality, the whole message is a forgery. The e-mail sender's details are forged and the seemingly harmless attached document contains the attack code. If the recipient does not realize the e-mail is a forgery, the whole case will probably go unnoticed, forever.

Program files like Windows EXE files do not get through firewalls and filters, so the attackers commonly use PDF, DOC, XLS, and PPT document files as the attachment. These are also more likely to be viewed as safe documents by the recipient. In their standard form these file types do not contain executable code, so the attackers use vulnerabilities in applications like Adobe Reader and Microsoft Word to infect the computer when the booby-trapped documents are opened.

The structure of these attack files has been deliberately broken so that it crashes the office application in use when opened, while simultaneously executing the binary code inside the document. This code usually creates two new files on the hard disk and executes them. The first is a clean document that opens up on the user's monitor and distracts the user from the crash.

The second new file is a backdoor program that starts immediately and hides itself in the system, often using rootkit techniques. It establishes a connection from the infected computer to a specific network address, anywhere in the world. With the help of the backdoor the attacker gains access to all the information on the target computer, as well as the information in the local network that the targeted person has access to.

The attacks often use backdoor programs like Gh0st RAT or Poison Ivy to remotely monitor their targets. With such tools, they can do anything they want on the target machine. This includes logging the keyboard to collect passwords and a remote file manager to search documents with interesting content. Sometimes the attackers can eavesdrop on their target by remotely controlling the microphone of the infected computer.

I've been tracking targeted spying attacks since they were first observed in 2005. Targets have included large companies, governments, ministries, embassies, and nonprofit organizations like those who campaign for the freedom of Tibet, support minorities in China, or represent the Falun Gong religion. It would be easy to point the finger at the government of China. But we don't have the smoking gun. Nobody can conclusively prove the origin of these attacks. In fact, we know with a high degree of certainty that several governments are engaging in similar attacks.

It's also clear that what we've seen so far is just the beginning. Online espionage and spying can only become a more important tool for intelligence purposes in the future. Protecting against such attacks can prove to be very difficult.

The most effective method to protect data against cyber spying is to process confidential information on dedicated computers that are not connected to the Internet. Critical infrastructure should be isolated from public networks.

And isolation does not mean a firewall: it means being disconnected. And being disconnected is painful, complicated, and expensive. But it's also safer.

Exploits

A very big part of criminal or governmental cyber attacks use exploits to infect the target computer.

Without a vulnerability, there is no exploit. And ultimately, vulnerabilities are just bugs: programming errors. And we have bugs because programs are written by human beings and human beings make errors. Software bugs have been a problem as long as we've had programmable computers, and they aren't going to disappear.

Before the Internet became widespread, bugs weren't very critical. You would be working on a word processor and would open a corrupted document file and your word processor would crash. While annoying, such a crash wasn't too big of a deal. You might lose any unsaved work in open documents, but that's it. But as soon as the Internet entered the picture, things changed. Suddenly bugs that used to be just a nuisance could suddenly be used to take over your computer.

We have different classes of vulnerabilities and their severity ranges from a nuisance to critical.

First, we have local and remote vulnerabilities. Local vulnerabilities can only be exploited by a local user who already has access to the system. But remote vulnerabilities are much more severe as they can be exploited from anywhere over a network connection.

Vulnerability types can then be divided by their actions on the target system: *denial-of-service*, *privilege escalation*, or *code execution*. Denial-of-service vulnerabilities allow the attacker to slow down or shut down the system. Privilege escalations can be used to gain additional rights on a system, and code execution allows running commands.

The most serious vulnerabilities are remote code execution vulnerabilities. And these are what the attackers need.

But even the most valuable vulnerabilities are worthless if the vulnerability gets patched. So the most valuable exploits are targeting vulnerabilities that are not known to the vendor behind the exploited product. This means that the vendor cannot fix the bug and issue a security patch to close the hole. If a security patch is available and the vulnerability starts to get exploited by the attackers five days after the patch came out, users had five days to react. If there is no patch available, they users had no time at all to secure themselves: literally zero days. This is where the term *zero-day vulnerability* comes from: users are vulnerable, even if they had applied all possible patches.

The knowledge of the vulnerabilities needed to create these exploits is gathered from several sources. Experienced professionals search for vulnerabilities systematically by using techniques like fuzzing or by reviewing the source code of open-source applications, looking for bugs. Specialist tools have been created to locate vulnerable code from compiled binaries. Less experienced attackers can find known vulnerabilities by reading security-themed mailing lists or by reverse engineering security patches as they are made available by the affected vendors. Exploits are valuable even if a patch is available, as there are targets that don't patch as quickly as they should.

Originally, only hobbyist malware writers were using exploits to do offensive attacks. Worms like Code Red, Sasser, and Blaster would spread around the world in minutes as they could remotely infect their target with exploits.

Things changed as organized criminal gangs started making serious money with keyloggers, banking trojans, and ransom trojans. As money entered the picture, the need for fresh exploits created an underground marketplace.

Things changed even more as governments entered the picture. As the infamous Stuxnet malware was discovered in July 2010, security companies were amazed to notice this unique piece of malware was using a total of four different zero-day exploits—which remains a record in its own field. Stuxnet was eventually linked to an operation launched by the governments of the United States and Israel to target various objects in the Middle East and to especially slow down the nuclear program of the Islamic Republic of Iran.

Other governments learned of Stuxnet and saw the three main take-aways of it: attacks like these are effective, they are cheap, and they are deniable. All of these qualities are highly sought after in espionage and military attacks. In effect, this started a cyber arms race that today is a reality in most of the technically advanced nations. These nations weren't just interested in running cyber defense programs to protect themselves against cyber attacks. They wanted to gain access to offensive capability and to be capable of launching offensive attacks themselves.

To have a credible offensive cyber program, a country will need a steady supply of new exploits. Exploits don't last forever. They get found out and patched. New versions of the vulnerable software might require new exploits, and these exploits have to be weaponized and reliable. To have a credible offensive cyber program, a country needs a steady supply of fresh exploits.

As finding the vulnerabilities and creating the weaponized exploits is hard, most governments would need to outsource this job to experts. Where can they find such expertise from? Security companies and antivirus experts are not providing attack code: they specialize in defense, not attacks. Intelligence agencies and militaries have always turned to defense contractors when they need technology they can't produce by themselves. This applies to exploits as well.

Simply by browsing the websites of the largest defense contractors in the world, you can easily find out that most of them advertise offensive capability to their customers. Northrop Grumman even runs radio ads claiming that they "provide governmental customers with both offensive and defensive solutions."

However, even the defense contractors might have a hard time building the specialized expertise to locate unknown vulnerabilities and to create attacks against them. Many of them seem to end up buying their exploits from one of the several boutique companies specializing in finding zero-day vulnerabilities. Such companies have popped up in various countries. These companies go out of their way to find bugs that can be exploited and turned into security holes. Once found, the exploits are weaponized. In this way, they can be abused effectively and reliably. These attackers also try to make sure that the company behind the targeted product will never learn about the vulnerability—because if they did, they would fix the bug. Consequently, the customers and the public at large would not be vulnerable any more. This would make the exploit code worthless to the vendor.

Companies specializing in selling exploits operate around the world. Some of the known companies reside in the United States, the United Kingdom, Germany, Italy, and France. Others operate from Asia. Many of them like to portray themselves as being part of the computer security industry. However, we must not mistake them for security companies, as these companies do not want to improve computer security. Quite the opposite, these companies go to great lengths to make sure the vulnerabilities they find do not get closed, making all of us more vulnerable.

In some cases, exploits can be used for good. For example, sanctioned penetration tests done with tools like Metasploit can improve the security of an organization. But that's not what we're discussing here. We're talking about creating zero-day vulnerabilities just to be used for secret offensive attacks.

The total size of the exploit export industry is hard to estimate. However, looking at public recruitment ads of the known actors as well as various defense contractors, it's easy to see there is much more recruitment happening right now for offensive positions than for defensive roles. As an example, some U.S.-based defense contractors have more than a hundred open positions for people with Top Secret/SCI clearance to create exploits. Some of these positions specifically mention the need to create offensive exploits targeting iPhones, iPads, and Android devices.

If we look for offensive cyber attacks that have been linked back to a known government, the best known examples link back to the governments of the United States and Israel. When the *New York Times* ran the story linking the U.S. Government and the Obama administration to Stuxnet, the White House started an investigation on who had leaked the information. Note that they never denied the story. They just wanted to know who leaked it.

As the U.S. is engaging in offensive cyber attacks on other countries, certainly other countries feel that they are free to do the same. This cyber arms race has created an increasing demand for exploits.

Government Surveillance

When the Internet became commonplace in the mid-1990s, the decision makers ignored it. They didn't see it as important or in any way relevant to them. As a direct result, global freedom flourished in the unrestricted online world. Suddenly people all over the world had in their reach something truly and really global. And suddenly, people weren't just consuming content; they were creating content for others to see.

But eventually politicians and leaders realized just how important the Internet is. And they realized how useful the Internet was for other purposes—especially for the purposes of doing surveillance on citizens.

The two arguably most important inventions of our generation, the Internet and mobile phones, changed the world. However, they both turned out to be perfect tools for the surveillance state. And in a surveillance state, everybody is assumed guilty.

Internet surveillance really become front-page material when Edward Snowden started leaking information on PRISM, XKeyscore, and other NSA programs in the summer of 2013.

But don't get me wrong. I do understand the need for doing both monitoring and surveillance. If somebody is suspected of running a drug ring, or planning a school shooting, or participating in a terror organization, he should be monitored, with a relevant court order.

However, that's not what PRISM is about. PRISM is not about monitoring suspicious people. PRISM is about monitoring everyone. It's about monitoring people that are known to be innocent. And it's about building dossiers on everyone, eventually going back decades. Such dossiers, based on our Internet activity, will build a thorough picture of us. And if the powers-that-be ever need to find a way to twist your hand, they would certainly find something suspicious or embarrassing on everyone, if they have enough of their Internet history recorded.

United States intelligence agencies have a full legal right to monitor foreigners. Which doesn't sound too bad—until your realize that most of us are foreigners to the Americans. In fact, 96 percent of the people on the planet turn out to be such *foreigners.* And when these people use U.S.-based services, they are legally under surveillance.

When the PRISM leaks started, U.S. intelligence tried to calm the rest of the world by explaining how there's no need to worry, and about how these programs were just about fighting terrorists. But then further leaks proved the U.S. was using their tools to monitor the European Commission and the United Nations as well. It's difficult for them to argue that they were trying to find terrorists at the European Union headquarters.

Another argument we've heard from the U.S. intelligence apparatus is that everyone else is doing Internet surveillance too. And indeed, most countries do have intelligence agencies, and most of them do monitor what other countries are doing. However, the U.S. has an unfair advantage. Almost all of the common Internet services, search engines, webmails, web browsers, and mobile operating systems come from the U.S. To put in another way: How many Spanish politicians and decision makers use American services? Answer: all of them. And how many American politicians and decision makers use Spanish services? Answer: none of them.

All this should make it obvious that we foreigners should not use U.S.-based services. They've proven to us that they are not trustworthy. Why would we voluntarily hand our data to a foreign intelligence agency?

But in practice, it's very hard to avoid using services like Google, Facebook, LinkedIn, Dropbox, Amazon, Skydrive, iCloud, Android, Windows, iOS, and so on. This is a clear example of the failure of Europe, Asia, and Africa to compete with the U.S. on Internet services. And when the rest of the world does produce a global hit—like Skype or Nokia—it typically ends up acquired by an American company, bringing it under U.S. control.

But if you're not doing anything wrong, why worry about this? Or, if you are worrying about this, what do you have to hide? My answer to this question is that I have nothing to hide... but I have nothing in particular that I'd want to share with an intelligence agency either. In particular, I have nothing to share with a foreign intelligence agency. If we really need a big brother, I'd much rather have a domestic big brother than a foreign big brother.

People have asked me if they really should worry about PRISM. I've told them that they should not be worried—they should be outraged instead. We should not just accept such blanket and wholesale surveillance from one country on the rest of the world.

Advancements in computing power and data storage have made wholesale surveillance possible. But they've also made leaking possible. That's how Edward Snowden could steal three laptops which contained so much information that, printed out, it would be a long row of trucks full of paper.

Leaking has become so easy that it will keep organizations worrying about getting caught over any wrongdoing. We might hope that this would force organizations to avoid unethical practices.

While governments are watching over us, they know we are watching over them.

Summary

We've seen massive shifts in cyber attacks over the last two decades: from simple viruses written by teenagers to multimillion-dollar cyber attacks launched by nation-states.

All this is happening right now, during our generation. We were the first generation that got online. We should do what we can to secure the net and keep it free so that it will be there for future generations to enjoy.

Society, Community, Individuals

The Impact of the Internet on Society:
A Global Perspective

Manuel Castells

Wallis Annenberg Chair Professor of Communication Technology and Society,
University of Southern California

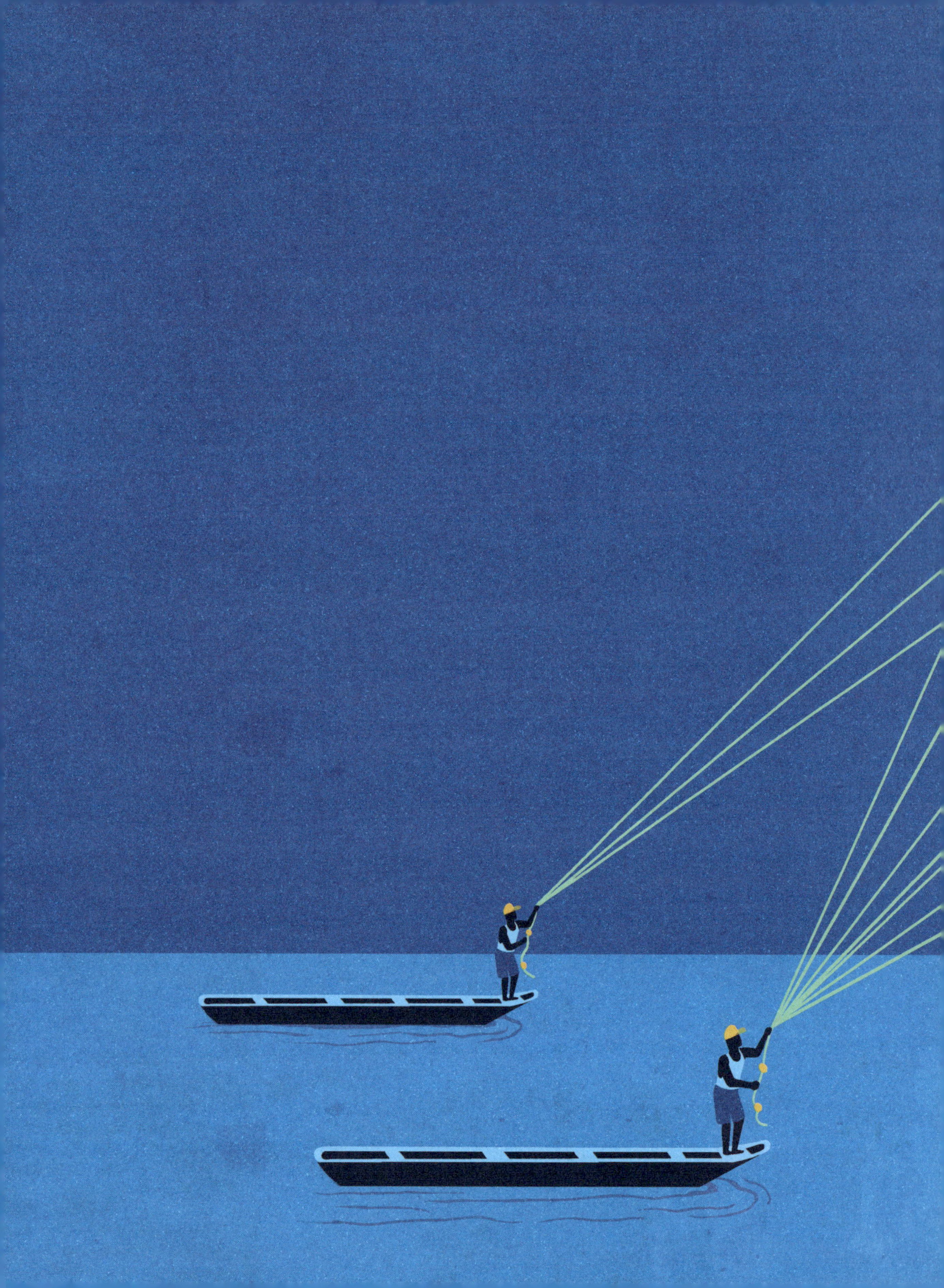

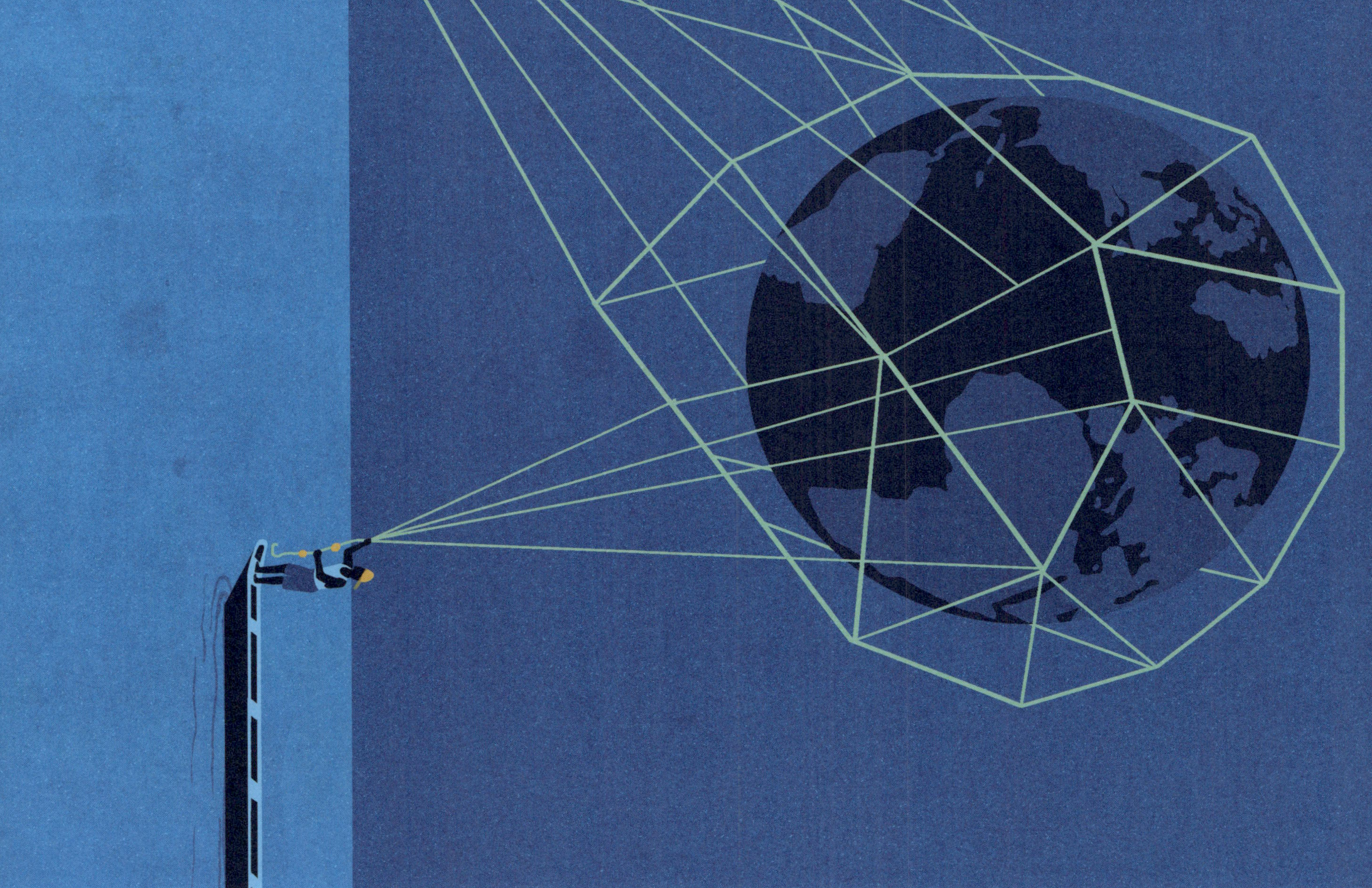

Manuel Castells

manuelcastells.info

Illustration
Emiliano Ponzi

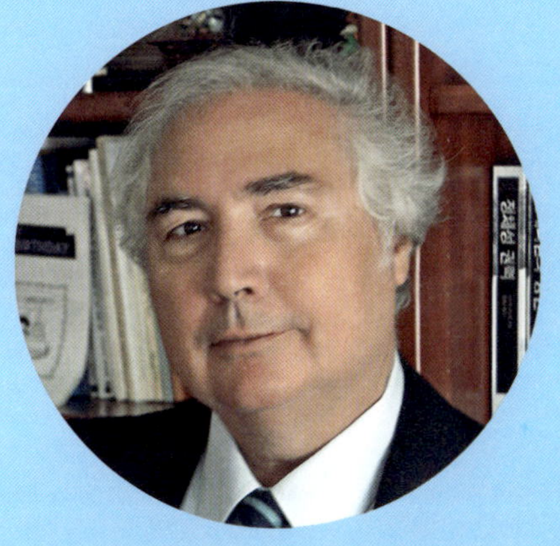

Manuel Castells is the Wallis Annenberg Chair Professor
of Communication Technology and Society at the University of
Southern California, Los Angeles. He is also Professor Emeritus
of Sociology at the University of California, Berkeley; director of
the Internet Interdisciplinary Institute of the Open University
of Catalonia (UOC); director of the Network Society Chair at the
Collège d'études mondiales in Paris, and director of research
in the Department of Sociology at the University of Cambridge.
He is académico numerario of the Spanish Royal Academy of
Economics and Finance, fellow of the American Academy
of Political and Social Science, fellow of the British Academy,
and fellow of the Academia Europea. He was also a founding
board member of the European Research Council and of
the European Institute of Innovation and Technology of the
European Commission. He received the Erasmus Medal in
2011, and the 2012 Holberg Prize. He has published 25 books,
including the trilogy *The Information Age: Economy, Society
and Culture* (Blackwell, 1996–2003), *The Internet Galaxy*
(Oxford University Press, 2001), *Communication Power* (Oxford
University Press, 2009), and *Networks of Outrage and Hope*
(Polity Press, 2012).

The Impact of the Internet on Society:
A Global Perspective

Introduction

The Internet is the decisive technology of the Information Age, as the electrical engine was the vector of technological transformation of the Industrial Age. This global network of computer networks, largely based nowadays on platforms of wireless communication, provides ubiquitous capacity of multimodal, interactive communication in chosen time, transcending space. The Internet is not really a new technology: its ancestor, the Arpanet, was first deployed in 1969 (Abbate 1999). But it was in the 1990s when it was privatized and released from the control of the U.S. Department of Commerce that it diffused around the world at extraordinary speed: in 1996 the first survey of Internet users counted about 40 million; in 2013 they are over 2.5 billion, with China accounting for the largest number of Internet users. Furthermore, for some time the spread of the Internet was limited by the difficulty to lay out land-based telecommunications infrastructure in the emerging countries. This has changed with the explosion of wireless communication in the early twenty-first century. Indeed, in 1991, there were about 16 million subscribers of wireless devices in the world, in 2013 they are close to 7 billion (in a planet of 7.7 billion human beings). Counting on the family and village uses of mobile phones, and taking into consideration the limited use of these devices among children under five years of age, we can say that humankind is now almost entirely connected, albeit with great levels of inequality in the bandwidth as well as in the efficiency and price of the service.

At the heart of these communication networks the Internet ensures the production, distribution, and use of digitized information in all formats. According to the study published by Martin Hilbert in *Science* (Hilbert and López 2011), 95 percent of all information existing in the planet is digitized and most of it is accessible on the Internet and other computer networks.

The speed and scope of the transformation of our communication environment by Internet and wireless communication has triggered all kind of utopian and dystopian perceptions around the world.

As in all moments of major technological change, people, companies, and institutions feel the depth of the change, but they are often overwhelmed by it, out of sheer ignorance of its effects.

The media aggravate the distorted perception by dwelling into scary reports on the basis of anecdotal observation and biased commentary. If there is a topic in which social sciences, in their diversity, should contribute to the full understanding of the world in which we live, it is precisely the area that has come to be named in academia as Internet Studies. Because, in fact, academic research knows a great deal on the interaction between Internet and society, on the basis of methodologically rigorous empirical research conducted in a plurality of cultural and institutional contexts. Any process of major technological change generates its own mythology. In part because it comes into practice before scientists can assess its effects and implications, so there is always a gap between social change and its understanding. For instance, media often report that intense use of the Internet increases the risk of alienation, isolation, depression, and withdrawal from society. In fact, available evidence shows that there is either no relationship or a positive cumulative relationship between the Internet use and the intensity of sociability. We observe that, overall, the more sociable people are, the more they use the Internet. And the more they use the Internet, the more they increase their sociability online and offline, their civic engagement, and the intensity of family and friendship relationships, in all cultures—with the exception of a couple of early studies of the Internet in the 1990s, corrected by their authors later (Castells 2001; Castells et al. 2007; Rainie and Wellman 2012; Center for the Digital Future 2012 et al.).

Thus, the purpose of this chapter will be to summarize some of the key research findings on the social effects of the Internet relying on the evidence provided by some of the major institutions specialized in the social study of the Internet. More specifically, I will be using the data from the world at large: the World Internet Survey conducted by the Center for the Digital Future, University of Southern California; the reports of the British Computer Society (BCS), using data from the World Values Survey of the University of Michigan; the Nielsen reports for a variety of countries; and the annual reports from the International Telecommunications Union. For data on the United States, I have used the Pew American Life and Internet Project of the Pew Institute. For the United Kingdom, the Oxford Internet Survey from the Oxford Internet Institute, University of Oxford, as well as the Virtual Society Project from the Economic and Social Science Research Council. For Spain, the Project Internet Catalonia of the Internet Interdisciplinary Institute (IN3) of the Universitat Oberta de Catalunya (UOC); the various reports on the information society from Telefónica; and from the Orange Foundation. For Portugal, the Observatório de Sociedade da Informação e do Conhecimento (OSIC) in Lisbon. I would like to emphasize that most of the data in these reports converge toward similar trends. Thus I have selected for my analysis the findings that complement and reinforce each other, offering a consistent picture of the human experience on the Internet in spite of the human diversity.

Given the aim of this publication to reach a broad audience, I will not present in this text the data supporting the analysis presented here. Instead, I am referring the interested reader to the web sources of the research organizations mentioned above, as well as to selected bibliographic references discussing the empirical foundation of the social trends reported here.

Technologies of Freedom, the Network Society, and the Culture of Autonomy

In order to fully understand the effects of the Internet on society, we should remember that technology is material culture. It is produced in a social process in a given institutional environment on the basis of the ideas, values, interests, and knowledge of their producers, both their early producers and their subsequent producers. In this process we must include the users of the technology, who appropriate and adapt the technology rather than adopting it, and by so doing they modify it and produce it in an endless process of interaction between technological production and social use. So, to assess the relevance of Internet in society we must recall the specific characteristics of Internet as a technology. Then we must place it in the context of the transformation of the overall social structure, as well as in relationship to the culture characteristic of this social structure. Indeed, we live in a new social structure, the global network society, characterized by the rise of a new culture, the culture of autonomy.

Internet is a technology of freedom, in the terms coined by Ithiel de Sola Pool in 1973, coming from a libertarian culture, paradoxically financed by the Pentagon for the benefit of scientists, engineers, and their students, with no direct military application in mind (Castells 2001). The expansion of the Internet from the mid-1990s onward resulted from the combination of three main factors:

- The technological discovery of the World Wide Web by Tim Berners-Lee and his willingness to distribute the source code to improve it by the open-source contribution of a global community of users, in continuity with the openness of the TCP/IP Internet protocols. The web keeps running under the same principle of open source. And two-thirds of web servers are operated by Apache, an open-source server program.

- Institutional change in the management of the Internet, keeping it under the loose management of the global Internet community, privatizing it, and allowing both commercial uses and cooperative uses.

- Major changes in social structure, culture, and social behavior: networking as a prevalent organizational form; individuation as the main orientation of social behavior; and the culture of autonomy as the culture of the network society.

I will elaborate on these major trends.

Our society is a network society; that is, a society constructed around personal and organizational networks powered by digital networks and communicated by the Internet. And because networks are global and know no boundaries, the network society is a global network society. This historically specific social structure resulted from the interaction between the emerging technological paradigm based on the digital revolution and some major sociocultural changes. A primary dimension of these changes is what has been labeled the rise of the Me-centered society, or, in sociological terms, the process of individuation, the decline of community understood in terms of space, work, family, and ascription in general. This is not the end of community, and not the end of place-based interaction, but there is a shift toward the reconstruction of social relationships, including strong cultural and personal ties that could be considered a form of community, on the basis of individual interests, values, and projects.

The process of individuation is not just a matter of cultural evolution, it is materially produced by the new forms of organizing economic activities, and social and political life, as I analyzed in my trilogy on the Information Age (Castells 1996–2003). It is based on the transformation of space (metropolitan life), work and economic activity (rise of the networked enterprise and networked work processes), culture and communication (shift from mass communication based on mass media to mass self-communication based on the Internet); on the crisis of the patriarchal family, with increasing autonomy of its individual members; the substitution of media politics for mass party politics; and globalization as the selective networking of places and processes throughout the planet.

But individuation does not mean isolation, or even less the end of community. Sociability is reconstructed as networked individualism and community through a quest for like-minded individuals in a process that combines online interaction with offline interaction, cyberspace and the local space. Individuation is the key process in constituting subjects (individual or collective), networking is the organizational form constructed by these subjects; this is the network society, and the form of sociability is what Rainie and Wellman (2012) conceptualized as networked individualism. Network technologies are of course the medium for this new social structure and this new culture (Papacharissi 2010).

As stated above, academic research has established that the Internet does not isolate people, nor does it reduce their sociability; it actually increases sociability, as shown by myself in my studies in Catalonia (Castells 2007), Rainie and Wellman in the United States (2012), Cardoso in Portugal (2010), and the World Internet Survey for the world at large (Center for the Digital Future 2012 et al.). Furthermore, a major study by Michael Willmott for the British Computer Society (Trajectory Partnership 2010) has shown a positive correlation, for individuals and for countries, between the frequency and intensity of the use of the Internet and the psychological indicators of personal happiness. He used global data for 35,000 people obtained from the World Wide Survey of the University of Michigan from 2005 to 2007. Controlling for other factors, the study showed that Internet use empowers people by increasing their feelings of security, personal freedom, and influence, all feelings that have a positive effect on happiness and personal well-being. The effect is particularly positive for people with lower income and who are less qualified, for people in the developing world, and for women. Age does not affect the positive relationship; it is significant for all ages. Why women? Because they are at the center of the network of their families, Internet helps them to organize their lives. Also, it helps them to overcome their isolation, particularly in patriarchal societies. The Internet also contributes to the rise of the culture of autonomy.

The key for the process of individuation is the construction of autonomy by social actors, who become subjects in the process. They do so by defining their specific projects in interaction with, but not submission to, the institutions of society. This is the case for a minority of individuals, but because of their capacity to lead and mobilize they introduce a new culture in every domain of social life: in work (entrepreneurship), in the media (the active audience), in the Internet (the creative user), in the market (the informed and proactive consumer), in education (students as informed critical thinkers, making possible the new frontier of e-learning and m-learning pedagogy), in health (the patient-centered health management system) in e-government (the informed, participatory citizen), in social movements (cultural change from the grassroots, as in feminism or environmentalism), and in politics (the independent-minded citizen able to participate in self-generated political networks).

There is increasing evidence of the direct relationship between the Internet and the rise of social autonomy. From 2002 to 2007 I directed in Catalonia one of the largest studies ever conducted in Europe on the Internet and society, based on 55,000 interviews, one-third of them face to face (IN3 2002–07). As part of this study, my collaborators and I compared the behavior of Internet users to non-Internet users in a sample of 3,000 people, representative of the population of Catalonia. Because in 2003 only about 40 percent of people were Internet users we could really compare the differences in social behavior for users and non-users, something that nowadays would be more difficult given the 79 percent penetration rate of the Internet in Catalonia. Although the data are relatively old, the findings are not, as more recent studies in other countries (particularly in Portugal) appear to confirm the observed trends. We constructed scales of autonomy in different dimensions. Only between 10 and 20 percent of the population, depending on dimensions, were in the high level of autonomy. But we focused on this active segment of the population to explore the role of the Internet in the construction of autonomy. Using factor analysis we identified six major types of autonomy based on projects of individuals according to their practices:

a) professional development
b) communicative autonomy
c) entrepreneurship
d) autonomy of the body
e) sociopolitical participation
f) personal, individual autonomy

These six types of autonomous practices were statistically independent among themselves. But each one of them correlated positively with Internet use in statistically significant terms, in a self-reinforcing loop (time sequence): the more one person was autonomous, the more she/he used the web, and the more she/he used the web, the more autonomous she/he became (Castells et al. 2007). This is a major empirical finding. Because if the dominant cultural trend in our society is the search for autonomy, and if the Internet powers this search, then we are moving toward a society of assertive individuals and cultural freedom, regardless of the barriers of rigid social organizations inherited from the Industrial Age. From this Internet-based culture of autonomy have emerged a new kind of sociability, networked sociability, and a new kind of sociopolitical practice, networked social movements and networked democracy. I will now turn to the analysis of these two fundamental trends at the source of current processes of social change worldwide.

The Rise of Social Network Sites on the Internet

Since 2002 (creation of Friendster, prior to Facebook) a new socio-technical revolution has taken place on the Internet: the rise of social network sites where now all human activities are present, from personal interaction to business, to work, to culture, to communication, to social movements, and to politics.

> *Social Network Sites are web-based services that allow individuals to (1) construct a public or semi-public profile within a bounded system, (2) articulate a list of other users with whom they share a connection, and (3) view and traverse their list of connections and those made by others within the system.*
>
> (Boyd and Ellison 2007, 2)

Social networking uses, in time globally spent, surpassed e-mail in November 2007. It surpassed e-mail in number of users in July 2009. In terms of users it reached 1 billion by September 2010, with Facebook accounting for about half of it. In 2013 it has almost doubled, particularly because of increasing use in China, India, and Latin America. There is indeed a great diversity of social networking sites (SNS) by countries and cultures. Facebook, started for Harvard-only members in 2004, is present in most of the world, but QQ, Cyworld, and Baidu dominate in China; Orkut in Brazil; Mixi in Japan; etc. In terms of demographics, age is the main differential factor in the use of SNS, with a drop of frequency of use after 50 years of age, and particularly 65. But this is not just a teenager's activity. The main Facebook U.S. category is in the age group 35–44, whose frequency of use of the site is higher than for younger people. Nearly 60 percent of adults in the U.S. have at least one SNS profile, 30 percent two, and 15 percent three or more. Females are as present as males, except when in a society there is a general gender gap. We observe no differences in education and class, but there is some class specialization of SNS, such as Myspace being lower than FB; LinkedIn is for professionals.

Thus, the most important activity on the Internet at this point in time goes through social networking, and SNS have become the chosen platforms for all kind of activities, not just personal friendships or chatting, but for marketing, e-commerce, education, cultural creativity, media and entertainment distribution, health applications, and sociopolitical activism. This is a significant trend for society at large. Let me explore the meaning of this trend on the basis of the still scant evidence.

Social networking sites are constructed by users themselves building on specific criteria of grouping. There is entrepreneurship in the process of creating sites, then people choose according to their interests and projects. Networks are tailored by people themselves with different levels of profiling and privacy. The key to success is not anonymity, but on the contrary, self-presentation of a real person connecting to real people (in some cases people are excluded from the SNS when they fake their identity). So, it is a self-constructed society by networking connecting to other networks. But this is not a virtual society. There is a close connection between virtual networks and networks in life at large. This is a hybrid world, a real world, not a virtual world or a segregated world.

People build networks to be with others, and to be with others they want to be with on the basis of criteria that include those people who they already know (a selected sub-segment). Most users go on the site every day. It is permanent connectivity. If we needed an answer to what happened to sociability in the Internet world, here it is:

There is a dramatic increase in sociability, but a different kind of sociability, facilitated and dynamized by permanent connectivity and social networking on the web.

Based on the time when Facebook was still releasing data (this time is now gone) we know that in 2009 users spent 500 billion minutes per month. This is not just about friendship or interpersonal communication. People do things together, share, act, exactly as in society, although the personal dimension is always there. Thus, in the U.S. 38 percent of adults share content, 21 percent remix, 14 percent blog, and this is growing exponentially, with development of technology, software, and SNS entrepreneurial initiatives. On Facebook, in 2009 the average user was connected to 60 pages, groups, and events, people interacted per month to 160 million objects (pages, groups, events), the average user created 70 pieces of content per month, and there were 25 billion pieces of content shared per month (web links, news stories, blogs posts, notes, photos). SNS are living spaces connecting all dimensions of people's experience. This transforms culture because people share experience with a low emotional cost, while saving energy and effort. They transcend time and space, yet they produce content, set up links, and connect practices. It is a constantly networked world in every dimension of human experience. They co-evolve in permanent, multiple interaction. But they choose the terms of their co-evolution.

Thus, people live their physical lives but increasingly connect on multiple dimensions in SNS.

Paradoxically, the virtual life is more social than the physical life, now individualized by the organization of work and urban living.

But people do not live a virtual reality, indeed it is a real virtuality, since social practices, sharing, mixing, and living in society is facilitated in the virtuality, in what I called time ago the "space of flows" (Castells 1996).

Because people are increasingly at ease in the multi-textuality and multi-dimensionality of the web, marketers, work organizations, service agencies, government, and civil society are migrating massively to the Internet, less and less setting up alternative sites, more and more being present in the networks that people construct by themselves and for themselves, with the help of Internet social networking entrepreneurs, some of whom become billionaires in the process, actually selling freedom and the possibility of the autonomous construction of lives. This is the liberating potential of the Internet made material practice by these social networking sites. The largest of these social networking sites are usually bounded social spaces managed by a company. However, if the company tries to impede free communication it may lose many of its users, because the entry barriers in this industry are very low. A couple of technologically savvy youngsters with little capital can set up a site on the Internet and attract escapees from a more restricted Internet space, as happened to AOL and other networking sites of the first generation, and as could happen to Facebook or any other SNS if they are tempted to tinker with the rules of openness (Facebook tried to make users pay and retracted within days). So, SNS are often a business, but they are in the business of selling freedom, free expression, chosen sociability. When they tinker with this promise they risk their hollowing by net citizens migrating with their friends to more friendly virtual lands.

Perhaps the most telling expression of this new freedom is the transformation of sociopolitical practices on the Internet.

Communication Power: Mass-Self Communication and the Transformation of Politics

Power and counterpower, the foundational relationships of society, are constructed in the human mind, through the construction of meaning and the processing of information according to certain sets of values and interests (Castells 2009).

Ideological apparatuses and the mass media have been key tools of mediating communication and asserting power, and still are. But the rise of a new culture, the culture of autonomy, has found in Internet and mobile communication networks a major medium of mass self-communication and self-organization.

The key source for the social production of meaning is the process of socialized communication. I define communication as the process of sharing meaning through the exchange of information. Socialized communication is the one that exists in the public realm, that has the potential of reaching society at large. Therefore, the battle over the human mind is largely played out in the process of socialized communication. And this is particularly so in the network society, the social structure of the Information Age, which is characterized by the pervasiveness of communication networks in a multimodal hypertext.

The ongoing transformation of communication technology in the digital age extends the reach of communication media to all domains of social life in a network that is at the same time global and local, generic and customized, in an ever-changing pattern.

As a result, power relations, that is the relations that constitute the foundation of all societies, as well as the processes challenging institutionalized power relations, are increasingly shaped and decided in the communication field. Meaningful, conscious communication is what makes humans human. Thus, any major transformation in the technology and organization of communication is of utmost relevance for social change. Over the last four decades the advent of the Internet and of wireless communication has shifted the communication process in society at large from mass communication to mass self-communication. This is from a message sent from one to many with little interactivity to a system based on messages from many to many, multimodal, in chosen time, and with interactivity, so that senders are receivers and receivers are senders. And both have access to a multimodal hypertext in the web that constitutes the endlessly changing backbone of communication processes.

The transformation of communication from mass communication to mass self-communication has contributed decisively to alter the process of social change. As power relationships have always been based on the control of communication and information that feed the neural networks constitutive of the human mind, the rise of horizontal networks of communication has created a new landscape of social and political change by the process of disintermediation of the government and corporate controls over communication. This is the power of the network, as social actors build their own networks on the basis of their projects, values, and interests. The outcome of these processes is open ended and dependent on specific contexts. Freedom, in this case freedom of communicate, does not say anything on the uses of freedom in society. This is to be established by scholarly research. But we need to start from this major historical phenomenon: the building of a global communication network based on the Internet, a technology that embodies the culture of freedom that was at its source.

In the first decade of the twenty-first century there have been multiple social movements around the world that have used the Internet as their space of formation and permanent connectivity, among the movements and with society at large. These networked social movements, formed in the social networking sites on the Internet, have mobilized in the urban space and in the institutional space, inducing new forms of social movements that are the main actors of social change in the network society. Networked social movements have been particularly active since 2010, and especially in the Arab revolutions against dictatorships; in Europe and the U.S. as forms of protest against the management of the financial crisis; in Brazil; in Turkey; in Mexico; and in highly diverse institutional contexts and economic conditions. It is precisely the similarity of the movements in extremely different contexts that allows the formulation of the hypothesis that this is the pattern of social movements characteristic of the global network society. In all cases we observe the capacity of these movements for self-organization, without a central leadership, on the basis of a spontaneous emotional movement. In all cases there is a connection between Internet-based communication, mobile networks, and the mass media in different forms, feeding into each other and amplifying the movement locally and globally.

These movements take place in the context of exploitation and oppression, social tensions and social struggles; but struggles that were not able to successfully challenge the state in other instances of revolt are now powered by the tools of mass self-communication. It is not the technology that induces the movements, but without the technology (Internet and wireless communication) social movements would not take the present form of being a challenge to state power. The fact is that technology is material culture (ideas brought into the design) and the Internet materialized the culture of freedom that, as it has been documented, emerged on American campuses in the 1960s. This culture-made technology is at the source of the new wave of social movements that exemplify the depth of the global impact of the Internet in all spheres of social organization, affecting particularly power relationships, the foundation of the institutions of society. (See case studies and an analytical perspective on the interaction between Internet and networked social movements in Castells 2012.)

Conclusion

The Internet, as all technologies, does not produce effects by itself. Yet, it has specific effects in altering the capacity of the communication system to be organized around flows that are interactive, multimodal, asynchronous or synchronous, global or local, and from many to many, from people to people, from people to objects, and from objects to objects, increasingly relying on the semantic web. How these characteristics affect specific systems of social relationships has to be established by research, and this is what I tried to present in this text. What is clear is that without the Internet we would not have seen the large-scale development of networking as the fundamental mechanism of social structuring and social change in every domain of social life. The Internet, the World Wide Web, and a variety of networks increasingly based on wireless platforms constitute the technological infrastructure of the network society, as the electrical grid and the electrical engine were the support system for the form of social organization that we conceptualized as the industrial society. Thus, as a social construction, this technological system is open ended, as the network society is an open-ended form of social organization that conveys the best and the worse in humankind. Yet, the global network society is our society, and the understanding of its logic on the basis of the interaction between culture, organization, and technology in the formation and development of social and technological networks is a key field of research in the twenty-first century.

We can only make progress in our understanding through the cumulative effort of scholarly research. Only then we will be able to cut through the myths surrounding the key technology of our time. A digital communication technology that is already a second skin for young people, yet it continues to feed the fears and the fantasies of those who are still in charge of a society that they barely understand.

Selected Bibliographic References

These references are in fact sources of more detailed references specific to each one of the topics analyzed in this text.

Abbate, Janet.
A Social History of the Internet. Cambridge, MA: MIT Press, 1999.

Boyd, Danah M., and Nicole B. Ellison.
"Social Network Sites: Definition, History, and Scholarship." *Journal of Computer-Mediated Communication* 13, no. 1 (2007).

Cardoso, Gustavo, Angus Cheong, and Jeffrey Cole (eds).
World Wide Internet: Changing Societies, Economies and Cultures. Macau: University of Macau Press, 2009.

Castells, Manuel.
The Information Age: Economy, Society, and Culture. 3 vols. Oxford: Blackwell, 1996–2003.
———. *The Internet Galaxy: Reflections on the Internet, Business, and Society.* Oxford: Oxford University Press, 2001.
———. *Communication Power.* Oxford: Oxford University Press, 2009.
———. *Networks of Outrage and Hope: Social Movements in the Internet Age.* Cambridge, UK: Polity Press, 2012.

Castells, Manuel, Imma Tubella, Teresa Sancho, and Meritxell Roca.
La transición a la sociedad red. Barcelona: Ariel, 2007.

Hilbert, Martin, and Priscilla López.
"The World's Technological Capacity to Store, Communicate, and Compute Information." *Science* 332, no. 6025 (April 1, 2011): pp. 60–65.

Papacharissi, Zizi, ed.
The Networked Self: Identity, Community, and Culture on Social Networking Sites. Routledge, 2010.

Rainie. Lee, and Barry Wellman.
Networked: The New Social Operating System. Cambridge, MA: MIT Press, 2012.

Trajectory Partnership (Michael Willmott and Paul Flatters).
The Information Dividend: Why IT Makes You "Happier." Swindon: British Informatics Society Limited, 2010. http://www.bcs.org/upload/pdf/info-dividend-full-report.pdf

Selected Web References

Used as sources for analysis in the chapter

Agência para a Sociedade do Conhecimento.
"Observatório de Sociedade da Informação e do Conhecimento (OSIC)." http://www.umic.pt/index.php?option=com_content&task=view&id=3026&Itemid=167

BCS, The Chartered Institute for IT.
"Features, Press and Policy." http://www.bcs.org/category/7307

Center for the Digital Future.
The World Internet Project International Report. 4th ed. Los Angeles: USC Annenberg School, Center for the Digital Future, 2012. http://www.worldinternetproject.net/_files/_Published/_oldis/770_2012wip_report4th_ed.pdf

ESRC (Economic & Social Research Council).
"Papers and Reports." Virtual Society. http://virtualsociety.sbs.ox.ac.uk/reports.htm

Fundación Orange.
"Análisis y Prospectiva: Informe eEspaña." Fundación Orange. http://fundacionorange.es/fundacionorange/analisisprospectiva.html

Fundación Telefónica.
"Informes SI." Fundación Telefónica. http://sociedadinformacion.fundacion.telefonica.com/DYC/SHI/InformesSI/seccion=1190&idioma=es_ES.do

IN3 (Internet Interdisciplinary Institute). UOC.
"Project Internet Catalonia (PIC): An Overview." Internet Interdisciplinary Institute, 2002–07. http://www.uoc.edu/in3/pic/eng/

International Telecommunication Union.
"Annual Reports." http://www.itu.int/osg/spu/sfo/annual_reports/index.html

Nielsen Company.
"Reports." 2013. http://www.nielsen.com/us/en/reports/2013.html?tag=Category:Media+and+Entertainment

Oxford Internet Surveys.
"Publications." http://microsites.oii.ox.ac.uk/oxis/publications

Pew Internet & American Life Project.
"Social Networking." Pew Internet. http://www.pewinternet.org/Topics/Activities-and-Pursuits/Social-Networking.aspx?typeFilter=5

The Internet, Politics, and the Politics of Internet Debate

Evgeny Morozov

Writer and journalist

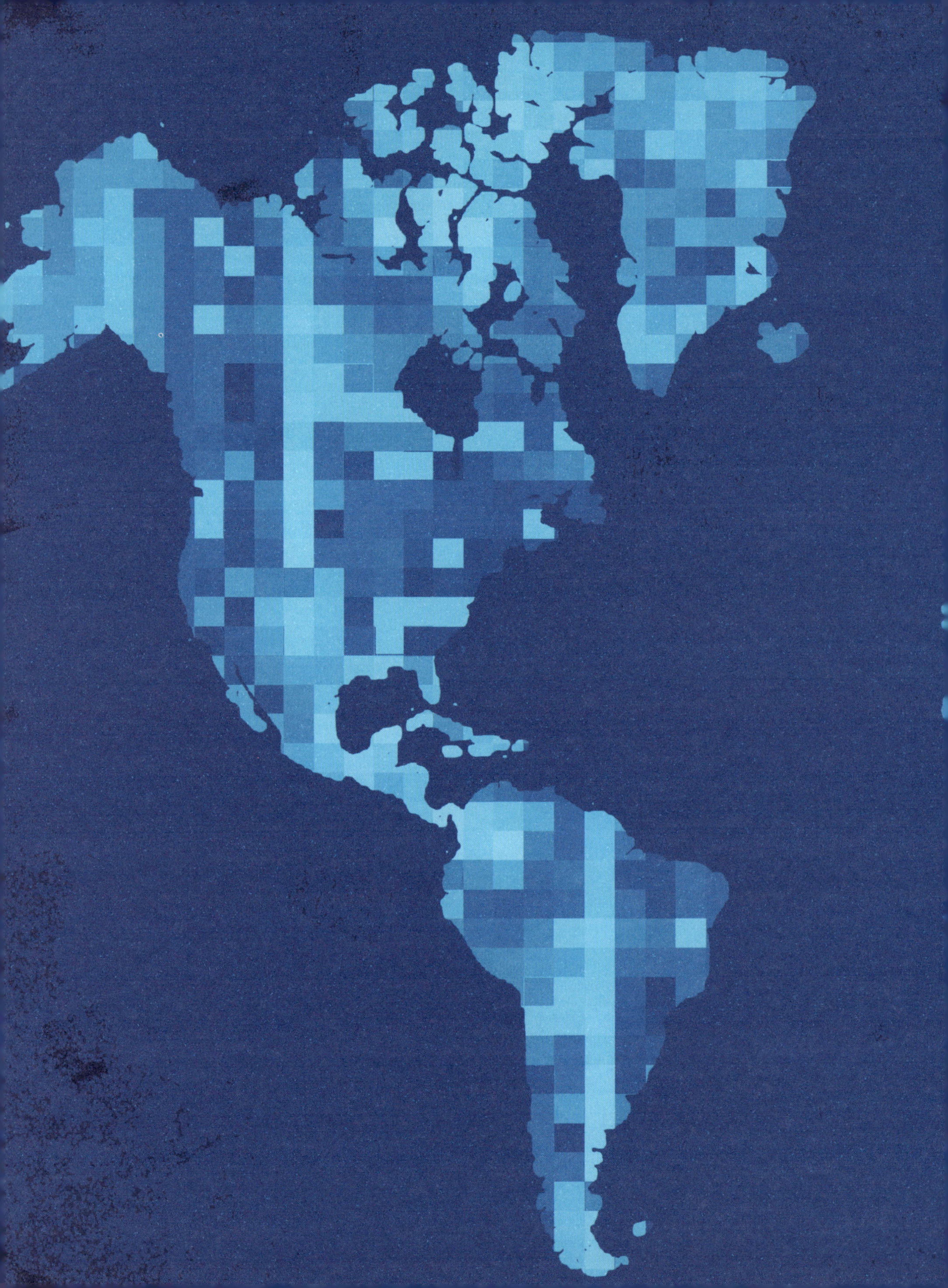

Evgeny Morozov

The Internet, Politics, and the Politics of Internet Debate

Evgeny Morozov
evgenymorozov.com

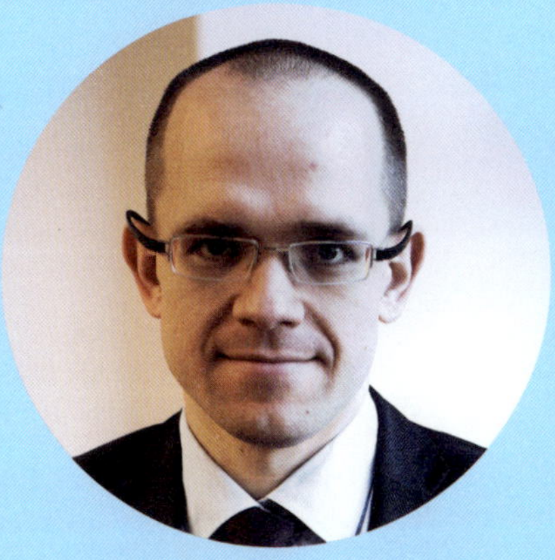

Evgeny Morozov is a contributing editor at the *New Republic* and the author of *The Net Delusion: The Dark Side of Internet Freedom* (PublicAffairs, 2011) and *To Save Everything, Click Here: The Folly of Technological Solutionism* (PublicAffairs, 2013). In 2010–12 he was a visiting scholar at Stanford University and a Schwartz Fellow at the New America Foundation. In 2009–10 he was a fellow at Georgetown University and in 2008–09 was a fellow at the Open Society Foundations (where he was on the board of the Information Program between 2008 and 2012). Between 2006 and 2008 he served as Director of New Media at Transitions Online. He has written for the *New York Times*, the *Economist*, the *Wall Street Journal*, *Financial Times*, *London Review of Books*, *Times Literary Supplement*, and other publications. His monthly *Slate* column is syndicated in *El País*, *Corriere della Sera*, *Frankfurter Allgemeine Zeitung*, *Folha de S. Paulo*, and several other newspapers.

Sites and services that have changed my life
thebrowser.com
scholar.google.com
Kindle
Instapaper

The Internet, Politics, and the Politics of
Internet Debate

The Internet, Politics, and the Politics of Internet Debate

What does it mean to reflect on the "political implications of the Internet" today—a most challenging task that I've been asked to accomplish in the present essay? One easy answer—all too easy perhaps—is to simply follow the intellectual path beloved by the media, the pundits, and the cultural critics: we can just assume that we all know what *the Internet* is. Like the proverbial judge asked to define pornography, we might have great difficulty defining it but we know it when we see it.

If that's the path we want to take, then our inquiry into the political implications of the Internet is likely to be contentious, inconclusive, and most likely infinite. For every invocation of some positive aspect to the Internet—"Look, the Internet was good for the Arab Spring: just look at how many people showed up to topple Mubarak!"—our imaginary interlocutor is likely to bring up some equally negative aspect—"Look, the Internet was bad for the Arab Spring: just look at all the surveillance and the failure to mobilize the digital masses after the first wave of protests in 2011."

Such intellectual ping-pong—with one side finding a suitable positive example, only to be challenged by the other side finding a suitable negative example—has been going on, in one form or another, for the past 15 years. The impact of the Internet on both authoritarian states and democracies has been analyzed this way—down to very minute details about how specific political regimes operate. So debates about the *filter bubble* (courtesy of Eli Pariser) or audience polarization (courtesy of Cass Sunstein) or the brain-wrecking/brain-boosting aspects of social media (courtesy of Nicholas Carr and Clay Shirky, respectively) can all be nicely framed as part of this broader conversation about whether—to simplify our initial question even further—"The Internet is good or bad for democracy and politics as such?"

As an active participant in some of these debates over the last five years, I've quickly reached a depressing conclusion that, on many of the highly contested issues, it's not uncommon for both parties to be wrong and right—simultaneously! Often, the opponents are either talking past each other or are focusing on two (or several) quite different aspects of the problem, somehow oblivious to the fact that once we abandon our quest to arrive at some ultimate score—if we stop comparing the negative side of our *Internet* ledger with the positive one—we might actually accommodate both perspectives—or reject them. The reason why we don't do that is because there seems to exist some strange gravitational pull within our debates about technology—and that pull drags every single conversation toward teasing out some implications for *the Internet at large*. Forget about learning about the world: let's just learn something about *the Internet*! Now, that's a trendy subject.

In my two books, I've dubbed this gravitational pull *Internet-centrism* and, for my money, this is by far the most important "political consequence of the Internet"—not least because it erects a barely perceptible set of barriers and intellectual traffic lights of sorts that guides our debates toward certain outcomes or, in the worst case, gets them stranded in all sorts of intellectual traffic jams where they tend to remain for decades. The only way out of this intellectual impasse is to clear away those traffic jams; we shouldn't be making things worse by continuing to traffic in dubious metaphysical assumptions of our own.

Consider an example that I've already mentioned: the debate about the impact of the Internet on the Arab Spring—a high-profile debate that is made all the more complex by the fact that those revolutions are still ongoing. Why is it so hard for us to accept that the proliferation of digital technologies could—given the favorable political, economic, and social conditions—allow a group of highly motivated young people to mobilize their supporters and advertise their protests while at the same time enabling those in power—and, above all, the secret police—to get a better handle on tracking the movements of their opponents? Or why can't we accept that, in the absence of those favorable political, economic, and social conditions, those in power are likely to exploit the same digital technologies for their own gain, be it to spread propaganda or surveillance or harassment or censorship or espionage? Or that there might be an important role that these digital technologies are playing in creating both favorable political, economic, and social conditions—by allowing access to more information, creating new jobs, weakening the role of dogmatic authority—for enabling democratization while at the same time creating political, economic, and social conditions—the weakening of mainstream political parties, the further marginalization of the disconnected lower classes, the ability to spread religious propaganda—that might further inhibit it? Why can't we seem to hold all these multiple perspectives on *the Internet* in mind at the same time?

The broader point I'm making here is that, as virtually every one of our social activities is being digitized, it's very arrogant of us to expect that, somehow, we would be able to figure out what the role of *the Internet* in all of this is. Given how ubiquitous and cheap both digitization and connectivity are, what we call *the Internet*—and I here I don't just mean computers, laptops, and routers but also smartphones and the Internet of Things and cheap sensors—is invading every single corner of our existence. This is not by any means a bad thing in itself. Properly designed and governed, this can actually be extremely emancipatory and be a healthy development for democracy. But what we need to come to grips with is that, once the Internet is everywhere, a question like "What are the political implications of the Internet?" loses much meaning, in part because it's like asking "What are the political implications of everything for everything?" A giant supercomputer might answer this question but, alas, we don't have it yet.

Consider an intriguing, even if a bit odd, parallel. Suppose we take the same case study—the Arab Spring—but instead of the *Internet*, we want to figure out the political implications of *money*. So everyone—the military, the dictators, the secular opposition, the Islamic opposition, the religious institutions—are given $100 million to spend as they wish. Now, it's obvious that, if we only rely on theory and speak in the abstract, we won't be able to predict what the impact of this cash infusion would be. Perhaps the opposition will use it to print more leaflets or establish stronger alliances with the trade unions. Or perhaps they will send some of their leaders for training abroad. Or maybe they will just steal some of the money. Perhaps the government will use it to buy more weapons. Or perhaps they will hire more police. Or maybe they will buy more surveillance equipment. But then maybe the religious institutions will use the money to build a splendid mosque that would somehow relieve the tensions.

To answer a question like "What are the political implications of money?" in this case would require knowing everything about how a given society operates, having an excellent grasp of its social fabric, being able to predict what alliances are likely to emerge and when. Clearly, this question is much harder than it appears at first sight; otherwise, the billions that the American government—and it's not exactly short on Middle East experts—poured into foreign aid to some of the regimes in the Middle East would have resulted in democracy long time ago. In retrospect, this looks like a silly question—and few of us would ever seriously pose it.

But why don't we feel the same constraints when it comes to inquiring into the "political implications of the Internet"? And is there a better way to preserve the spirit of this question—and still get some answers—even if we pose it differently? Tackling the first question would give us a clue to the second one. The reason why we keep asking "So, on the whole, is the Internet good or bad?" type of questions has to do with our strong belief that it's a medium and, as a medium, it has some coherence—a logic of sorts—that, once applied to political and social institutions, can meld them in accordance with what the *logic of the Internet* demands.

One can counter that, when it comes to money, we are dealing with a medium as well—its *logic*, some might say, is to create markets. This is trivially true but our set of assumptions about the Internet and its logic runs much deeper and wider. For example, most of us to believe that it's an *either/or* type of medium: it's either a tool of enslavement (i.e., it would favor the governors) or emancipation (i.e., it would favor the governed). That it might do both—and that it might do it differently at different times, depending on the exact historical conditions in a given country—is an insight that is hard to square with how we think of this medium.

For what is this *Internet*? It's a set of services, platforms, standards, and user behaviors. It might seem that the platforms, to take just one example, are the same everywhere—but, of course, they aren't. And it's not just a matter of digital device. Online platforms that are popular in Russia—LiveJournal or VK—have different modes of governance, different policies with regards to free speech, different functionality—than platforms that are popular in either America or China. Yes, we might call all of them *online* platforms or *blogging* platforms but, at the micro-level—the

level that shapes user interaction and user behavior—these are profoundly different.

These platforms—whose evolution has been shaped by the peculiar-
ity of political conditions in which they emerged—give rise to different
citizens and different politics. This is not to say that they can't give rise
to democratic politics, protests, and manifestations of public anger—as
we all know from the news, they do it regularly—but even if they do, they
probably do it via different routes and modalities of behavior. All of this is
to say that it's probably not a good idea to take a snapshot of the totality
of such platforms, behaviors, and users in one country, call it *the Internet*,
and then compare it with a snapshot of the totality of other platforms, other
behaviors, and other users in another country on the false assumption that
all of this too is somehow the same *Internet*. This is not the same Internet,
it never was and it never will be.

But even in the context of a single country, it seems impossible to answer
our initial question about the "political consequences of the Internet." If,
say, *the Russian Internet* is made of platforms, standards, user behaviors,
and so on—and if we grant that both their individual shape and the form
of their mutual entanglement are themselves the product of history, politics, economics, and culture—then we are essentially asking about the
"political consequences of politics," a tautology if there ever was one.
The Internet, as this term exists in popular discourse, is not the *Internet*
as it's experienced by users on the ground. There's no Platonic idea of the
Internet or a stable abstract object around which we can build a philosophy or a social science or on which implications we can *reflect*. That is, it
certainly exists as a ubiquitous presence in our public debate but this is
not the *Internet* as it is experienced by actors on the ground—those who
are actually making politics.

What we tend to forget about the history of computing and
digital networks is that the modes of behavior that we currently
practice on the Internet today—sending e-mails, looking up
information, shopping, engaging in debate—predate the idea
of the Internet as such.

The myth that most of us have bought into is that, in the middle of the Cold War, a bunch of wise people with funding from the U.S. Defense Department got together, thought through about everything that *the Internet* could do, and then simply started implementing that agenda item by item, as if they had it all figured out.

But these people had no idea what *the Internet* was for, what it would be, or that it would soon be imagined as *global village* or *cyberspace*. For much of the 1970s and early 1980s, this *Internet* coexisted with many other similar networks. Even when the World Wide Web came into existence in the early 1990s, it coexisted with several other approaches—Gopher and WAIS were the most prominent ones—that, under somewhat different conditions, could have given us a digital environment that is very different from the one we have today. There's simply no teleological logic leading to the World Wide Web; much of it wasn't built according to a grand master plan. Different practices give rise to different technological infrastructures to enable them and it just happens that the network that links these infrastructures—the Internet—is now thoroughly confused with the plurality of both infrastructures and practices.

So, if we really want to be very specific about our language—a prerequisite, as I would argue, to talking about politics—we should state the following:

The practice of social networking in Egypt is different from the practice of social networking in China, even though both have some functional similarities.

Users in Egypt do and expect different things from social networks than do people in China—which makes perfect sense given that they live in different cultures, with different political, social, and cultural concerns.

Now, the actual social-technological infrastructures that enable social networking in Egypt are almost certainly different from those in China; in the former case, much of this social networking probably happens on Facebook—an American site that might have a complicated outlook toward its Egyptian users—whereas in China, much of social networking activity happens on local sites that are tightly controlled by the government. Their servers are probably located inside the country, not outside. They probably have a team of native speakers to do censorship—not necessarily the case in Egypt/Facebook. Such differences in socio-technical infrastructures that enable the practice of social networking have profound implications on how much freedom users have in each case; how they relate to each other; how subversive they have to get to express their discontent; how easy it is for state authorities to monitor their actions, and so forth.

Finally, there's one final network—*the Internet*—which is actually of rather trivial importance in this comparison, as Egyptian users in Facebook and Chinese users on a local Chinese social network probably do not have much to say to each other. Yes, it's true that they are all wired by the same *network*—and that network does have the same standards and protocols—but this insight is of little consequence here. Once we switch to a practice-based view of the world, we discover that, even though the Egyptian users and the Chinese users browse *the same Internet* for the purposes of social networking, their experience on it is profoundly different. Moreover, as already noted, even within each country, we are likely to see lots of other variations that depend on where and when we look: in times of upheaval, social networking could be more or less useful for protesters depending on what their goals are and how much surveillance and censorship power the authorities have.

To believe that we can collapse all these differences into just one *Internet* and then study its political implications seems naïve and actually irresponsible. As enjoyable as it has been, this debate—about whether "the Internet is good or bad for dictators"—must end, in part because there's simply nothing interesting to be said about this abstract *Internet* thing. This doesn't just work for dictators, by the way; it applies for studying political changes in democratic regimes as well. Anyone who has enough knowledge and patience to map out the political culture of a given democratic regime—and then do a similar mapping of its media-technological-knowledge infrastructures—would discover the impossibility of predicting—and then aggregating—the totality of changes in political culture that are triggered by shifts, even tiny ones, in how the media-technological-knowledge infrastructures operate.

A few examples might suffice. A country with strong freedom of information laws might suddenly discover that, thanks to search engines, the documents that were previously public but stored in a library are now widely accessibly online, at no cost and extra effort. Is it good or bad for democracy? This is not a question we can answer in the abstract. Or we might discover that, suddenly, search engines and their autocomplete function allow us to see which politicians are believed—or speculated—to be taking bribes as the word *bribe* follows their name in the search query. Is it good or bad for democracy? This again is hard to say in the abstract. And this is just the *search engines*—but think about *social networking*, databases, Wikipedia, smartphones, sensors, Big Data, algorithms—all of this is part of *the Internet* too. The idea that, somehow, all of these technologies will have similar effects—and those effects will hold regardless of the political culture where these technologies are put to use—seems delusional.

The only way forward for responsible researchers who are actually interested in figuring out the connections between media-technological-knowledge infrastructures and politics is to proceed slowly and carefully and without operating with such ambiguous concepts like *the Internet*. Yes to the study of individual practices, yes to the study of particular segments of the media-technological-knowledge infrastructures—no to the totalizing language of *the Internet debate*, with its assumption that it's a single and coherent medium—"just like the printing press," as the pundits like to say—which is manifesting the same effects everywhere it goes.

How and why we have settled on this language and set of metaphors—i.e., the idea that *the Internet* is an agent of change that is similar to the *printing press*—is itself a profoundly important question that our digital intellectuals shouldn't shy away from tackling in full force.

For if we do want to understand the "political implications of the Internet," we can see them right here, in the way in which most of the debates about *the Internet* are set up: in framing questions in a particular manner—"Tell us how the Internet affects X…"—we make certain answers and certain modes of thinking impossible. We take them off the table, so to say, and instead prefer to continue with the exciting game of intellectual ping-pong where we are constantly asked to update the score. Twitter enabling new protests in Russia? Great: score one for "the Internet is good for democracy." American firms selling surveillance equipment to dictators in the Middle East? Too bad: score one for "the Internet is bad for democracy."

We must learn to register such developments—Twitter-based protests, after all, are as important as the murky sales of powerful surveillance software—without feeling any need to update the score in that ping-pong game. For if we are truly concerned with the future of democracy in the world, we must make sure that (a) Twitter is most useful to protesters worldwide and that its commercial ethos doesn't undermine its utility for activists, and (b) Western governments have enough regulations in place that would prohibit their own firms from shipping dangerous tools of surveillance to dictatorial regimes; in most cases, this would be a very difficult problem to solve, in part because these tools are built to satisfy the surveillance needs in democracies—we got a painful reminder of this thanks to Edward Snowden's revelations.

Both of these questions—the utility of Twitter for protest and the challenges involved in containing the sprawling surveillance apparatus built by democracies—would require a lot of soul-searching and force us to task lots of uncomfortable questions: about the future of capitalism, privacy, personal data, responsibility of companies and governments, the Western obsession with the war on terror, and so forth. None of these questions will be easy to answer on their own but they would get maddeningly difficult to answer if we also confuse ourselves with an unnecessary urge to somehow make sure that our answers cohere to some vision of *the Internet* as a singular network, a single medium with coherent logics and demands. No, this vision won't serve us any good and we might as well abandon it from the very start; the questions we need to answer already look complicated enough.

It would be naïve to think that, as we move forward, our intellectual predicaments will become lighter and our challenges easier. Of course not: we'll face even more practices, more infrastructures, more techniques of creating, manipulating, and disseminating knowledge. All of them will change the political culture of each and every state in ways that no one can really predict. Yes, there might be similarities and the ongoing inter-networking and the intercommunication enabled by the English language would yield certain homogenization in practices. But it would be incorrect to expect that such occasional homogenizations would trigger more dif-ferentiations or result in completely new actors, practices, or techniques. That Islamist groups use Twitter to publicize their terrorist acts does tell us something about globalization but it doesn't tell us much about the direction in which it would be moving, let alone about what it has in store for democ-racy or cosmopolitanism. For all we know, the global exposure enabled by the internetworking might spawn more local copycats who would pursue their own highly localized projects of terror.

The great intellectual mistake that we could make in this regard is to assume that, somehow, if only we think hard enough about *the Internet*, we would arrive at the right answer as to what would happen to the world once everything is interconnected and digital.

To reiterate: this is a false hope. Such intellectual mastery would never happen—in part because digitization or connectivity are not like physical or chemical processes whose consequences we can predict. And this has nothing to do with the protean nature of *the Internet* or it being the most complex force in history; no, it simply has to do with the fact that what is being digitized and connected are various parts of our society—and it's those parts that defy any logic of prediction.

Think about it this way: the Arab Spring has proved as impossible to predict in advance as the Cold War—all of this despite the fact that almost everyone carries a mobile phone, there's plenty of *Big Data* on social media sites, and the computing power available for churning out predictions is much more impressive than it was in the 1980s. And yet, with all this data and with all this computing power, even the CIA, with its impressive mod-els and its penchant for game theory and data collection, failed to even remotely predict it in advance. Actually, given these immense technological resources, the failure to predict the Arab Spring looks far more remarkable than the failure to predict the fall of the Soviet Union and the eventual end of the Cold War. So don't hold your breath for anyone being able to work out "the political implications of the Internet" any time soon.

Does it all mean that we should just abandon all hope and do nothing, hoping that, somehow, now that everyone has access to a smartphone and Google, things will work themselves out and democracy will eventually prevail? Well, no: this would be too irresponsible. The best we can do is to develop a better set of optical tools—the ones that would allow us to zoom in on particular practices and notice the actual bits and pieces of the many infrastructures hiding behind the *Internet* label—and embrace a form of epistemological modesty, where, every time we are asked to opine on "What does the Internet do to Subject X?" we politely decline and stay silent. Or, if we are of a more dissenting breed, we point out the explicit danger of asking such questions.

Designing Connections

Federico Casalegno

Director of the MIT Mobile Experience Lab and Associate Director of
the MIT Design Laboratory at the Massachusetts Institute of Technology

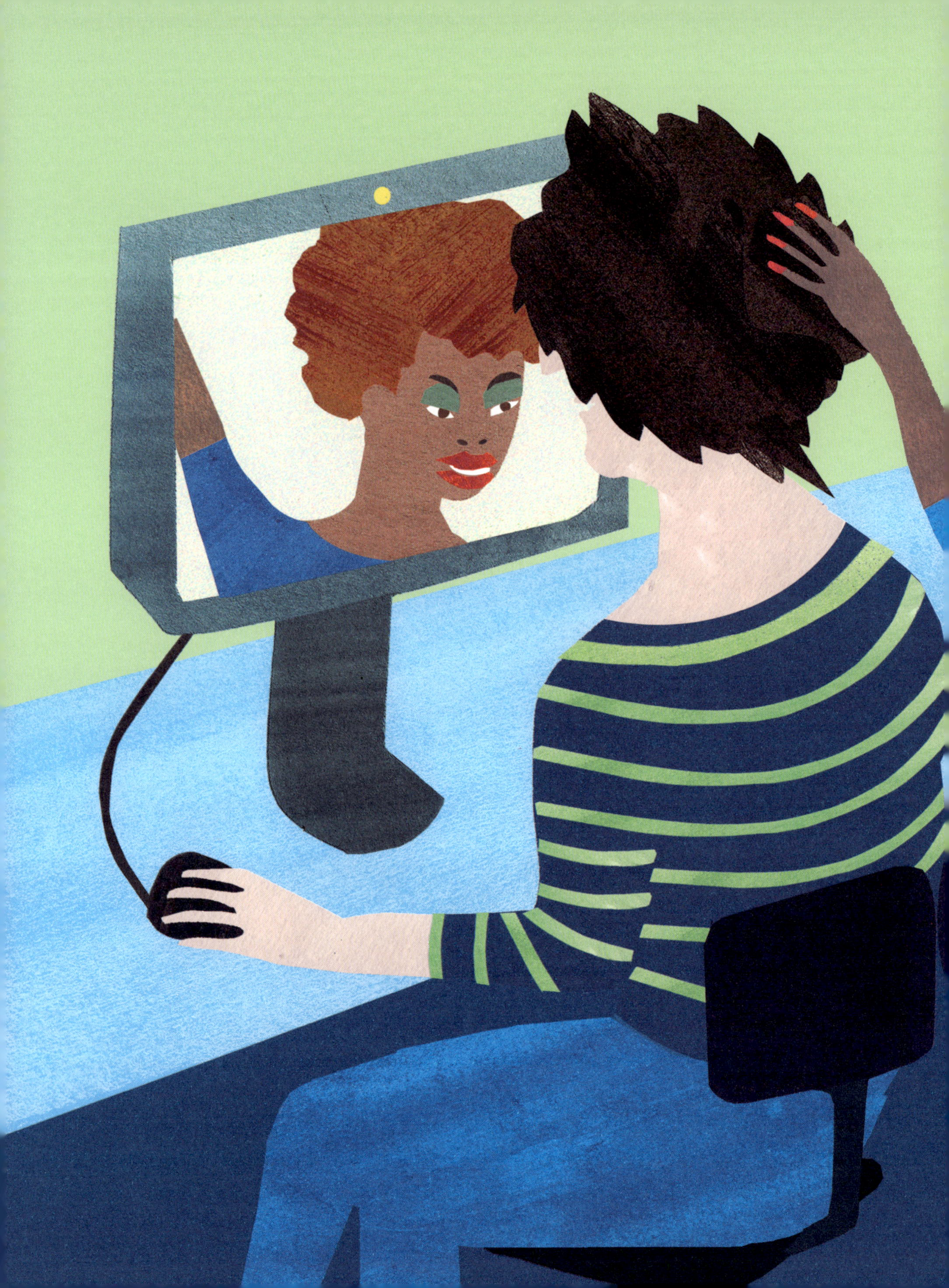

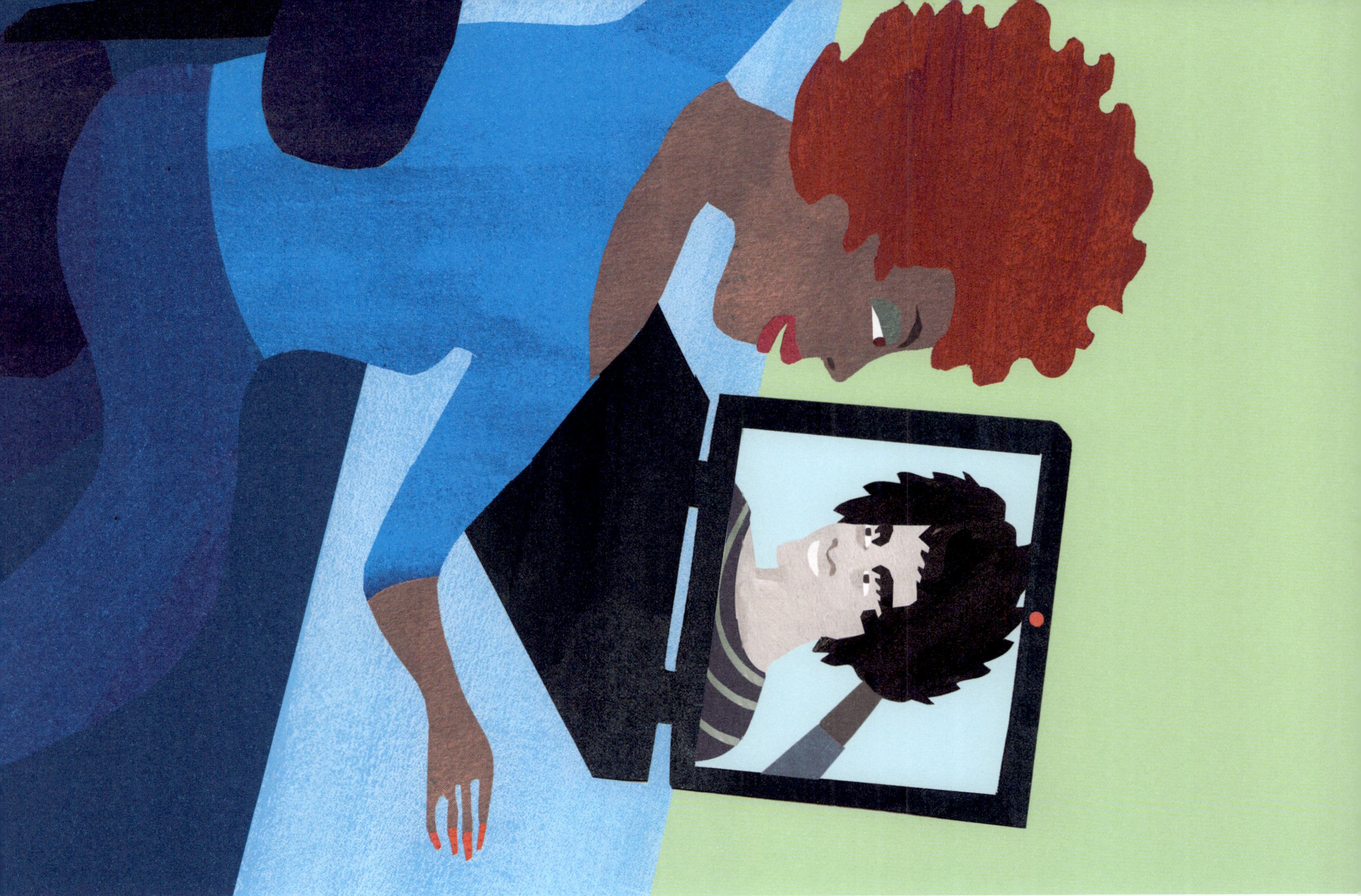

Federico Casalegno

mobile.mit.edu/people/federico

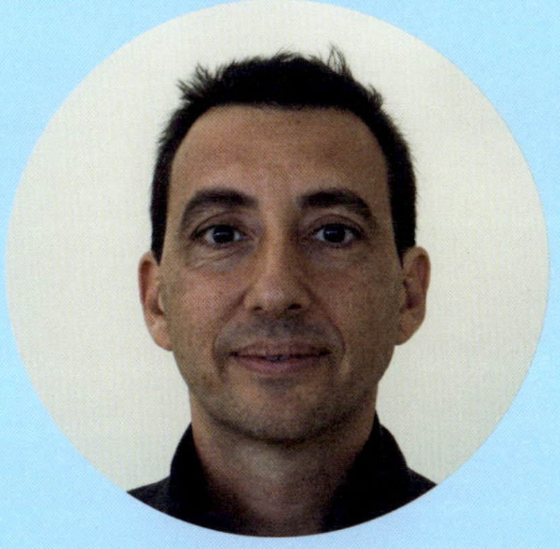

Federico Casalegno is Director of the MIT Mobile Experience
Lab and Associate Director of the MIT Design Laboratory at
the Massachusetts Institute of Technology. Since 2008, he
is the director of the Green Home Alliance between MIT and the
Fondazione Bruno Kessler in Italy. He is adjunct full professor at IMT
Institute for Advanced Studies, Lucca, Italy, and has been awarded
an honorary professorship at the University of Glasgow, Glasgow
School of Art. Dr. Casalegno both teaches and leads advanced
research at MIT and designs interactive media to foster connections
between people, information, and physical places using cutting-
edge information technology. Since 2004, he has also held a position
as lecturer at the MIT Media Lab Smart Cities group. From 2004
to 2007, he worked at Motorola, Inc. as a technology and product
innovation analyst, and from 1994 to 2000 worked at Philips Design
on connected communities and new media environments. He has
published several scientific papers in peer-reviewed journals, books,
and articles. For the Living Memory connected community project
he was awarded the Best Concept prize by I.D. Magazine and the
Silver Prize for design concept by the Industrial Designers Society
of America (IDSA). He holds a PhD in Sociology of Culture and
Communication from the Sorbonne University, Paris V.

Sites and services that have changed my life
google.com
mit.edu
wikipedia.org
kiva.org
skype.com
ted.com

Designing Connections

No one disputes that new technologies, including the ubiquitous Internet and World Wide Web along with social media, have changed our lives and how we work and play. Most people who use these technologies can point to many positive things that have resulted. What we tend not to focus on, though, is the primary downside of our digital connectivity. While we're all busy using our various devices, doing everything from finding a restaurant nearby to sharing an experience we've had with acquaintances to working from home and thus avoiding contributing to a clogged highway, we may also be separating ourselves from direct human contact. And that may exact a severe price on society.

As Sherry Turkle (2011, xx) has written, "Technology proposes itself as the architect of our intimacies." She warns that humans are falling prey to the "illusion of companionship" as we amass Facebook and Twitter "friends" and treat tweets and wall posts as "authentic" communication.

The challenge today, then, is to design technologies we can use, but not let them use us. No one disputes that remote interaction not only has positive attributes but that in certain cases is necessary. No one disputes that remote interaction may, in many cases, be more efficient and in some instances may achieve better results. Still, though, our use of digital technologies, today and tomorrow, poses a question. It is a question we may not have thought about but that is pressing nonetheless: How do we make technological advances without disconnecting from direct human interaction?

Consider this question in the context of some of the most recent amazing advances in technological capabilities.

- There has been a huge uptick in the number of consumer wearable and sensing technologies that do everything from tracking physical activity, dietary choices and calories, sleep habits and cycles, to sensing mood changes, where you gaze, and whether your posture needs correcting. Many of the devices are linked to smartphones applications and websites where goals can be set, progress monitored, and even competitions can be set up with friends and strangers.

- Edible and nanotechnologies in the years to come will become more popular and diffused in our societies. In June, the head of Google-owned Motorola's research division announced the development of an ingestible vitamin prototype that will transform the human body into an authentication passcode. Once swallowed, the pill creates an individual 18-bit ECG light signal detectable by external devices such as a personal computer or smartphone. The small chip in the pill is switched on and off by stomach acid (Ferro 2013). We can already foresee many areas where this type of technology can be beneficial.

- With a grain-of-rice-size RFID chip implanted in his hand, artist Anthony Antonellis has created what some are calling the first-ever digital tattoo. The chip functions like a floppy disk: it stores 1KB of data and the content it holds can be swapped out and replaced with any text file or image of a size less than its storage capability. The content is viewable only on a smartphone (Zolfagharifard 2013).

- Professor Hugh Herr, who heads the Biomechatronics research group at the MIT Media Lab (2013), has developed physically assistive technologies that allow what he calls "intimate extensions" of the human body "structurally, neurologically, and dynamically," with a focus on orthotics and prosthetics. His inventions include a computer-controlled knee and a robotic ankle-foot prosthesis that mimics the action of a biological ankle and allows an amputee to have a natural gait.

These are but a few of many examples of how technologies have not only progressively become part of our lives, not only extensions of our bodies, but integral parts of us and our bodies. There is an emergent and increasingly symbiotic relationship between humans, networks, and technologies, which poses the earlier question a different way: How do we continue to progress and reap all the potential benefits of what digital technologies have to offer without turning ourselves into cyborgs?

What follows is not a Luddite manifesto, nor a screed against human progress. Rather, consider it in the tradition of cautionary tales. In this case, it is a tale about what we, as humans, lose as we increasingly move our interactions with others to our digital technologies and eliminate, more and more, the human activity of talking with others face to face, in shared physical space. It is a tale about the decline of *Dasein*, or "being there," which philosophers (notably Heidegger [1927]) have identified as a uniquely human experience that helps shape us as social beings. It is these human interactions that are being subverted, even if inadvertently, by digital technologies.

And further: Can we actually build trust, engagement, and even social sustainability using digital technologies... things that seem antithetical to their use?

More than a hundred years ago, German sociologist and philosopher Ferdinand Tönnies (1887) provided a kind of guide for answering that question. He described two types of social groupings: the *Gemeinschaft* (or community) and the *Gesellschaft* (or society). The former refers to "emphatic" groupings of people in which feelings of togetherness and mutual bonds are shared, like a family or a neighborhood. In the latter, cohesiveness among group members is more mechanical and based on individual aims and goals.

Increasingly, it appears that the severing of direct human interaction that occurs with the use of so many digital technologies makes for a more efficient *Gesellschaft*, but perhaps at the expense of the *Gemeinschaft*. We need to find a balance.

This issue of balancing advances in digital technology with maintaining, and indeed strengthening, human interaction and human connections at the *Gemeinschaft* level has informed the work of the MIT Mobile Experience Lab[1] from its beginning. The aim of the lab's research has been to creatively design new media and technology to connect people, places, and information, always with a human-centric approach in which technology is a tool, not the driver of innovation. While it may seem a cliché, the goal truly is to design technology around people, not the other way around. So, the complexity of our questions has evolved over time, from how to build in a way to promote

1. http://mobile.mit.edu

direct connections while taking advantage of new technologies that enable new personal devices, to an outlook today that encompasses the entire digital ecosystem of a home or, beyond, an entire city. What we've tried to do, in a sense, is grow along with the expansion of how *smart* is used with respect to technology: from smart personal devices to smart cities, reflecting back on what we might call the *smart individual* in a digital world. And not just smart in using digital technology, but smart in not allowing that technology to disconnect us from each other as it is seeming to connect us.

It is this context within which the digital technology applications described below have been designed and employed under circumstances where human connectivity may be between individuals, neighbors, schoolmates, or communities and the institutions on which they depend and that exist to serve their interests.

Trust and Engagement Through a Wearable Device

Brescia is a province in northern Italy, situated at the foot of the Alps. The city of Brescia has about 200,000 people, and it was facing a big problem in the mid-2000s: a big increase in the number of automobile accidents involving young, drunk drivers. The Councilor of Innovation and government workers involved with running the province's information and communication systems believed that digital technology might provide part of a solution to the problem. The objective was to help create an environment in which the incidence of drunk driving would not only decrease, but would do so while drawing young drivers into a closer relationship with government institutions. Put differently, the institutions wanted to be seen not just as the enforcers of laws, but as a component of a social circle that could help lead young drivers to better outcomes. That would, by definition, mean using technology as a tool to strengthen human connections.

To begin to find a digital *solution* to a social problem, though, required not simply going through the catalogue of digital technologies and choosing something that seemed apt, but bringing civic engagement to the effort from the beginning. Students in Brescia joined with students from MIT to explore the local issues and social culture to ensure that any solution would unfold in a local context that would build connections. They did background research, interviewed residents of Brescia, and explored the city. They conducted a design charette and met with Brescia government representatives in a workshop, building a portfolio of ideas for how to go beyond the simple application of technology. The students from Brescia, in particular, became conduits between the local Brescian citizenry and the laboratory.

Ultimately, what the lab designed as a technology *solution* to the drunk driving problem (based on what had been learned about Brescians and on the outcome of the earlier design charette) was a system that combined wearable technology, mobile phones, and a web infrastructure specifically aimed at establishing a peer-to-peer trust network in which Brescian youth address the social issue of drunk driving themselves, but aided by government institutions. Thus, the system builds direct human connections based on trust while at the same time promoting civic engagement.

Each user of what is called Ride.Link[2] becomes a registered member of an online social networking platform with a personalized profile. From there, a network of friends is established. Users wear smart bracelets when out partying or at clubs. The bracelets are equipped with simple breathalyzers; the user blows on the bracelet to determine whether driving would be safe. If not, the bracelet sends a message through the system, via the cell phone, to contact a friend who can drive.

The more sophisticated social component is found in how the technological tool aims to strengthen trust. The online social network has components of reputation management; the system facilitates matching a group of designated drivers with their friends who need a safe ride home if they consume alcohol and are unable to drive themselves, and over time reputations for reliability, based on trust, grow. Once home safely, drinkers and drivers are rewarded with incentive points redeemable at an e-commerce store integrated into the system.

Notably, in the Ride.Link demonstration project the users themselves identified all manner of potential new directions in which the technology could be used.

2. http://mobile.mit.edu/p/ridelink/

Building social trust was at the very core of the conception of the Ride. Link system, as a step toward strengthening human relationships and social connections among a peer group and empowering a local community to develop solutions to its own problems. UNICEF's Youth-Led Digital Mapping project in the favelas (slums) of Rio de Janeiro, Brazil, also using a technology developed by the MIT Mobile Experience Lab, takes this empowerment to a new, higher level (Caparelli, Palazzo, and Kone 2012).

Creating Community Change Through Digital Engagement

The UNICEF country office in Brazil trains young people to gather stories and data about their communities using a smartphone-based application called UNICEF-GIS, which is based on the underlying technology Open Locast, a location-based media framework. With it, youth can map their neighborhoods, identify where governmental and nongovernmental services exist or may be missing and address issues of accessibility for young people, point specifically to places where young people face particular risks or hazards (actionable items related to infrastructure and the environment), and locate public social spaces where the community is coming together.

Locast was developed as the Mobile Experience Lab sought to gain a better understanding of how evolving media technologies could be used to improve connections between people and their social, cultural, and physical spaces. Its development benefits from what we learned in 2005 with a project in Manresa, a small city in Catalonia (Spain) that began with an exploration of how governments and civic institutions can improve the way they communicate with citizens using networked technologies and new media, and how governments might become more responsive and offer better services through the use of wireless, interactive, and location-aware technologies. Back then, we were trying to provide Manresa's citizens with a sort of magnifying glass that would allow them to see into civic institutions, thus making them transparent, as well as allow citizens to investigate and explore their urban environment. We called the device we developed (a modified cell phone) the electronic lens, or eLens.[3]

3. http://mobile.mit.edu/p/elens

With eLens, users could post messages in physical locations, tag buildings and places, create social networks based on common interests and social empathy, and share information, opinions, experiences, and passions. Tagging was central to eLens; it was a way to enrich the physical environment by combining formal and institutional information with informal communication and personal annotations. People from local communities who posted their ideas, information, and experiences in their physical environment could create affinity based on social networks. In short, digital technology was used to strengthen *Gemeinschaft*.

In the initial experiment, Manresa teens were organized into teams to redesign the city's three famous architectural walks, which are a tourist attraction. Using the technology and working together, they would provide on-the-spot contextual information about the city's attractions and resources. They could tag buildings with formal messages about history, architecture, and the city, or about their own subjective interactions with their community and its people.

eLens was a clear effort to merge digital information into the built environment and merge user-generated communication and annotation with top-down information. The project was an exploration in embedding human memories and making them accessible as a way to humanize cities and physical places. This had already been done with art (e.g., sculptures in public places), but we wanted to do it with human communication. And while the technology may not have been perfect for the objective, we made the effort.

In much the same way today, Locast allows for rapid prototyping and quick deployment of location-based media platforms, and has two primary components: a web application and a mobile application that act in unison to provide a platform that can be tailored to specific users. In the Brazil case, Locast—as part of UNICEF-GIS—is tailored to build human connections among the youth while, at the same time, identifying to service providers (including governmental and nongovernmental institutions) where they can disseminate information and assistance face-to-face.

This digital technology, and the way it's being used, supports not only bottom-up communication from favela residents to institutions that can help them, but also horizontal communication within the community among activists and non-activists alike. Before the UNICEF-GIS project was rolled out in Rio, there was already some community self-organization to address many of the problems residents encounter. Requiring face-to-face engagement in physical space, the tool helps reinforce the community self-organization and thus strengthen human interaction.

The Brazil project is by no means the first use of Locast to build civic engagement and human connections. In northern Italy, the technology was at the center of the Locast H2Flow project, in which students used templates on their mobile phones to construct video reports and documentaries about sustainable water issues in their community. Working in groups to conduct interviews, survey the public, and uncover issues *in the field*, the teens not only learned through participation but also drew closer together to each other and to the local authorities responsible for water in their region. This engendered a new level of civic engagement, one that required much more than sitting at a desk and working at a personal computer. The students were freed from those shackles, compelled to go outside and work with others, face-to-face.

A digital technology like Locast also reinforces the transmission of knowledge, culture, history, and memory, all of which are key components of *Gemeinschaft*. In the Boston area, the lab undertook the Memory Traces project to explore the potential of digital storytelling using mobile devices.[4] Interviewing prominent first-, second-, and third-generation Italian Americans, the project produced 150 *episodes* relaying memories, made the stories *visual* by overlaying them on a map of the city, and made it possible to access stories by person, time, place, period, or theme. A mobile application allows users to follow the stories as they travel through the city of Boston, linking them directly to the physical urban environment.

It turns out that geo-referenced media has the potential to enrich learning and create strong links between people, places, and information. The technology can also help empower people, young and old, to become public advocates and even decision makers, as in Brazil. In Boston, Memory Traces is demonstrating how embedding information into physical spaces

4. http://locast.mit.edu/memorytraces/

and then unleashing digital technology to bring people together around that information can strengthen human connections.

Smart People, Not Just Smart Technology

The Locast projects just described point to how much of what futurists predicted about digital technologies has come to pass, and also how carefully we must tread to ensure that these technologies don't engulf us.

Today, powerful little computers that we carry around in our pockets allow us to make recordings, take high-quality pictures, listen to more music than is almost imaginable, access the Internet at high speeds, process a variety of data, organize our personal information, and employ sensors that tell us where we are, how to get where we need to go, what the weather is, how fast we're moving, where the next coffee shop might be, deposit and withdraw funds and pay, share a plethora of things with other devices thanks to embedded near field communications capabilities, tag just about anything…

The advances in digital technology have brought computational capability directly into our physical surroundings, where once we had to sit at our computers at work or home to do not even half of what we can do today.

These same advances, as the Ride.Link project illustrates, are beginning to create an ecosystem of wearable digital technology.

Yet, we still ride subways on which dozens of people, despite their physical proximity, are completely engrossed in their personal digital *spaces*, reading e-books, playing games, surfing the web, talking on the phone to someone else similarly ensconced in a personal digital space, but not co-located. So, the risk remains: our human connections become more and more severed, with real physical interaction in physical spaces replaced with, well, the sort of *cyborgian* life alluded to earlier.

It turns out this question of connections to physical space is as important as the earlier question posed about taking advantage of digital technologies without disconnecting from direct human interaction, which takes place in shared physical places—as the Brazil project shows. So, then, how do we employ digital technologies without isolating ourselves from others in real physical spaces?

Digital Connections in Physical Space

Some years back, the Mobile Experience Lab began to work in France with the Régie Autonome des Transports Parisiens (Autonomous Transit Operator of Paris, or RATP) to engage people there in thinking about the bus line of the future.[5] The RATP operates a multimode system that includes extensive bus lines, regional trains, trams, and even the subway service, and is today the major provider of public transportation in the Greater Paris area. A lot of effort was put into the future of the physical buses, how bus routes should be designed, and how riders should access and even help design the bus schedules. All of these considerations led to the bus stop, where the issue of human connections in a digitally enabled world once again arose.

First, the lab explored several questions. How can we connect the bus stop more organically to the bus? To its environment? How can we create a seamless fluidity between the bus stop and the neighborhood? What can be done at the bus stop to help people put the public bus system to better use? To have a better understanding of the bus lines and how they can be used? To provide more portals into the urban environment between physical stops? What might be a good design for the bus stop of the future? These questions were considered in the context of human connections, not simply digital technologies and how they might be employed in a bus stop of the future.

The resulting design of a bus stop had lots of digital capabilities, from digital display technology to sensors that allowed it to become a herald

5.   http://mobile.mit.edu/p/smartmobility/

of neighborhood environmental conditions. But in the context of strengthening connections, the lab took some counterintuitive steps specifically designed to compel face-to-face interaction in physical spaces. It was an early experiment in what this article is all about.

The lab sought to establish the bus as a kind of *outdoor living room*, a space between a bus rider's home and work or destination that can build stronger social ties between people and between people and their physical surroundings. It is the same idea behind the increasing prevalence of interactive furniture in public spaces, where digital technologies and new media are used to help people find what they need—information, services, whatever—locally. Such applications intensify a physical space, making it richer and denser and capitalizing on opportunities to connect people.

In Paris, the bus stop was designed not just to help people use the bus system itself, but also to serve as a local information kiosk for its local community, as an information portal through which citizens can access fundamental resources offered by the city of Paris and, in particular, neighbors and the neighborhood. In addition, it was designed to do so by creating a kind of collective intelligence that would enable the local community to build its own human connections independent of the bus line.

Facing waiting passengers, the bus stop (called the Electronic Guimard, after Paris Métro designer Hector Guimard) has an interior that provides displays and interaction screens for way-finding and schedule information, news, information about local businesses and points of interest, and local community networking. It is in the networking that the human connection-building becomes most pronounced. So, for instance, someone in the community may be able to access the bus stop from home, digitally, to post a notice about starting a neighborhood book club, but eventually the system will require that person and other interested people to continue their organizing efforts in real time, face-to-face, maybe at a neighborhood café that has been enabled with access to the bus stop and further digital tools needed to extend the initial organizing efforts until a real book club exists, with people physically present in a shared space.

In this way, the conception the lab realized was to strengthen the real links between commuters, visitors, neighbors, and, on a larger scale, the city's citizens—at the very local level, but also promoting face-to-face interaction by promoting local conversations, all while helping RATP keep current with the latest in digital technologies. The Electronic Guimard, while by now perhaps eclipsed by more recent technological advances, keeps alive the key notion of an interactive urban artifact that reinforces social interactions.

A Connected Home

The Paris project addressed human interaction, connections, and physical space on a community-wide, even citywide scale. So it may seem a step back to take on the questions posed earlier at the level of an individual family's domicile. After all, one function of our homes, beyond shelter, is to offer a refuge from the world outside, a place to rest, refresh, and renew.

This does not negate, though, that even the physical space of a home can employ the most advanced digital technologies while strengthening human connections beyond the walls.

Typically today, designers of technologically advanced housing are addressing a common set of issues: transcending shelter to make the home a potential workplace easily connected to the online world; employing building methods that are environmentally sound; using materials that are sustainable; and embedding digital technologies that support and encourage efficient use of resources (electricity, water, and so on). These are not specifically issues of strengthening human connections.

What might it look like to design a home with digital technologies that create the potential for social interaction between the house and its inhabitants, other dwellings and residents, and the larger community and world?

In Trentino, a province in northern Italy, the Mobile Experience Lab has worked in concert with other researchers and designers to answer that question. Part of doing so has meant expanding the notion of sustainability from the environmental and energy contexts to something more akin to social sustainability: designing what is called the Connected Sustainable Home in a way that allows it to be smoothly integrated within its specific community given a specific social, cultural, and economic *context*. Coupled with physical space, that context is the arena within which human connections unfold. After all, physical spaces carry history, memory, and culture just as people do, and these are the building blocks of human connections.

An example of the solution can be found in the dynamic façade of the Connected Sustainable Home, which operates using digital technology. The façade is a matrix of 4 × 9 digitally controlled windows, each with three degrees of freedom that allow it to function as a filter between exterior and interior controlling air, daylight, and heat flow. Twenty-seven of the windows in the façade contain an electronic actuator hidden in the frame to allow automated operability. Each windowpane is operable independently so that the permeability to airflow is adjustable with precision. Cross-ventilation becomes possible when house windows facing north and windows of the dynamic façade facing south are open at the same time. The windows themselves are made of radically new materials in a radically new design. An artificial intelligence system optimizes the production, management, and distribution of the renewable energy the connected home utilizes.

While at first blush the dynamic façade may seem a purely technological advance, its design has two main aspects of sustainability that function together and that are linked directly to our broader objective of human connectivity. The first is performance, and the need to achieve natural ventilation. This is eminently *human* in the context of where the home is built; open windows have specific social and cultural implications for the site in Italy, and so making the windows operable was a given. Italians build human connections in part through their interactions through windows, from the outside to the inside and vice versa. A home without windows that can open to the outside world and to neighbors and strangers who may pass by, no matter how technologically advanced, energy efficient, and *sustainable* it may be, is a home that weakens human connections.

The second aspect of sustainability in the Connected Sustainable Home is aesthetics. How, for instance, is the house perceived from the public street? The windows change positions and each serves as a light filter, becoming transparent or opaque. Does the look of the dynamic façade matter in strengthening human connections?

We found the ability to achieve different visual patterns with the windows (open/closed, degrees of interior illumination, average light, etc.) provides an aesthetic advantage. The house can reflect different levels of comfort; the façade can show to the outside world the *behavior* of the residents. Diverse patterns can be aesthetically pleasing. Overall, the combination of performance and aesthetics in the dynamic façade creates a Connected Sustainable Home that looks different depending on external conditions. The windows allow the winter sun to enter. In times of warmer weather, fresh air enters the house. At night, visibility into the house can be blocked for privacy, while still maintaining light and air characteristics. The dynamic façade functions as a responsive, programmable skin between exterior and interior. And in doing all of this, it engages the inhabitant, the neighbor, and the passerby at the aesthetic level to make a connection.

Beyond the Conventional Definition of Smart Technology

When technologists use the word *smart* to describe their inventions and applications, they typically mean harnessing a whole host of digital technologies—monitoring systems, automated controls, sensors—in combination with modeling and decision support to do some things more efficiently and to do some things that have never been done before. That's what is meant by the smart electricity grid, smart transportation networks, and so on. While the objective may more often than not be to figure out how to correct for erratic demand that makes constrained supply difficult to manage, which by its definition centers on human activity, it is not about humans as humans making human connections.

As the lab's projects show, though, the potential for expanding this conventional definition of smart to transcend devices and systems and encompass people certainly exists.

For instance, in the case of the Connected Sustainable Home, the objective was not to create a *smart* home in a completely techno-centric sense, although there is a lot of digital technology (far more than described in this article) involved in the design. The house's own intelligence does not make decisions for the inhabitants. Instead, the design of all the efficiency-related technologies in the house work as a kind of *personal trainer* to encourage efficiency and thus sustainability, and in a context where the technology *relationship* between the house and its inhabitants can be extended beyond the physical building to a wider world. Just as with the Nike wristband, neighbors might playfully connect as they *compete* to create the most efficient community.

In the book *Connected Sustainable Cities*, this idea is taken further and writ larger. The idea of such a city begins with employing "ubiquitous, networked intelligence to ensure the efficient and responsible use of the scarce resources … that are required for a city's operation, together with the effective management of waste products that a city produces, such as carbon emissions to the atmosphere" (Mitchell and Casalegno 2008, 1). But its end is not simply to be technologically smart. It is predicated on the conviction that "pervasive connectivity and related services can encourage new ways of planning, working, and living that make social connections stronger and lead to cooperative sustainable behavior" (Mitchell and Casalegno 2008, 1).

In the context of an entire city, human connections are a foundational aspect of both the smart city and its smart inhabitants, along with technology, to enable "coordinated, efficient, and sustainable urban policies across neighborhoods, institutions and, indeed, the entire social fabric of an urban area" (Mitchell and Casalegno 2008, 1).

How do we avoid becoming cyborgs in a city that takes full advantage of advanced digital technologies in a city, in applications ranging from mobility to work to living and playing? The interactive bus stops described earlier are a start. Self-organized ridesharing, enabled by smartphones, is another. In residences and offices, sustainable agriculture on rooftops can flourish with the help of digital technologies that can not only guide planting and growing decisions, but also help organize the work and bring people together to sow and reap. On a larger scale, neighborhoods can be designed as connected live-work villages that use digital technologies to take advantage of flex time, telecommuting, cloud computing and other collaborative tools, and shared work and meeting spaces as needed. Systems can be established that leverage everything digital technologies have to offer while still putting humans in direct contact within physical spaces.

First Step: Admitting the Challenge Exists

It seems that a lot of technologists either avoid or perhaps have never even considered that their designs and inventions are pulling people apart. It's easy to be seduced into believing that ubiquitous connectivity with your far-flung family through Facebook has only positive ramifications. It's easy to miss the isolation that comes from sitting alone at a computer, seemingly connected to an entire world but absent any physical contact with others in a real physical space. Do we really want to get to a point where a smiling emoticon sent by text or posted online is the norm for showing glee, where once we saw the real smile?

Again, this is about striking a balance.

Digital technology has reinvented our expectations for staying connected at the cost of severing some of our most important human connections—the ones that happen face-to-face.

How often have you communicated digitally with someone over a period that could have just as easily been spent sitting down together for a cup of coffee?

This problem is real, and there's a strong argument that as our devices grow more and more capable we had better do something about reversing the trend. It doesn't have to mean stopping the advance of technological progress. There's no way to impose a rule that every use of digital technology has to create opportunities for the kind of human interaction that technology tends to suppress, but we do need to think more carefully about how to ensure that we can all reap the benefits of digital technology without losing those interactions and… well… becoming something like the cyborgs mentioned earlier.

The correction of our course can begin with a recognition of the problem and a pledge to make sure our progress is being driven by what people need as people, not by what is possible with the next technological development in a sort of vacuum. An iPhone today has more technological capabilities built into it than existed in the first space shuttle. We don't need to halt the expansion of iPhone capabilities, but can we at least keep asking ourselves, at each juncture, whether we actually need the next new thing, and what are its implications for advancing or subverting human connections?

The massive uprisings of the Arab Spring have taught an important lesson. Enabled in large part by digital technology, they still showed that humans have to make physical connections to hope to create a better world. For all the amazing interactions possible on, say, Twitter, it was to the streets of Tunis, Cairo, and elsewhere that hundreds of thousands of people came to make their difference. Yes, they could broadcast content around the world at the proverbial flip of a switch, but they could not take down a dictator without relegating digital technology to its rightful place as a tool of human action, not a substitute for human action.

References

Caparelli, Maria Estela, Ludmilla Palazzo, and Rhazi Kone.
"In Brazil, Adolescents Use UNICEF's New Digital Mapping Technology To Reduce Disaster Risks in the Favelas." UNICEF: Newsline. March 19, 2012. http://www.unicef.org/infobycountry/brazil_62043.html

Ferro, Shaunacy.
"New Motorola Vitamin Pills Could Be Edible Stomach-Acid-Powered Passwords." *Popular Science*, May 30, 2013. http://www.popsci.com/gadgets/article/2013-05/motorola-debuts-vitamin-authentication-powered-stomach-acid

Heidegger, Martin.
Sein und Zeit. Tübingen: Max Niemeyer Verlag, 1927. English: *Being and Time*, 1962.

MIT Media Lab.
"Hugh Herr Biography." MIT Media Lab. www.media.mit.edu/people/hherr (accessed September 9, 2013).

Mitchell, William J., and Federico Casalegno.
Connected Sustainable Cities. Cambridge, MA: MIT Mobile Experience Lab Publishing, 2008. http://connectedsustainablecities.org/downloads/connected_sustainable_cities.pdf

Tönnies, Ferdinand.
Gemeinschaft und Gesellschaft [1887]. 2nd ed.. Leipzig: Fues's Verlag, 1912. English: *Community and Society*, 1957.

Turkle, Sherry.
Alone Together: Why We Expect More from Technology and Less from Each Other. New York: Basic Books, 2011.

Zolfagharifard, Ellie.
"Would You Have Tattoo Implanted Under Your Skin? Artist Has Chip Placed Inside His Hand That Reveals Artwork When Read by a Smartphone." *Daily Mail*, August 29, 2013. http://www.dailymail.co.uk/sciencetech/article-2405596/Artist-Anthony-Antonellis-creates-digital-tattoo-implanting-RFID-chip-hand.html

The Internet and Education

Neil Selwyn

Professor in the Faculty of Education, Monash University

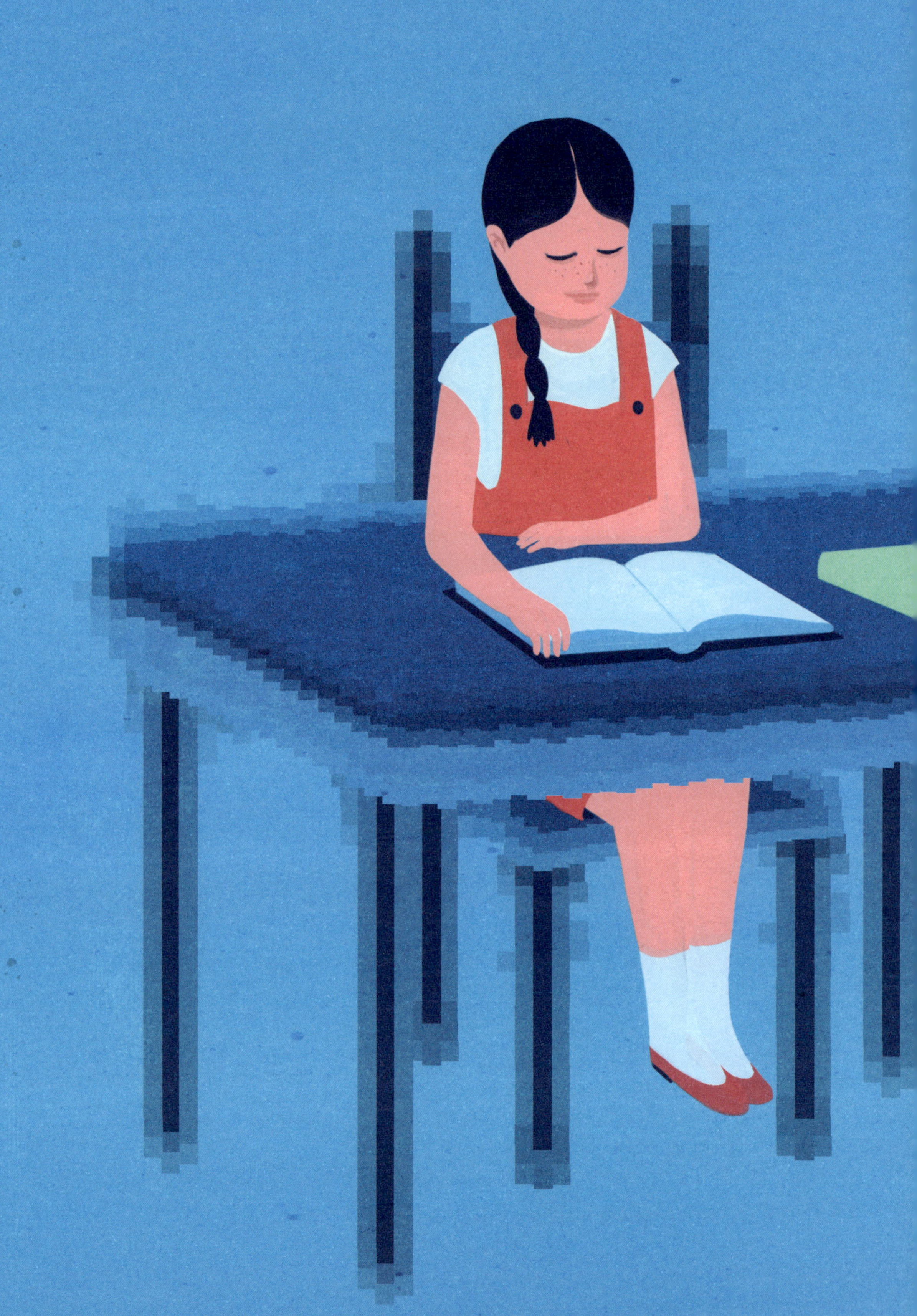

Neil Selwyn
ioe.ac.uk/staff/lklb_48.html

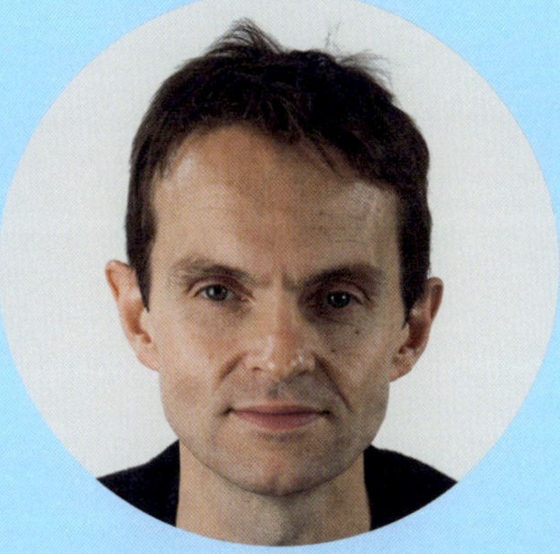

Neil Selwyn is a professor in the Faculty of Education, Monash University, Melbourne, Australia. Over the past 20 years his research and writing has focused on many different aspects of education and digital media—from students' experiences to the political economy of *ed tech.* Recent books include *Education in a Digital World* (Routledge, 2013), *The Politics of Education and Technology* (Palgrave Macmillan, 2013), and *Distrusting Educational Technology* (Routledge, 2014). His latest book, *Degrees of Digitization. Digital Technology and the Contemporary University* (Routledge), will be published in the summer of 2014.

Sites and services that have changed my life
twitter.com
wikipedia.org
archive.org/web

The Internet and Education

Introduction

In many ways, it is difficult to discuss any aspect of contemporary society without considering the Internet. Many people's lives are saturated so thoroughly with digital technology that the once obvious distinction between either being *online* or *offline* now fails to do justice to a situation where the Internet is implicitly *always on*. Indeed, it is often observed that younger generations are unable to talk about *the Internet* as a discrete entity. Instead, online practices have been part of young people's lives since birth and, much like oxygen, water, or electricity, are assumed to be a basic condition of modern life. As Donald Tapscott (2009, 20) put it, "to them, technology is like the air." Thus, in many ways, talking about *the Internet and education* simply means talking about contemporary *education*. The Internet is already an integral element of education in (over)developed nations, and we can be certain that its worldwide educational significance will continue to increase throughout this decade.

That said, the educational impact of the Internet is not straightforward. At a rudimentary level, it is important to remember that well over half the world's population has no direct experience of using *the Internet* at all. While this is likely to change with the global expansion of mobile telephony, the issue of unequal access to the most enabling and empowering forms of Internet use remains a major concern. Moreover—as the continued dominance of *traditional* forms of classroom instruction and paper-and-pencil examinations suggest—the educational changes being experienced in the Internet age are complex and often compromised. In addressing the topic of "the Internet and education" we therefore need to proceed with caution. As such, this chapter will consider the following questions:

- What are the potential implications of the Internet for education and learning?

- What dominant forms of Internet-based education have emerged over the past 20 years?

- How does the educational potential of the Internet relate to the realities of its use?

- Most importantly, how should we understand the potential gains and losses of what is being advanced?

The Internet as an Educational Tool

For many commentators, the Internet has always been an inherently educational tool. Indeed, many people would argue that the main characteristics of the Internet align closely with the core concerns of education. For instance, both the Internet *and* education are concerned with information exchange, communication, and the creation of knowledge.

The participatory, communal nature of many social Internet applications and activities is aligned closely with the fundamental qualities of how humans learn, not least the practices of creating, sharing, collaborating, and critiquing.

Thus, in light of the Internet's capacity to allow these activities to take place on a vast and almost instantaneous scale, the educational implications of the Internet are understandably often described in grand terms. Take, for example, this recent pronouncement from Jeb Bush:

> *The Internet isn't just a powerful tool for communication. It's arguably the most potent force for learning and innovation since the printing press. And it's at the center of what is possibly America's mightiest struggle and greatest opportunity: How to reimagine education for a transformative era.*
>
> (Bush and Dawson 2013)

Beyond such hyperbole, the implications of the Internet for education and learning can be understood in at least four distinct ways. First, is the potential of the Internet to offer individual learners increased freedom from the physical limitations of the *real world*. This is often expressed in terms of reducing constraints of place, space, time, and geography, with individuals able to access high-quality learning opportunities and educational provision regardless of local circumstances. The Internet is therefore portrayed as allowing education to take place on an *any time, any place, any pace* basis. Many commentators extend these *freedoms* into a transcendence of social and material disadvantage, with the Internet perceived as an inherently democratizing medium. The ability to support *freer* and *fairer* educational interactions and experiences is seen to reflect the Internet's underpinning qualities as "a radically democratic zone of infinite connectivity" (Murphy 2012, 122).

Secondly, the Internet is seen to support a *new culture of learning*—i.e., learning that is based around *bottom-up* principles of collective exploration, play, and innovation rather than *top-down* individualized instruction (Thomas and Seely-Brown 2011). The Internet allows learning to take place on a *many-to-many* rather than *one-to-many* basis, thereby supporting *socio-constructivist* modes of learning and cognitive development that are profoundly social and cultural in nature. Many educators would consider learners to benefit from the socially rich environments that the Internet can support (see Luckin 2010). For example, it is often argued that the Internet offers individuals enhanced access to sources of knowledge and expertise that exist outside of their immediate environment. In this sense, there is now considerable interest in the ability of the Internet to support powerful forms of *situated learning* and digitally dispersed *communities of practice*. The Internet is therefore seen as a powerful tool in supporting learning through *authentic* activities and interactions between people and extended social environments.

Thirdly, the capacity of the Internet to support a mass *connectivity* between people and information is felt to have radically altered the relationship between individuals and knowledge. It is sometimes argued that the Internet supports forms of knowledge creation and knowledge consumption that differ greatly from the epistemological presumptions of formal schooling and mass instruction. The networked relationships that Internet users have with online information have prompted wholesale reassessments of the nature of learning. Some educationalists are now beginning to advance ideas of *fluid intelligence* and *connectivism*—reflecting the belief that learning via the Internet is contingent on the ability to access and use distributed information on a *just-in-time* basis. From this perspective, *learning* is understood as the ability to connect to specialized information nodes and sources as and when required. Thus being *knowledgeable* relates to the ability to nurture and maintain these connections (see Chatti, Jarke, and Quix 2010). As George Siemens (2004) puts it, learning can therefore be conceived in terms of the "capacity to know more" via the Internet rather than relating to the individual accumulation of prior knowledge in terms of "what is currently known."

Fourthly, the Internet is seen to have dramatically *personalized* the ways in which people learn—thereby making education a far more individually determined process than was previously the case. The Internet is associated with an enhanced social autonomy and control, offering individuals increased choice over the nature and form of what they learn, as well as where, when, and how they learn it. Education is therefore a wholly controllable aspect of one's personal life, with the Internet facilitating a *digital juggling* of educational engagement alongside daily activities and other commitments (Subrahmanyam and Šmahel 2011). Indeed, Internet users are often celebrated as benefiting from an enhanced capacity to self-organize and *curate* educational engagement for themselves, rather than relying on the norms and expectations of an education *system*.

The Educational Implications of the Internet

All these various shifts and realignments clearly constitute a fundamental challenge to the *traditional* forms of educational provision and practice that were established throughout the nineteenth and twentieth centuries, especially institutionalized modes of *formal* schooling and university education. For many commentators, therefore, the Internet contradicts the monopoly of state education systems and the vested interests of the professions that work within them. In all of the ways just outlined, the Internet would certainly seem to test established educational boundaries between *experts* and *novices*, the production and consumption of knowledge, as well as the timing and location of learning. In terms of how education is provided, the Internet is associated with a range of radically different learning practices and altered social relations.

The Internet has certainly prompted ongoing debate and concern within the educational community. On one hand, many educationalists are busying themselves with rethinking and reimagining the notion of *the school* and *the university* in ways that respond to the demands of the Internet age. There have been various proposals over the past decade for the development of educational institutions that are better aligned with the characteristics of Internet-adept learners and online knowledge. As Collins and Halverson (2009, 129) put it, the task of reinventing schools and universities for the Internet age involves not only "rethinking what is important to learn" but also "rethinking learning." This has seen modes of schooling being developed that are built around the communal creation (rather than individual consumption) of knowledge, in an attempt to imbue learning with a sense of play, expression, reflection, and exploration. The past ten years has seen a rash of ideas from enthusiastic educators proposing the development of new pedagogies and curricula built around social interaction, exploration, *gaming*, and *making*. All of these proposals for *school 2.0* reflect what Whitby (2013, 9–11) describes as *new models* of education provision based around "openness to learning and masterful tech-savvy."

However, in contrast to these *re-schooling* proposals has been a countermovement to align the Internet with more radical forms of educational deinstitutionalization. These *de-schooling* arguments have proven popular with groups outside of the traditional *education establishment*, framing the Internet as capable of usurping the need for educational institutions altogether. Key concepts here include self-determination, self-organization, self-regulation, and (in a neat twist on the notion of *do-it-yourself*) the idea of *do-it-ourselves*. All these ideas align the Internet with a general rejection of institutionalized education—especially what has long been critiqued as the obsolete *banking model* of accumulating *knowledge content*. Instead, Internet-based education is conceived along lines of open discussion, open debate, radical questioning, continuous experimentation, and the sharing of knowledge.

As with other aspects of digital activity, education is therefore imagined as something that is now open to reprogramming, modification, and hacking to better suit one's individual needs.

As Dale Stephens (2013, 9) reasons:

The systems and institutions that we see around us—of schools, college, and work—are being systematically dismantled.... If you want to learn the skills required to navigate the world—the hustle, networking, and creativity—you're going to have to hack your own education.

These are all highly contestable but highly seductive propositions. Indeed, whether one agrees with them or not, these arguments all highlight the fundamental challenge of the Internet to what was experienced throughout the past one hundred years or so as the dominant mode of education. It is therefore understandable that the Internet is now being discussed in terms of inevitable educational change, transformation, and the general *disruption* of twentieth-century models of education provision and practice. As the noted technology commentator Jeff Jarvis (2009, 210) concluded in an acclaimed overview of the Internet's societal significance, "education is one of the institutions most deserving of disruption—and with the greatest opportunities to come of it." Bold statements such as these are now being made with sufficient frequency and conviction that talk of an impending *digital disruption* of education is now rarely contested. Many people, therefore, see the prospect of the Internet completely reinventing education not as a matter of *if*, but as a matter of *when*.

Prominent Forms of Internet-Based Education

In the face of such forceful predictions of what *will* happen, it is perhaps sensible to take a step back and consider the realities of what has already happened with the Internet and education. As was suggested at the beginning of this chapter, amidst these grand claims of transformation and disruption, it is important to ask how the educational potential of the Internet is *actually* being realized in practice. In this sense, we should acknowledge that the Internet has been long used for educational purposes, and a number of prominent models of Internet-based education have emerged over the past 20 years. Perhaps the most established of these are various forms of what has come to be known as *e-learning*—ranging from online courses through to virtual classrooms and even virtual schools. Many early forms of e-learning involved the predominantly one-way delivery of learning content, thereby replicating traditional *correspondence* forms of distance education. These programs (which continue to the present day) tend to rely on online content management systems, albeit supported by some form of interactivity in the form of e-mail, bulletin boards, and other communications systems. Alongside these forms of content delivery is the continued development of so-called virtual classrooms—usually spatial representations of classrooms or lecture theaters that can be *inhabited* by learners and teachers. Often these virtual spaces are designed to support synchronous forms of *live* instruction and feedback, with learners able to listen to lectures and view videos and visual presentations while also interacting with other learners via text and voice. Other asynchronous forms of virtual classroom exist in the form of digital spaces where resources can be accessed and shared—such as audio recordings and text transcripts of lectures, supplementary readings, and discussion forums. These forms of e-learning have continued to be developed since the 1990s, with entire *cyber schools* and online universities now well-established features of educational systems around the world.

While these examples of *e-learning* tend to replicate the basic structure and procedures of *bricks-and-mortar* schools and universities, a variety of other models of Internet-supported education have emerged over the past 20 years. One of the most familiar forms of Internet-based education is the collective *open* creation of information and knowledge, as exemplified by the online encyclopedia Wikipedia. Despite ongoing debates over its accuracy and coverage, the educational significance of Wikipedia is considerable. As well as being a vast information resource, the ability of users to contribute and refine content is seen to make *wiki* tools such as Wikipedia a significant educational tool. The belief now persists amongst many educators that mass user-driven applications such as Wikipedia allow individuals to engage in learning activities that are more personally meaningful and more publically significant than was ever possible before. As John Willinsky (2009, XIII) reasons:

> *Today a student who makes the slightest correction to a Wikipedia article is contributing more to the state of public knowledge, in a matter of minutes, than I was able to do over the course of my entire grade school education, such as it was.*

These characteristics of wiki tools correspond with the wider *Open Educational Resource* movement which is concerned with making professionally developed educational materials available online for no cost. In this manner, it is reckoned that content from almost 80 percent of courses at the Massachusetts Institute of Technology are available on this free-to-use basis. Similar commitments can be found in institutions ranging from world-class universities such as Yale and Oxford to local community colleges. In all these cases, course materials such as seminar notes, podcasts, and videos of lectures are shared online with a worldwide population of learners, most of whom could otherwise not attend. Crucially (as with Wikipedia), the emphasis of Open Educational Resources is not merely permitting individuals to use provided materials, but encouraging the alteration and amendment of these resources as required. For example, the UK Open University's extensive OpenLearn project provides free online access to all of the institution's curriculum materials with an invitation for individual users to adapt these resources as they wish.

Other forms of online content sharing involve the open distribution of educational content that has been created by individuals as well as institutions. For example, the YouTube EDU service offers access to millions of educational videos produced by individual educators and learners. Similarly, Apple Computers' collection of educational media—the so-called iTunes U—is designed to allow learners to circumvent traditional educational lectures and classes in favor of on-demand free mobile learning (Çelik, Toptaş, and Karaca 2012). Describing itself as "possibly the world's greatest collection of free educational media available to students, teachers, and lifelong learners," iTunes U offers free access to hundreds of thousands of educational audio and video podcast files. Most recently, there has been considerable praise for the Khan Academy's online provision of thousands of bespoke educational videos alongside interactive quizzes and assessments covering a range of subject areas and topics. The aim of Khan Academy is to support individuals to learn at their own pace and to revisit learning content on a repeated basis. This so-called flipped classroom model is intended to allow individuals to engage with instructional elements of learning *before* entering a formal classroom. Face-to-face classroom time can be then be devoted to the practical application of the knowledge through problem solving, discovery work, project-based learning, and experiments (Khan 2012).

Another notable *open* example of Internet-based education has been the development of *MOOCs* (Massively Open Online Courses) over the past five years or so. Now, most notably through successful large-scale ventures such as Coursera and Ed-X, MOOCs involve the online delivery of courses on a free-at-the-point-of-contact basis to mass audiences. At its heart, the MOOC model is based on the idea of individuals being encouraged to learn through their own choice of online tools—what has been termed *personal learning networks*—the collective results of which can be aggregated by the course coordinators and shared with other learners. This focus on individually directed discovery learning has proved especially appropriate to college-level education. Now it is possible for individuals of all ages to participate in mass online courses run by professors from the likes of Stanford, MIT, and Harvard universities in subjects ranging from a Yale elective in Roman architecture to a Harvard course in the fundamentals of neuroscience.

Another radical application of the Internet to support self-directed, non-institutional learning are initiatives such as the *hole-in-the-wall* and *School in the Cloud* initiatives. These programs are built around an ethos of *minimally invasive education* where children and young people can access digital technology at any time, and teach themselves how to use computers and the Internet on an individually paced basis. The guiding ethos for the original hole-in-the-wall program was to locate Internet access in what Arora (2010, 691) characterizes as "out-of-the-way, out-of-the-mind locations" rather than in formal settings such as schools or universities. Indeed, the program's credo of minimally invasive education is an avowedly non-institutionalized one, with children expected to engage with the Internet as an educative tool "free of charge and free of any supervision" (Mitra 2010). This approach is seen to be especially applicable to locations such as slum communities in India and Cambodia where Internet access is otherwise lacking. The recent elaboration of the initiative into the School in the Cloud marks an attempt to use online communication tools to allow older community members in high-income countries to act as mentors and *friendly but knowledgeable* mediators to young autonomous learners in lower-income communities. The provision of such access and support is therefore seen to underpin what the project team term "self-organized learning environments" and "self-activated learning"—thus providing an alternative "for those denied formal schooling" in low-income countries (Arora 2010, 700).

These programs, projects, and initiatives are indicative of the variety of ways in which education and the Internet have coalesced over the past 20 years. Yet perhaps the most significant forms of Internet-based education are the completely *informal* instances of learning that occur in the course of everyday Internet use. In this sense the Internet's implicit support of various forms of *informal learning* could be seen as its most substantial educational impact (see Ünlüsoy et al. 2014). As the cultural anthropologist Mimi Ito has described, there are various different genres of everyday Internet-based practice that can be said to involve elements of learning (see Ito et al. 2009). At a basic level is the popular practice of using the Internet to simply *hang out* with others. Often these forms of *hanging out* can spill over into more focused instances of what Ito terms *messing around*—i.e., activities that are interest-driven and more centered on peer sociability, often involving fortuitous searching, experimentation, and playing with resources. This messing around can then sometimes lead to the more intense commitment of what Ito has described as *geeking out*. These are bouts of concentrated and intense participation within defined communities of like-minded and similarly interested individuals driven by common and often specialized interests. In supporting all these forms of *learning*, everyday use of the Internet can be seen as an inherently educational activity.

The Reality of the Internet and Education

These examples—and many more like them—are now seen as proof of the Internet's growing contribution to what it means to learn and be educated in the twenty-first century. Undoubtedly, developments such as MOOCs, flipped classrooms, and self-organized learning could well turn out to be educational *game changers* (Oblinger 2012). Yet the history of educational technology over the past one hundred years or so warns us that change is rarely as instantaneous *or* as totalizing as many people would like to believe. Indeed, the history of *modern* educational technologies (starting with Thomas Edison's championing of educational filmstrips in the 1910s) has usually been characterized by sets of complex mutually shaping relationships between education and technology (see Cuban 1986). In other words, *new* technologies rarely—if ever—have a direct one-way *impact* or predictable *effect* on education. Rather, established cultures and traditions of education also have a profound reciprocal influence on technologies. As the historian Larry Cuban (1993, 185) observed succinctly of the remarkable resilience of schools to the waves of successive technological developments throughout the 1980s and 1990s, "computer meets classroom—classroom wins." In asking how the Internet is shaping education in the 2010s, we therefore need to also ask the corresponding question of how education is shaping the Internet.

From this perspective, it is not surprising to see the most successful forms of Internet-based education and *e-learning* being those that reflect and even replicate *pre-Internet* forms of education such as classrooms, lectures, and books. It is also not surprising to see the long-established *grammar* of formal education and educational institutions having a strong bearing on emerging forms of Internet-based education (Tyack and Cuban 1995). Take, for instance, the persistence of familiar practices such as dividing knowledge into distinct subject areas, using graded individual assessments, or relying on *expert* teachers. While understandable, these continuities certainly belie claims of radical transformation and disruption of the educational status quo. Thus in contrast to the revolutionary zeal of some commentators, it could be observed that the Internet is having most *impact* on education where it is *not* causing radically new patterns of participation or practice. For instance, rather than extending educational opportunities to those who previously were excluded, the recent rise of the MOOC in countries such as the U.S. and UK appears primarily to be supporting well-resourced, highly motivated, and already well-educated individuals to engage in more education (thereby replicating a trend referred to by some social commentators as the *Matthew Effect*). This is not to say that MOOCs are an insignificant form of education—however, it does suggest that their main *impact* is that of increasing rather than widening educational participation. Indeed, this view does imply that some of the more *radical* claims of social transformation and change that surround MOOCs (and other forms of Internet-based education) require careful consideration.

This leaves any attempts to predict the likely influence of the Internet on future forms of education on uncertain ground. Of course, it is unwise to adapt an overtly cynical view that there is nothing *new* about Internet-based education at all—i.e., that the educational effects of the Internet are simply a case of *old wine in new bottles*. Yet it is equally unwise to presume that any of the examples given so far in the chapter necessarily herald a fundamental shift in education. The Internet is certainly associated with educational changes—yet these changes are complex, contradictory, convoluted and decidedly *messy*.

In this respect, perhaps the most significant issues that need to be considered about the Internet and education are sociological, rather than technical, in nature.

In this sense, the Internet prompts a range of ideological questions (rather than purely technical answers) about the nature of education in the near future. Thus, as this chapter draws to a close we should move away from the optimistic speculation that pervades most educational discussions of the Internet. Instead, there are a number of important but less often acknowledged social, cultural, and political implications that also merit attention:

I) The Internet and the increased individualization of education

First, then, is the way in which Internet-based education promotes an implicit individualization of practice and action. The Internet is celebrated by many educationalists as increasing the responsibility of individuals in terms of making choices with regards to education, as well as dealing with the consequences of their choice. All the forms of Internet education outlined in this chapter demand increased levels of self-dependence on the part of the individual, with educational success dependent primarily on the individual's ability to self-direct their ongoing engagement with learning through various preferred means. Of course, this is usually assumed to work in favor of the individual and to the detriment of formal institutions. Yet the idea of the self-responsibilized, self-determining learner is based upon an unrealistic assumption that all individuals have a capacity to act in an agentic, empowered fashion throughout the course of their day-to-day lives. In Bauman's (2001) terms, the successful online learner is someone able to act as an empowered individual *de facto* rather than an individual *de jure* (i.e., someone who simply has individualism *done to* them). Of course, only a privileged minority of people are able to act in a largely empowered fashion. As such this individualization of action leads to education becoming an area of increased risk as well as opportunity.

These issues raise a number of important questions. For instance, just how equal are individuals in being able to make the educational *choices* that the Internet actually offers? How are the apparent educational freedoms of the Internet resulting in enhanced *unfreedoms* (such as the intensification and extension of educational *work* into domestic settings)? To what extent are *personalized* forms of Internet education simply facilitating the *mass customization* of homogenous educational services and content? What is the nature of the collective forms of Internet-based education? How do *communities* of learners established through the Internet differ in terms of social diversity, obligation, or solidarity? Is the Internet undermining or even eroding notions of education as a public good?

II) The Internet and the growth of data-driven education

Another significant issue related to the increased educational significance of the Internet is the ways in which online data and information are now defining, as well as describing, social life. The Internet has certainly extended the significance of databases, data mining, analytics, and algorithms, with organizations and institutions functioning increasingly through the ongoing collection, aggregation, and (re)analysis of data. Crucially, the Internet allows this *data work* to take place on a mass, aggregated scale. We are now seen to be living in an era of *Big Data* where computerized systems are making available "massive quantities of information produced by and about people, things, and their interactions" (Boyd and Crawford 2012, 662).

The collection and analysis of online data is now a key aspect of how actions are structured and decisions are made in many areas of education. Now, for example, masses of online data are being generated, collected, and collated as a result of the Internet-based activities that take place within educational institutions—ranging from *in-house* monitoring of system conditions to the *public* collection of data at local, state, and federal levels. These data are used for a variety of purposes—including internal course administration, target setting, performance management, and student tracking. Similar processes and practices exist in terms of use of data *across* educational systems—from student databases to performance *league tables*. There are, of course, many potential advantages to the heightened significance of online data. There has been much recent enthusiasm for the potential of *learning analytics*—i.e., "the measurement, collection, analysis and reporting of data about learners and their contexts, for purposes of understanding and optimizing learning and the environments in which it occurs" (Siemens et al. 2011, 4). Similarly, there is growing discussion of *educational data mining* and *academic analytics*. All of these uses of digital data are seen to lead to more efficient and transparent educational processes, as well as supporting individuals to self-monitor and *self-diagnose* their learning (Eynon 2013).

Yet, there is a clear need for caution amidst these potential advantages—not least how the increased prevalence of online data in education is implicated in the shaping of what people can and cannot do. For example, how are individuals and their learning being represented by data collected online? How does the Internet support the connection, aggregation, and use of these data in ways not before possible? To what extent are individuals' educational engagements now being determined by *data profiles*? How are these online data being used in forms of *predictive surveillance* where educators and educational institutions use data relating to past performance and behavior to inform expectations of future behaviors? What aspects of educational engagement are *not* represented in the online data being collected and analyzed?

III) The Internet and the increased commercialization and privatization of education

Thirdly, is the need to recognize the role of commercial and private actors in the growth of Internet-based education. Indeed, the role of the private sector is integral to many of the forms of Internet-based education described in this chapter. For example, it is estimated that the global education/technology market is worth upwards of $7 trillion, with burgeoning levels of private capital investment in online education. A range of multinational commercial interests such as Pearson, Cengage, and McGraw-Hill are now involved heavily in the business of e-learning and online provision of teaching and training—competing with countless smaller commercial concerns and a range of nonprofit organizations. Clearly Internet-based education marks a distinct move away from a *planned economy* model where education provision is largely the preserve of state-run, public-sector institutions (see Picciano and Spring 2013).

Of course, the increased involvement of commercial interests in online education could be seen to have many potential benefits. The private sector is able to focus considerable technological resources and expertise on educational issues. It is often assumed that commercially provided education is more responsive to the demands of its *customers*—be it the immediate preferences of learners or the longer-term workforce requirements of business and industry. Moreover, as Chubb and Moe (2012) reason, improvement can arise from market competition between private and public education providers: "in time, [for-profit institutions] may do amazing things with computerized instruction—imagine equivalents of Apple or Microsoft, with the right incentives to work in higher education—and they may give elite nonprofits some healthy competition in providing innovative, high-quality content." Indeed, the appeal of many of the forms of Internet-based education described in this chapter is predicated upon bringing the innovation of the private sector to bear on the inefficiencies of public education. As Sebastian Thrun (the computer scientist credited with the popularization of the MOOC concept) argued recently: "Education is broken. Face it. It is so broken at so many ends, it requires a little bit of Silicon Valley magic" (Wolfson 2013).

Yet the possibilities for commercial innovation and *magic* notwithstanding, there are a number of reasons to challenge the growing influence of private interests in shaping education agendas in these ways. For example, how committed are IT producers and vendors to the public good of educational technology above and beyond matters of profit and market share? Given that education is an integral element in determining the life chances of the most vulnerable members of society, how appropriate is a Silicon Valley, venture-capitalist mindset of high-risk *start-ups* with expected high rates of failure? What are the moral and ethical implications of reshaping education along the lines of market forces and commercial values? Why should education correspond automatically with the needs of the digital economy?

IV) The Internet and the changing values of education

Finally—and perhaps less tangibly—there is also a sense that the Internet might be altering the psychological, emotional, and spiritual bases of education. For example, many of the forms of online education discussed in this chapter imply an increased expansion of education into unfamiliar areas of society and social life—leading to an *always-on* state of potential educational engagement. Indeed, the *anytime, anyplace* nature of online education clearly involves the expansion of education and learning into domestic, work, and community settings where education and learning might previously have not been prominent. There are clear parallels here with what Basil Bernstein (2001) identified as the "total pedagogization of society"—i.e., a modern society that ensures that pedagogy is integrated into all possible spheres of life. This raises questions of what is perhaps lost when one is able to engage with education at all times of the day and in all contexts? Is there something to be said for being able to disconnect from the pressures of education? Is learning best suited to some contexts and circumstances than others?

Many of the forms of online education described in this chapter could also be said to frame learning (often inadvertently) as a competitive endeavor. Thus in contrast to allowing individuals to learn harmoniously alongside others, the Internet could be seen as placing individuals in "personal formative cycles, occupied in unison within individual feedback-action loops. They learn to become industrious self-improvers, accepting and implementing external goals" (Allen 2011, 378). Thus while a sense of achievement at the expense of others may not be immediately apparent, the Internet could be seen as a means of humanizing, disguising, and intensifying the competitive connotations of learning. Continuing this line of thinking, the partial, segmented, task-orientated, fragmented, and discontinuous nature of online education could perhaps even be seen as a form of *spiritual alienation*—i.e., alienation at the level of meaning, where *conditions of good work* become detached from the *conditions of good character* (Sennett 2012).

All these points also relate to the correspondences between the Internet and the altered emotional aspects of educational engagement. In particular, many of the forms of Internet-based education described earlier in this chapter (such as the virtual school or the MOOC) could be said to involve learning being experienced on less immediate, less intimate, and perhaps more instrumental grounds. These points were explored in Jonathan Wolff's (2013) recent reflections on what might be lost when a lecture takes place online as opposed to in a face-to-face lecture theater. While these diminishments are often difficult to pinpoint, Wolff suggested qualities such as the immediacy, the serendipity, and the *real-ness of the live experience* of learning alongside other people. Certainly, the remote, virtual sense of learning online is qualitatively different to the embodied sense of face-to-face learning—both in advantageous and disadvantageous ways.

Conclusions

Whether one agrees with any of these latter arguments or not, it is clear that the topic of "the Internet and education" needs to be approached in a circumspect manner. The predominantly optimistic rhetoric of transformation and change that currently surrounds the Internet and education distracts from a number of significant conflicts and tensions that need to be better acknowledged and addressed. This is not to say that we should adopt a wholly antagonistic *or* wholly pessimistic stance. Indeed, many of the *issues* just outlined should not be assumed automatically to be cause for concern. There are, after all, many people who will be advantaged by more individualized, elitist, competitive, market-driven, omnipresent, and de-emotionalized forms of educational engagement. The Internet clearly works for the millions of people who are learning online at this very moment.

Yet while it may well be that the Internet is helping *some* individuals to engage with education in more convenient, engaging, and useful ways, we would do well to acknowledge that this is unlikely to be the case for all. Any Internet-led changes in education are accompanied by a variety of unintended consequences, *second-order effects*, and unforeseen implications. Perhaps the most important point to consider is the well-worn tendency of digital technology to reinforce existing patterns of educational engagement—helping already engaged individuals to participate further, but doing little to widen participation or reengage those who are previously disengaged. In particular, any discussion of the educational *potential* of the Internet needs to remain mindful of the limited usefulness of a *technical-fix* approach to understanding contemporary education. The Internet should not be seen as a ready *solution* to apparent inefficiencies of *twentieth-century* education institutions or practices—it will not lead automatically to more engaged or motivated learners, more highly skilled workforces, or rising levels of national intelligence and innovation. Instead, it is likely that many of the *problems* of contemporary education are primarily social and cultural in nature, and therefore require social and cultural responses.

As such, while there is plenty of scope for the increased use of the Internet within education, any claims for *change* and *improvement* should be seen as contentious and debatable matters, rather than inevitable trends that educators have no choice but to adapt to. To reiterate a key theme that has emerged throughout our discussion, underlying all of the issues raised in this chapter are questions of what sort of future education one believes in. As such, the role of the Internet in *improving, transforming, or even disrupting* education is a deeply complex and ideologically loaded matter that goes well beyond technical issues of how to personalize the delivery of educational content, or support the production and consumption of online content. The future of education may well involve increased use of the Internet—but will not be determined by it.

References

Allen, Ansgar.
"Michael Young's *The Rise of the Meritocracy*: A Philosophical Critique." *British Journal of Educational Studies* 59, no. 4 (2001): 367–82.

Arora, Payal.
"Hope-in-the-Wall? A Digital Promise for Free Learning." *British Journal of Educational Technology* 41 (2010): 689–702.

Bauman, Zygmunt.
The Individualized Society. Cambridge, UK: Polity Press, 2001.

Bernstein, Basil.
"From Pedagogies to Knowledges." In Ana Morais, Isabel Neves, Brian Davies, and Harry Daniels, eds., *Towards a Sociology of Pedagogy: The Contribution of Basil Bernstein to Research*. New York: Peter Lang, 2001. 363–68.

Boyd, Danah, and Kate Crawford.
"Critical Questions for Big Data." *Information, Communication, & Society* 15, no. 5 (2012): 662–79.

Bush, Jeb, and Rosario Dawson.
"Internet Brings Historic Shift in Learning." *Miami Herald*, June 25, 2013. http://www.miamiherald.com/2013/06/25/3470108/internet-brings-historic-shift.html#storylink=cpy (accessed September 6, 2013).

Çelik, Serkan, Veli Toptaş, and Tuğçe Karaca.
"iTunes University: Potentials and Applications." *Procedia—Social and Behavioral Sciences* 64 (2012): 412–16.

Chatti, Mohammed Amine, Matthias Jarke, and Christoph Quix.
"Connectivism: The Network Metaphor of Learning." *International Journal of Learning Technology* 5, no. 1 (February 15, 2010): 80–99.

Chubb, John, and Terry Moe.
"Higher education's online revolution" *Wall Street Journal*, May 30, 2012. http://online.wsj.com/article/SB10001424052702304019404577416631206583286.html (accessed September 6, 2013).

Collins, Allan, and Richard Halverson.
Rethinking Education in the Age of Technology. New York: Teachers College Press, 2009.

Cuban, Larry.
Teachers and Machines: The Classroom Use of Technology Since 1920. New York: Teachers College Press, 1986.
———. "Computer Meets Classroom: Classroom Wins" *Teachers College Record* 95, no. 2 (1993): 185–210.

Eynon, Rebecca.
"The Rise of Big Data: What Does It Mean for Education, Technology, and Media Research?" *Learning, Media and Technology* 38, no. 3 (2013).

Ito, Mizuko, Sonja Baumer, Matteo Bittanti, Danah Boyd, Rachel Cody, Becky Herr-Stephenson, Heather A. Horst et al.
Hanging Out, Messing Around, and Geeking Out: Kids Living and Learning with New Media. Cambridge, MA: MIT Press, 2009.

Jarvis, Jeff.
What Would Google Do? London: Collins, 2009.

Khan, Salman.
The One World Schoolhouse. London: Hodder, 2012.

Luckin, Rosemary.
Re-designing Learning Contexts: Technology-Rich, Learner-centred Ecologies. London: Routledge, 2010.

Mitra, Sugata.
"Give Them a Laptop and a Group of Pupils Will Teach Themselves." *Guardian*, Educational Supplement, October 19, 2010.

Murphy, Douglas.
The Architecture of Failure. Winchester, UK: Zero, 2012.

Oblinger, Diana G.
Game Changers: Education and Information Technologies. Washington, D.C.: Educause, 2012.

Picciano, Anthony G., and Joel Spring.
The Great American Education-Industrial Complex: Ideology, Technology and Profit. London: Routledge, 2013.

Sennett, Richard.
*Together: The Ritual, Pleasures
    and Politics of Cooperation*.
    London: Allen Lane, 2012.

Siemens, George.
"Connectivism: A Learning
    Theory for the Digital Age,"
    eLearnSpace, December 12,
    2004. http://www.elearnspace.
    org/Articles/connectivism.htm
    (accessed September 6, 2013).

Siemens, George, Dragan Gašević,
Caroline Haythornthwaite, Shane
Dawson, Simon Buckingham
Shum, Rebecca Ferguson, Erik
Duval, Katrien Verbert, and Ryan
S. J. d. Baker.
Open Learning Analytics. N.p.:
    Society for Learning Analytics
    Research, 2011.

Stephens, Dale J.
Hacking Your Education. London:
    Penguin Press, 2013.

Subrahmanyam, Kaveri, and
David Šmahel,
*Digital Youth: The Role of Media in
    Development*. Berlin: Springer,
    2011.

Tapscott, Don.
*Grown Up Digital: How the Net
    Generation is Changing Your
    World*. New York: McGraw Hill,
    2009.

Thomas, Douglas, and Seely
Brown, John.
A New Culture of Learning.
    Charleston, SC: Createspace,
    2011.

Tyack, David, and Cuban, Larry.
*Tinkering Toward Utopia: A Century
    of Public School Reform*.
    Cambridge, MA: Harvard
    University Press, 1995.

Ünlüsoy, Asli, Mariëtte de Haan,
Kevin Leander, and Beate Volker.
"Learning Potential in Youth's
    Online Networks." *Computers &
    Education* (forthcoming, 2014).

Whitby, Greg.
*Educating Gen Wi-Fi: How We Can
    Make Schools Relevant for
    21st Century Leaders*. Sydney:
    Harper Collins, 2013.

Willinsky, John.
"Forward" in Charalambos
    Vrasidas, Michalinos
    Zembylas, and Gene V. Glass,
    eds., *ICT for Education,
    Development and Social
    Justice*. Charlotte, NC:
    Information Age, 2009. XI-XIV.

Wolff, Jonathan.
"It's Too Early to Write Off the
    Lecture." *Guardian*, June 25,
    2013. http://www.guardian.
    co.uk/education/2013/
    jun/24/university-lecture-
    still-best-learning (accessed
    September 6, 2013).

Wolfson, Lisa.
"Venture Capital Needed for
    'Broken' US Education,
    Thrun Says." *Bloomberg
    Businessweek*, June 18, 2013.
    http://www.businessweek.
    com/news/2013-06-18/
    venture-capital-needed-
    for-broken-u-dot-s-dot-
    education-thrun-says
    (accessed September 6,
    2013).

The Way of the Dodo

Lucien Engelen

Director of the Radboud REshape & Innovation Center, Radboud University Medical Center

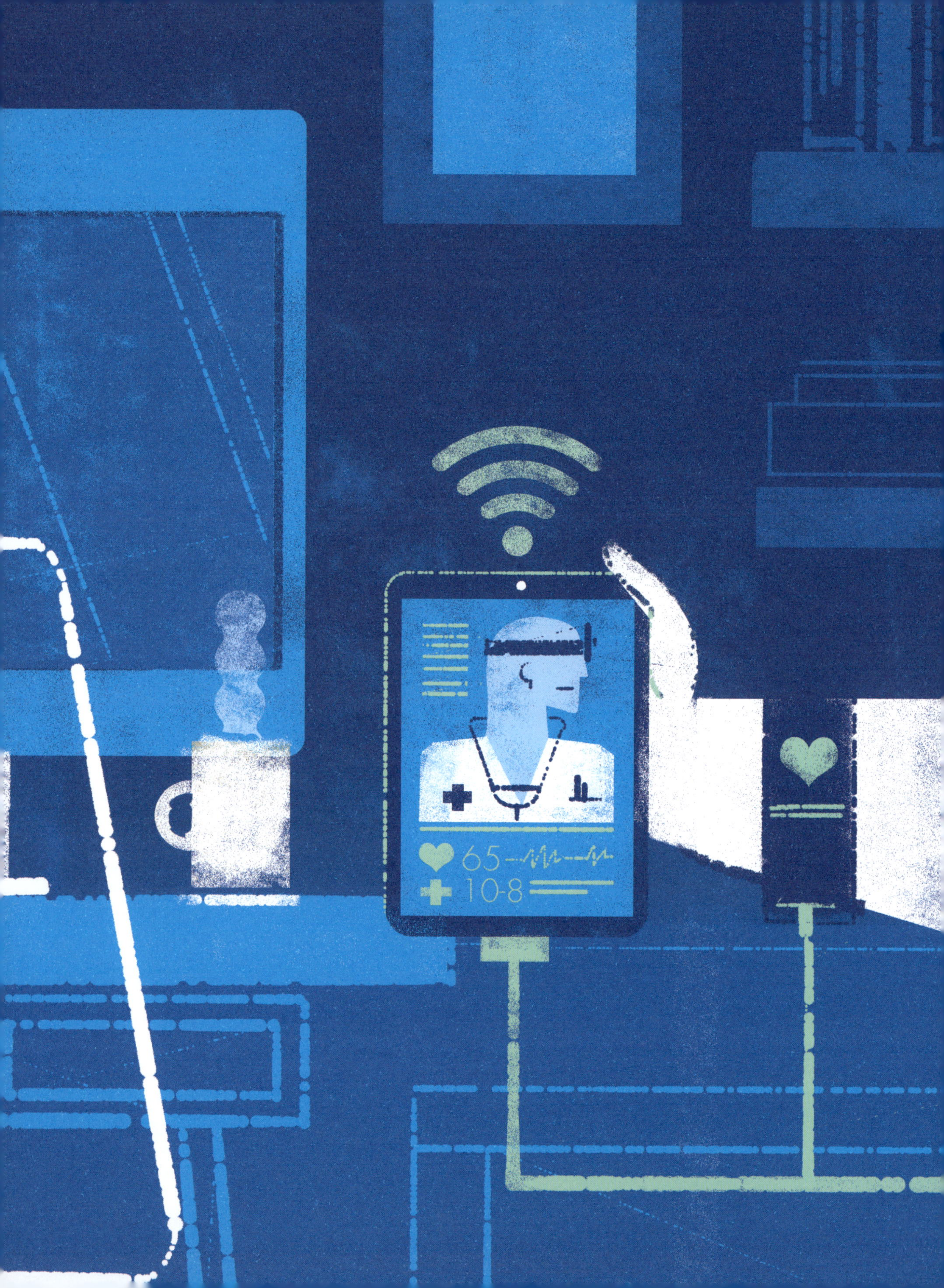

65
10-8

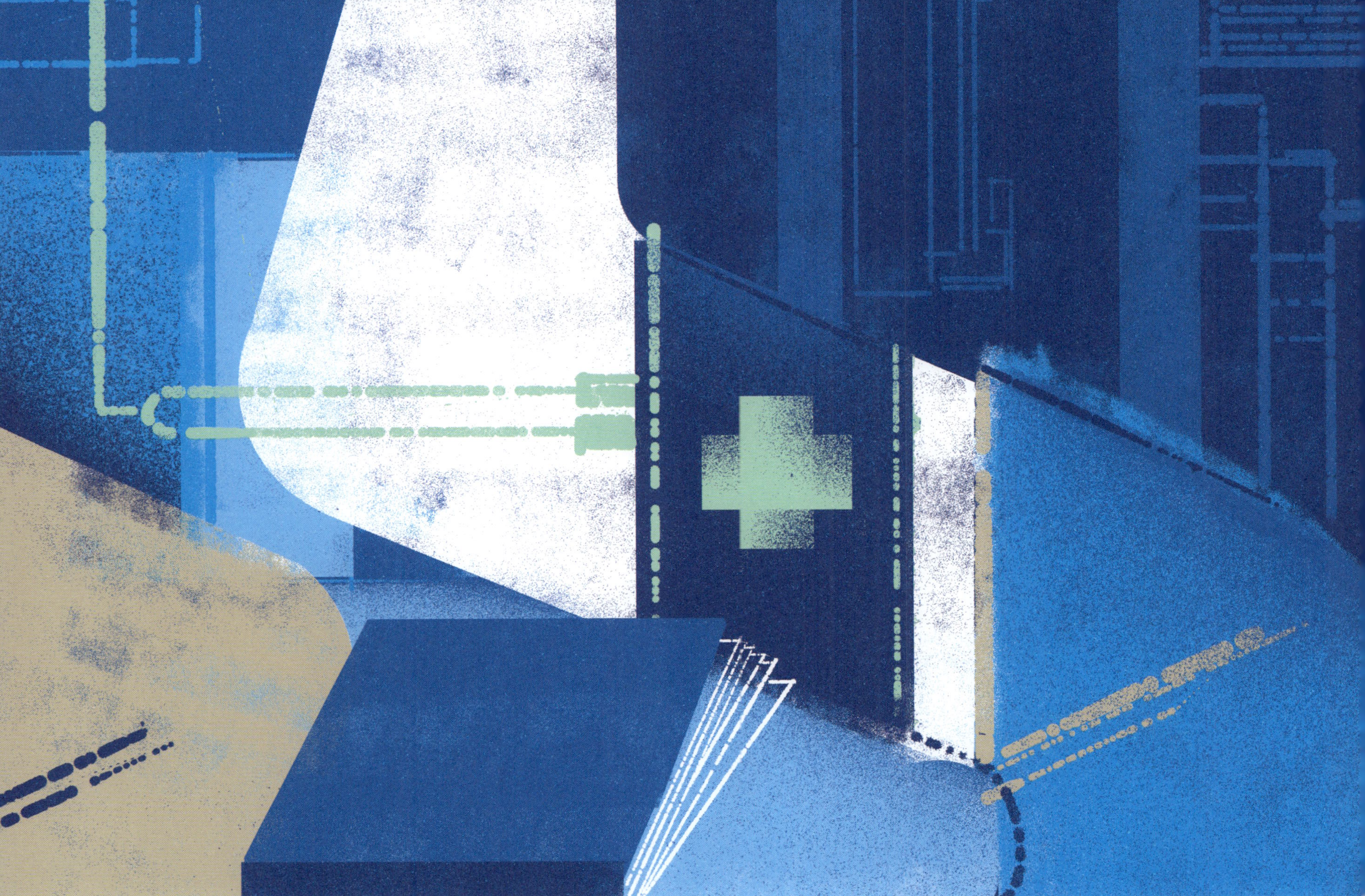

Lucien Engelen

futuremed2020.com/lucien-engelen

Illustration
Ignacio Molano

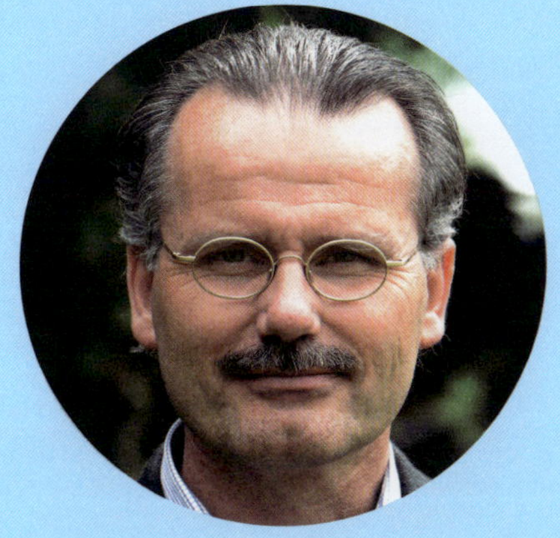

Lucien Engelen is the head of the Regional Acute Healthcare Network at Radboud University Nijmegen Medical Center in the Netherlands, as well as an advisor to the executive board on questions relating to changes in healthcare, enhancing patient participation, and working toward participatory healthcare. He is the founding director of the Radboud REshape & Innovation Center, an institution that creates, develops, and implements healthcare innovations. He is also the founder and curator of TEDxMaastricht "The Future of Health," an independently organized TEDTalks event, and the subsequent TEDxMaastricht and TEDxRadboudU. He is currently on the faculty at Singularity University / FutureMed in Silicon Valley, California.

The Way of the Dodo

"The Internet has revolutionized our lives!" is an often heard exclamation. The Internet has added a lot to our lives indeed, and has also made a few things disappear. Think of all the things that became obsolete due to the Internet, such as letter writing, privacy, and all kinds of brokers and middlemen.

These developments make me think about the dodo, the notorious one-meter-tall, pigeon-like, flightless bird, last spotted by a Dutch mariner in 1662 near Mauritius. Of all the species that became extinct, the dodo has become a kind of metaphor for extinction. To "go the way of the dodo" means that something is destined to go out of existence. In this era of Internet and technology, this goes not only for flora and fauna, but also for stuff we use or things we do. Many futurists have already predicted that things like post offices, taxi drivers, manual labor, and even death itself will go the way of the dodo.

So what about healthcare? What will vanish in the field of medicine? Will technology and the Internet take over like they did in the music and travel industries? Will nurses be replaced by robots? Will the doctor be replaced by a smartphone app? Will we no longer go to a hospital or to the doctor's office? A shift is surely occurring, and some things in healthcare have already began their march on the way of the dodo. But, in my opinion, we will still need medical professionals. Real people with real compassion giving great care.

The challenges that healthcare faces are huge; that is no breaking news. Financial mismatches, doubling of healthcare demand, and the shortage of skilled personnel (the Netherlands will lack 400,000 professionals by 2040) will drive healthcare systems to *reinvent themselves*. Moreover, there are two developments awaiting *at the gate* to disrupt many of the current care models: the assertive patient is here to stay, and new technologies are developing at exponential rates. The impact of new communication paradigms, such as social media and transparency of performance, is just as underrated as is the role of e-health overrated. Medical professionals need to think big, act small, dare to fail, stop talking… and start acting NOW.

If medical professionals still want to be a relevant cog in the healthcare system in, let's say the next five years, they should be concentrating on these three topics, for themselves, for their institutions, and most of all for their patients:

1. Engaging patients
2. Exponentially growing technology, including the Internet
3. Social media

I will now address a selection of future healthcare dodos. With the power of the three topics above, the Radboud REshape & Innovation Center has initiated a range of innovations. Among these are (in random order):

- HereIsMyData™—A service that consists of a Personal Health Record, a community aspect, and an eHealth connector.

- AED4US—As of 2009 we are crowdsourcing the locations of automatic electronic defibrillators (AEDs) in the Netherlands. The program currently has the largest database in the world, with over 18,500 units and nearly 300,000 downloads, and benefits from the assistance of the public.

- FaceTalk—A videoconference system we've developed that allows health-care professionals to consult with patients and colleagues in an easy and secure way without additional hardware other than regular computers or tablet PCs.

- AYA4—An online community for young adult cancer patients (18–35 years of age) to share, in a secure fashion, intimate details about their life with cancer, about challenges such as relationship, work, finances, etc. Enrollment currently has a national reach.

- TEDxMaastricht, TEDxNijmegen—Every year we hold a high-level con-ference—twice in Maastricht (2011 and 2012) and twice in Nijmegen (2012 and 2013)—to share ideas, dreams, and examples; that is, over the Internet. For 2014 we are organizing 360andabove,[1] a conference that will run virtually on the Internet, connecting patient-centered innovations

1.   http://www.linkedin.com/today/post/article/ 20130908153807-19886490-the-24-hours-of-health?

in a new format. For 24 hours in a row, starting in Nijmegen, traveling with the daylight one time zone at a time. From Nijmegen to London, the East Coast and Midwest U.S., California, Canada, Australia, Japan, India, Hungary, France, and back to Nijmegen for the finale.

With these projects we try to outsmart the dodo; otherwise we will become living (or extinct) examples in the near future for others that do indeed innovate in a way that creates *futureproof* health (care).

Location

One of the major shifts in healthcare is that location is becoming less important. Due to new (mobile) technology and cheaper testing methods, things are already changing. And yet, rising healthcare costs are forcing all stakeholders to become much more efficient with regards to processes, staff, and overhead. The number of mergers and takeovers is increasing. Whether or not that is the way to go is still to be seen. We at the Radboud University Nijmegen Medical Center think there are other ways to become more efficient. For example, by creating a network based on collaboration instead. With different points of care nearby, and with the help of new technology, a great of number of things can be achieved. We will be able to monitor our patients at locations just around the corner, or even in their own homes. More specialist procedures will be performed farther away. Over the past decades we have tended to take healthcare away from the people themselves. This started with bringing people into hospitals rather than caring for them in their homes. Healthcare has become centralized in institutions rather than in networks, as it was in the old days. But new technology is enabling us to reverse that while keeping the same high standards. So, this means that trusted, well-known hospitals with doctors we are now so familiar with will increasingly disappear. On the other hand, we will bring health(care) back into people's homes.

Duration of the Stay

A decade ago, some procedures required up to 15 days of hospitaliza-tion. Now, they take 3 days. This is due to new technologies, innovations in medicines, logistics, and protocols, and new insights on rehabilitation. A median stay in U.S. hospitals at present is about 5 days. Long stays for regular procedures will become unnecessary, and prohibitively expensive. Monitoring at home, enabled by the Internet, is increasingly assuming an important position in this field.

Individual, Unorganized Healthcare Professionals

Healthcare is becoming even more complex than it already was. This is caused by increasing legislation and severe budget cuts.

There are many constraints on medical education and the overload of information that has to be digested makes it hard to keep up. In addition, the administrative burden is increasingly distracting medical personal from delivering actual healthcare. The part-time ratio for healthcare workers is increasing. The number of female professionals entering healthcare adds to this tendency (Graham 2012). More and more tasks are delegated from doc-tors to nurse practitioners and physicians' assistants; next up is *delegating* to the patients and their network. In order to maintain quality standards and to be able to keep collaborating on complex issues, working in groups or setting up strategic partnerships could benefit healthcare processes.

I believe that within one or two decades, individual, unorganized health-care professionals will become a minority.

Two-Party Research in a Three-Party World

Up until now, health research has mainly been done by the pharmaceutical industry and researchers. Patients were merely a passive object. I often say, "Doing (as in designing) medical research without the cooperation of patients is like racing a car backwards... blindfolded." Now, we have the tools at hand to involve patients. New communication techniques have democratized the media, and we have even seen regimes forced from power through revolutions—and the role of the Internet was crucial. The same tools will also be employed to organize patients around research on matters they care deeply about, namely their own health or the health of a family member. Research with patients in co-control will transform traditional research and create a pathway for (applied) research through new systems that will change the situation forever. It will just be a matter of time before these kinds of tools will become available to patients. We hope to contribute to this goal with MedCrowdFund™, a social platform (like a medical Kickstarter) where patients can design and find funding for innovation and research. Let's see how long it takes for a two-party health research system to be transformed into a three-party one. Patients will swap roles: they will go from being the object, to being the subject, to acting as a partner in research. A very good example is my friend Jack Andraka, born in 1997(!). After countless rejections by traditional institutions, and with a lot of perseverance, Jack developed a pancreatic cancer test "just by using Google and Wikipedia." It is designed as an early detection test to determine whether or not a patient has early-stage pancreatic cancer. The test is over 90 percent accurate, and is 168 times faster, 26,000 times less expensive (costing around $0.03), and over 400 times more sensitive than the current diagnostic tests, and takes only five minutes to perform. He says that the test is also effective for detecting ovarian and lung cancer, due to the same biomarker they all have in common. Truly inspiring! So medical professionals must look carefully at these new initiatives; they need to judge them not on *what* they are doing, but on *why* and *how*. They need to reach out, explore, and challenge diseases together!

Being a Good Doctor Won't Be Good Enough Anymore

We have gotten used to submitting and finding customer opinions on almost every kind of service online. Reviews and ratings of tourist hotspots, travel agencies, restaurants, financial products, and so on are now in the public sphere. And of course, healthcare professionals are part of this trend.

The Way of the Dodo

A treatment has become an experience, and the customer's satisfaction with it in general might become equally important as the quality of the medicine practiced.

According to Pew Research, 50 percent of smartphone users in the U.S. use their device to look up health information; a recent study for the Netherlands showed that this figure was 60 percent. This means that they will probably have researched their physician online while they were sitting in the waiting room, and that they will review him or her as soon as they have left the building. "Hospital-ity" has regained its vital meaning.

Not only text-based web content, but also informational videos will become increasingly important. Healthcare could benefit from adopting the use of video as well. It offers great opportunities for providers to present themselves and their services.

A caveat! The quality of strictly medical care will no longer be the only indicator people compare in order to choose healthcare providers.

The Patient Is Not in the Middle

Many healthcare providers are pivoting their service by putting the patient in the middle, in their ambition to change healthcare into a more open, co-creative environment. Putting patients in the center, however, seems to me to be one of the most paternalistic approaches a patient might have to deal with. Patients are not objects around which healthcare providers perform their duty. Patients should be(come) partners. They are equals in the team that collaborates to sustain or achieve their optimal health.

If patients want to take control of their health but are unable to, we must teach them. If they want to but can not because there is no system or technology, we must build it for and with them.

And if they do not want to, we must deliver healthcare in the traditional way.

In the center, however, is something else: it is an ear. A very important organ (that's why we have two, right?)—it is the sense of hearing that many healthcare systems have stopped using. As healthcare professionals know what's best for patients—at least that's what they think—they make choices *on behalf of* instead of *with* the patient and their families.

We often grab at *innovation* as the big solution for everything. We start innovating without having looked closely at existing procedures and at how optimizing these existing systems could bring great benefit and improvement. That (at least in my opinion) starts with really listening to what is truly needed. Healthcare providers need to stop assuming, they need quit thinking they "know" what patients need; or from a industry perspective, what healthcare professionals need. Listening is asking. I highly recommend appointing a CLO into every healthcare team; I created and appointed this position back in 2009: a Chief Listening Officer. Employed both online and offline, every time we intend to change our healthcare delivery the CLO will interview patients, family members, and informal caregivers: "How can we help you?" Not being a healthcare professional like a doctor or nurse, it appeared that patients were more open to the CLO, and more candid than with the focus groups, surveys, etc. we have used until now. Every project we kick off begins with the CLO listening to what the target groups really want. In almost every project that we have run the original plan our colleagues came up with changed, and through that process of adaptation benefitted significantly.

Partnerships

One should not underestimate the power of collaboration. At our medical center, we love to team up with other parties, nationally as well as internationally. It is imperative that healthcare providers do not suffer from the not-invented-here syndrome. They need to open up, and unlock the gates surrounding their domains. It is hard to find likeminded collaborators, but they are out there! In the Netherlands we mostly come across the usual suspects, and thus we broadened our horizons and contacted numerous international innovators. In other countries one finds different cultures and mentalities. We are impressed by the pace we are able to maintain in our international teams, and a bit ashamed that it is quite clearly impossible to develop and implement quickly in our own country. The importance of the Internet in this respect is also crucial. Connections are being made through social media, based on slideshows we have put online, with people often reflecting on photos we have published in social media of the things we are doing. Entrepreneurship, leadership, decisive action, and speed are important assets for implementing innovations successfully. Without them, one cannot evolve. And the fate of the dodo is one step closer.

Rules and Regulations

The thing with exponential developments is that they take little time to develop, but more time for laws and ethics to catch up. How should the regulatory agencies prepare for an ever-changing world in which technology is growing exponentially and changing the arena? In the *old* days, it took big companies years of innovation before they could launch a new medical device. Nowadays, with the time to market dramatically shorter, new devices are released on a daily basis. Does this actually change the way regulatory agencies should act? In the Netherlands, regulatory requirements for digital healthcare innovations are hot at the moment; it is at the center of attention of the Dutch Health Care Inspectorate. And that's a good thing. The certification of medical applications will contribute to a rise in quality. I do not think, however, that this is enough. I strongly believe that the appliance of open technical standards, such as for information exchange and the reuse of existing and proven applications, should be made mandatory by policy makers. The software industry has powerful interests. They operate defensively and are far from eager to open up their systems and thereby implicitly grant access to competition.

Furthermore, the financial system must be improved. If financial compensation does not end up in the tills of the developers and producers of (digital) healthcare innovations, the dodo will soon be joined by many talented peers.

e-Go Systems

At the moment, huge amounts of data are being generated by information systems, medical records, tracking devices, lab results, image resources, etc. What we need is the ability to mine these different types of data and be able to understand their meaning, the relation between them, and how they interact. We need a central repository where anyone (not only patients, but any citizen) can access their own data in a comprehensive way—not only health data, but also other kinds, such as financial data. The patient (or citizen) must be able to decide with whom to share it. A patient could share data with his physician or siblings, so that they may both use it on relevant occasions. The reality is that almost all healthcare information systems are focused on the healthcare professional. It is not an open system, but closed, with data stored in hidden silos. It is usually very unattractive and the user experience is poor. I call these *e-Go systems*. They are egoistic, hierarchical systems that do match up with contemporary demand, and mostly do not connect to other systems in the healthcare chain outside of their own. They somehow still manage to profit from business models that have already failed in other markets. These systems should have gone the way of the dodo a long time ago, but still manage to survive, as yet.

We have to work on open, transparent, user-friendly, and cooperative systems based on open technology standards that actively promote interoperability. We have to move on from e-Go systems to e-Co systems. Now is the time for an e-Co system that sees and treats the patient as the linchpin: a system that is the constant factor in any health-related action and intervention; a transparent system that services patients and their networks independently. Putting people in charge of their own personal health data, of course, also creates co-responsibility. I believe—and have also witnessed it—that a lot of people are able to and want to be in that position. Giving patients control over their own data is an important step in making patients partners.

Here Is Your Data!

This is exactly the reason why we at the Radboud REshape & Innovation Center decided to start a *noncommercial* service to boost the process of creating these e-Co systems, setting them up, validating them through scientific research, and making them widely available. Just like our other tools—FaceTalk™,[2] MedCrowdFund™ (e-Patient Dave 2012),[3] our AYA4-community (Tucker 2012), and AED4US (Root 2012)—we sometimes set up services or products ourselves if we think the market acts too slow or at too high a price. We recently announced an e-Co system HereIsMyData™.[4]

HereIsMyData™ consists of:

1. a Personal Health Record;
2. a community system that gives patients, caregivers, and families the opportunity to talk about a specific disease;
3. and connectivity tools for many kinds of personal health devices like Withings,[5] Fitbit,[6] Jawbone-Up,[7] Scout,[8] etc., and great data visualization tools. Of course, we'll connect our FaceTalk™ and MedCrowdFund™ to it.

So it is not a platform; it is more like a service combining the best of three worlds. This service will give people the power to combine a lot of their personal health (measurement) data in one place. If this data is needed for one's health(care), it also can be used in one's own Personal Health Record (PHR). How it differs from a great many platforms and systems is that with HereIsMyData™ people decide for themselves who is granted access and subscription to their data. In addition, it is possible for a healthcare professional to subscribe to connected services of patients, such as scales and other barometers of clinical measurements; and the other way around, patients can subscribe to data from the hospital, such as blood values or clinical notes (from their electronic medical record [EMR]). In addition, they can grant healthcare professionals like their general practitioner but also family caretakers access to their personal data, for instance their weight history. At the moment, this project is our main spearhead and participation is open to all.

2. http://en.facetalk.nl/
3. http://www.medcrowdfund.org/?_locale=en
4. http://www.hereismydata.com/
5. http://www.withings.com/
6. http://www.fitbit.com/
7. https://jawbone.com/up
8. http://www.scanadu.com/scout/

Reshaping Radboud

In almost all of my keynote presentations I emphasize "stop talking, start doing." And by living up to this mantra we have been able to realize many innovative projects. Inevitably, not all of them were successful, but we always ran a number of projects simultaneously. So quite a few managed to survive evolution (so far). We incubated these projects in our Radboud REshape & Innovation Center, and when they reached adulthood, we let them go—back home, to the Radboud University Nijmegen Medical Center, where they could be implemented and incorporated into regular process flows. Of course we stay in touch, to perform maintenance and to evaluate. And it is very nice to see how these projects have found their way into the daily routine of nurses, physicians, managers, and board members. We collect evidence by researching the effectiveness scientifically and we incorporate our vision, experience, and innovations into the curriculum. So now our innovation flywheel is in perpetual motion. For instance, we discovered that at this moment (Summer 2013) the viewing angle of Google Glass prevents surgeons from using it optimally. We provide the Google Glass team with valuable feedback and at the same time brace ourselves for impact. Because we now receive so many ideas from inspired medical professionals on how to improve their work by using Google Glass. This gives us the opportunity to keep innovating. Because we *will* beat the dodo!

References

e-Patient Dave,
"'The Patient as Partner,'
    in Medical Research at
    Radboud University."
    e.Patients.net, December
    29, 2012. http://e-patients.
    net/archives/2012/12/
    the-patient-as-partner-
    in-medical-research-at-
    radboud-university.html

Graham, Ruth.
"44% Of Female Doctors
    Work Part-Time. Are
    They Betraying Their
    Profession?" The Grindstone,
    March 27, 2012. http://
    www.thegrindstone.
    com/2012/03/27/
    career-management/
    almost-half-of-all-female-
    doctors-work-part-time-
    are-they-betraying-their-
    profession-535/

Root, Anton.
"Crowdmapping Life-
    Saving Apparatuses: A
    Discussion with AED4.US
    Founder Lucien Engelen."
    Crowdsourcing.org,
    August 7, 2012. http://www.
    crowdsourcing.org/editorial/
    crowdmapping-life-saving-
    apparatuses-a-discussion-
    with-aed4us-founder-lucien-
    engelen/17662

Tucker, Ian,
"Lucien Engelen: How Social
    Networks Can Solve the
    Healthcare Crisis." *Guardian*,
    March 4. 2012. http://
    www.theguardian.com/
    technology/2012/mar/04/
    bright-idea-engelen-
    healthcare-network

How the Internet Has Changed Everyday Life

Zaryn Dentzel

CEO, Tuenti

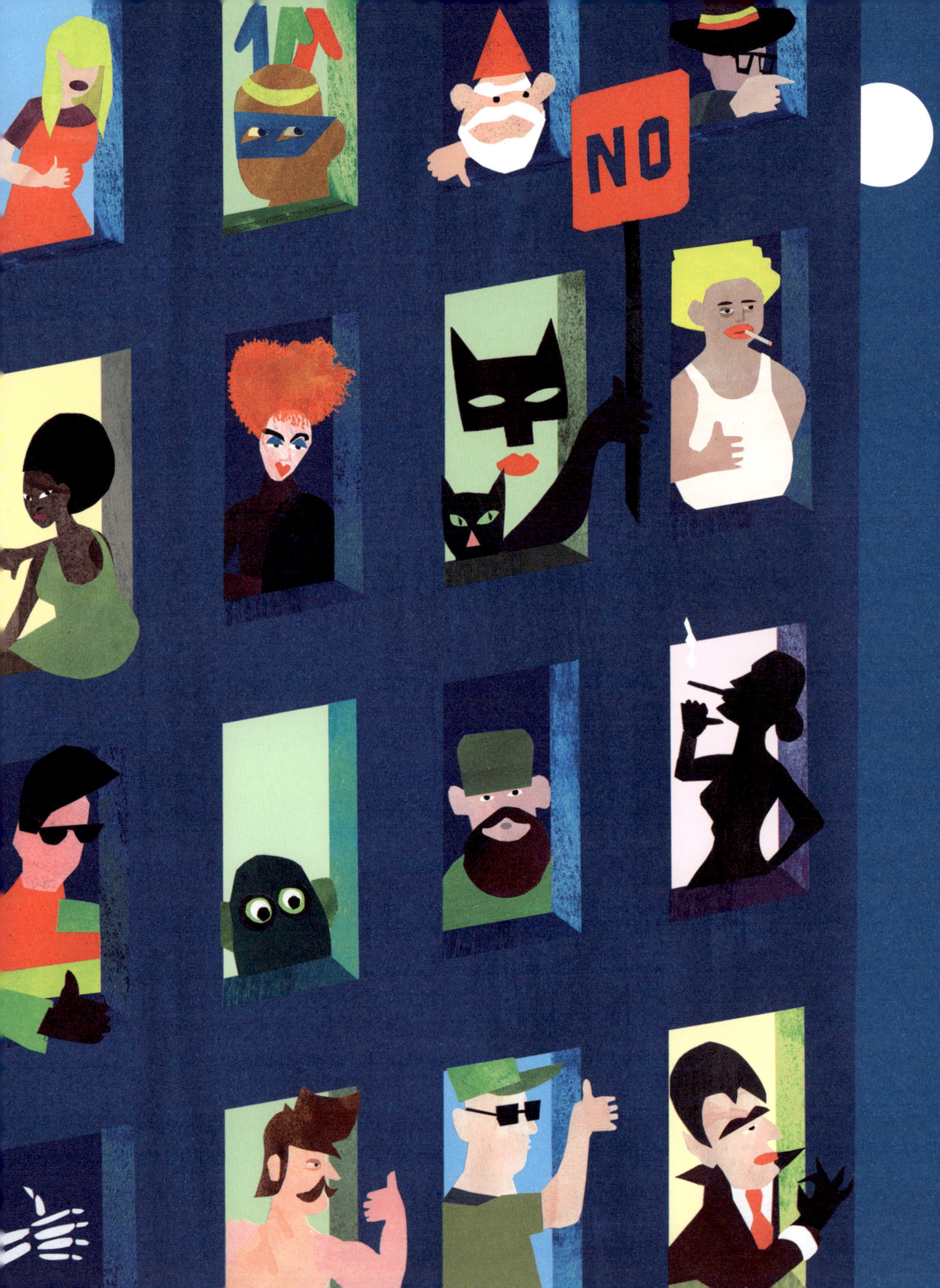

NO

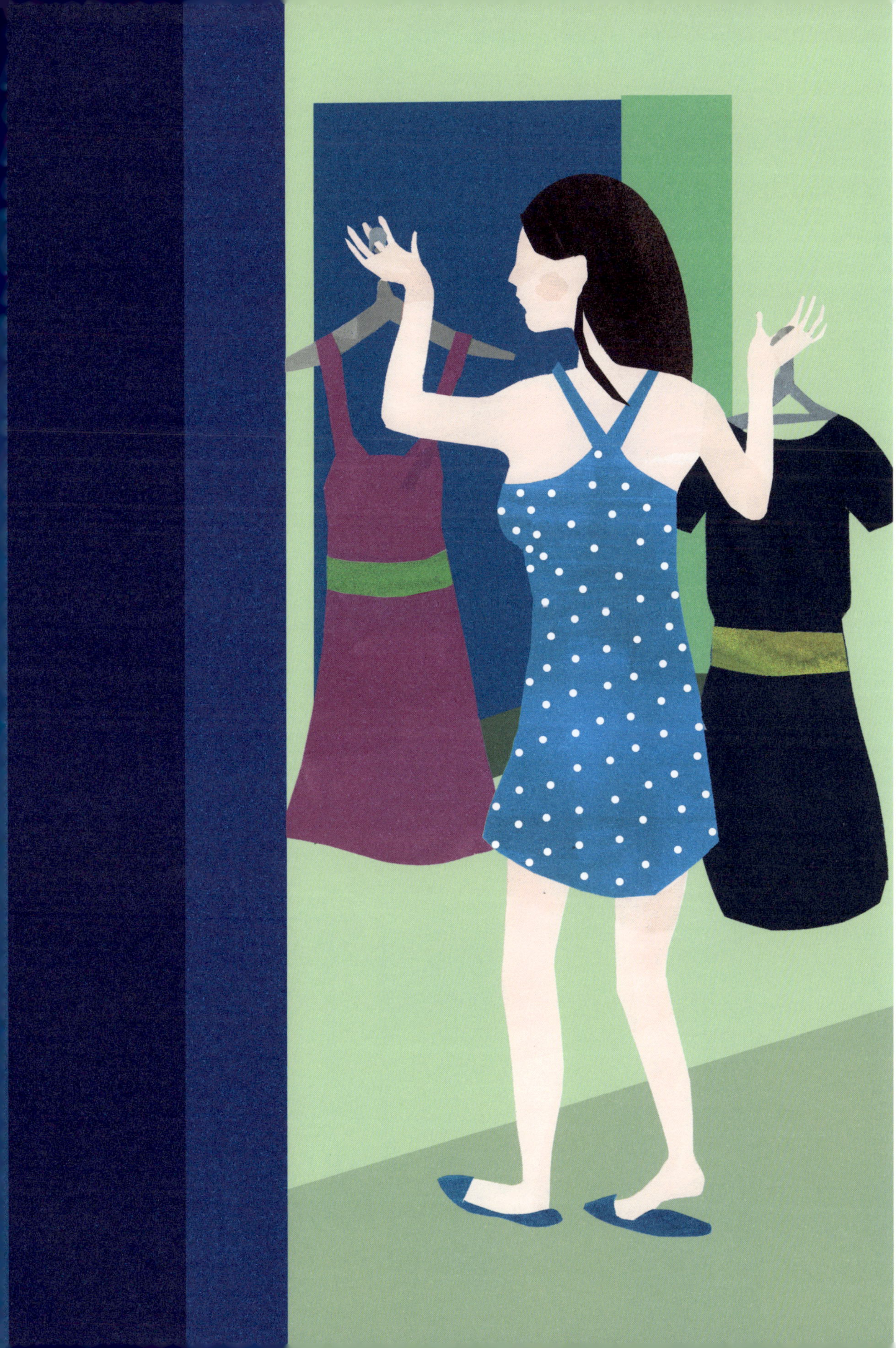

236/237
Zaryn Dentzel
How the Internet Has Changed Everyday Life
Society, Community, Individuals

Zaryn Dentzel

es.wikipedia.org/wiki/Zaryn_Dentzel

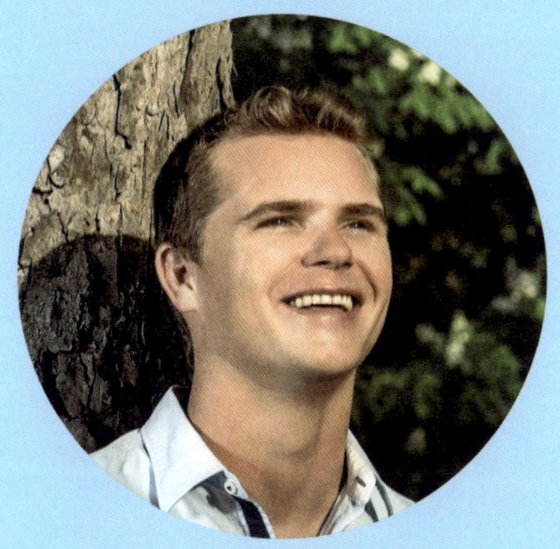

Zaryn Dentzel is the founder and CEO of Tuenti, a Spanish tech company centered on mobile communications whose multi-platform integrates the best of instant messaging and the most private and secure social network. Also a member of the cabinet of advisors to Crown Prince Felipe for the Principe de Girona Foundation, Dentzel is involved in promoting education and entrepreneurship among young people in Spain. He studied at UC Santa Barbara and Occidental College, graduating with a degree in Spanish Literature, and Diplomacy and World Affairs.

Sites and services that have changed my life
tuenti.com
techcrunch.com
spotify.com
Kinect Training

How the Internet Has Changed Everyday Life

What Happened?

The Internet has turned our existence upside down. It has revolutionized communications, to the extent that it is now our preferred medium of everyday communication. In almost everything we do, we use the Internet. Ordering a pizza, buying a television, sharing a moment with a friend, sending a picture over instant messaging. Before the Internet, if you wanted to keep up with the news, you had to walk down to the newsstand when it opened in the morning and buy a local edition reporting what had happened the previous day. But today a click or two is enough to read your local paper and any news source from anywhere in the world, updated up to the minute.

The Internet itself has been transformed. In its early days—which from a historical perspective are still relatively recent—it was a static network designed to shuttle a small freight of bytes or a short message between two terminals; it was a repository of information where content was published and maintained only by expert coders. Today, however, immense quantities of information are uploaded and downloaded over this electronic leviathan, and the content is very much our own, for now we are all commentators, publishers, and creators.

In the 1980s and 1990s, the Internet widened in scope to encompass the IT capabilities of universities and research centers, and, later on, public entities, institutions, and private enterprises from around the world. The Internet underwent immense growth; it was no longer a state-controlled project, but the largest computer network in the world, comprising over 50,000 sub-networks, 4 million systems, and 70 million users.

The emergence of *web 2.0* in the first decade of the twenty-first century was itself a revolution in the short history of the Internet, fostering the rise of social media and other interactive, crowd-based communication tools.

The Internet was no longer concerned with information exchange alone: it was a sophisticated multidisciplinary tool enabling individuals to create content, communicate with one another, and even escape reality. Today, we can send data from one end of the world to the other in a matter of seconds, make online presentations, live in parallel "game worlds," and use pictures, video, sound, and text to share our real lives, our genuine identity. Personal stories go public; local issues become global.

The rise of the Internet has sparked a debate about how online communication affects social relationships. The Internet frees us from geographic fetters and brings us together in topic-based communities that are not tied down to any specific place. Ours is a networked, globalized society connected by new technologies. The Internet is the tool we use to interact with one another, and accordingly poses new challenges to privacy and security.

Information technologies have wrought fundamental change throughout society, driving it forward from the industrial age to the networked era. In our world, global information networks are vital infrastructure—but in what ways has this changed human relations? The Internet has changed business, education, government, healthcare, and even the ways in which we interact with our loved ones—it has become one of the key drivers of social evolution.

The changes in social communication are of particular significance. Although analogue tools still have their place in some sectors, new technologies are continuing to gain ground every day, transforming our communication practices and possibilities—particularly among younger people. The Internet has removed all communication barriers. Online, the conventional constraints of space and time disappear and there is a dizzyingly wide range of communicative possibilities. The impact of social media applications has triggered discussion of the "new communication democracy."

The development of the Internet today is being shaped predominantly by instant, mobile communications. The mobile Internet is a fresh revolution. Comprehensive Internet connectivity via smartphones and tablets is leading to an increasingly mobile reality: we are not tied to any single specific device, and everything is in the cloud.

People no longer spend hours gazing at a computer screen after work or class; instead, they use their mobile devices to stay online everywhere, all the time.

Anyone failing to keep abreast of this radical change is losing out on an opportunity.

Communication Opportunities Created by the Internet

The Internet has become embedded in every aspect of our day-to-day lives, changing the way we interact with others. This insight struck me when I started out in the world of social media. I created my first social network in 2005, when I was finishing college in the United States—it had a political theme. I could already see that social media were on the verge of changing our way of communicating, helping us to share information by opening up a new channel that cuts across conventional ones.

That first attempt did not work out, but I learned from the experience. I get the feeling that in many countries failure is punished too harshly—but the fact is, the only surefire way of avoiding failure is to do nothing at all. I firmly believe that mistakes help you improve; getting it wrong teaches you how to get it right. Creativity, hard work, and a positive attitude will let you achieve any goal.

In 2006, after I moved to Spain, I created Tuenti. Tuenti (which, contrary to widespread belief, has nothing to do with the number 20; it is short for "tu entidad," the Spanish for "your entity") is a social communication platform for genuine friends. From the outset, the idea was to keep it simple, relevant, and private. That's the key to its success.

I think the real value of social media is that you can stay in touch from moment to moment with the people who really matter to you. Social media let you share experiences and information; they get people and ideas in touch instantly, without frontiers. Camaraderie, friendship, and solidarity—social phenomena that have been around for as long as humanity itself—have been freed from the conventional restrictions of space and time and can now thrive in a rich variety of ways.

Out of all the plethora of communication opportunities that the Internet has opened up, I would highlight the emergence of social media and the way they have intricately melded into our daily lives. Social media have changed our personal space, altering the way we interact with our loved ones, our friends, and our sexual partners; they have forced us to rethink even basic daily processes like studying and shopping; they have affected the economy by nurturing the business startup culture and electronic commerce; they have even given us new ways to form broad-based political movements.

The Internet and Education

The Internet has clearly impacted all levels of education by providing unbounded possibilities for learning. I believe the future of education is a networked future. People can use the Internet to create and share knowledge and develop new ways of teaching and learning that captivate and stimulate students' imagination at any time, anywhere, using any device. By connecting and empowering students and educators, we can speed up economic growth and enhance the well-being of society throughout the world. We should work together, over a network, to build the global learning society.

The network of networks is an inexhaustible source of information. What's more, the Internet has enabled users to move away from their former passive role as mere recipients of messages conveyed by conventional media to an active role, choosing what information to receive, how, and when. The information recipient even decides whether or not they want to stay informed.

We have moved on from scattergun mass communication to a pattern where the user proactively selects the information they need.

Students can work interactively with one another, unrestricted by physical or time constraints. Today, you can use the Internet to access libraries, encyclopedias, art galleries, news archives, and other information sources from anywhere in the world: I believe this is a key advantage in the education field. The web is a formidable resource for enhancing the process of building knowledge.

I also believe the Internet is a wonderful tool for learning and practicing other languages—this continues to be a critical issue in many countries, including Spain, and, in a globalized world, calls for special efforts to improve.

The Internet, in addition to its communicative purposes, has become a vital tool for exchanging knowledge and education; it is not just an information source, or a locus where results can be published, it is also a channel for cooperating with other people and groups who are working on related research topics.

The Internet and Privacy and Security

Another key issue surrounding Internet use is privacy. Internet users are becoming more sensitive to the insight that privacy is a must-have in our lives.

Privacy has risen near the top of the agenda in step with an increasing awareness of the implications of using social media. Much of the time, people started to use social media with no real idea of the dangers, and have wised up only through trial and error—sheer accident, snafus, and mistakes. Lately, inappropriate use of social media seems to hit the headlines every day. Celebrities posting inappropriate comments to their profiles, private pictures and tapes leaked to the Internet at large, companies displaying arrogance toward users, and even criminal activities involving private-data trafficking or social media exploitation.

All this shows that—contrary to what many people seem to have assumed—online security and privacy are critical, and, I believe, will become even more important going forward. And, although every user needs privacy, the issue is particularly sensitive for minors—despite attempts to raise their awareness, children still behave recklessly online.

I have always been highly concerned about privacy. On Tuenti, the default privacy setting on every user account is the highest available level of data protection. Only people the user has accepted as a "friend" can access their personal details, see their telephone number, or download their pictures.

This means that, by default, user information is not accessible to third parties. In addition, users are supported by procedures for reporting abuse. Any user can report a profile or photograph that is abusive, inappropriate, or violates the terms of use: action is taken immediately. Security and privacy queries are resolved within 24 hours.

We need to be aware that different Internet platforms provide widely different privacy experiences. Some of them are entirely open and public; no steps whatsoever are taken to protect personal information, and all profiles are indexable by Internet search engines.

On the other hand, I think the debate about whether social media use should be subject to an age requirement is somewhat pointless, given that most globally active platforms operate without age restrictions. The European regulatory framework is quite different from the United States and Asian codes. Companies based in Europe are bound by rigorous policies on privacy and underage use of social media. This can become a competitive drawback when the ground rules do not apply equally to all players—our American and Japanese competitors, for instance, are not required to place any kind of age constraint on access.

Outside the scope of what the industry or regulators can do, it is vital that users themselves look after the privacy of their data. I believe the information is the user's property, so the user is the only party entitled to control the collection, use, and disclosure of any information about him or herself. Some social networks seem to have forgotten this fact—they sell data, make it impossible to delete an account, or make it complex and difficult to manage one's privacy settings. Everything should be a lot simpler and more transparent.

Social networks should continue to devote intense efforts to developing self-regulation mechanisms and guidelines for this new environment of online coexistence to ensure that user information is safe: the Internet should be a space for freedom, but also for trust. The main way of ensuring that social media are used appropriately is awareness. But awareness and user education will be of little use unless it becomes an absolute requirement that the privacy of the individual is treated as a universal value.

The Internet and Culture

As in the sphere of education, the development of information and communication technologies and the wide-ranging effects of globalization are changing what we are, and the meaning of cultural identity. Ours is a complex world in which cultural flows across borders are always on the rise. The concepts of space, time, and distance are losing their conventional meanings. Cultural globalization is here, and a global movement of cultural processes and initiatives is underway.

Again, in the cultural arena, vast fields of opportunity open up thanks to online tools. The possibilities are multiplied for disseminating a proposal, an item of knowledge, or a work of art. Against those doomsayers who warn that the Internet is harming culture, I am radically optimistic. The Internet is bringing culture closer to more people, making it more easily and quickly accessible; it is also nurturing the rise of new forms of expression for art and the spread of knowledge. Some would say, in fact, that the Internet is not just a technology, but a cultural artifact in its own right.

In addition to its impact on culture itself, the Internet is enormously beneficial for innovation, which brings progress in all fields of endeavor—the creation of new goods, services, and ideas, the advance of knowledge and society, and increasing well-being.

The Internet and Personal Relationships

The Internet has also changed the way we interact with our family, friends, and life partners. Now everyone is connected to everyone else in a simpler, more accessible, and more immediate way; we can conduct part of our personal relationships using our laptops, smart phones, and tablets.

The benefits of always-online immediate availability are highly significant. I would find a long-distance relationship with my life partner or my family unthinkable without the communication tools that the network of networks provides me with. I'm living in Madrid, but I can stay close to my brother in

California. For me, that is the key plus of the Internet: keeping in touch with the people who really matter to me.

As we have seen, the Internet revolution is not just technological; it also operates at a personal level, and throughout the structure of society. The Internet makes it possible for an unlimited number of people to communicate with one another freely and easily, in an unrestricted way.

Just a century ago, this was unimaginable. An increasing number of couples come together, stay together, or break up with the aid—or even as a consequence—of social communication tools. There are even apps and social networks out there that are purposely designed to help people get together for sex.

Of course, when compared to face-to-face communication, online communication is severely limited in the sense impressions it can convey (an estimated 60 to 70 percent of human communication takes place nonverbally), which can lead to misunderstandings and embarrassing situations—no doubt quite a few relationships have floundered as a result. I think the key is to be genuine, honest, and real at all times, using all the social media tools and their many advantages. Let's just remember that a liar and a cheat online is a liar and a cheat offline too.

The Internet and Social and Political Activism

Even before the emergence of social media, pioneering experiments took place in the political sphere—like *Essembly*, a project I was involved in. We started to create a politically themed platform to encourage debate and provide a home for social and political causes; but the social networks that have later nurtured activism in a new way were not as yet in existence.

Research has shown that young people who voice their political opinions on the Internet are more inclined to take part in public affairs. The better informed a citizen is, the more likely they will step into the polling booth, and the better they will express their political liberties. The Internet has proved to be a decisive communication tool in the latest election campaigns. It is thanks to the Internet that causes in the social, welfare, ideological, and political arenas have been spoken up for and have won the support of other citizens sharing those values—in many cases, with a real impact on government decision making.

The Internet and Consumer Trends

New technologies increase the speed of information transfer, and this opens up the possibility of "bespoke" shopping. The Internet offers an immense wealth of possibilities for buying content, news, and leisure products, and all sorts of advantages arise from e-commerce, which has become a major distribution channel for goods and services. You can book airline tickets, get a T-shirt from Australia, or buy food at an online grocery store. New applications support secure business transactions and create new commercial opportunities.

In this setting, it is the consumer who gains the upper hand, and the conventional rules and methods of distribution and marketing break down. Consumers' access to information multiplies, and their reviews of their experience with various products and services take center stage. Access to product comparisons and rankings, user reviews and comments, and recommendations from bloggers with large followings have shaped a new scenario for consumer behavior, retail trade, and the economy in general.

The Internet and the Economy

The Internet is one of the key factors driving today's economy. No one can afford to be left behind. Even in a tough macroeconomic framework, the Internet can foster growth, coupled with enhanced productivity and competitiveness.

The Internet provides opportunities for strengthening the economy: How should we tackle them? While Europe—and Spain specifically—are making efforts to make the best possible use of the Internet, there are areas in which their approach needs to improve. Europe faces a major challenge, and risks serious failure if it lets the United States run ahead on its own. The European Commission, in its "Startup Manifesto," suggests that the Old World be more entrepreneur-friendly—the proposal is backed by companies like Spotify and Tuenti. Europe lacks some of the necessary know-how. We need to improve in financial services and in data privacy, moving past the obsolete regulatory framework we now have and making a bid to achieve a well-connected continent with a single market for 4G mobile connections. We need to make it easier to hire talent outside each given country.

The use of e-commerce should be encouraged among small and medium-sized enterprises so that growth opportunities can be exploited more intensely. Following the global trend of the Internet, companies should internalize their online business. And much more emphasis should be placed on new technologies training in the academic and business spheres.

Modern life is global, and Spain is competing against every other country in the world. I do not believe in defeatism or victim culture. Optimism should not translate into callousness, but I sincerely believe that if you think creatively, if you find a different angle, if you innovate with a positive attitude and without fear of failure, then you can change things for the better. Spain needs to seize the moment to reinvent itself, grasping the opportunities offered up by the online world. We need to act, take decisions, avoid "paralysis through analysis." I sometimes feel we are too inclined to navel-gazing: Spain shuts itself off, fascinated with its own contradictions and local issues, and loses its sense of perspective. Spain should open up to the outside, use the crisis as an opportunity to do things differently, in a new way—creating value, underlining its strengths, aspiring to be something more.

In the United States, for instance, diving headfirst into a personal Internet-related startup is regarded as perfectly normal. I'm glad to see that this entrepreneurial spirit is beginning to take hold here as well. I believe in working hard, showing perseverance, keeping your goals in view, surrounding yourself with talent, and taking risks. No risk, no success. We live in an increasingly globalized world: of course you can have a Spain-based Internet startup, there are no frontiers.

We need to take risks and keep one step ahead of the future. It is precisely the most disruptive innovations that require radical changes in approach and product, which might not even find a market yet ready for them—these are the areas providing real opportunities to continue being relevant, to move forward and "earn" the future, creating value and maintaining leadership. It is the disruptive changes that enable a business, product, or service to revolutionize the market—and, particularly in the technology sector, such changes are a necessity.

The Future of Social Communications, Innovation, Mobile Technologies, and Total Connectivity in Our Lives

The future of social communications will be shaped by an *always-online* culture. *Always online* is already here and will set the trend going forward. Total connectivity, the Internet you can take with you wherever you go, is growing unstoppably. There is no turning back for global digitalization.

Innovation is the driving force of growth and progress, so we need to shake up entrenched processes, products, services, and industries, so that all of us together—including established businesses, reacting to their emerging competitors—can move forward together.

Innovation is shaping and will continue to shape the future of social communications. It is already a reality that Internet connections are in-creasingly mobile. A survey we conducted in early 2013 in partnership with Ipsos found that 94 percent of Tuenti users aged 16 to 35 owned cell phones, 84 percent of users connected to the Internet using their phones, and 47 percent had mobile data subscriptions for connecting to the Internet. A total of 74 percent of users reported connecting to the Internet from their phone on a daily basis, while 84 percent did so at least weekly. Only 13 percent did not use their phones to connect to the Internet, and that percentage is decreasing every day.

Mobile Internet use alters the pattern of device usage; the hitherto familiar ways of accessing the Internet are changing too. The smartphone activities taking up the most time (over three hours a day) include instant messaging (38%), social media use (35%), listening to music (24%), and web browsing (20%). The activities taking up the least time (under five minutes a day) are: SMS texting (51%), watching movies (43%), reading and writing e-mail (38%), and talking on the phone (32%). Things are still changing.

Smartphones are gaining ground in everyday life. Many of the purposes formerly served by other items now involve using our smartphones. Some 75 percent of young people reported having replaced their MP3 player with their phone, 74 percent use their phone as an alarm clock, 70 percent use it as their camera, and 67 percent use it as their watch.

We have been observing these shifts for a while, which is why we decided to reinvent ourselves by placing smartphones at the heart of our strategy. I want to use this example as a showcase of what is happening in the world of social communication and the Internet in general: mobile connectivity is bringing about a new revolution. Tuenti is no longer just a social network, and social media as a whole are becoming more than just websites. The new Tuenti provides native mobile apps for Android, iPhone, Blackberry, Windows Phone, as well as the Firefox OS app and the mobile version of the website, m.tuenti.com. Tuenti is now a cross-platform service that lets users connect with their friends and contacts from wherever they may be, using their device of choice. A user with a laptop can IM in real time with a user with a smartphone, and switch from one device to another without losing the thread of the conversation. The conversations are in the cloud, so data and contacts are preserved independently of the devices being used. This means the experience has to be made uniform across platforms, which sometimes involves paring down functionalities, given the processing and screen size limitations of mobile devices. Facebook, Twitter, Instagram, LinkedIn, and so on are all evolving to become increasingly cross-platform experiences. But Tuenti is the first social network that has also developed its own Mobile Virtual Network Operator (MVNO)—the company is an Internet service provider over the mobile network. Tuenti is an MVNO with a social media angle, and this may be the future path of telecommunications.

Social media are evolving to become something more, and innovation must be their hallmark if they are to continue being relevant. Tuenti now embraces both social communications and telecom services provision, offering value added by letting you use the mobile app free of charge and without using up your data traffic allowance, even if you have no credit on your prepaid card—this is wholly revolutionary in the telecom sector. The convergence of social media with more traditional sectors is already bringing about a new context for innovation, a new arena for the development and growth of the Internet.

Just about everything in the world of the Internet still lies ahead of us, and mobile communications as we know them must be reinvented by making them more digital. The future will be shaped by innovation converging with the impact of mobility. This applies not just to social media but to the Internet in general, particularly in the social communications field. I feel that many people do not understand what we are doing and have no idea of the potential development of companies like ours at the global level. Right now, there may be somebody out there, in some corner of the world, developing the tool that will turn the Internet upside down all over again. The tool that will alter our day-to-day life once more. Creating more opportunities, providing new benefits to individuals, bringing more individual and collective well-being. Just ten years ago, social media did not exist; in the next ten years, something else radically new will emerge. There are many areas in which products, processes, and services can be improved or created afresh. The future is brimming with opportunities, and the future of the Internet has only just begun.

The Economy, Business, and Work

The Internet and Business

Dan Schiller

Professor of Library and Information Science and of Communication,
University of Illinois

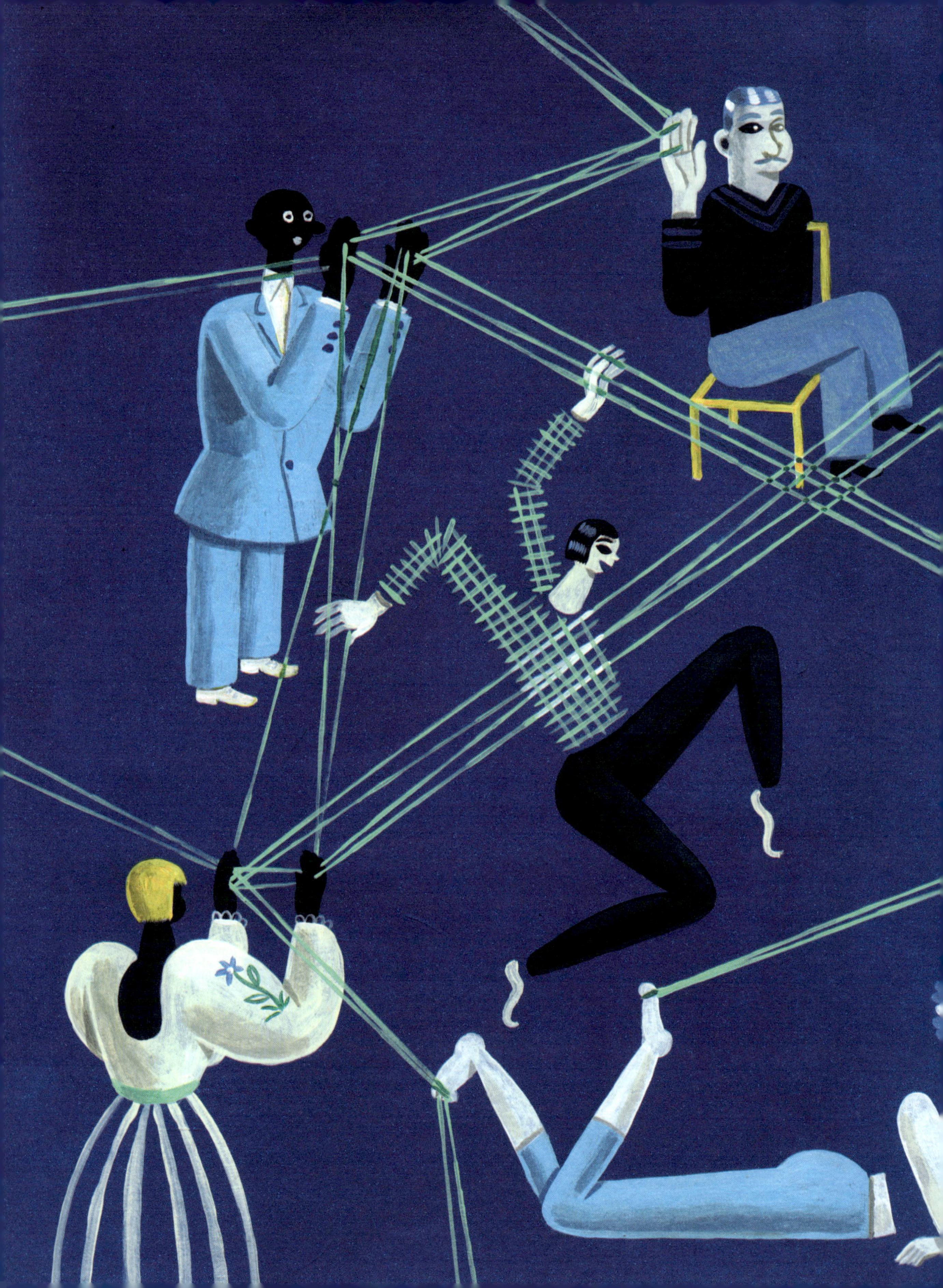

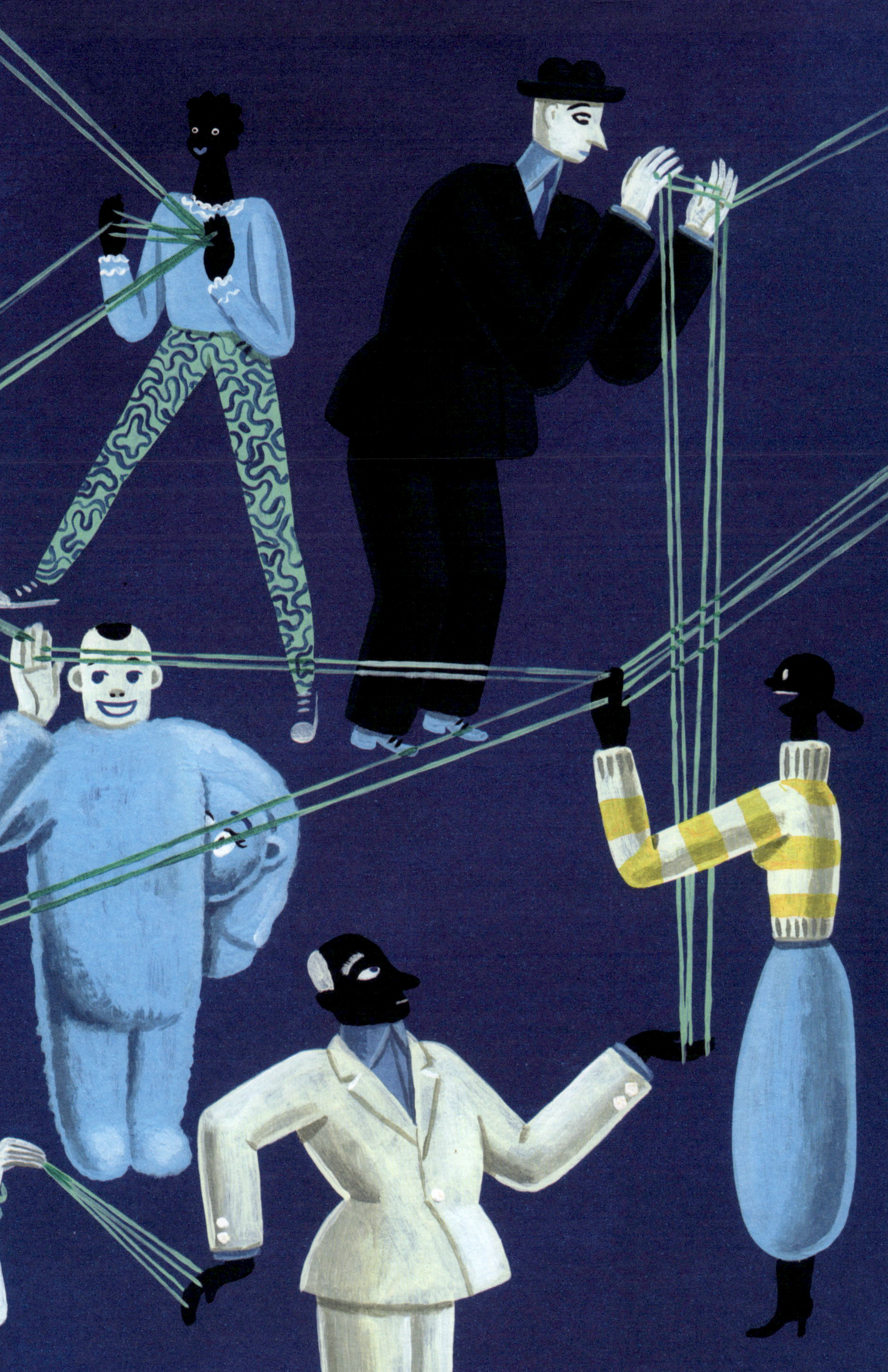

Dan Schiller

lis.illinois.edu/people/faculty/dschille

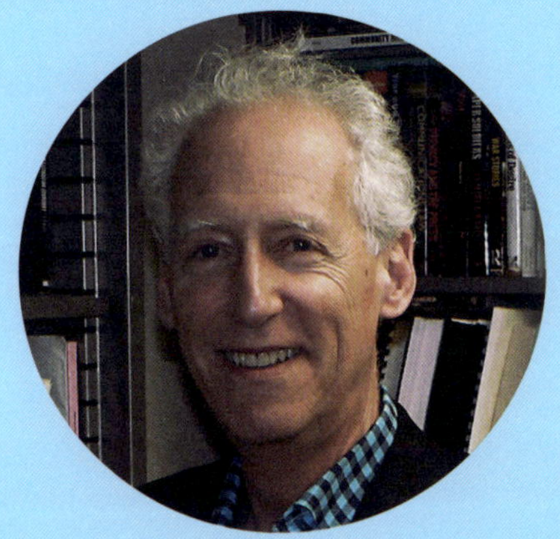

Dan Schiller is a historian of communication and information who works broadly within the tradition of political economy. He was Professor of Library and Information Science at UCLA and then Professor of Communication at UCSD before assuming his present position as Professor of Library and Information Science and of Communication at the University of Illinois at Urbana-Champaign. Among his books are *Telematics and Government* (Ablex Publishing, 1982), *Digital Capitalism* (MIT Press, 1999), *How to Think about Information* (University of Illinois Press, 2007), and the forthcoming *Digital Depression: The Crisis of Digital Capitalism*. He has contributed articles about Internet structure and policy to *Le Monde diplomatique* since the 1990s, and he co-edits the book series Geopolitics of Information for the University of Illinois Press.

Sites and services that have changed my life
counterpunch.org
freegovinfo.info
wikileaks.org
tomdispatch.com
eff.org

The Internet and Business

Given the historical significance of business as a social and political force, one might assume that there would exist ample and incisive scholarship into how business has shaped today's Internet—implementing systems and services and advocating policies for what has become an essential infrastructure. Such an assumption would be incorrect.

With some notable exceptions (including Aspray and Ceruzzi 2008; Cortada 2004–08), academic analysts have elevated individual Internet users and foregrounded their network links and online behaviors. Nearly forty years after the Internet Protocol was conceived, the structure and policy of the Internet remain secondary topics.

Journalism offers a partial corrective. In the trade and financial press we find ongoing documentation of leading indices: share prices, quarterly profits, executive reshufflings. Market forays on the supply side also generate welcome coverage. Is Facebook up to the competition with Google for mobile advertising? When will Apple introduce a television set? Might investors abandon Microsoft?

But this still is not sufficient for clarifying basic issues of structure and function and policymaking power. How did the Internet become entrenched as a business infrastructure? How has business shaped the Internet's wider social function? What are the primary features of the Internet's own institutional coordination and control? Is this mechanism for Internet governance broadly accepted by the international community? What have been the macroeconomic consequences of business's take-up of Internet systems and services?

These are among the questions for which we possess, at best, incomplete answers. In this essay I will only begin to scrutinize some of them.

This article includes material drawn from my forthcoming book, *Digital Depression: The Crisis of Digital Capitalism*.

Corporate outlays make up most of the investment in Internet systems and services (Schiller 2001). This is true also for the overall market for information processing and communications where, in one estimate, the consumer share accounts for barely one-third of what is perhaps a $4.5 trillion global market (WITSA 2010, 15, fig. 5). Business users' dominance of network investment has given them an important and little-studied role—both political and market-based—in shaping the history of network system development: the reach, the pricing, and the character of service options.

During the 1960s and 1970s U.S. policymakers authorized specialized new data communications carriers on terms that afforded them—and their customers—preferential access to the public telecommunications infrastructure (Schiller 1982). What would be called the Internet took shape in this policy environment. However, for some decades after it was devised in 1975, Internet systems continued to denominate just one of several rival approaches to data communications. Internetworking could boast of important advantages: it was dominated by U.S. corporate and university military contractors and by U.S. government agencies, which enabled it to be expanded internationally as a research network supporting U.S. military alliances led by NATO.

Throughout the late 1980s, and above all after the rollout of the World Wide Web early in the 1990s, the Internet became the predominant mode of data transfer. Businesses harbored a seemingly insatiable appetite for Internet systems and services (though many also continued to rely on networks that were not part of the Internet). Connecting to the Internet was relatively easy, and it enabled companies to mesh what often had been multiple incompatible networks. An additional attraction came with the innovation of *intranets*, software shields to conceal proprietary systems from unauthorized users. Internet use widened dramatically, making it an increasingly ubiquitous channel for business-to-business (B2B) and business-to-consumer (B2C) exchanges. As points of network access multiplied to include not only desktop computers during the 1980s but notebooks during the 1990s and 2000s and smartphones and tablets during the 2010s, services and applications proliferated. Internet data traffic seemed prospectively boundless, and network modernization projects mushroomed globally—even, after 2008, amid a depressed economy.

The profile of business use remained uneven; financial services generated heavy expenditures and extractive industries proportionally lighter ones. However, Internet functionality continued to be absorbed across the entire length and breadth of the business system, from mines and utilities to banks, from wholesalers and retailers to agribusinesses, and from durable and nondurable goods manufacturers to communications media (USDOC 2013, table 2a).[1]

All sectors made ever-increasing use of the Internet, so that information processing and communications outlays by U.S. companies comprised the greatest single portion of corporate capital investment overall.

A brief historical sketch of network innovation within three different business sectors will be sufficient to point out the contradictory patterns of assimilation.

Finance

Big banks, pivots of the capitalist political economy, have transformed throughout the past few decades, to constitute a concentrated and diversified industry possessing a multifaceted global reach. Large international banks offer diverse means of payment and credit; grease the wheels of corporate mergers and acquisitions; devise fee-based speculative instruments both for their customers and on their own account; and operate as outsourcers for large non-financial companies, for whom they have increasingly taken over payroll deposits, taxes, foreign exchange hedges, trade finance, and other financial functions (Nolan 2012, 111–12).

Massive bank investments in information technology interlace through all of this, as James W. Cortada (2006, 37–112) details. In 1966, the financial sector as a whole—inclusive of finance, insurance, and real

---

1. The most recent year for which official statistics are available is 2011.

estate—operated an estimated 17 percent share of the nation's computer installations, less than half the total then in use in U.S. manufacturing (Schiller 1982, 24, table 4). Computer systems had been introduced initially to process ever-growing volumes of checks, and to coordinate and control savings and lending (Cortada 2006, 60–73). But their range grew dramatically as the circuits of finance lengthened and diversified, and as debt was pushed on every social institution.

Credit and debit cards, ATMs and Electronic Funds Transfer systems, stock-exchange trading, point-of-sale systems used by retail chains, e-commerce, and mobile payment systems each built upon existing network capabilities and in turn stimulated additional innovation around bank and interbank networks. Beginning in the 1970s and 1980s, big banks devoted an ever-increasing share of their operating expenses to data processing and telecommunications; in turn, the largest banks accounted for a disproportionate share of the industry's ICT expenditures. These investments grew alongside bank deregulation, which ushered in gigantic diversified financial intermediaries possessing both motive and means to pump up consumer, corporate, and government debt.

By 2006, JP Morgan boasted an IT staff of 20,000 and a $7 billion annual IT budget; recent investments had focused "on building sophisticated trading platforms for institutional investors and hedge fund clients," and "[a] clutch of quants with PhDs have been hired to create algorithmic models that speed up trading" (Der Hovanesian 2006).[2] Its peers did the same. At about $50 billion, overall investment in ICTs by U.S. financial institutions including insurance companies was the second largest of any sector, and accounted for some 17 percent of total U.S. corporate ICT investment in 2011 (DOC 2013, table 2a). Internet channels took over an increasing range of services within more complex financial network architectures.

The reciprocal hold exercised by finance over network development was vital. Not only were banks and other lenders needed to supply funding guarantees for networking projects in the now-privatized environment of global telecommunications. They also garnered a major role in determining the social functions performed by these network systems. Peter

2. Thanks to Shinjoung Yeo for this reference.

Nolan notes how, in a general way, "intense pressure from the banks has helped to stimulate enormous structural change and technical progress in the IT industry" (Nolan 2012, 113). A company called Hibernia supplied a salient illustration. Hibernia announced in Fall 2010 its plan to construct a new transatlantic submarine cable. This seemed audacious, even enigmatic: the transatlantic market had been heavily overbuilt between 1998 and 2001, when seven additional cables had been laid; the severe price competition that followed, as the Internet bubble popped, bankrupted some operators. It led also to spectacular price drops by surviving networks, so that even in 2010 bandwidth prices remained among the lowest in the world. Hibernia's was the first cable project for a decade in this seemingly still-inauspicious market. What was its rationale?

Hibernia anticipated that by using a more direct physical route across the ocean floor, its "Project Express" cable would cut five milliseconds off what is called *return-path latency*—the time required by a message to transit back and forth, in this case between New York and London. Once completed, it promised to be the fastest available path between these two cities.

For ordinary users such a marginal gain made no difference. For one group, however, it brought an irresistible advantage. "Financial institutions engaged in high-velocity trading are speed demons," explained an analyst: "They claim that shaving off just a few milliseconds of connectivity between two trading locations can earn them tens of millions of dollars a year—so they're willing to pay extra for the fastest path" (TeleGeography 2010, quoting TeleGeography vice president of research Tim Stronge).

This was decisive. By 2011 high-frequency trading by hedge funds, exchanges, and megabanks made up as much as 70 percent of U.S. equity trading (Patterson 2012, 8), and about one-third of Europe's (Lex Column 2011, 14). Playing the market no longer revolved merely around more or less shrewd estimates of different companies' earning potential, but also on exploiting innovations in the network infrastructure to get ahead of other traders. Goldman Sachs, Barclays, Credit Suisse, and Morgan Stanley had instituted trading systems built around algorithms for capturing profits by tracing microsecond stock-price movements. "They scan the different exchanges, trying to anticipate which direction individual stocks are likely to move in the next fraction of a second based on current market conditions and statistical analysis of past performance" (Kroft 2010). Then they issue buy and sell orders of their own. For these mostly unregulated high-speed networks, one analyst observes, "location is critical; the servers are placed as close as possible to those of the exchange" (Lex Column 2011, 14; Grant and Demos 2011, 21). Hibernia planned to reroute network plumbing so as to build in advantages for a tiny group of preferred customers.[3] Similar ultra-fast links were being constructed elsewhere, such as between New York and the great commodity exchanges in Chicago (Miller 2011).

Such projects accounted for a colossal financial investment in network technology. Though this investment was not the underlying cause of the 2008 crisis, it did help spread the panic through innumerable channels, as far-flung as they were also opaque. The assimilation of networks by manufacturers, to which we turn now, generated different pathways toward this same crisis.

Manufacturing

It is still sometimes thought that manufacturing industry constitutes a *stage of economic growth* that was, in its turn, supplanted by a new epoch of information and communications during the late twentieth century. Such a conception may be faulted on at least two counts. First, it abstracts particular national economies—typically, that of the U.S.—from the transnational political-economic relationships in which they are enmeshed. Second, it misrepresents the history of network innovation.

Big industrial manufacturers actually constituted a leading site of computer network development. "In general," writes James W. Cortada (2004, 120), "manufacturing industries were early adopters of computers, spending nearly half of what all American industries did on this technology in the

3.   Set up as a unit in Hibernia's so-called Global Financial Network, Project Express was supported by $250 million in financing from a three-year-old joint venture between Chinese network vendor Huawei and Britain's Global Marine Systems— long the largest global operator of cable ships (Business Wire 2011). However, as U.S.-China tension mounted over *cyber security* issues in 2012 and 2013, the U.S. Government used its large, lucrative contracts with key U.S. carriers as leverage to force Hibernia to suspend work on the cable (TeleGeography 2013b).

1950s and, even two decades later, nearly a quarter." Numerical control, computer-aided design and manufacturing, manufacturing information systems, robotics, and plant-wide data networks were expressions of this impulse; transportation equipment manufacturers, in automotive, trucking, and aerospace were especially prominent early innovators (Cortada 2004, 99–113, 120–21). As in other sectors, therefore, networking followed an evolutionary trajectory; when it developed, the Internet was assimilated into what was already a network-intensive industry. In 2011, U.S. manufacturers' investments in information processing and communications equipment were the third largest of any sector: $34.7 billion, or around 12 percent of the total (DOC 2013, table 2a).

Manufacturing applications of networks were grouped along two axes. One pertained to the reorganization of the labor processes on which manufacturing depended, including not only fabrication and assembly, but also design and engineering and management. Along this axis, the role of digital networks was to enable the automation of a continuing succession of tasks, and to enlarge the range of collaborative communication for production across the technical division of labor. The second pertained to enabling the dispersion of manufacturing operations: network links are among the "permissive technologies," as Bluestone and Harrison (1982) called them 30 years ago, that enabled surging foreign direct investment by U.S. and European manufacturers throughout the final decades of the twentieth century.

Under different names, export processing zones characterized by low wages, loose environmental restrictions, and lax oversight of occupational safety and health became sites of surging growth (for an early study, see Shaiken 1990). The countries that hosted this movement of capital often saw few substantial contributions to their domestic economic well-being; the same movement of capital also ravaged working-class communities at its source. Even as it shuttered high-wage plants in its U.S. *home* market, for example, in 1998 General Motors began to open auto-making plants in China. Already selling more cars in China than in the U.S. by 2010 (Meiners 2010), GM brought in two new plants there in 2012, and in 2013 announced a further multibillion-dollar investment with its Chinese joint-venture partners to launch four more Chinese plants. Some of this augmented manufacturing capacity ultimately might be used, GM forecast, to export automobiles back to the United States (Woodall 2013).

These two sets of changes radically reconfigured the manufacturing production systems. Country-of-origin thinking (and the statistics used to validate it) has been steadily supplanted: complex consumer commodities, from automobiles to smartphones, today are the final outcome of administratively coordinated production systems aiming at the world market and binding together suppliers and sub-suppliers in multiple countries. The iPhone was in this way, as in others, emblematic, as was shown by a well-publicized report for the Asian Development Bank (Xing and Detert 2011). Just-in-time inventories and co-located plants, characteristic forms of contemporary manufacturing, are utterly reliant on advanced digital networks. This becomes starkly evident when a natural or human-induced calamity—an earthquake, a flood, or a nuclear accident—interrupts the ordinary sequence.

We should be wary of attributing to manufacturers' assimilation of networks any transcendent rationality. General Motors has spent monumental sums—tens of billions of dollars—on information and communications technology since the 1970s, even for a time trying to integrate forward by becoming a supplier of data processing services through acquisitions of EDS and Hughes Aircraft. This did not prevent GM from plunging into bankruptcy and government receivership in 2009. Networks helped GM, akin to major manufacturers generally, to reorganize production; but this network investment paradoxically contributed to two destabilizing trends. First, overcapacity deepened throughout most of the world automotive market, as network-enabled production resulted in a chronic surfeit. Second, what David Harvey (2012) calls "wage repression" lowered the standard of living in working-class communities throughout the United States and Western Europe—which hit economic demand, in turn helping to induce today's depressed conditions.

Communications and Information

The information industry accounts for the largest single share of overall U.S. investment in ICTs—$80 billion in 2011, or about 28 percent of the total. The Internet here again became the pivot of a far-reaching process of market recomposition.

Transnational providers of Internet services consolidated down into three primary segments. Giant network operators, such as Telefónica, Verizon, Deutsche Telekom, China Mobile, and América Móvil, made up one such group. Comcast, Time-Warner, Disney, and a few other multimedia conglomerates possessing troves of programming and tens of thousands of copyrights presided over a second. A third segment encompassed a handful of large, dynamic Internet intermediaries, from Google and Apple to Alibaba (McChesney 2013).

Relations across and within these three segments were volatile. As this was written, proliferating *over-the-top* services for voice, video, and other communications were enabling the big Internet intermediaries to pounce on conventional media offerings, rearranging what had been long-engraved distribution channels. Apple, Intel, Netflix, and Google, the latter already much the largest Internet video company through its ownership of YouTube, were each moving to introduce over-the-top video channels (Stelter 2013a, B1, B6; 2013b, B1, B6). Because, however—akin to cable, satellite, and broadcast distributors—online video distributors turned out to require professionally produced content, they also needed to cut deals with the seven media conglomerates that still control around 95 percent of U.S. TV viewing hours (GOA 2013, 6–7).

Voice-over-Internet (VoI) applications proved even more disruptive. Cross-border traffic routed by Skype (purchased by Microsoft in 2011) grew by 45 billion minutes in 2010, 47 billion in 2011, and 51 billion in 2012: that is more than twice the volume added during this interval by all of the world's phone companies combined (TeleGeography 2011, 2012, 2013a). In just five years, Skype became the world's largest supplier of cross-border voice communications, with more than one-third of all international telephone traffic (TeleGeography 2013a). This cut to the bone of the market for conventional telephone service, jeopardizing gigantic infrastructure investments and impelling network operators to find means of integrating with—or charging more to carry—these and other Internet applications.

The recomposition of communications around Internet technology, however, spanned beyond disruptions to existing markets. The continuing dynamism of Internet systems, services, and applications signified that leading Internet intermediaries were trying to coordinate not a one-off shift, but an ongoing transition whose character and limits remain substantially open-ended. In close relation with corporate and organizational users, as well as with consumers, suppliers advanced three interrelated programs of development.

Cloud computing—distribution of content and of software as a service from centralized data centers—was the first. With precursors going back to 1960s-era plans for a *computer utility*, cloud computing is a model for distributing data, software applications, and automated labor services to users wherever they are located. Much of this innovation was occurring within major businesses, which adopted *private cloud* services in search of added efficiencies. A second initiative cohered around the so-called Internet of Things: arrays of sensors are being embedded in roads, industrial plants and equipment, and consumer goods—and all of these appliances are being assigned unique Internet addresses to enable *machine-to-machine* communication. (Devices connected to the Internet are expected to outnumber human users by 10 to 1 within just a few years [Cortada 2011, 10].) Surging market growth for smartphones and other handheld computing devices likewise continued, alongside a prospective take-up of *smartwear* such as wristbands, glasses, and watches (Nuttall 2013, 7).

The volume of data produced as an adjunct of these different types of machine-to-machine and human-machine interaction increased, and became omnipresent. To capture and manipulate it, a third initiative took shape: *Big Data*, which centered on the analysis and feedback of data into products and services. Predictive models received intensive cultivation (Cain Miller 2013b, A1, A3); and companies from Amazon to IBM invested billions in data analytics (Lohr 2013, B9).

The Internet industry's "colossal public relations machine," as one journalist called it (Glanz 2013, 5), was set in overdrive to popularize these initiatives. Prospectively more important, however, were the online product lines that were being readied for Internet distribution: in education, cultural heritage, biotechnology, and medicine. The Internet's function as a critical business infrastructure was thus matched or even surpassed by its importance as a site of commodification, that is, as a site of new industries capable of generating profit growth.

And, across the entire landscape of Internet systems and services, U.S. companies built up such a comparative advantage that what I call digital capitalism (Schiller 1999) itself became a lopsided construction.

Aggregate figures tell the story. U.S. expenditures on ICTs in 2010, at $1.2 trillion, exceeded those of China, Japan, the UK, and Russia combined. This skew was likely to persist, because the U.S. accounted for more than half of global ICT research and development spending. A high-level 2013 U.S. report underlined, finally, that "The United States captures more than 30 percent of global Internet revenues and more than 40 percent of net income" (Negroponte and Palmisano 2013, 9).

This did not mean that digital capitalism was uncontested; sometimes, though, even the competition was U.S.-based. Unquestionably, search engines were dominated by Google, but with the extension of navigational services to mobile devices and with search functions becoming embedded in e-commerce, competition from Apple, Amazon, and others was escalating (Cain Miller 2013a, A1, A4). Google's lead in digital advertising met competition from marketing super-groups, as well as from Facebook and Twitter; Google's Android mobile operating system won a firmer hold after it was taken up by Samsung—which also began to match Apple in its take of the global profits generated by smartphones and tablets (Bulard 2013, 1–3; Garside 2013; Dilger 2013). Microsoft reaped disproportionate earnings from PC operating systems, but as PCs gave way to other computing platforms, Google and Apple bulked larger here, too. The same transition to mobile devices saw Qualcomm supplant Intel as the leading chipmaker (Nuttall 2013, 14). Throughout much of the world, consumer e-commerce was channeled through Amazon (which also led in cloud services); however, China's Alibaba was poised to be a competitive threat going forward. Transnational supply of corporate routing equipment was led by Cisco, but China's Huawei was snapping at its heels. Facebook's billion users friended one another in 70 languages (Facebooknol 2009). Oracle competed with SAP for business software, while IBM morphed into a top purveyor of computer services and data analytics. U.S. multimedia companies, typically active in publishing, film, recording, and television, continued to straddle the world market. U.S.-headquartered companies were not only leaders in supply, finally, but also in demand and application: from Wal-Mart to General Electric, U.S. corporations had built transnational network-based systems and applications that aspiring rivals found difficult to surpass (Nolan and Zhang 2010).

As battles over Internet markets continued to unfold, however, the movement of the transnational political economy was shaped not only by corporations but also by states.

In a trend that heightened as a result of the economic depression that began in 2008, Internet systems and services constituted a rare and much-coveted pole of economic dynamism. This fact conferred on the Internet a profound political importance.

States vied with one another to set the ground rules for the development of Internet industries. Businesses turned to political intervention, hoping to accomplish what they had not able to via private market interaction.

I turn now to consider some of the resulting patterns of political engagement.

Despite years of rhetoric about the virtues of market freedom, historically the U.S. Government had been the most important structuring force behind the Internet. Not only did U.S. military contracts underwrite the research and development on which the Internet's underlying technology is based; not only did the Government supply an unrivaled market for Internet equipment and services; not only did the U.S. contrive policy through which to privatize the Internet's backbone networks (Abbate 1999). The U.S. Government also played a crucial role in the migration of the sales effort—advertising, marketing, and e-commerce—to the Internet during the 1990s. Close coordination between the upper echelons of the Clinton Administration and U.S. business, as Matthew Crain (2013) shows, enabled the World Wide Web's assimilation into the commercial media-marketing system. The installation of lax privacy strictures allowed technical inno-vations—*cookies*—to be introduced and widely deployed, empowering marketers to track consumers as they surfed online. The Internet thus morphed into a "surveillance engine," as Wikileaks' Julian Assange later called it (2012), as a consequence of deliberate policy. Only the U.S. Government's active support enabled business to incorporate the Internet so fully into its sales effort.

The U.S. also established the Internet as an extraterritorial system with the United States itself as its hub. By brokering, or at least facilitating, agreements to exchange data traffic between organizations sited in different countries, and by ensuring that the agencies charged with managing critical Internet resources (unique identifiers, including autonomous system numbers, generic domain names, and Internet addresses) were accountable to its own Executive Branch, the U.S. Government helped establish a U.S.-centric Internet.

U.S. power over the Internet is not comprehensive; it is also opaque. Formally, this power is expressed through legal contracts that bind a nonprofit contractor—a California corporation called ICANN (as well as a shadowy for-profit U.S. company called VeriSign, which not only manages the dotcom franchise but also manages crucial Internet address system functions) to the Commerce Department. A key part of its attempt to downplay its structured relationship with U.S. state power has been ICANN's much-heralded "multi-stakeholder model": multi-stakeholderism confers formal representation on corporations and civil society groups as well as governments, but absents Internet governance from the sphere of multilateral institutions. A comparable veneer obscures the activities of the Internet Engineering Task Force (IETF), an independent organization charged with developing Internet architecture and system engineering and possessing no formal obligations to U.S. authorities. IETF operations are sheltered behind an ideological cloak of neutral technocratic expertise, supposedly cut free of corporate or state interests. The organization, however, is disproportionately staffed by employees of U.S. companies and U.S. state agencies. Can it be inconsequential that (data from 2007) 71 percent of the 120 specialized working groups whose remit is to improve Internet technology were chaired by individuals from the United States, while developing country representatives counted for 6 percent of this total? Or that nearly four-fifths of these experts were employed by private companies such as Cisco Systems (Mathiason

2008, 36)?[4] As Milton Mueller (2010, 240) sums it up, the coordination and control of today's extraterritorial Internet add up to "unilateral globalism" exercised by a single superstate: the U.S.

Even as it became institutionalized during the 1990s, this skew gave rise to political contention. Foreign states—Brazil and China were prominent—pushed to alter existing arrangements. Some asserted that the cost structure, the technical features, and the management of the Internet prevented them from exercising their own jurisdictional authority over national political-economic and cultural space. Some recognized that the U.S. preemption of the extraterritorial Internet hindered, even foreclosed, profitable participation by non-U.S. interests along what had become a decisive frontier of economic growth. The appearance of unilateral U.S. power seemed to signify an absence of comity with respect to *global Internet governance.* The conflict simmered, and periodically boiled up. At the World Summit on the Information Society between 2003 and 2005, unhappiness was transmuted into concrete initiatives; but these efforts stumbled in the face of U.S. recalcitrance.

The U.S. Government continued to make a privileged U.S. role in cyberspace a cornerstone of its economic diplomacy. Resisting attempts to place oversight and management of the Internet in multilateral organizations, the U.S. instead tolerated merely cosmetic changes to the existing U.S.-centric system. Concurrently, U.S. authorities campaigned to defend and, if possible, to extend U.S. businesses' already massive exploitation of transborder data flows (TDF).

The U.S. had engaged TDF controversies concertedly throughout the 1970s and early 1980s, in response to threats made by Western European and *Third World* countries to restrict the uses made by big companies of transnational computer networks (Schiller 1982, 1984). By the time the Internet exploded on the scene in the 1990s, effective limits on international data flows had been mostly repulsed or, where this proved necessary, finessed. (Some U.S. trading partners, notably the EU, instituted data protection policies that needed to be—and were—worked around.)

4.   Thanks to Hong Shen for this reference.

Heightened dependence by transnational companies on a technologically dynamic Internet, however, portended further conflicts over TDF.

The U.S. sought to outflank prospective resistance to this technological transition. Again, a covering shield was used, as the Executive Branch resurrected the "free flow of information" rhetoric that had stood service for decades in draping hard-edged U.S. economic and strategic interests in an appealing language of universal human rights (Schiller 1976). A proceeding launched by the U.S. Department of Commerce in 2010 provided clues to this application of the policy, and also revealed an overarching corporate consensus behind it. In announcing its inquiry, the Commerce Department underlined how the ongoing movement toward centralized data centers would be essentially contingent on unrestricted flows of proprietary data: "The rise of globally-accessible cloud computing services—everything from Web-based mail and office productivity suites, to more general purpose computing, storage and communications services available through the cloud—raises a new set of questions regarding local restrictions that countries may impose on services accessible, though not physically located, in their country" (DOC 2010, 60071).

Respondents included the membership of the United States Council for International Business (USCIB): "top U.S.-based global companies and professional services firms from every sector of our economy, with operations in every region of the globe." USCIB expressed an avowed "user orientation." It sought to elicit U.S. Government aid in helping to counter "restrictions on collecting, using or transferring personal information, encryption regulations, restrictions on location or sensor-based information, quotas on digital content among others." It specifically aimed to repel foreign government polices that might "preclude companies from gaining the economies and efficiencies of global platforms." Service providers must not be compelled to store or process data in any and every country, "effectively requiring local investment and placing data under local jurisdictions" (USCIB 2010). Another big trade association, TechAmerica (2010, 1–2), this time representing ICT suppliers, expressly singled out a need to safeguard emerging cloud services. "As cloud computing continues to grow, so, too, will the amount of data crossing national borders. If divergent claims to jurisdiction over user content remain then it becomes quite difficult for providers to manage their legal obligations and their global technology operations while at the same time protect their customers" (TechAmerica 2010, 7).

This policy demand for unrestricted proprietary data flows garnered support from a great array of corporations. "As the software industry moves increasingly to a cloud computing model, where software and IT functionality is delivered to customers over the Internet," stated the Business Software Alliance, "the imperative to reduce barriers to cross-border data flows becomes clear. A key element of the economics of cloud computing is the unrestrained ability to move data and workloads wherever the computing resources to service them are available" (Holleyman 2010, 6–7). Global harmonization was needed to support unrestricted data flows and, as the Entertainment Software Association disclosed in its submission, implementing free trade agreements could contribute to this goal (ESA 2010, 3, 7). The Computer & Communications Industry Association underlined that, "When we discuss the global free flow of information over the Internet, there are potentially trillions of dollars of U.S. economic activity at stake." To elevate the status of digital goods and services into "a central feature of our trade policy," the multilateral framework of the World Trade Organization and bilateral free-trade agreements alike would be needed (CCIA 2010, 2, 22–23). In their individual submissions, vendors including Microsoft (2010, 1), eBay (2010), and Google concurred. Google (2010, 15) expressly rejected any assumption of jurisdiction over the Internet by other states, such as through multilateral intergovernmental agencies like the UN-affiliated International Telecommunication Union. Declaring that it had invested "tens of billions of dollars" to supply global IP services covering 159 countries to 98 percent of Fortune 1000 businesses, Verizon (2010, 1, 2) went on to agree that "the U.S. government's international advocacy should continue to promote a single, global, interoperable Internet that is free of government restrictions that interfere with the ability of informed consumers to drive continued development of services and content." However, "different policies and national operating requirements" threatened Verizon with "country-specific" fragmentation. This jeopardized not only Verizon's profit strategy but also those of its transnational enterprise customers, who "demand a uniform set of integrated services from a single supplier."

Policies to ensure unrestricted proprietary data flows thus constituted a fundamental general demand by transnational businesses, including both users and suppliers of the Internet. This, however, did not guarantee that U.S. "unilateral globalism" over the Internet would persist.

The structure and policy of the Internet instead became sites of wrenching political conflict, as inter-state opposition to the status quo widened. The demand to make global Internet governance a formal multilateral undertaking turned into a majority position at a meeting of the International Telecommunication Union in December 2012—a meeting from which the U.S. delegation walked out (Schiller 2013, 6). Midway through 2013, a task force report to the U.S. Council on Foreign Relations affirmed that "*A global Internet increasingly fragmented into national Internets is not in the interest of the United States*," and suggested that "by building a cyber alliance, making the free flow of information a part of all future trade agreements, and articulating an inclusive and robust vision of Internet governance, Washington can limit the effects of a fragmenting Internet." However, the report conceded that "The trends do not look good" (Negroponte and Palmisano 2013, 13, 67 [emphasis in the original]). U.S. policies had begun to seem brittle—even stale. In a blog post review of the Council on Foreign Relations report, a U.S. expert asked: "Has the U.S. run out of ideas about Internet governance?" (Mueller 2013) A U.S. academic conference in June 2013 accorded serious attention to the idea that a "federated Internet" in which different national Internets were somehow linked might soon supplant the existing U.S.-centric extraterritorial system (CITI 2013).

It was in this context that Edward J. Snowden's disclosures about NSA spying on the world's peoples made their sensational appearance. News stories in London's *Guardian* newspaper in June 2013 reverberated through the world's press, and cascaded into public opinion. As awareness of the U.S.'s singular power over the Internet finally burst into widespread view, it also crashed into international politics and diplomacy (Kelley 2013).

Within days, France found new footing for its longstanding "cultural exception" policy—which aimed to protect music and film from U.S. transnational media conglomerates—as it insisted that the EU should reserve the domain of audiovisual culture from Trans-Atlantic Trade pact negotiations (Fontanella-Khan and Politi 2013, 2). Within weeks, Snowden's revelations were figuring in German electoral politics (Eddy 2013, A5). Across the Atlantic, a Washington, D.C. policy group convened a meeting to discuss "digital trade policy," on the assumption that the U.S.'s "widespread, clandestine surveillance of digital communications ... will likely have an impact on the ability of the U.S. government and tech sector to fight back against anti-competitive policies, such as server localization, that impede the global free flow of information while potentially legitimizing countries who wish to engage in such practices" (ITIF 2013). Might states place restrictions on transborder data flows? Might data protection policies be strengthened, to compel network services offered within a national jurisdiction to be stored on local servers? In early August, the president of Argentina, allied with representatives of Mercosur countries, denounced U.S. espionage at the United Nations, and issued calls to reinstate multilateral accountability (Stea 2013). The U.S. Obama Administration reverted to crisis management (Savage and Shear 2013, A1, A11).

The furor erupted over U.S. Government surveillance programs, but the underlying issue was actually U.S. corporate and state power over the extraterritorial Internet. The long-standing international conflict over the Internet's skewed structure in turn became freighted with new contingency. In an insurrectionary world, the question of how the Internet might be restructured—and with what ramifications for business—was not only increasingly palpable but also vital.

References

This article includes material drawn from my forthcoming book, *Digital Depression: The Crisis of Digital Capitalism*.

Lex Column.
"Slaves to the Algorithm." *Financial Times*, July 13, 2011.

Abbate, Janet.
Inventing The Internet. Cambridge, MA: MIT Press, 1999.

Aspray, William, and Paul E. Ceruzzi, eds.
The Internet and American Business. Cambridge: MIT Press, 2008.

Assange, Julian.
CypherPunks: Freedom and the Future of the Internet. New York: O/R Books, 2012.

Bluestone, Barry, and Bennett Harrison.
The Deindustrialization of America. New York: Basic Books, 1982.

Bulard, Martine.
"South Korea's Corporate Dynasty." *Le Monde diplomatique*, July 2013: 1–3 (English Edition).

Business Wire.
"Hibernia Atlantic Achieves an Important Milestone for Project Express." Unified Communications, January 5, 2011. http://unified-communications.tmcnet.com/news/2011/01/05/5225567.htm (accessed January 14, 2011).

Cain Miller, Claire.
"As Web Search Goes Mobile, Apps Chip at Google's Lead." *New York Times*, April 4, 2013a.
———. "New Generation of Apps Knows What You Want, Before You Do." *New York Times*, July 30, 2013b.

CITI (Columbia Institute for Tele-Information).
"The Future of Internet Governance After Dubai: Are We Heading To A Federated Internet?" June 20, 2013.

CCIA (Computer & Communications Industry Association).
"Comments before the United States Department of Commerce, In the Matter of the Notice of Inquiry on 'Global Free Flow of Information on the Internet.'" December 6, 2010.

Cortada, James W.
Information and the Modern Corporation. Cambridge, MA: MIT Press, 2011.
———. *The Digital Hand*. 3 vols. New York: Oxford University Press, 2004-2008.
———. *The Digital Hand*. Vol. 1: *How Computers Changed the Work of American Manufacturing, Transportation, and Retail Industries*. New York: Oxford University Press, 2004.
———. *The Digital Hand*. Vol. 2: *How Computers Changed the Work of American Financial, Telecommunications, Media, and Entertainment Industries*. New York: Oxford University Press, 2006.

Crain, Matthew.
"The Revolution Will Be Commercialized: Finance, Public Policy, and the Construction of Internet Advertising." PhD Thesis, University of Illinois. Urbana-Champaign, 2013.

Der Hovanesian, Mara.
"JP Morgan: The Bank Of Technology." *Business Week*, June 19, 2006.

Dilger, Daniel Eran.
"Samsung Electronics Has Not Dethroned Apple, Inc. in Mobile Profits." *AppleInsider*, July 27, 2013. http://appleinsider.com/articles/13/07/27/samsung-has-not-dethroned-apple-in-mobilo-profits

DOC (U.S. Department of Commerce), Census Bureau.
"ICT Expenditures and Percent Change for Companies With Employees by Major Industry Sector: 2011 and 2010 Revised," 2011 Information & Communication Technology Survey, March 28, 2013. http://www.census.gov/econ/ict/xls/2011/full_report.html (accessed September 6, 2013).

eBay, Inc.
"Comments before the United States Department of Commerce, In the Matter of the Notice of Inquiry on 'Global Free Flow of Information on the Internet.'" December 6, 2010.

Eddy, Melissa.
"Merkel Appears to Weather Anger Among German Voters Over N.S.A. Spying." *New York Times*. July 12, 2013.

ESA (Entertainment Software Association).
"Comments before the United States Department of Commerce, In the Matter of the Notice of Inquiry on 'Global Free Flow of Information on the Internet.'" December 6, 2010.

Facebooknol,
"70 Languages in Which Facebook Can Be Used." Facebook, October 7, 2009. Retrieved at http://www.facebook.com/note.php?note_id=147674353371

Fontanella-Khan, James, and James Politi.
"Data Scandal Clouds Trade Talks." *Financial Times*, June 10, 2013.

Garside, Juliette.
"Samsung Overtakes Apple As World's Most Profitable Mobile Phone Maker." *Guardian*, July 26, 2013. http://www.theguardian.com/technology/2013/jul/26/samsung-apple-profitable-mobile-phone?view=mobile

Glanz, James.
"Is Big Data an Economic Big Dud?" *New York Times*, August 18, 2013, Sunday Review.

Google.
"Comments before the United States Department of Commerce, In the Matter of the Notice of Inquiry on 'Global Free Flow of Information on the Internet.'" December 6, 2010.

Grant, Jeremy, and Telis Demos.
"Ultra-fast Traders Braced for Tough Curbs in Europe." *Financial Times*, October 14, 2011.

Harvey, David.
The Enigma of Capital. New York: Oxford, 2012.

Holleyman, Robert W., II, President and CEO, Business Software Alliance. Correspondence to The Honorable Gary Locke, Secretary of Commerce.
"Re: Inquiry on the Global Free Flow of Information on the Internet." December 6, 2010.

ITIF (Information Technology and Innovation Foundation).
"The Impact of PRISM on Digital Trade Policy." July 24, 2013, Washington, D.C. https://webmail.illinois.edu/owa/?ae=Item&t=IPM.Note&id=RgAAAAB7gIC89xbIRbWWbzd2rfqcBwCjf4nelht%2bRZTyq0cFTa5OABryJJZxAAA36aBTO02hTIgzuWp4z9R%2fAAAcKEFTAAAJ

Kelley, Caroline.
"A Competitive Disadvantage? American Businesses Fear the Fallout from Surveillance Leaks." *Time*, August 1, 2013. http://nation.time.com/2013/08/01/american-businesses-fear-the-fallout-from-surveillance-leaks/

Kroft, Steve.
"How Speed Traders Are Changing Wall Street." *CBS Sixty Minutes*, October 11, 2010. http://www.cbsnews.com/8301-18560_162-6936075.html

Lohr, Steve.
"Revenue Falls, but Profit Tops Forecast at I.B.M." *New York Times*, July 18, 2013.

Mathiason, John.
Internet Governance: The New Frontier of Global Institutions. New York: Routledge, 2008.

McChesney, Robert W.
Digital Disconnect. New York: Free Press, 2013.

Meiners, Jens.
"Ford and GM Battle for Sales in China." *Car And Driver*, October 2010. http://www.caranddriver.com/features/ford-and-gm-battle-for-sales-in-china-feature (accessed September 6, 2013).

Microsoft Corporation.
"Comments before the United States Department of Commerce, In the Matter of the Notice of Inquiry on 'Global Free Flow of Information on the Internet.'" December 6, 2010.

Miller, Rich.
"More Speed—at $80,000 a Millisecond." *DataCenter Knowledge*. January 24, 2011. http://www.datacenterknowledge.com/archives/2011/01/24/more-speed-at-80000-a-millisecond/ (accessed June 8, 2013).

Miller, Toby.
"French Say 'Non' To Planet Hollywood." *The Conversation*. June 2013. http://theconversation.com/french-say-non-to-planet-hollywood-15327 (accessed September 6, 2013).

Mueller, Milton L.
"Has The U.S. Run Out Of Ideas About Internet Governance? (Part 2)." *Internet Governance Project* (blog), June 18, 2013. http://www.internetgovernance.org/2013/06/18/has-the-usa-run-out-of-ideas-about-internet-governance-part-2/ (accessed September 6, 2013).
———. *Networks and States: The Global Politics of Internet Governance*. Cambridge, MA: MIT Press, 2010.

Negroponte, John D., and Samuel Palmisano, Chairs, Adam Segal, Project Director
"Defending an Open, Global, Secure, and Resilient Internet." Independent Task Force Report No. 70. New York: Council on Foreign Relations, June 2013: 9.

Nolan, Peter, and Jin Zhang.
"Global Competition After The Financial Crisis." *New Left Review* 64 (July/August 2010).

Nolan, Peter.
Is China Buying the World? London: Polity Press, 2012.

Nuttall, Chris.
"Qualcomm Forecasts Extra $600m in Revenues." *Financial Times*, April 25, 2013.
———. "Smartwear." *Financial Times*, March 22, 2013.

Patterson, Scott.
Dark Pools: High Speed Traders, A.I. Bandits, and the Threat to the Global Financial System. New York: Crown Business, 2012.

Savage, Charlie, and Michael D. Shear.
"President Moves To Ease Worries On Surveillance." *New York Times*, August 10, 2013.

Schiller, Dan.
"Masters of the Internet." *Le Monde diplomatique*, February 2013.
———."World Communications in Today's Age of Capital." *Emergences* 11, no. 1 (2001): 51–68.
———.*Digital Capitalism: Networking the Global Market System*. Cambridge, MA: MIT Press, 1999.
———.*Telematics and Government*. Norwood: Ablex Publishing, 1982.

Schiller, Herbert I.
Communication and Cultural Domination. White Plains, NY: International Arts & Sciences Press, 1976.
———.*Information and the Crisis Economy*. Norwood, NJ: Ablex Publishing, 1984.
———. *Who Knows: Information in the Age of the Fortune 500*. Norwood, NJ: Ablex Publishing, 1981.

Shaiken, Harley.
Mexico in the Global Economy: High Technology and Work Organization in Export Industries. La Jolla: University of California Center for U.S.-Mexico Studies, 1990.
Stea, Carla.
"Latin American Condemns U.S. Espionage at United Nations Security Council." *Global Research*. August 17, 2013. http://www.globalresearch.ca/latin-america-condemns-us-espionage-at-united-nations-security-council/5346120 (accessed September 6, 2013).

Stelter, Brian.
"Google Said To Weigh Supplying TV Channels." *New York Times*, July 17, 2013a.

Stelter, Brian.
"Pushing The Right Buttons." *New York Times*, July 18, 2013b.

TechAmerica.
"U.S. Department of Commerce Notice of Inquiry on Global Free Flow of Information on the Internet." December 6, 2010.

TeleGeography.
"CommsUpdate: "Hibernia Pulls Ahead in Trans-Atlantic Speed Race." TeleGeography, September 30, 2010. Quoting TeleGeography vice president of research Tim Stronge. http://www.telegeography.com/products/commsupdate/articles/2010/09/30/hibernia-pulls-ahead-in-trans-atlantic-speed-race/
———. "International Long-Distance Slumps, While Skype Soars." TeleGeography, January 6, 2011. http://www.telegeography.com/press/press-releases/2011/01/06/international-long-distance-slumps-while-skype-soars/
———. "International Call Traffic Growth Slows, as Skype's Volume Soars." TeleGeography, January 10, 2012. http://www.telegeography.com/press/press-releases/2012/01/09/international-call-traffic-growth-slows-as-skypes-volumes-soar/

———. "The Bell Tolls for Telcos?" TeleGeography, February 13, 2013a. http://www.telegeography.com/press/press-releases/2013/02/13/the-bell-tolls-for-telcos/

———. "China-US Security Tensions Force Hibernia To Down Tools on Express Cable." *CommsUpdate*, February 15, 2013b. http://www.telegeography.com/products/commsupdate/articles/2013/02/15/china-us-security-tensions-force-hibernia-to-down-tools-on-express-cable/

DOC (U.S. Department of Commerce). "Global Free Flow of Information on the Internet," *Federal Register* 75 (188), September 29, 2010. http://www.ntia.doc.gov/files/ntia/publications/fr_gffinoi_09292010.pdf

GAO (U.S. Government Accountability Office). "Video Marketplace: Competition Is Evolving, and Government Reporting Should Be Reevaluated," GAO-13-576, June 2013: 6-7.

USCIB (United States Council for International Business). "Response To Notice of Inquiry On Global Free Flow of Information on the Internet." http://www.ntia.doc.gov/federal-register-notices/2010/iptf-global-free-flow-information-internet-notice-inquiry

Verizon and Verizon Wireless. "Comments before the United States Department of Commerce, In the Matter of the Notice of Inquiry on 'Global Free Flow of Information on the Internet.'" December 6, 2010.

WITSA (World Information Technology and Services Alliance). "Digital Planet 2010." Executive Summary. October 2010.

Woodall, Bernie. "GM Plans To Add Four More Plants in China." *Automotive News*, April 20, 2103. http://www.autonews.com/article/20130420/GLOBAL03/130429994#axzz2Zmq1nHdX

Xing, Yuqing, and Neal Detert. "How the iPhone Widens the United States Trade Deficit with the People's Republic of China." ADB Working Paper Series No. 257. Tokyo: Asian Development Bank Institute, May 2011 (Revised). http://www.adbi.org/files/2010.12.14.wp257.iphone.widens.us.trade.deficit.prc.pdf

Distributed Innovation and Creativity, Peer Production, and Commons in Networked Economy

Yochai Benkler

Berkman Professor of Entrepreneurial Legal Studies, Harvard Law School

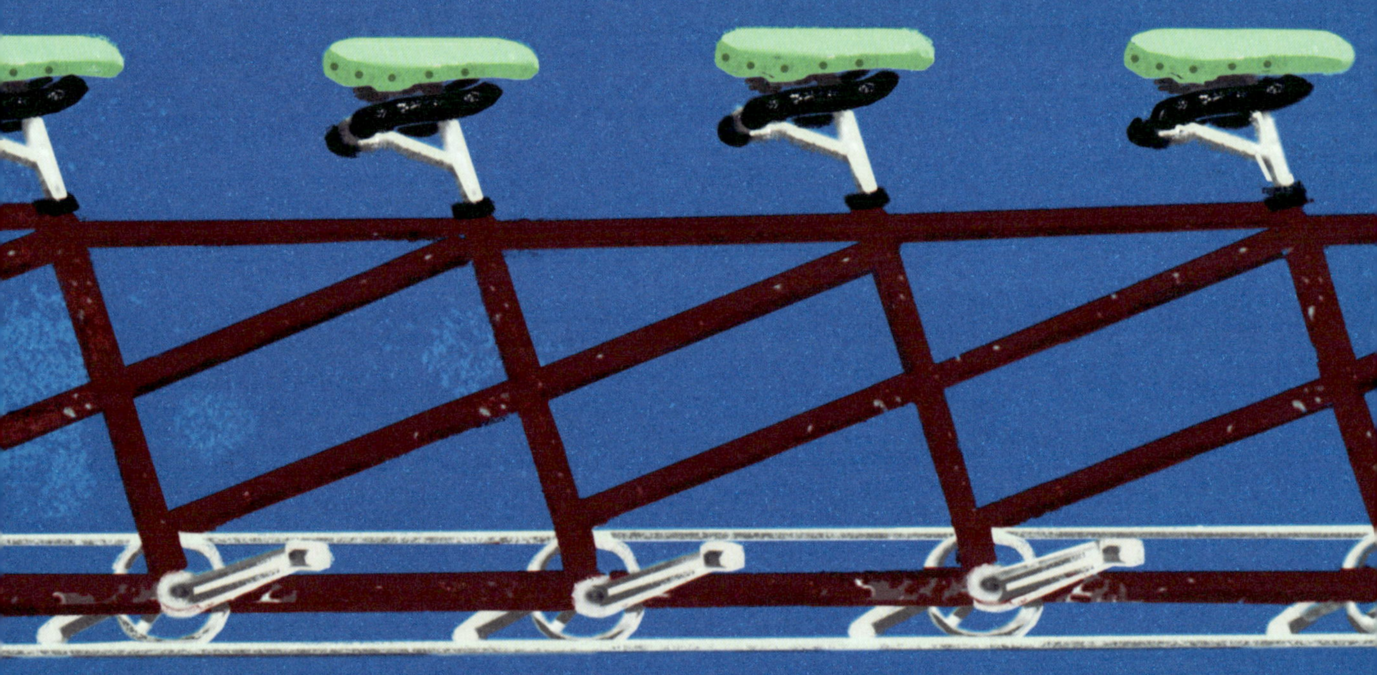

Distributed Innovation and Creativity, Peer Production, and Commons in Networked Economy

Yochai Benkler

The Economy, Business, and Work

Yochai Benkler

benkler.org

Illustration
Eva Vázquez

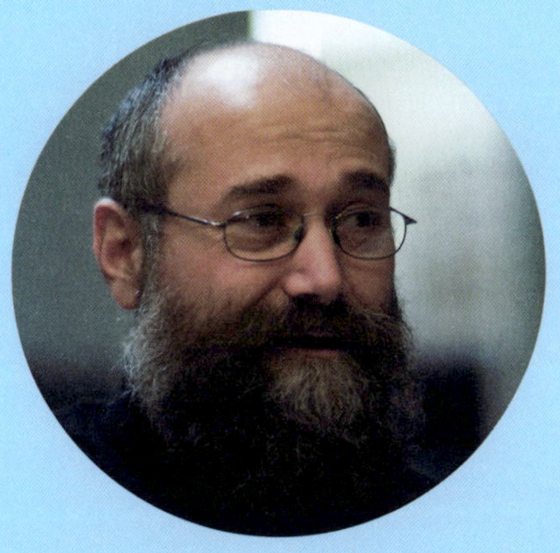

Yochai Benkler is the Berkman Professor of Entrepreneurial Legal Studies at Harvard Law School, and faculty co-director of the Berkman Center for Internet and Society at Harvard University. Since the 1990s he has played a role in characterizing the role of information commons and decentralized collaboration to innovation, information production, and freedom in the networked economy and society. His books include *The Wealth of Networks: How Social Production Transforms Markets and Freedom* (Yale University Press, 2006), which won academic awards from the American Political Science Association, the American Sociological Association, and the McGannon Award for Social and Ethical Relevance in Communications. In 2012 he received a lifetime achievement award from Oxford University "in recognition of his extraordinary contribution to the study and public understanding of the Internet and information goods." His socially engaged work has won him the Ford Foundation Visionaries Award in 2011, the Electronic Frontier Foundation's Pioneer Award for 2007, and the Public Knowledge IP3 Award in 2006. Also anchored in the realities of markets, it was cited as "perhaps the best work yet about the fast moving, enthusiast-driven Internet" by the *Financial Times* and named best business book about the future in 2006 by *Strategy and Business*. Benkler has advised governments and international organizations on innovation policy and telecommunications, and serves on the boards or advisory boards of several nonprofits engaged in working toward an open society.

Sites and services that have changed my life
E-mail
The World Wide Web
google.com
wikipedia.com
Free and Open Source Software

Distributed Innovation and Creativity, Peer Production, and Commons in Networked Economy

Imagine that in late 1995 someone told you that two groups of engineers were developing a critical piece of web infrastructure—the web server software that handles all the secure communications and payments, serves up pages, and runs the core functions of websites. The first group was Microsoft, then the most valuable software company in the world with a near monopoly hold over the operating system of personal computation; the second was a bunch of engineers, academics, amateurs, and people working for companies that were not engaged in this effort working in their spare time—who were developing the software and handing it out under a license that allowed anyone to copy the software, modify it, and distribute it as they pleased. Perhaps it is hard, as of this writing in 2013, to capture just how stupid the question "Who is going to win this race?" would have sounded to a reasonable person in 1995. And yet, the Apache web server, developed as Free and Open Source Software (FOSS) by the second group has systematically been adopted by a majority of websites over the past 18 years, through two boom and bust cycles. Microsoft trailed a distant second, while the third and fastest growing web server software, Nginx, was also FOSS. FOSS development has made inroads throughout the software platform. Mozilla Firefox has successfully cut into Microsoft Internet Explorer's browser lead; about 80 percent of most scripting languages, like PHP, Ruby, or Python, are FOSS, and the FOSS operating system Linux dominates in infrastructure applications like server farms or high-end applications like supercomputing, and has expanded to a variety of embedded devices like set-top boxes, and sits at the heart of the Android mobile phone operating system.

FOSS is a critical example because its success is technically measurable, and its adoption is a clear market signal of its superiority in many fields. But the success of FOSS is not unique. If in February 2001 someone had shown Jimmy Wales's new project, which consisted at the time of 900 stubs on the Web, stored on a web platform that allowed anyone to write and edit, but paid no one to do so, producing a product in which no one claimed exclusive proprietary rights, and claimed that within five years this product would be favorably compared to Britannica by the prestigious science magazine *Nature* and within less than a decade would put Microsoft's *Encarta* encyclopedia out of business, they would have been laughed out of the room. And yet she moves.

Wikipedia and FOSS have become the foundational narratives for explaining the remarkable transformation in the organization of information production that occurred in the past two decades. The basic dynamic is clear. For the first time since the Industrial Revolution, the most important inputs, into some of the most important economic sectors, of the most advanced economies in the world, are radically distributed in the population. The core capital resources necessary for these core economic production activities—computation, communications, electronic storage, and most recently sensors—have become widely available in the populations of all wealthy countries, as well as widely available in the middle and wealthier classes of emerging economies. What prevented automobile enthusiasts from competing with General Motors was the sheer capital cost barriers of an assembly line. That constraint does not prevent Wikipedians or FOSS developers from competing with Britannica or Microsoft, respectively. What we have seen in the past 15 years is the emergence of a third modality of production, what I have called *social production*. That is, people have always acted for social, emotional, or ideological reasons: talking to other people, taking photographs, singing, writing, helping each other move some furniture, or mobilizing for a common cause. The networked information economy has allowed some of these activities, driven by these same diverse motivations, to move from being extremely important socially but peripheral economically to occupying a significant space at the very heart of the most advanced economies in the world, at the very heart of the cultural and information production sectors, and increasingly at the heart of what it means to be citizens in a democratic society.

The emerging technological feasibility of social production generally, and peer production—the kind of large-scale collaboration of which Wikipedia is the most prominent example—more specifically, is interacting with the high rate of change and the increasing complexity of global innovation and production systems.

As complexity and the rate of change increase, twentieth-century organizational models are becoming too slow and too rigid to sense their environment, understand their limitations, to experiment with change, adapt to it, and adopt the innovations it necessitates.

Increasingly, in the business literature and practice, we see a shift toward a range of *open* innovation and production techniques—techniques that accept that you can never assume that the best person or resource set for any given job is one that you already employ or with whom you have a well-defined contractual relationship. Instead, we see firms and other organizations adopting a range of models that permit for more fluid flows of information, talent, and projects across and among organizations depending on the degree of uncertainty associated with their activities. Social production in the commons becomes the outer fringe of these open strategies; where experimentation under conditions of extreme uncertainty and high complexity can be done on models that require no clear appropriation model, and therefore can be carried on with very high rates of failure.

Technology is not destiny. The possibility of radically distributed production of information, knowledge, and culture is continuously competing with strong centralizing trends. Pervasive monitoring of consumer behavior and the development of behavioral advertising seek to use the same networked technologies to achieve much greater control by companies that sit on Big Data repositories of the consumption and payment patterns of consumers. As free software matures, its advantages are being recognized by firms, and its practices are adopted and subtly altered so as to moderate some of the more radical effects on industrial organization its emergence presented. Government surveillance has improved dramatically in the past several years, and similarly presents serious opportunities for increased control, rather than increased decentralization, emerging from the adoption of ubiquitous, networked computation. It is important not to read this essay as a utopia that claims to be a prediction. Rather, it is a characterization of one possible future among several, a future that is a reasonably good description of the near past and of a future that could, but will not necessarily, stabilize in the years to come.

Information is a very unusual economic good. If a furniture factory makes a chair and I want it, I can buy it from them. If you then want a chair as well, the factory has to buy more wood, spend more energy on cutting and shaping it, and pay a carpenter to make a second chair. But information goods are not like that. Once Tolstoy wrote *War and Peace*, it doesn't matter if three people or a million want to read it. Tolstoy need not spend one more second on writing the book (although the publisher needs to buy more paper, etc.). So too with the design of the lightbulb or a set of instructions on what the best way for surgeons to wash their hands before surgery. Once someone has figured out how to do something, everyone can learn it at the cost of duplication: the cost of printing another copy of the book; the cost of following the instructions to make a lightbulb. The information or innovation itself, once produced, is as Justice Louis Brandeis of the U.S. Supreme Court wrote a century ago, "free as the air to common use." Now, if artists, inventors, or writers all gave their work away for free, we would have to find some other system to allow them to make a living, otherwise they would starve. The most common way we do so today is to grant them limited rights to license their insights and creations: copyrights or patents. Economists have long known and written that when these copyrights and patents are asserted, and consumers have to pay for a book or a lightbulb more than the simple cost of manufacturing the next copy, the consumers will be using that information less than would be most socially efficient in the short term. This is what in economics we call a *public goods problem*. But we usually are willing to give up some of the efficiency in order to make sure that writers and inventors can make a living, and we try to make up for the inefficiency by also having information produced with government funding: primarily for scientific and other scholarly research and for the arts.

What the quirky nature of information means in the networked environment, however, is that if there is a group of volunteers who can get together and create something—a video, an encyclopedia, or a software program—without having to be paid directly for it, they have solved the public goods problem in a way that doesn't require them to close it up and charge for it.

More important than the availability of information at its efficient cost for consumers is its availability for subsequent innovators or creators.

Existing information is one of the most important resources used to create new information goods. Newspaper stories are made of fresh reporting on the background of prior articles; academic articles require those that preceded them. Books, movies, music are all influenced by prior works, incorporating elements, ideas, or references and always operating within the same cultural conversation. And software perhaps more than all of these is a field typified by incremental innovation.

What ubiquitous computers and networked communications did in the 1990s was reduce the cost of communications and copying to near zero. Given that the information itself, once produced, is a public good (its marginal cost is zero), and that there were now millions of people who could use their time in socially fun, meaningful, or productive ways, and who could also use massive repositories of existing materials to make their own new products, the Internet created a new urgency to recognizing the role of commons in market society.

The commons is a way of allocating access and use rights in resources that does not give anyone exclusive rights to exclude anyone else.

A city street is a commons: anyone who has a car or a bicycle can drive on the road; anyone who can walk or use a wheelchair can travel the sidewalks. No individual or company has the right to exclude anyone or charge them for access. From streets and highways, to canals and waterways, major shipping lanes and navigable rivers; basic scientific knowledge, mathematical algorithms, basic ideas; all these have been kept as commons in modern market economies because they provide enormous freedom of action to a wide range of productive behaviors—both economic and social.

By the middle of the first decade of the twenty-first century, commons-based information, knowledge, and cultural production was flourishing. Much of it was with implied or express permission. Software developers in particular led the way with the development of Free and Open Source Software (FOSS). The major legal innovation of FOSS was that the software always came with a license that made it legal for anyone to take the software and not only use it but develop it further and release their improvements back into the commons. Effectively FOSS developed in a world in which all software is born exclusive property and gave developers a way to share their software with the world, to dedicate it to the commons of software developers. Ever since the late 1990s, there has been a powerful movement among academics to do the same thing; and there is a large and growing number of people who share their music, videos, photos, and online writings under a Creative Commons license, which takes the idea developed in FOSS and applies it well beyond software to all information goods that would otherwise be subject to the exclusive rights of copyright. Beyond the formal ways in which users created commons by licensing, there was a tremendous amount of sharing that happened without any formal rights. Remix culture emerged by people taking materials, often from the formal, rights-based entertainment world but not exclusively, and creating their own versions which were, in turn, remixed by others. Implicit permissions coupled with a background culture of open sharing and rising rhetoric of openness and commons made these practices universally adopted. It is important to note here that when I refer to the rise of commons-based production, I am not including the purely consumption uses—in particular peer-to-peer file sharing for no reason other than consumption without payment. While these practices have been demonized beyond their real cost, they are not themselves properly seen as part of the emergence of commons-based production.

What the adoption of commons-based practices allowed was a massive increase in the number, range, and diversity of actors engaged in production, rather than consumption, of information, knowledge, and culture. Beginning in the late nineteenth century, a series of technologies and organizational practices combined to train three generations in the habits of passive reception. Starting with the large-scale mechanical presses and automated typesetting innovations that led to the large-circulation, professionalized, advertising-supported newspapers in the late nineteenth century, through radio and the pinnacle of this culture—television—the cost of being a producer of information increased, as did the reach of those who were in a position to produce at such high costs. These developments were complemented by recorded music and film, both of which reduced the need for more widely distributed (and less hyper-qualified) musicianship, storytelling, and acting capacities. For three generations, audiences lost the capacity to make their own music, perform their own games and entertainment, or pass information and opinion locally and informally, and replaced these with an increasing dependence on a professionalized, mostly commercial model of production: the industrial information economy.

What ubiquitous networked computation has done is to reverse the technical, material conditions that led to that highly asymmetric information production structure.

But had all existing information been exclusive property, and had the practices of the newly creative people who had been passive audiences before not adopted widespread, promiscuous mutual borrowing—a commons—the potential of the technology would likely have been narrower. Only those who could make from scratch would have been able to transition from consumers to producers; and much of the culture of remixing, quoting, and curating materials for one another would have been too expensive and transactions costs too high to allow it to flourish.

Peer Production

One important practice within the domain of commons-based production was the emergence of peer production: large-scale collaborative engagement by groups of individuals who come together to produce products more complex than they could have approached on their own. Wikipedia is the most widely visible and best-known example of peer production: a self-governing community of thousands of highly engaged contributors, and tens of thousands of individuals with lower but still active levels of participation. While it accounts for only a slice of the universe of social production in the networked commons, peer production is the most significant organizational innovation that has emerged from Internet-mediated social practice. Organizationally, it combines three core characteristics: (a) *decentralization of conception and execution* of problems and solutions, (b) *harnessing diverse motivations*, and (c) *separation of governance and management from property and contract*. First, unlike traditional organization, the question of what people should work on, what projects, subprojects, and intermediate steps, is not determined by an institutional hierarchy, but by self-selection and discussion among participants. Second, peer production allows many different people, with many different motivations, to collaborate on projects they share. This is particularly valuable in approaching problems that do not have a well-defined economic payoff. Such problems include those that are highly innovative and the likelihood of commercial success too low to fund participation, problems whose social value is high but whose nature prevents them from being delivered in a format that would support commercial appropriation, or because the sheer scope and diversity of human interest they seek to serve is too great for any single company to identify and serve on a paid model. The third aspect—the separation of management and governance from contract and property—is merely the organizational equivalent of the commons. Even within the organization or networked enterprise that is a peer-production community, the fact that the inputs and outputs are treated as commons allows the prior two elements—diversely motivated individuals—to act on the resource and project set without asking permission, because no property and contract rights need be negotiated to act.

Functionally, these components make peer-production practices highly adept at learning and experimentation, innovation, and adaptation in rapidly changing, persistently uncertain, and complex environments. Under high rates of technological innovation, and the high diversity of sources of uncertainty typical of early twenty-first-century global markets, the functional advantages of peer production have made it an effective organizational model in diverse domains. From free software through Wikipedia to video journalism, peer production plays a more significant role in the information production environment than predicted by standard models at the turn of the millennium.

The basic model of peer production simply focuses on minimizing transactions costs. Any production project requires the coordination of people, resources, and projects. In a classic perfect market, prices on each of these three components lead to matching. A firm expecting a given price for a project will be able to determine how much it can afford to pay for agents and resources for the project. The values of the competing projects, the value of the various people and resources to competing projects, will determine the market-clearing price for any given resource or person, and in turn will decide whether, when, and at what quality the project can be pursued given the market valuation of its output. Ronald Coase's (1937) highly influential theory of the firm posited that for some resources, people, and projects, the cost of market clearance—finding the right people and resources, contracting for them, overcoming bargaining impasses, and so forth—would be so high that it is more efficient to have managers simply assign people and resources to projects, rather than running continuous auctions for how to get more paper to the printer on the third-floor suite. That is why we have firms.

Once one understands that social exchange is also a transactional framework widely used for a broad range of goods and services it is trivial to expand the classic transactions costs theory of the firm to social exchange networks. A market model of fixing a paper jam on the third-floor printer would be one where the person at the desk whose printer fails goes online, finds a printer tech support service, and pays them to come fix the printer. A managerial model would be one where it turns out to be more efficient for a manager to appoint a logistics person, who hires a tech support team once and then not every person who has a technical program needs to go to the market and run a search and service auction. Instead, the person on the third floor with the broken printer knows that all they need to is make a call to tech support. A social transactional model would posit the problem at home. The person with the broken printer walks over to their technology savvy neighbor and asks for help, which the neighbor gives willingly. Next week, maybe the first neighbor will reciprocate by watering the techie neighbor's plants when he is away at a conference. There is no systematic reason why the transactions costs model cannot apply seamlessly to social exchange, which we use all the time in our everyday life without thinking about it. We have long used it extensively to solve economic problems with highly localized characteristics, from childcare and cooking, through other social insurance concerns against relatively minor disruption, to mundane things like short-distance moving of furniture within a home or a short-distance move between homes. But for most problems of economic significance, the motivations were too weak and the transactions costs too high to allow these networks to play a truly significant economic role. Ubiquitous networked communications and the unique properties of information as an economic good make that transactional framework more widely applicable to sophisticated economic production problems than was feasible during the earlier industrial era.

Complexity, Uncertainty, and Open Innovation

The simple transactions cost model of peer production can be supplemented with a more specific view of information and learning that explains why distributed innovation, creativity, or problem solving would have a transactions costs advantage over proprietary and managed systems. A more complete explanation requires a clearer model of how organizations learn. Both managerial control and price clearance require formalization of descriptions of resources, people (that is, their diverse capabilities and availabilities for a given project at a given juncture/time), and projects into units capable of transmission through the communications system these organizational models represent. The organizational and transactions costs associated with perfectly defining price, or perfectly defining for managerial assessment and decision making, over every potential resource or person that somewhat diverges from its neighbor in context and time, require abstraction, generalization, and standardization of the characteristics of the resources, people, and projects. Knowing what John or Jane specifically are able to do, given their hobbies or what they read last week, is an overwhelming information problem for a centralized managerial system, and is also an extremely difficult problem for a system that has to translate these capabilities into standardized prices—wages offered and demanded. Instead, what we see is both markets and organizations abstracting from the particularities of the individuals and the discrete resources to relatively stable markers of classes or types of resources—say, setting salaries based on education level or seniority. In that abstraction process, both administrative descriptions and prices are what technologists dealing in communications systems call *lossy* media: the formalization strips information out of the real-world characteristics of the relevant resources and projects. The lost information, in turn, leads systems whose functioning depends on discarding that information to underperform relative to systems able to bring a more refined fit of potential resources and agents to better-defined projects.

A global, networked economy in which there is enormous investment in innovation and in which innovation in one place can be used to compete in most other places is one in which complexity and uncertainty are increasing dramatically and at a rapid pace.

Complexity and uncertainty, in turn, make the information problem of matching people, resources, and projects less amenable to managerial or price-based solutions. Complexity and uncertainty put pressure on both neoclassical markets and the new institutional models of firms because the actual properties of resources, people, and projects are highly diverse and interconnected; and the interactions among them are complex, in the sense that small differences in initial conditions or perturbations over time can significantly change the qualities of the interactions and outcomes at the system level. These lead to the known phenomenon of path dependence, both technological and institutional. That is, divergence from efficient and effective practice can persist in the face of systematic, observed inefficiency. The fine-grained, diverse qualities of people, projects, and resources, and the relatively significant divergences that can occur because of relatively fine-grained differences in input combinations or local interactions, mean that it is impossible to abstract and generalize the process into communications units available for managerial decision or price clearance without significant loss of information, control, and, ultimately, effectiveness.

Note that *knowledge* and *learning* in the presence of complexity and uncertainty refers to more than a classic notion of innovation, such as creating a new way of doing something that was impossible to do before. Importantly, it also includes problem solving, or iterative improvement in how something is done given persistent absence of complete knowledge about the problem and the solution. If creating the WWW or writable web software like Wiki was *innovation* on a commons-based model, Wikipedia's organizational innovation is in problem solving more than innovation: how to maintain quality contributions together with potentially limitless expansion, a problem that scarcity absolved Britannica from solving. User-generated content similarly solves for serving more diverse tastes than a more centralized system can; user-created restaurant or hotel accommodations solve a complexity-in-implementation problem with highly diverse sites to review and tastes of people who may want to use the places reviewed. In each case, the peer approach allowed the organizations to explore a space of highly diverse interests and tastes that was too costly for more traditional organizations to explore.

In this model, a critical part of the advantage of peer production incorporates the importance of knowledge that you simply cannot contract for or manage well: either because it is tacit knowledge, or because the number and diversity of people with knowledge that needs to be brought to bear on an implementation problem is too great to contract for. Tacit knowledge is knowledge people possess, but in a form that they cannot communicate. Once you learn how to ride a bicycle, you know how to do so. Yet if you were to sit down and write a detailed memorandum, your reader would not know how to ride a bicycle. It is increasingly clear that tacit knowledge is critical in actual human systems. And peer production allows people to deploy their tacit knowledge directly, without losing much of it in the effort to translate it into the communicable form (an effort as futile as teaching how to ride a bike by writing a memo) necessary for decision making through prices or managerial hierarchies. Where knowledge is explicit, but highly distributed in forms that need to be collated to be effective, the barrier is a simple transactions costs problem. A system that allows agents to explore their environment for problems and solutions, experiment, learn, and iterate on solutions and their refinement without requiring intermediate formalizations to permit and fund the process will have an advantage over a system that does require those formalizations; and that advantage will grow as the uncertainty of what path to follow, who is best situated to follow it, and what class of solution approaches are most promising becomes less clearly defined.

Peer production more generally, in particular when it relies on commons—that is, on symmetrical access privileges (with or without use rules) to the resource without transaction—allows (a) diverse people, irrespective of organizational affiliation or property/contract nexus to a given resource or project, (b) dynamically to assess and reassess the available resources, projects, and potential collaborators, and (c) to self-assign to projects and collaborations. By leaving all these elements of the organization of a project to self-organization dynamics, peer production overcomes the lossiness of markets and bureaucracies, whether firm or governmental. It does so, of course, at the expense of incurring new kinds of coordination and self-organization costs. Where the physical capital requirements of a project are either very low, or capable of fulfillment by utilizing pre-existing distributed capital endowments (like personally owned computers), where the project is susceptible to modularization for incremental production pursued by diverse participants, and where the diversity gain from harnessing a wide range of experience, talent, insight, and creativity in innovation, quality, speed, or precision of connecting outputs to demand is high, peer production can emerge and outperform markets and hierarchies.

The benefits of peer production are sufficient that the practice has been widely adopted by firms and other more traditional organizations, including governments. In one study, for example, Josh Lerner and Mark Schankerman (2010) documented that 40 percent of commercial software firms develop some FOSS software. In another book, Charles Schweik and Robert English (2012) laid out the institutional motivations of both firms and governments to adopt these models. In these cases, the access to the diverse developer body and the openness of standards outweighs, for these organizations, the cost of lost appropriability. But the effect holds beyond software. Firms like Yelp or TripAdvisor succeeded against more established competitors in their businesses—restaurant reviews and travel guides, respectively—by building sophisticated platforms that allowed a much more diverse range of nonprofessionals to identify and review their respective targets. Again, in both cases, firms that built platforms for peer production outperformed firms that used more traditional managerial and contract-based approaches.

Commons-based production and peer production are edge cases of a broader range of openness strategies that trade off the freedom to operate that typifies these two approaches and the manageability and appropriability that many more traditional organizations seek to preserve. Some firms are increasingly using competitions and prizes, such as Pfizer's use of the Innocentive system, to diversify the range of people who work on their problems, without ceding proprietary or contractual control over the project. The prize model allows a firm to specify with greater or lesser degree of generality the problem they are trying to solve, place it on a platform that manages the competition, and allows anyone, from anywhere, to submit solutions. The firm then still gets to select its preferred solution and retain control, while paying anyone who is willing to work on the problem and does so successfully. This approach offers firms the core benefit of being able to attract a person whom the firm could never have identified through its own networks to work on a problem the firm has identified; what it loses is the diagnostic power of having many diverse people looking at the resource and project space in which the firm is situated, and identifying the potential for a new project, or diagnosing a problem the firm does not yet know it has. For that, more thoroughly open strategies are necessary.

Another increasingly critical strategic choice of many firms is participation in networks of firms engaging in a range of open collaborative innovation practices. *Open collaborative innovation* is a term used to describe a set of productive practices developed by firms operating in complex product and innovation-rich markets. These practices share with peer production the recognition that the smartest and best people to solve any given problem are unlikely to work in a single firm, the firm facing the challenge, and that models of innovation and problem solving that allow diverse people, from diverse settings, to work collaboratively on the problem will lead to better outcomes than production models that enforce strict boundaries at the edge of the firm and do not allow collaboration based on fit of person to task rather than based on employment contract and ownership of the problem. Firms might share employees, designs, and collocate employees for extensive periods in a project. They are likely to share intellectual property in the project, or often adopt open standards models that assure each that neither can defect from the collaborative arrangement. Legal scholars Ron Gilson, Hal Scott, and Charles Sabel (2008, 2010) have documented how these approaches have developed looser, more open contractual models than traditional supply contracts created in the past, a looseness that replicates some of the benefits of peer production and commons-based production that removes contractual encumbrances altogether. Open collaborative practice in networks of firms trades off the benefits of a fully open-to-the-world project definition that peer production or prize systems have, in exchange for having a more manageable set of people, resources, and projects to work with.

A final model of openness that mixes commons with property is the entrepreneurial model at the edge of academia and business. This is the model that typifies Silicon Valley, Cambridge, Massachusetts, and many self-consciously designed "innovation clusters" anchored around universities. On one side of this academia/entrepreneurship boundary sits the academic model that allows for investment in highly uncertain innovation at the very boundaries of science. The level of uncertainty and high social returns is such, that the initial funding for the work comes from government funding and is not intended to be captured commercially. The status-based economy of academia, the public funding, and the publication and presentation norms of academic science contribute both to experimentation and to wide dissemination of the findings under terms that allow others to build on and develop the work. They are the commons side of the interface. This, at least, is the idealized model, one that with declining research budgets and an increasing focus of universities on technology transfer revenues seems far from perfectly true. On the other side of the university-centered innovation cluster model are entrepreneurial firms: small, agile, and highly disposable. These allow for high-risk, high-reward investment models, which can experiment, prototype, adopt, and fail or grow on a much more rapid basis than traditional firms. They also provide a membrane for academics and young academic trainees, recent doctoral or postdoctoral students, to cycle out of the academic and into the market system, and back. Some of the larger firms with roots in this model, like Microsoft, Google, or Yahoo, have created research centers that seem to honor the academic model of free exploration to at least as great a degree as the more budget-constrained academic programs do, and increasingly people collaborate across this membrane. These models, in particular in the information technology side and less so in the biotechnology side, include much greater fidelity to commons-based models, free publication, free exchange with individuals without any contractual relations than do the open collaborative innovation models, and in turn they give up a degree of control and manageability.

What is important to understand about all these models is that they are diverse strategies for dealing with the same core set of challenges that increased complexity and uncertainty present. They all mark different points in a solution space that trades off manageability, effectiveness, and crisp definition of inputs, outputs, and processes for ease of experimentation, freedom to operate without constraint and permission processes, and the harnessing of diverse motivations, including in particular those that do not require translation into monetary terms that are themselves lossy.

Commons-based practices and open innovation offer freedom to operate in the face of the extreme challenges of planning under uncertainty and complexity. They provide an evolutionary model, typified by repeated experimentation, failure and survival, and adoption of successful adaptation rather than the more traditional, engineering-style approaches to building

optimized systems with well-understood responses to well-behaved and reasonably predictable change. This model is built on experimentation and
adaptation to a highly uncertain and changing environment, emphasizing
innovation, resilience, and robustness over efficiency.

A decade ago, Wikipedia or FOSS were widely treated in mainstream
economics and business circles as mere curiosities. Anyone who continues
to think of them in these terms in the middle of the second decade of the
twenty-first century does so at their own peril. Their success represents a
core challenge to how we have thought about property and contract, organization theory and management over the past 150 years. Understanding why
they have succeeded and what their particular strengths and limitations
are has become indispensable for anyone who thinks about organizations
in a networked information economy.

References

Coase, Ronald.
"The Nature of the Firm."
  Economica 4, no. 16 (1937):
  386–405.

Gilson, Ronald J., Charles F.
Sabel. and Robert E. Scott.
"Contracting for Innovation:
  Vertical Disintegration and
  Interfirm Collaboration."
  November 19, 2008. *Columbia
  Law Review* 109, no. 3 (April
  2009); Columbia Law and
  Economics Working Paper
  No. 340; ECGI - Law Working
  Paper No. 118/2009. http://
  ssrn.com/abstract=1304283
———. "Braiding: The Interaction
  of Formal and Informal
  Contracting in Theory,
  Practice and Doctrine."
  Stanford Law and Economics
  Olin Working Paper No. 389;
  Columbia Law and Economics
  Working Paper No. 367.
  January 11, 2010. http://ssrn.
  com/abstract=1535575 or
  http://dx.doi.org/10.2139/
  ssrn.1535575

Lerner, Josh, and Mark
Schankerman.
*The Comingled Code: Open Source
  and Economic Development*.
  Cambridge, MA: MIT Press,
  2010.

Schweik, Charles M., and Robert
C. English.
*Internet Success: A Study of
  Open-Source Software
  Commons*. Cambridge, MA:
  MIT Press, 2012.

How Is the Internet Changing the Way We Work?

Thomas W. Malone

Patrick J. McGovern Professor of Management, MIT Sloan School of Management

and Director of the MIT Center for Collective Intelligence

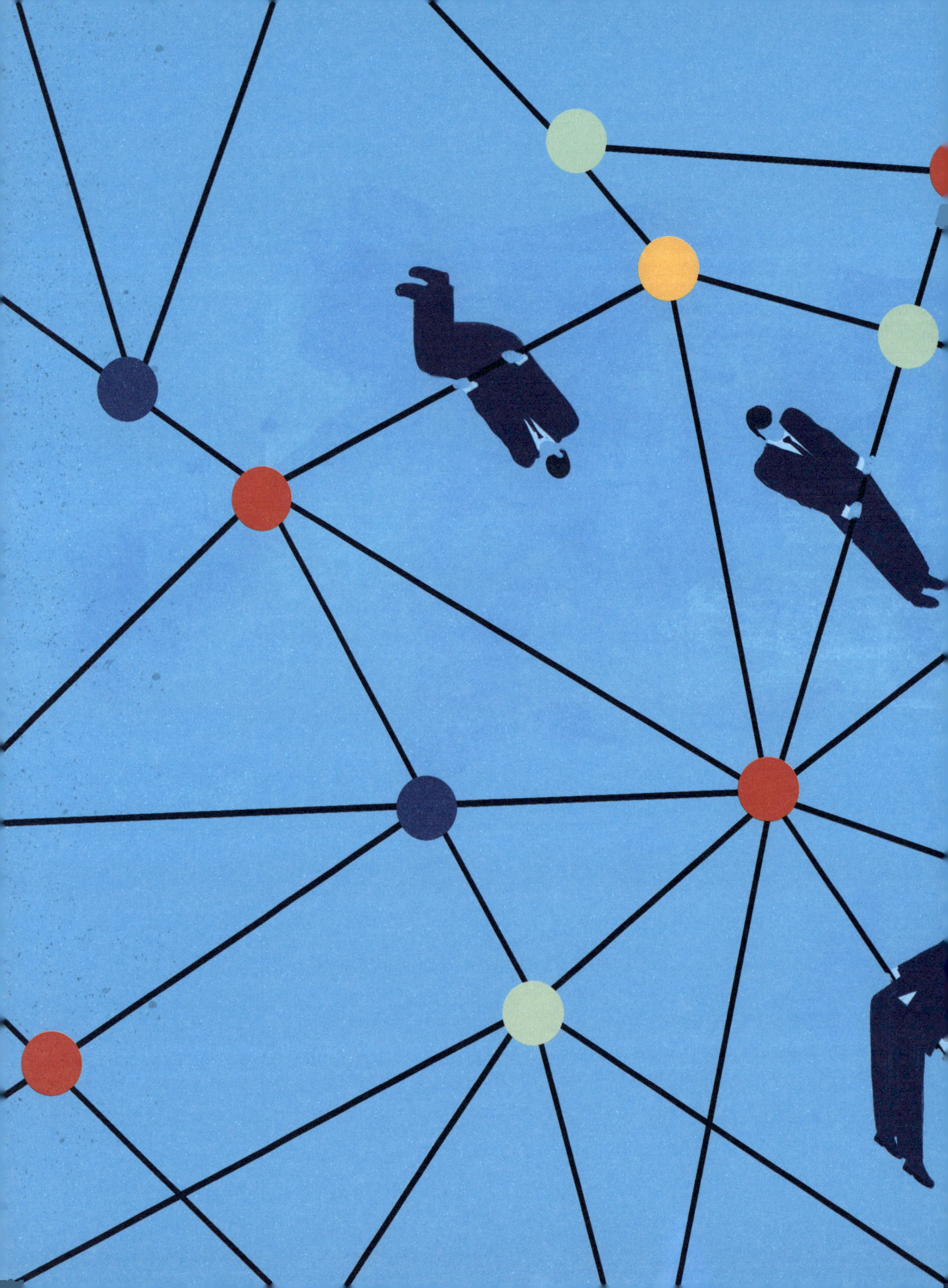

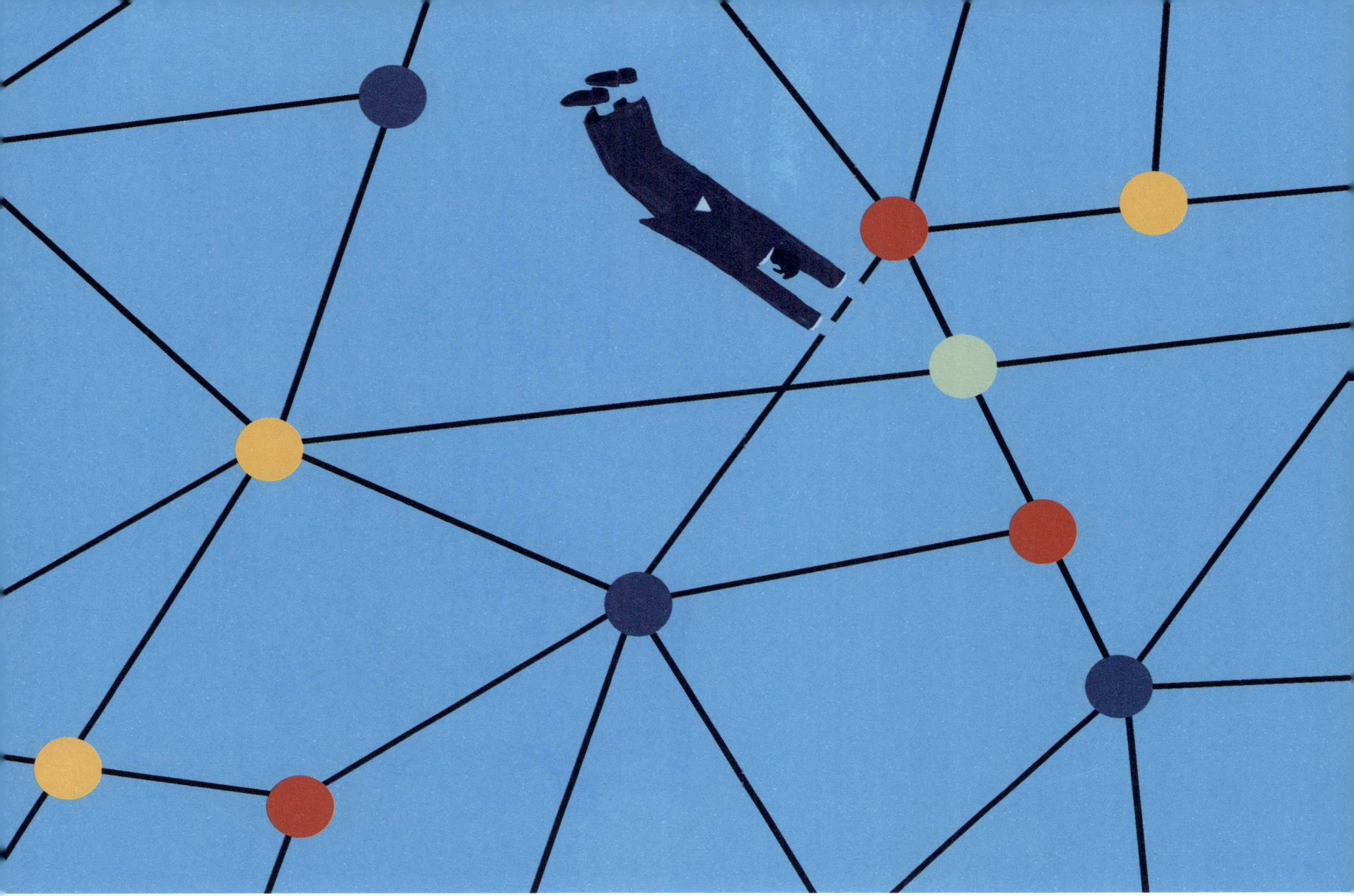

Thomas W. Malone

cci.mit.edu/malone

Illustration
Emiliano Ponzi

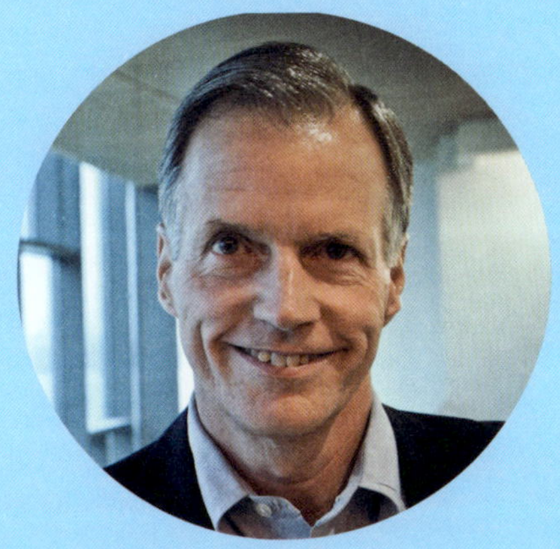

Thomas W. Malone is the Patrick J. McGovern Professor of Management at the MIT Sloan School of Management and the founding director of the MIT Center for Collective Intelligence. He was also the founder and director of the MIT Center for Coordination Science and one of the two founding co-directors of the MIT Initiative on "Inventing the Organizations of the 21st Century." In 2004 he summarized two decades of his groundbreaking research on how work can be organized in new ways to take advantage of the possibilities provided by information technology in the critically acclaimed book *The Future of Work* (translated into six languages). He has published over 100 articles, research papers, and book chapters, and is also an inventor with 11 patents and the co-editor of three books: *Coordination Theory and Collaboration Technology* (Psychology Press, 2001), *Inventing the Organizations of the 21st Century* (MIT Press, 2003), and *Organizing Business Knowledge: The MIT Process Handbook* (MIT Press, 2003). In 2012, he received an honorary doctorate from the University of Zurich. He was cofounder of three software companies and has consulted and served as a board member for a number of other organizations. He speaks frequently for business audiences around the world and is often quoted in the media. Before joining MIT in 1983, he was a research scientist at the Xerox Palo Alto Research Center (PARC). He has a BA in Mathematical Sciences from Rice University, an MS in Engineering-Economic Systems from Stanford University, and a PhD in Cognitive and Social Psychology from Stanford University.

Sites and services that have changed my life
E-mail
google.com
wikipedia.com
climatecolab.org

Imagine you are a shopkeeper, living somewhere in Spain, in 1795. You no longer believe, as did the ancient Egyptians, that your king, Carlos IV, is literally a god, living on earth. But you still believe that he has a *divine right* to rule over you. You can't imagine any country being governed well without a king who is responsible for the protection and control of his subjects.

You have heard of the strange rebellion in North America where the British colonists claimed that they could govern themselves without any king at all. You've also heard about the recent violent bloodshed in France where a group of so-called revolutionaries killed their king, replaced the government, and destroyed, almost overnight, so many good things. But these experiments seem to you like profound mistakes, bound to fail.

It just doesn't make sense to say—as these democratic revolutionaries do—that people could ever really *govern themselves.* That's a contradiction in terms, like saying that children could raise themselves or farm animals could run a farm. People can try it, you think, but it certainly couldn't work as well as a wise and just king.

Well, of course, today we know what happened to those strange democratic experiments. They worked. Really well. Over the past two hundred years those democratic ideas have triumphed in Europe, America, and many other parts of the world. While democratic governments are not everywhere in the world today, their economic, political, and military successes have far surpassed what almost anyone would have predicted in the late 1700s. And, perhaps more importantly, our whole way of thinking about many things—the role of government, the rights of people, the importance of public opinion—has profoundly changed, even in countries that don't themselves have democratic governments.

Now, we are in the early stages of another revolution—a revolution in business—that may ultimately be as profound as the democratic revolution in government. Like the democratic revolution, the revolution in business will lead to a transformation in our thinking about control: Where does power come from? Who should be in control? Who is responsible?

And, once again, the result of this revolution will be a world where people have more freedom. A world in which power and control in business are spread more widely than our industrial age ancestors would have ever thought possible. A world in which more and more people are at the *center* of their own organizations.

In this new world of business, lots of highly connected individuals will each make their own decisions using information from many other places. In fact, this revolution is now possible because new information technologies make it feasible—on a scale never before possible in human history—for vastly more people to have the information they need to make well-informed choices.

But the real impetus for this revolution will not come from these new technologies. It will come from our own human desires—our desires for economic efficiency and flexibility, certainly, but also our desires for non-economic values like personal satisfaction and fulfillment.

In other words, one of the most important drivers of the revolution is this: for the first time in history, new technologies allow us to have the economic benefits of large organizations— like economies of scale and knowledge—without giving up the human benefits of small ones—like freedom, creativity, motivation, and flexibility.

This revolution has already begun. We saw its harbingers in the final decades of the twentieth century in talk about *empowering* workers, *outsourcing* almost everything, creating *networked* or *virtual* corporations. We saw it in the premature—but partly correct—enthusiasm for new ways of doing business in the *dot.com* bubble and in the slogan that "the Internet changes everything." We see it all around us today in the increasing amount of choice many people have in how they do their work.

But, like the loyal subjects of King Carlos IV in 1795, most of us don't yet begin to understand how far-reaching these changes may eventually be. We still assume, without even really thinking about it, that someone always needs to be *responsible* and *accountable* in business. We assume that the managers of well-run companies should always be *in control* of what's happening. We assume that power should always come from the *top* of an organization and be delegated *down.*

But the underlying technological and economic forces all around us today are making these beliefs less useful. New ways of organizing work are now becoming possible. Management is changing. And that gives all of us more choices in how we shape the world that is being created.

What Will These New Ways of Organizing Work Look Like?

There's a technical term for the kind of organization this revolution will make more common. The word is *decentralized.* But most people have a very limited view of what this word means. If you're like many people in business today, when you hear the word *decentralized*, you assume that it means delegating more power to lower-level managers inside traditional organizations. It might mean, for instance, letting divisional vice-presidents make product strategy decisions that used to be made by the CEO.

But this limited kind of decentralization barely scratches the surface of what's possible. Let's define decentralization as the *participation of people in making the decisions that matter to them*. In this sense, decentralization means roughly the same thing as *freedom.* Decentralized organizations are those where more people have more freedom. And from this point of view, as you can see in figure 1, there's a much wider range of possibilities for decentralization.

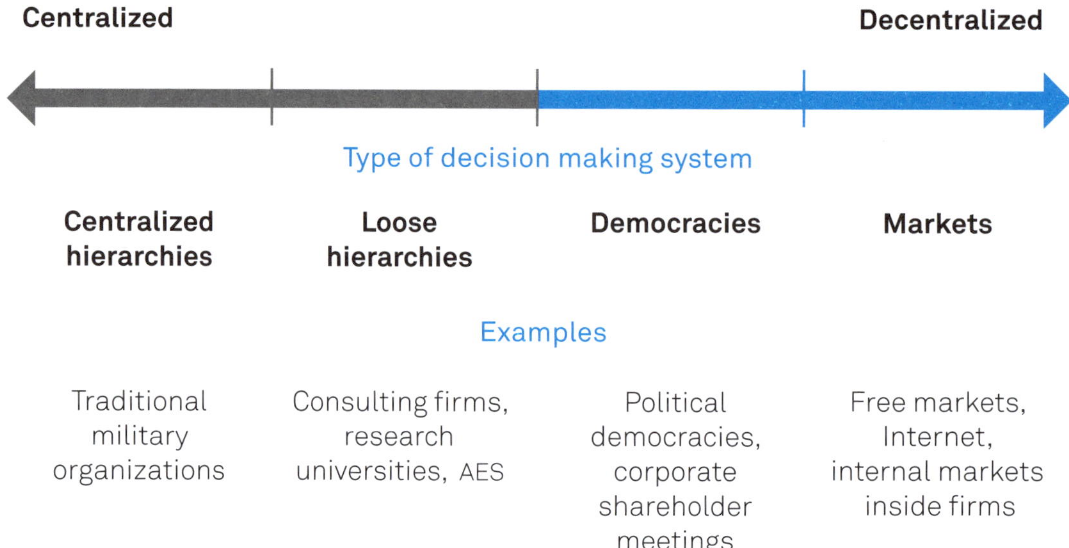

Fig. 1
The decentralization continuum.
Organizations can be placed on a continuum based how much people participate in making decisions that matter to them.

At the far left of the continuum are highly centralized organizations. If all important decisions are made by high-level centralized decision-makers (as in traditional military organizations, for instance), then the organization is highly centralized. The rest of the continuum shows three important kinds of decision-making structures where people have more freedom: *loose hierarchies*, *democracies*, and *markets*. As you progress along the continuum, from loose hierarchies to democracies to markets, the amount of freedom people have in decision-making increases.

For example, some companies today already have *loose hierarchies* where they delegate huge amounts of decision-making authority to very low levels in their organization. Many management consulting firms, for instance, let the individual partners and consultants on a project make almost all operational decisions about the project. And AES Corp., one of the world's largest electric power producers, has let very low-level workers make critical multimillion-dollar decisions about things like acquiring new subsidiaries. In an even more extreme example, one of the most important computer operating systems in the world today—Linux—was written by a loosely coordinated hierarchy of thousands of volunteer computer programmers all over the world.

When most people think about decentralization, they stop at this point—delegating lots of decisions to lower levels in hierarchies. But what if power didn't get *delegated* to lower levels? What if, instead, it originated there? How much energy and creativity might it be possible to unlock if everyone in an organization felt they were *in control?*

The right half of the continuum shows the possibilities for what this more extreme kind of freedom can look like in business. For example, some businesses already act like miniature democracies where decisions are made by voting. Many good managers today, for instance, informally poll their employees about key decisions, and some companies do more formal polling of employees for many purposes. In a few cases, like the cooperative Mondragon Corporation in Spain, the workers own the company and, therefore, can elect the equivalent of a board of directors and vote on other key issues. What if companies begin to take this notion of democratic decision-making even more seriously? What if, for instance, professional partnerships and other worker-owned businesses let workers elect (and fire) their own managers at every level, not just at the top? And what if these employee-owners could vote on any other key questions on which they wanted to express opinions?

The most extreme kind of business freedom occurs in markets because, in markets, no one is bound by a decision to which he or she doesn't agree. In a pure market, for instance, no one *on top* delegates decisions about what to buy and sell to the different players in the market. Instead, all the individual buyers and sellers make their own mutual agreements, subject only to their own financial constraints, their abilities, and the overall rules of the market.

For instance, companies can use this form of organization by outsourcing things they used to do inside. Many companies today are already outsourcing all kinds of things, from manufacturing, to sales, to human resource management. In some cases, large companies may not even need to exist in the first place. Flexible webs of small companies or even temporary combinations of electronically connected freelancers ("e-lancers") can sometimes do the same things more effectively. This way of organizing is already common in the film industry, for example, where a producer, a director, actors, cinematographers, and others come together for the purpose of making one movie and then disband and rearrange in different combinations to make others.

In other cases, you can get many of the benefits of markets *inside* the boundaries of large companies. For example, some companies today are beginning to experiment with micro-level *internal markets* where employees of the company *buy* and *sell* things among themselves, and their internal trading is just another way of allocating resources for the company as a whole. One semiconductor company, for instance, has looked at letting individual salespeople and plant managers *buy* and *sell* individual products directly to each other in an internal electronic market. This gives the plants very immediate and dynamic feedback about which products to make each day, and it helps the salespeople continually set prices for external customers.

To understand why decentralized things like these are likely to happen more often in the future, you need to understand what leads to centralization and decentralization in the first place.

Why Is This Happening?

Of course, there are many factors that affect how and where decisions are made in a business, or for that matter, in any organization. Here are just a few of the factors that sometimes matter: Who already has the information needed to make good decisions? Who already has the power to make the decisions, and whom do they trust to make decisions on their behalf? What specific individuals are potential decision makers, and what are their capabilities and motivations? What are the cultural assumptions in the company and its country about what kinds of people should make decisions? All these factors vary widely from situation to situation, but in general, they aren't changing dramatically in any single direction overall.

There is, however, another factor that affects where decisions are made in businesses, and this factor is changing dramatically in the same direction almost everywhere. In fact, when we look back carefully at the history of humanity, we can see that this very same factor has been implicated, time after time, in some of the most important historical changes in where decisions were made, not just in businesses, but in human societies, too.

What could this factor possibly be?

It's the *cost of communication*.

When the only form of communication was face-to-face conversation, our distant hunting and gathering ancestors organized themselves in small, egalitarian, decentralized groups called bands. Over many millennia, as hunting and gathering gave way to agriculture, and as our ancestors learned to communicate over long distances more cheaply by writing, they were able to form larger and larger societies ruled by kings, emperors, and other centralized rulers (see fig. 2). These larger societies had many economic and military advantages over the hunting and gathering bands, but their members had to give up some of their freedom to get these benefits.

Then, only a few hundred years ago, our ancestors invented a new communication technology, the printing press, which reduced even further the

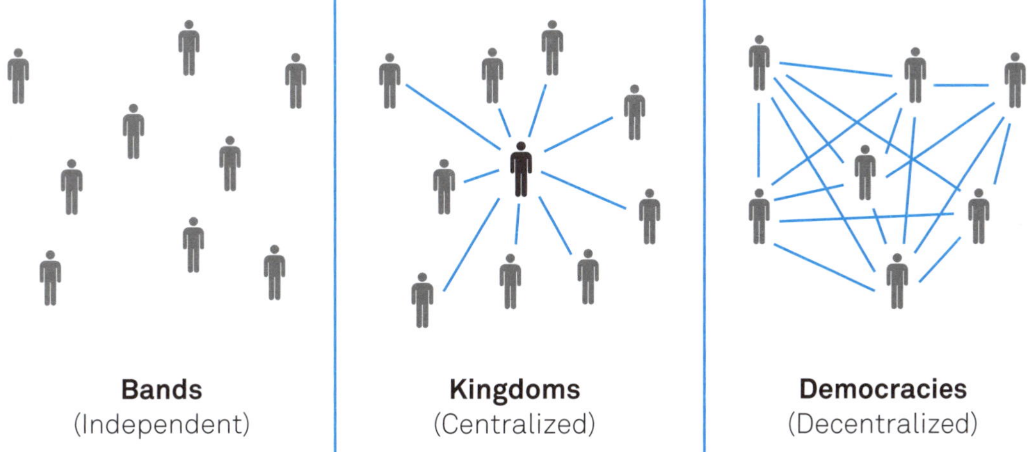

Fig. 2
The major ways human societies have been organized throughout history reveal a remarkably simple pattern that foreshadows how businesses are changing now.

costs of communicating to large numbers of people. This time, the declining costs of communication allowed our ancestors to reverse their millennia-long march toward greater centralization. Instead, soon after the printing press came into wide use, the democratic revolution began. Then, ordinary people—who could now be much better informed about political matters—came to have more say in their own government than they had usually had in all the millennia since our hunting and gathering days.

Was the declining cost of communication the only factor that caused all these societal changes? Of course not. Each of these changes arose from complex combinations of forces involving many other factors as well. For instance, our human desires for individual freedom—and for the motivation and flexibility that often accompany individual freedom—were critical. But the declining costs of communication allowed by new *information technologies* like writing and printing played a key role in *enabling* each of these changes. And it is certainly interesting, to say the least, that the very same underlying factor is implicated in such diverse and important changes in human societies as the rise of kingdoms and the rise of democracies.

Even more remarkable still is the fact that this very same pattern appears to be repeating itself now—at a much faster rate—in the history of business organizations as well!

Throughout most of human history, up until the 1800s, most businesses were organized as small, local, often family affairs, similar in many ways to the bands of our hunting and gathering ancestors. But by the 1900s, new communication technologies like telegraph, telephone, typewriters, and carbon paper finally provided enough communication capacity to allow businesses to grow and centralize on a large scale like governments had begun to do many millennia earlier (see fig. 3). By taking advantage of economies of scale and knowledge, these large business *kingdoms* were able to achieve an unprecedented level of material prosperity.

As a result of this massive—and successful—move toward centralization of business in the twentieth century, many of us still unconsciously associate success in business with bigness and centralization. But in order to achieve these economic benefits of bigness, many of the individual workers in these large companies had to give up some of the freedom and flexibility they had in the farms and small businesses of the previous era.

It's obvious that new information technologies can still be used to continue this trend—to keep creating ever-larger and more centralized business kingdoms. And some of the important business changes in the years to come will still be continuations of this previous trend—integrating larger and larger groups of people to take advantage of economies of scale or knowledge.

But just as the rise of democracies reversed a trend toward centralization in societies that had lasted for millennia, we are now beginning to see signs of a similar reversal in business.

With new technologies like e-mail, instant messaging, and the Internet, it's now becoming economically feasible—for the first time in human history—to give huge numbers of people the information they need to make more choices for themselves.

In the places where this makes economic sense, that means many more people can have the kinds of freedom and flexibility in business that used

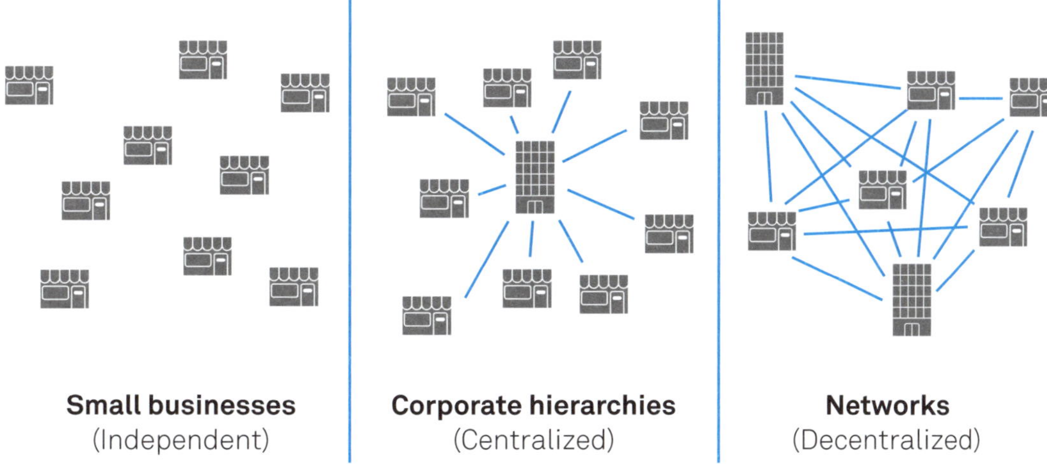

Fig. 3
The major changes in how businesses were organized through history echo similar changes in the ways societies were organized.

to be common only in small organizations. When people are making their own decisions, for instance, rather than just following orders, they are often more dedicated, more creative, and more innovative.

Decentralized businesses can usually be more flexible, too—both with their customers and with their own workers. Because they give people more choices, decentralized businesses just plain have a lot more chances to give people the things they really want. In other words, they give people more freedom.

But these new decentralized businesses don't have the limitations that small, isolated businesses did in the past. Because these new organizations have access to the best information available anywhere in the world, they can also benefit from many of the advantages of large organizations, too. If there are economies of scale in parts of their business, for instance, they can find the best suppliers in the world for those things. They can find customers all over the world, and they can use electronic reputation systems to establish credibility with potential customers who've never heard of them. And if someone on the other side of the globe has figured out how to do something better, they can learn from that experience, too.

Of course, this kind of decentralization doesn't work well in all situations. In some places, for instance, like making certain kinds of semiconductors, the critical factors in business success are just economies of scale. And, in these places, we should expect cheaper communication to lead to more centralization in order to take advantage of these economies of scale.

But in our increasingly knowledge-based and innovation-driven economy, the critical factors in business success are often precisely the same as the benefits of decentralized decision making: motivation, creativity, flexibility, and innovation.

So even though it won't happen everywhere, we should expect this change to more decentralized decision-making to happen in more and more parts of our economy over the coming decades.

Even where decentralization is desirable, however, the changes won't all happen overnight. Just as the democratic transformation of societies evolved in fits and starts over a period of centuries, these changes in business will take decades to play out fully. And every time there is a setback in one place, or a failure to move forward somewhere else, there will be people who say that things aren't going to change after all. When people over-invested in e-business and the speculative *new economy* bubble burst, for instance, many people thought that the *old economy* had won, and we were going back to business as usual.

But the relentless improvements in the cost of communication, year after year, and decade after decade, mean that there will continue to be more and more opportunities for decentralization. These fundamental changes in the economics of communication and decision-making will continue working their way through our economy, company after company, and industry after industry, for many, many years to come.

What Does This Mean for You?

If decentralization becomes desirable in more and more places in business, then we'll need to manage in new ways. But no matter how much we talk about new kinds of management, most of us still have—deep in our minds—models of management based on the classic centralized philosophy of *command and control.* To be successful in the world we're entering, you'll need a new—broader—set of mental models. While these new models shouldn't exclude the possibility of commanding and controlling, they need to also encompass a much wider range of possibilities—both centralized and decentralized.

Here's one way of summarizing this new perspective: we need to move from thinking about *command and control* to *coordinate and cultivate.* For example, when you *coordinate*, you organize work so that good things happen, whether you are *in control* or not. Some kinds of coordination are centralized; others are decentralized. But either way, coordinating focuses on the *activities* that need to be done and the relationships among them.

When you *cultivate*, you bring out the best in a situation by the right combination of controlling and letting go. Sometimes, for example, you need to give people top-down commands, but sometimes you just need to help them find and develop their own natural strengths. Good cultivation, therefore, involves finding the right balance between centralized and decentralized control. In fact, sometimes—paradoxically—the best way to gain power is to give it away.

In both these cases, coordinating and cultivating are not the *opposites* of commanding and controlling; they are the *supersets*. That is, they include the whole range of possibilities from completely centralized to completely decentralized.

And that is a key part of how the world of management is changing: to be an effective manager in the world we're entering, you can't be *stuck* in a centralized mindset. You need to be able to move flexibly back and forth on the decentralization continuum as the situation demands. Since most of us already understand centralization pretty well, the thing that's new—the thing we need to understand better—is decentralization.

The Choices

Like the democratic revolution that preceded it, the business revolution we have entered is a time of dramatic change in the economies, the organizations, and the cultural assumptions of our society. And, as in any time of dramatic change, small choices can often have big effects. Whether you participate in events as significant as writing the American Declaration of Independence or whether you just make lots of daily decisions about what work to do and how to do it, you will be shaping the world in which we and our descendants will live for the rest of this century.

If you choose to, you can use the new possibilities enabled by information technology to help create a world that is both more economically efficient and more flexible than has ever before been possible in human history. There are many powerful economic forces that will lead us to do just that, to combine the economic benefits of bigness—like global scale and diverse knowledge—with the human benefits of smallness—like flex-ibility, creativity, and motivation.

But that isn't the end of the possibilities these new technologies provide. Because more people will have more choices, they can bring more of their own values into business. And that means you can put a broader range of your human values, not just your economic ones, at the center of your thinking about business.

In other words, you can—if you choose—use your work to help create a world that is not just richer, but also a world that is better.

That is the choice before you.

Communication and Culture

The Internet: Changing the Language

David Crystal

Honorary Professor of Linguistics, Bangor University

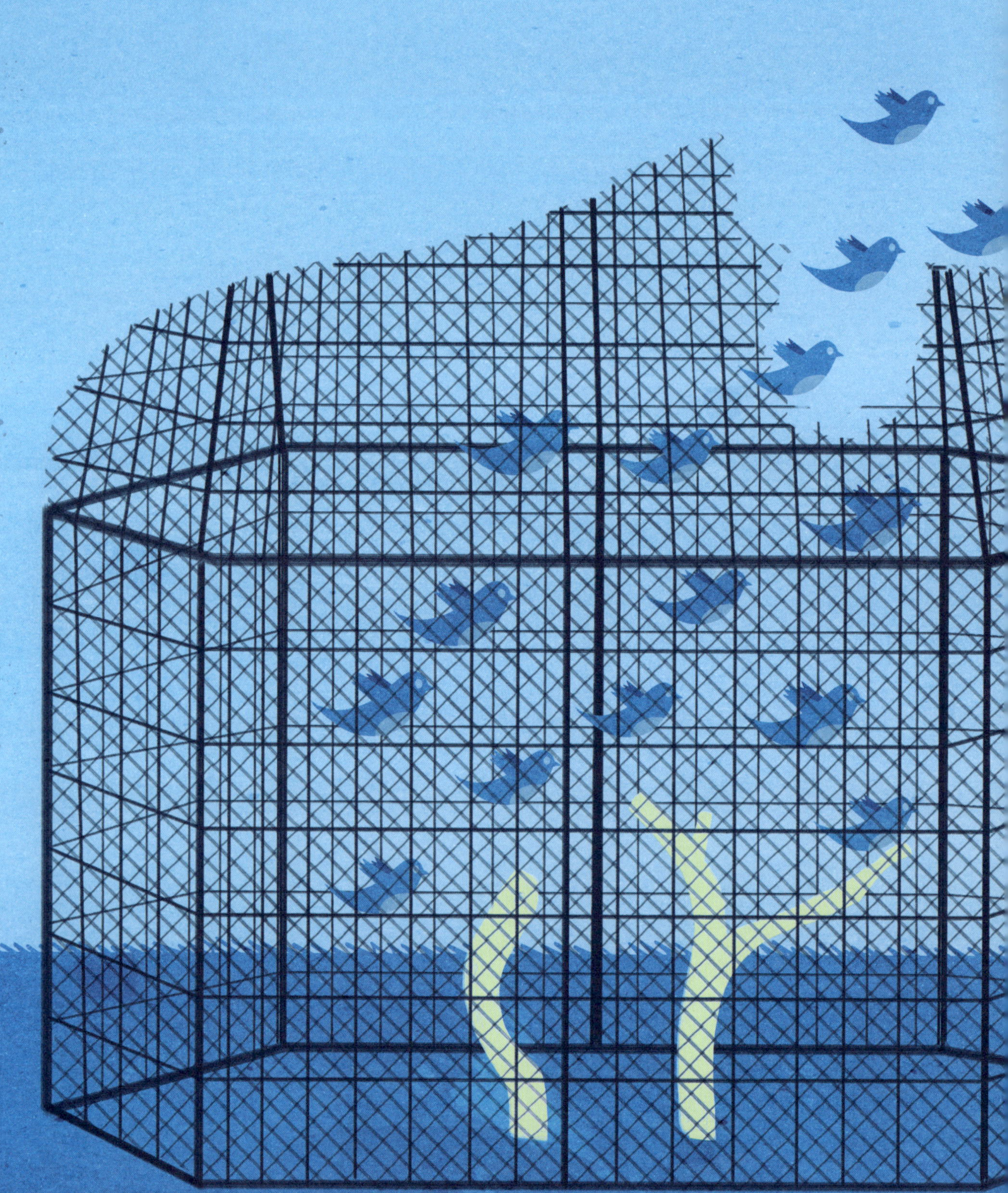

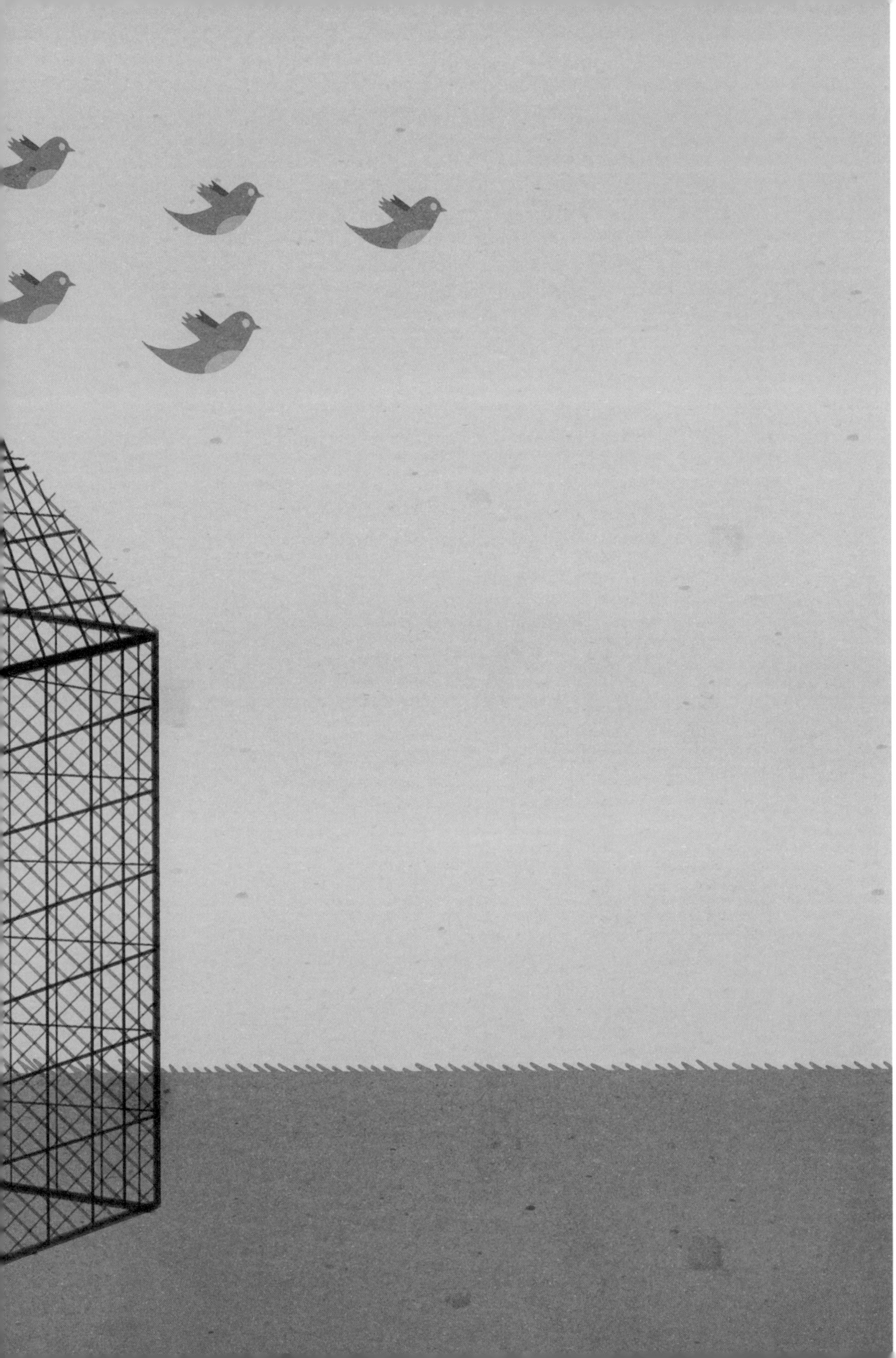

David Crystal

davidcrystal.com

Illustration
Emiliano Ponzi

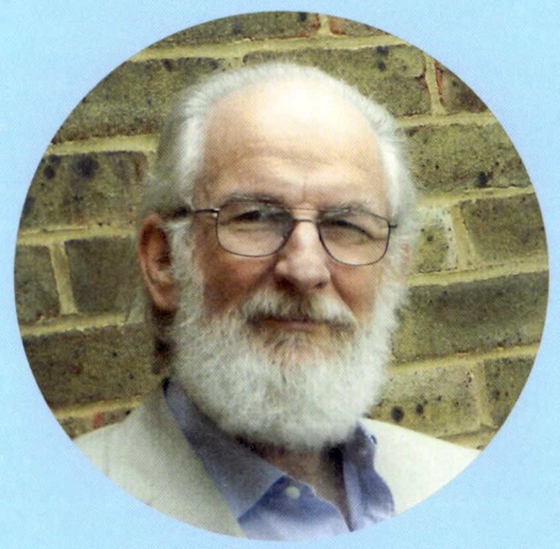

David Crystal is Honorary Professor of Linguistics at the
University of Bangor, and works from his home in Holyhead,
North Wales, as a writer, editor, lecturer, and broadcaster.
He read English at University College London, specialized
in English language studies, then joined academic life as
a lecturer in linguistics, first at Bangor, then at Reading,
where he became professor of linguistics. His books related
to his article include *Language and the Internet* (Cambridge
University Press, 2001) and *Internet Linguistics* (Routledge,
2011), and he is the inventor of the semantic targeting
approaches to online advertising, iSense and Sitescreen.
An autobiographical memoir, *Just a Phrase I'm Going Through:
My Life in Language*, was published in 2009 by Routledge.

Sites and services that have changed my life
oed.com
davidcrystal.com
shakespeareswords.com
johnbradburnepoetry.com

The Internet: Changing the Language

It is, of course, too soon to say what permanent effect the Internet will have on languages. Electronically mediated communication (EMC) has been in routine use for only around twenty years, and this is an eyeblink in the history of a language. It takes time—a lot of time—for a change to emerge, for individuals to get used to its novelty, for them to start using it in everyday speech and writing, and for it eventually to become so widely used that it becomes a permanent feature of a language, recorded in dictionaries, grammars, and manuals of style. There are already some telltale signs of what may happen, but everything has to be tentative.

The Difficulty of Generalization

All general statements about EMC are inevitably tentative because of the nature of the medium. Its size, for a start, makes it difficult to manage: there has never been a corpus of language data as large as this one, containing more written language than all the libraries in the world combined. Then there is its diversity, which defies linguistic generalization: the stylistic range of EMC includes the vast outputs found in e-mail, chat rooms, the web, virtual worlds, blogging, instant messaging, text messaging, and Twitter, as well as the increasing amount of linguistic communication encountered in social networking forums such as Facebook, each output presenting different communicative perspectives, properties, strategies, and expectations.

The speed of change makes it difficult to keep pace. How can we generalize about the linguistic style of e-mails, for example? When it first became prevalent, in the mid-1990s, the average age of e-mailers was in the 20s, and it has steadily risen. To take one year at random: the average in the UK rose from 35.7 to 37.9 between October 2006 and October 2007 (Nielsen 2007). This means that many e-mailers, for example, are now senior citizens. The consequence is that the original colloquial and radical style of e-mails (with their deviant spelling, punctuation, and capitalization) has been supplemented by a more conservative and formal style, as older people introduce norms derived from the standard language. Similarly, the average age of a Facebook user has sharply risen in the past decade, from a predominantly young person's medium to a medium for everyone: in 2012 it was 40.5 years (Pingdom 2013).

But it is not solely a matter of age. The pragmatic purpose of a piece of EMC can alter, sometimes overnight. A good example is Twitter which, when it arrived in 2006, used the prompt "What are you doing?" The result was a range of tweets which were inward-looking, using lots of first-person pronouns and present tenses. Then in November 2009 Twitter changed its prompt to "What's happening?" This made the tweets outward-looking, with lots of third-person pronouns, and a wider range of tense forms. The result was a shift in the aims and linguistic character of Twitter, which took on more of the features of a news service, as well as attracting more advertising content.

EMC as Writing or Speech

EMC, for the moment, is predominantly a written medium. This will not always be so. Voice over Internet (VoI) is rapidly increasing, and already it is possible to engage in many kinds of interactions without the fingers touching the keyboard at all, using speech-to-text software. The technique is a long way from perfection: systems have recurrent problems with regional accents, speed of speech, background noise, and the interpretation of proper names. But these will reduce as time goes by.

Some people say that in 50 years' time keyboards will be redundant, but this is unlikely because speech and writing perform very different and complementary functions. EMC relies on characteristics belonging to both sides of the speech/writing divide.

The graphic character of EMC is best illustrated by the web, which in many of its functions (e.g., databasing, reference publishing, archiving, advertising) is no different from traditional situations which use writing; indeed, most varieties of written language (legal, religious, and so on) can now be found on the web with little stylistic change other than an adaptation to the electronic medium. In contrast, the situations of e-mail, chat groups, virtual worlds, and instant messaging, though expressed through the medium of writing, display several of the core properties of speech. They are time-governed, expecting or demanding an immediate response; they are transient, in the sense that messages may be immediately deleted (as in e-mails) or be lost to attention as they scroll off the screen (as in chat groups); and their utterances display much of the urgency and energetic force which is characteristic of face-to-face conversation. The situations are not all equally *spoken* in character. We *write* e-mails, not *speak* them. But chat groups are for *chat*, and people certainly *speak* to each other there—as do people involved in virtual worlds and instant messaging.

Another distinctive feature of EMC writing is that, apart from in audio/video interactions (such as Skype or iChat), it lacks the facial expressions, gestures, and conventions of body posture and distance which are so critical in expressing personal opinions and attitudes and in moderating social relationships. The limitation was noted early in the development of the medium, and led to the introduction of *smileys* or *emoticons*. Today there are some sixty or so emoticons offered by message exchange systems. It is plain that they are a potentially helpful way of capturing some of the basic features of facial expression, but their semantic role is limited. They can forestall a gross misperception of a speaker's intent, but an individual emoticon still allows a large number of readings (happiness, joke, sympathy, good mood, delight, amusement, etc.) which can only be disambiguated by referring to the verbal context. Without care, moreover, they can foster misunderstanding: adding a smile to an utterance which is plainly angry can increase rather than decrease the force of the *flame*. So it is not surprising to see the use of emoticons falling, as time goes by. People have realized that they do not solve all communication problems in EMC, and may even add to them.

When we consider EMC as a species of written language, and compare it with traditional modes of writing, certain novel properties are immediately apparent. However, these properties are nothing to do with the standard conception of writing as a combination of vocabulary, grammar, and orthography. EMC has certainly introduced a few thousand new words into English, for example, but these make up only a tiny fraction of the million+ words that exist in that language. There is nothing revolutionary here. Similarly, the grammar of written English, as seen in EMC, displays no novelty in comparison with what was used before—no radically different word orders (syntax) or word endings (morphology). And despite the way people manipulate certain features of the orthography, such as simplifying punctuation marks or using them excessively, or adding the occasional emoticon, the writing system on the whole looks very similar to what existed in pre-EMC days. The novelty of EMC writing lies elsewhere, in the opportunities it presents for fresh kinds of communicative activity, and in the development of new styles of discourse.

There is a contrast, first of all, with the space-bound character of traditional writing—the fact that a piece of text is static and permanent on the page. If something is written down, repeated reference to it will encounter an unchanged text. Putting it like this, we can see immediately that EMC is not by any means like conventional writing. A *page* on the web often varies from encounter to encounter (and all have the option of varying, even if page-owners choose not to take it) for several possible reasons: its factual content might have been updated, its advertising sponsor might have changed, or its graphic designer might have added new features. Nor is the writing that we see necessarily static, given the technical options available which allow text to move around the screen, disappear/reappear, change color, and so on. From a user point of view, there are opportunities to *interfere* with the text in all kinds of ways that are not possible in traditional writing. A page, once downloaded to the user's screen, may have its text cut, added to, revised, annotated, even totally restructured, in ways that nonetheless retain the character of the original. The possibilities are causing not a little anxiety among those concerned about issues of ownership, copyright, and forgery.

Secondly, EMC outputs display differences from traditional writing with respect to their space-bound presence. E-mails are in principle static and permanent, but routine textual deletion is expected procedure (it is a prominent option in the management system), and it is possible to alter messages electronically with an ease and undetectability which is not possible when people try to alter a traditionally written text. Messages in asynchronic chat groups and blogs tend to be long-term in character; but those in synchronic groups, virtual worlds, and instant messaging are not. In the literature on EMC, reference is often made to the *persistence* of a conversational message—the fact that it stays on the screen for a period of time (before the arrival of other messages replaces it or makes it scroll out of sight).

Thirdly, we see differences between some EMC outputs and traditional writing when we ask how complex, elaborate, or contrived they are. Certain outputs are very similar to what happened before. In particular, the web allows the same range of planning and structural complexity as would be seen in writing and printing offline. But for chat groups, virtual worlds, and instant messaging, where the pressure is strong to communicate rapidly, there is much less complexity and forward planning. Blogs vary greatly in their constructional complexity: some are highly crafted; others are wildly erratic, when compared with the norms of the standard written language. E-mails also vary: some people are happy to send messages with no revision at all, not caring if typing errors, spelling mistakes, and other anomalies are included in their messages; others take as many pains to revise their messages as they would in non-EMC settings.

Fourthly, traditional writing is visually decontextualized: normally we cannot see the writers when we read their writing, and we can give them no immediate visual feedback, as we could when talking to someone in face-to-face conversation. In these respects, EMC is just like traditional writing. But web pages often provide visual aids to support text, in the form of photographs, maps, diagrams, animations, and the like; and many virtual-world settings have a visual component built in. The arrival of web-cams is also altering the communicative dynamic of EMC interactions, especially in instant messaging, and some interesting situations arise. I observed an anomalous one recently, where A and B were attempting to use an audio/video link via iChat, but B's microphone was down. As a result B could hear A but A could not hear B, who thus had to resort to her keyboard. A's spoken stimulus was followed by B's written response.

After a somewhat chaotic start, the conversation settled down into a steady rhythm.

Fifthly, we can compare the factual content of EMC and traditional writing. The majority of the latter is factually communicative, as is evident from the vast amount of reference material in libraries. A focus on fact is also evident on the web, and in many blogs and e-mails; but other EMC situations are less clear. Within the reality parameters established by a virtual world, factual information is certainly routinely transmitted, but there is a strong social element always present which greatly affects the kind of language used. Chat groups vary enormously: the more academic and professional they are, the more likely they are to be factual in aim (though often not in achievement, if reports of the amount of flaming are to be believed). The more social and ludic chat groups, on the other hand, routinely contain sequences which have negligible factual content. Instant message exchanges are also highly variable, sometimes containing a great deal of information, sometimes being wholly devoted to social chitchat.

Sixthly, traditional writing is graphically rich, as we can immediately see from the pages of many a fashion magazine. The web has reflected this richness, but greatly increased it, the technology putting into the hands of the ordinary user a range of typographic and color variation that far exceeds the pen, the typewriter, and the early word processor, and allowing further options not available to conventional publishing, such as animated text, hypertext links, and multimedia support (sound, video, film). On the other hand, as typographers and graphic designers have repeatedly pointed out, just because a new visual language is available to everyone does not mean that everyone can use it well. Despite the provision of a wide range of guides to Internet design and desktop publishing, examples of illegibility, visual confusion, over-ornamentation, and other inadequacies abound. They are compounded by the limitations of the medium, which cause no problem if respected, but which are often ignored, as when we encounter screenfuls of unbroken text, paragraphs which scroll downwards interminably, or text which scrolls awkwardly off the right-hand side of the screen. The problems of *graphic translatability* are only beginning to be appreciated—that it is not possible to take a paper-based text and put it on a screen without rethinking the graphic presentation and even, sometimes, the content of the message.

EMC, then, offers new communicative possibilities in the way people can manipulate written language. And already we can see how these opportunities are creating new kinds of electronic discourse.

New Kinds of Text

Every time a new technology arrives, we see the growth of new kinds of discourse, reflecting the aims and intentions of the users. Printing introduced us to such notions as newspapers, chapter organization, and indexes. Broadcasting brought sports commentary, news reading, and weather forecasting. EMC is no different. The content displayed on a screen presents a variety of textual spaces whose purpose varies. There is a scale of online adaptability. At one extreme, we find texts where no adaptation to EMC has been made—a PDF of an article on screen, for example, with no search or other facilities—in which case, any linguistic analysis would be identical with that of the corresponding offline text. At the other extreme, we find written texts which have no counterpart in the offline world. Here are four examples.

Texts whose aim is to defeat spam filters

We only have to look in our e-mail junk folder to discover a world of novel texts whose linguistic properties sometimes defy analysis:

supr vi-agra online now znwygghsxp
VI @ GRA 75% off regular xxp wybzz lusfg
fully stocked online pharmac^y
Great deals, prescription d[rugs

It is possible to see a linguistic rationale in the graphological variations in the word *Viagra*, for example, introduced to ensure that it avoids the word-matching function in a filter. We may find the letters spaced (*V i a g r a*), transposed (*Viarga*), duplicated (*Viaggra*), or separated by arbitrary symbols (*Vi*agra*). There are only so many options, and these can to a large extent be predicted. There have been huge advances here since the early days when the stupid software, having been told to ban anything containing the string S-E-X, disallowed messages about Sussex, Essex, and many other innocent terms. There is also an anti-linguistic rationale, as one might put it, in which random strings are generated (*wybzz*). These too can be handled, if one's spam filter is sophisticated, by telling it to remove any message which does not respect the graphotactic norms of a language (i.e., the rules governing syllable structure, vowel sequence, and consonant clusters).

Texts whose aim is to guarantee higher rankings in web searches

How is one to ensure that one's page appears in the first few hits in a web search? There are several techniques, some nonlinguistic, some linguistic. An example of a nonlinguistic technique is the frequency of hypertext links: the more pages link to my site, the more likely my page will move up the rankings. An example of a linguistic technique is the listing of key words or phrases which identify the semantic content of a page in the page's metadata: these will be picked up by the search engine and given priority in a search. Neither of these techniques actually alters the linguistic character of the text on a page. Rather different is a third technique, where the text is manipulated to include keywords, especially in the heading and first paragraph, to ensure that a salient term is prioritized. The semantic difference can be seen in the following pair of texts (invented, but based on exactly what happens). Text A is an original paragraph; text B is the paragraph rewritten with ranking in mind, to ensure that the product name gets noticed:

The Crystal Knitting-Machine is the latest and most exciting product from Crystal Industries. It has an aluminum frame, comes in five exciting colors, and a wide range of accessories.

The Crystal Knitting-Machine is the latest and most exciting product from Crystal Industries.

- The Crystal Knitting-Machine has an aluminum frame.
- The Crystal Knitting-Machine comes in five exciting colors.
- The Crystal Knitting-Machine has a wide range of accessories.

Some search engines have got wise to this technique, and try to block it, but it is difficult, in view of the various paraphrases which can be introduced (e.g., *Knitting-Machine from Crystal*, *Crystal Machines for Knitting*).

Texts whose aim is to save time, energy, or money

Text messaging (a different sense of the term *text*, note) is a good example of a genre whose linguistic characteristics have evolved partly as a response to technological limitations. The limitation to 160 characters (for Roman alphabets) has motivated an increased use of nonstandard words (of the *c u l8r* type), using logograms, initialisms, shortenings, and other abbreviatory conventions. The important word is *partly*. Most of these abbreviations were being used in EMC long before mobile phones became a routine part of our lives. And the motivation to use them goes well beyond the ergonomic, as their playful character provides entertainment value as an end in itself as well as increasing rapport between participants. I have developed this point in my *Txtng: the Gr8 Db8*.

Another example of a new type of text arising out of considerations of convenience is the e-mail which uses *framing*. We receive a message which contains, say, three different points in a single paragraph. We can, if we want, reply to each of these points by taking the paragraph, splitting it up into three parts, and then responding to each part separately, so that the message we send back then looks a bit like a play dialogue. Then, our sender can do the same thing to our responses, and when we get the message back, we see his replies to our replies. We can then send the lot on to someone else for further comments, and when it comes back, there are now three voices framed on the screen. And so it can go on—replies within replies within replies—and all unified within the same screen typography. People find this method of response extremely convenient—to an extent, for there comes a point where the nested messages make the text too complex to be easily followed.

Related to framing is intercalated response. Someone sends me a set of questions, or makes a set of critical points about something I have written. I respond to these by intercalating my responses between the points made by the sender. For clarity, I might put my responses in a different color, or include them in angle brackets or some such convention. A further response from the sender might lead to the use of an additional color; and if other people are copied in to the exchange, some graphical means of this kind, to distinguish the various participants, is essential.

Texts whose aim is to maintain a standard

Although the Internet is supposedly a medium where freedom of speech is axiomatic, controls and constraints are commonplace to avoid abuses. These range from the excising of obscene and aggressive language to the editing of pages or posts to ensure that they stay focused on a particular topic. Moderators (facilitators, managers, wizards... the terminology is various) have to deal with organizational, social, and content-related issues. From a textual point of view, what we end up with is a sanitized text, in which certain parts of language (chiefly vocabulary) are excluded. It is not clear how far such controls will evolve, as the notion of textual responsibility relating to the libel laws is still in the process of being tested.

A good example of content moderation is in the online advertising industry, where there is a great deal of current concern to ensure that ads on a particular web page are both relevant and sensitive to the content of that page. Irrelevance or insensitivity leads to lost commercial opportunities and can generate extremely bad PR. Irrelevance can be illustrated by a CNN report of a street stabbing in Chicago, where the ads down the side of the screen said such things as "Buy your knives here"—the software being unaware that the weapons sense of *knife* in the news report did not match the cutlery sense of *knife* in the ad inventory. Insensitivity can be illustrated by a German page which was describing heritage visits to Auschwitz; the same silly software, having found "gas" mentioned several times on the page, linked this with a power company's ads for "cheap gas," much to the embarrassment of all concerned. One solution, known as *semantic targeting* (and now available in Ad Pepper Media's iSense and Sitescreen products) carries out a complete lexical analysis of web pages and ad inventories so that subject matter is matched and ad misplacements avoided. In extreme cases, such as a firm which does not want its ad to appear on a particular page (e.g., a child clothing manufacturer on an adult porn site), ads can be blocked from appearing. As a result, from a content point of view, the text that appears on a page appears more semantically coherent and pragmatically acceptable than would otherwise be the case.

Texts Sans Frontières

All the texts mentioned so far have one thing in common: they are easily identifiable and determinate. They have definable physical boundaries, which can be spatial (e.g., letters and books) or temporal (e.g., broadcasts and interviews). They are created at a specific point in time; and once created, they are static and permanent. Each text has a single authorial or presenting voice (even in cases of multiple authorship of books and papers), and that authorship is either known or can easily be established (except in some historical contexts). It is a stable, familiar, comfortable world. And what the Internet has done is remove the stability, familiarity, and comfort.

Written texts are defined by their physical boundaries: the edges of the page, the covers of the book, the border of the road sign… Spoken texts are defined by their temporal boundaries: the arrival and departure of participants in a conversation, the beginning and end of a broadcast, the opening and closing of a lecture… Internet texts are more problematic. Sometimes, as with a text message or an instant-message exchange, we can clearly identify the start and the finish. But with most Internet outputs there are decisions to be made, as the following examples show.

- Does a single e-mail message constitute a text, or is the text everything available on a screen at a particular point in time, including previously exchanged messages that have not been deleted and any framed or intercalated responses sent by the recipient? And does one include unchanging biodata, such as the sender's address, web links, and taglines?

- *A fortiori*, does an entire website constitute a text, or are the texts the individual elements of the menu (Home, About, Contact, Help…), or the individual pages, or the functional elements seen on these pages (main text, advertisements, comments…)? The distinction has commercial importance in online advertising, where an ad server is likely to serve a different range of ads to the top page of a site compared to its constituent pages. Sky TV, for example, at one point had a banking ad at the top of its home page, and a video games ad at the top of its sport page. And should we include translations? Many websites now are multilingual, with a list of language choices on the home page. Are these part of the same text, or are they different texts?

- If an e-mail, tweet, instant message, blog, or other output includes an obligatory hypertext link, is that link to be considered as part of the text? By *obligatory* I mean a link that forms part of the structure of a sentence or which provides information that is critical to the understanding of the page, such as "Please go to www… for details," or the links used in tweets.

- If security is an obligatory element (e.g., asking for user names, pass-words, or other authentication), is this to be considered as part of the text? Are the glosses or images which appear when a mouse hovers over a string to be considered as part of the text? And do we include the key-words which identify the page, and which may not appear on the screen, but are only visible when one looks at the underlying code, as here?

```
<HEAD>
<TITLE>Stamp Collecting World</TITLE>
<META name="description" content="Everything you wanted to know about stamps, from prices to history.">
<META name="keywords" content="stamps, stamp collecting, stamp history, prices, stamps for sale">
</HEAD>
```

- How are we to define a text in an Internet output which is continuously growing, as in a social networking site, a chat room, a blog forum, or a bulletin board, which might last indefinitely? In these cases there is a dynamic archive, which in some cases goes back many years. Are asso-ciated comments to be considered part of the text? As they are elicited by the main text, and are semantically (and sometimes grammatically) dependent on it, they cannot be taken as independent texts in their own right. There is an asymmetrical relationship: the main text has autonomy: it does not need comments to survive; but comments could not exist without a main text. And there is no theoretical limit to the number of comments a post might elicit.

- Similarly, how are we to define a text in an Internet output which is continually changing—where there is permanently scrolling data, regularly updated, such as stock-market reports and news headlines? Here there may be no archive: old information is deleted as it is replaced. The content comes from an inventory which is fixed at any one point in time, but frequently refreshed. Some sequences that appear on-screen are cyclical (such as the recurring headlines we see in a news-ticker service or a retail store); others are randomly generated (such as the pop-up ads or banner ads taken from a large inventory, which may change in front of your eyes every few seconds.

- What do we do with a message sequence (as in e-mails or a bulletin board) where the subject line identifies a semantic thread? Is the text the set of messages that relate to that thread (as in items 4 and 9 below)? They may be separated by other messages, as in this example from a Shakespeare forum:

    4   Arden3 The Merchant of Venice
    5   Thoughts on Double Falsehood
    6   Arden3 Sir Thomas More
    7   2011 Blackfriars Conference Announcement
    8   From New York to Santa Fe
    9   Arden3 The Merchant of Venice

- Do we follow the header? If so, what do we do with cases where (a) the discussion continues but someone changes the header in the subject line, or (b) the header in the subject line remains the same, but the discussion veers off-topic? Which takes priority?

- Are we to include in the text elements automatically inserted by cookies, such as site preferences, shopping cart contents, and visitor tracking, or the features which are available to users, such as helplines and analytics reports?

- How do we view texts rendered incomplete by the technology, as when a tweet exceeds the 140-character limit and is truncated by the software? This is shown by ellipsis dots on screen.

The traditional notion of *text* is inadequate to handle these cases. A broader, more inclusive notion is going to be needed. Clearly, what we see in all these examples are aggregates of functional elements, which interact in various ways in different Internet outputs. We need terms for both the elements and the aggregates. Dürscheid and Jucker (2011), for example, call the elements "communicative acts," and the aggregates "communicative act sequences." Doubtless other proposals will be forthcoming, as linguists explore these phenomena in more detail. In the meantime, here are some general observations.

Panchronicity

The above examples are not a complete list of the boundary decisions which have to be made when we are trying to identify Internet texts, but they are representative of what is *out there*. And they raise quite fundamental questions. In particular, Ferdinand de Saussure's classical distinction between synchronic and diachronic does not adapt well to these kinds of communication, where everything is diachronic, time-stampable to a micro-level. Texts are classically treated as synchronic entities, by which we mean we disregard the changes that were made during the process of composition and treat the finished product as if time did not exist. But with many electronically mediated texts there is no finished product. And in many cases, time ceases to be chronological.

For example, I can in 2011 post a message to a forum discussion about a page which was created in 2004. From a linguistic point of view, we cannot say that we now have a new synchronic iteration of that page, because the language has changed in the interim. I might use in my message vocabulary that has entered the language since 2004, or show the influence of an ongoing grammatical change. Content is inevitably affected. I might refer to Twitter—something which would not have been possible in 2004, for that network did not appear until 2006. I might even—as is possible with Wiki pages—insert information into the main text of a page which could not have been available at the time of the page's creation. In the case of my blog, I might go back to a post I wrote in 2004 and edit it to include material from 2013.

We need a new term for this curious conflation of language from different time periods. We are very familiar with texts which include language from earlier periods (archaisms). We need a way of describing features of texts which include language from later periods. The traditional term for a chronological mismatch is anachronism—when something from a particular point in time is introduced into an earlier period (before it existed) or a later period (after it ceased to exist). Anachronisms can be isolated instances—as when Shakespeare introduces striking clocks into ancient Rome (in *Julius Caesar*)—or a whole text can be anachronistic, as when a modern author writes a play about the seventeenth century and has everyone speak in a twenty-first-century way. But these cases don't quite capture the EMC situation, where a chronological anomaly has been introduced into an original text. This is a new take on the grammatical notion of *future in the past*—or, perhaps better, *back to the future*. And I think we need a new term to capture what is happening. A text which contains such futurisms cannot be described as synchronic for it cannot be seen as a single *état de langue* (Saussure's term for a state of the language at a particular point in time): it is a conflation of language from two or more *états de langue*. Nor can it be described as diachronic, for the aim is not to show language change between these different états. Such texts, whose identity is dependent on features from different time frames, I call panchronic.

Wiki pages, such as those seen on Wikipedia, are typically panchronic. They are the result of an indefinite number of interventions by an indefinite number of individuals over an indefinite number of periods of time (which become increasingly present as time goes by). We are only 20 or so years into the web, so the effect so far is limited; but think ahead 50 or 100 years, and it is obvious that panchronicity will become a dominant element of Internet presence. From a linguistic point of view, the result is pages that are temporally and stylistically heterogeneous. Already we find huge differences, such as standard and nonstandard language coexisting on the same page, often because some of the contributors are communicating in a second language in which they are not fluent. Tenses go all over the place, as this example illustrates (reproduced exactly as it appeared in Wikipedia):

Following his resignation, Mubarak did not make any media appearances. With the exception of family and a close circle of aides, he reportedly refused to talk to anyone, even his supporters. His health was speculated to be rapidly deteriorating with some reports even alleging him to be in a coma. Most sources claim that he is not longer interested in performing any duties and wants to "die in Sharm El-Sheikh."

On 28 February 2011, the General Prosecutor of Egypt issued an order prohibiting Mubarak and his family from leaving Egypt. It was reported that the former president was in contact with his lawyer in case of possible criminal charges against him. As a result, Mubarak and his family had been under house arrest at a presidential palace in the Red Sea resort of Sharm el-Sheikh. On Wednesday 13 April 2011 Egyptian prosecutors said they had detained former president Hosni Mubarak for 15 days, facing questioning about corruption and abuse of power, few hours after he was hospitalized in the resort of Sharm el Sheik.

Note the way for example, we move from past tense to present tense in paragraph 1, and from *was* to *had* in paragraph 2. Note also the way *former president Hosni Mubarak* is introduced in the last sentence, as if this were a new topic in the discourse. Note the three different spellings of the Red Sea resort. And how are we to interpret such nonstandard usages as *was speculated*, *in case of*, and *few hours*?

In pages like this, traditional notions of stylistic coherence, with respect to level of formality, technicality, and individuality, no longer apply, though a certain amount of accommodation is apparent, either because contributors sense the properties of each other's style, or a piece of software alters contributions (e.g., removing obscenities), or a moderator introduces a degree of leveling. The pages are also semantically and pragmatically heterogeneous, as the intentions behind the various contributions vary greatly. Wiki articles on sensitive topics illustrate this most clearly, with judicious observations competing with contributions that range from mild through moderate to severe in the subjectivity of their opinions. And one never knows whether a change introduced in a wiki context is factual or fictitious, innocent or malicious.

The problem exists even when the person introducing the various changes is the same. The author of the original text may change it—refreshing a web page, or revising a blog posting. How are we to view the relationship between the various versions? This is not the first time we have encountered this problem. It is a familiar problem for medievalists faced with varying versions of a text. It is a routine question in the case of, say, Shakespeare: Did he (or someone else) go back and revise an earlier manuscript? It is something we see all the time in the notion of a *second edition*, where the two layers of text may be separated by many years. But what is happening on the Internet is hugely different from the traditional process of revision, because it is something that authors can do with unprecedented frequency and in unprecedented ways. A website page can be refreshed, either automatically or manually.

The issue is particularly relevant now that print-on-demand texts are becoming common. It is possible for me to publish a book very quickly and cheaply, printing only a handful of copies. Having produced my first print run, I then decide to print another, but make a few changes to the file before I send it to the POD company. In theory (and increasingly common in practice), I can print just one copy, make some changes, then print another copy, make some more changes, and so on. The situation is beginning to resemble medieval scribal practice, where no two manuscripts were identical, or the typesetting variations between copies of Shakespeare's First Folio. The traditional terminology of *first edition*, *second edition*, *first edition with corrections*, ISBN numbering, and so on, seems totally inadequate to account for the variability we now encounter. The same problem is also present in archiving. The British Library, for example, launched its Web Archiving Consortium a few years ago. My website is included. But how do we define the relationship between the various time-stamped iterations of this site, as they accumulate in the archive?

Anonymity

I mentioned five criteria above: texts have definable physical boundaries; they are created at a specific point in time; they are static and permanent; they have a single authorial or presenting voice; and—apart from in some historical contexts—authorship is either known or can easily be established. None of these criteria are necessarily present on the Internet. And in the case of the last of these, its absence presents linguists with a particularly difficult situation. When we classify texts into types we rely greatly on extralinguistic information. This is something we have learned from sociolinguistics and stylistics: the notion of a language variety (or register, or genre, or whatever) arises from a correlation of linguistic features with extralinguistic features of the situation in which it occurs, such as its formality or occupational identity. In principle we know the speaker or writer—whether male or female, old or young, upper class or lower class, scientist or journalist, and so on. And when we do research we try to take these variables into account in order to make our study comparable to others or distinguishable from others in controlled ways. In short, we know who we are dealing with.

But on the Internet, a lot of the time, we don't. The writer is anonymous. In a wide range of Internet situations, people hide their identity, especially in chat groups, blogging, spam e-mails, avatar-based interactions (such as virtual reality games and Second Life), and social networking. These situations routinely contain individuals who are talking to each other under nicknames (nicks), which may be an assumed first name, a fantasy description (topdude, sexstar), or a mythical character or role (rockman, elfslayer). Operating behind a false persona seems to make people less inhibited: they may feel emboldened to talk more and in different ways from their real-world linguistic repertoire. They must also expect to receive messages from others who are likewise less inhibited, and be prepared for negative outcomes. There are obviously inherent risks in talking to someone we do not know, and instances of harassment, insulting or aggressive language, and subterfuge are legion. Terminology has evolved to identify them, such as flaming, spoofing, trolling, and lurking. New conventions have evolved, such as the use of CAPITALS to express *shouting*.

While all of these phenomena have a history in traditional mediums, the Internet makes them present in the public domain to an extent that was not encountered before. But we do not yet have detailed linguistic accounts of the consequences of anonymity. All that is clear is that traditional theories don't account for it. Try using Gricean maxims of conversation to the Internet (Grice 1975): our speech acts, he says, should be truthful (the maxim of quality), brief (the maxim of quantity), relevant (the maxim of relation), and clear (the maxim of manner). Take quality: do not say what you believe to be false; do not say anything for which you lack evidence.

Which world was Grice living in? A pre-Internet world, evidently. Pragmatics people traditionally assume that human beings are nice. The Internet has shown that they are not. Is a pedophile going to be truthful, brief, relevant, and clear? Are the people sending us tempting offers from Nigeria—beautifully pilloried in Neil Forsyth's recent book, *Delete This at Your Peril* (2010)? Are extreme-views sites (such as hate racist sites) going to follow Geoffrey Leech's (1983) maxims of politeness (tact, generosity, approbation, modesty, agreement, sympathy)? And if brevity was the soul of the Internet, we would not have such coinages as blogorrhea and twitterrhea.

Electronically mediated communication is not the first medium to allow interaction between individuals who wish to remain anonymous, of course, as we know from the history of telephone and amateur radio; but it is certainly unprecedented in the scale and range of situations in which people can hide their identity, and exploit their anonymity in ways that would be difficult to replicate offline. And the linguist is faced with a growing corpus of data which is uninterpretable in sociolinguistic or stylistic terms. A different orientation needs to be devised, in which intention and effect become primary, and identity becomes secondary.

The Future

The biggest question marks to do with change on the Internet relate to the way EMC is developing—always difficult to predict as technology rapidly changes. Most of my observations about written language are based on what I have seen on the large screen of my computer. But it is a fact that Internet access is becoming increasingly mobile. Indeed, in some parts of the world, where a wired electricity supply is unreliable or absent (such as a great deal of Africa), the only way of reaching the Internet is via mobile phones. So what happens, in terms of legibility, when a page containing a large amount of visually encoded information is presented on a small screen? How is the information reorganized? What is lost and what is gained? If, as the mobile phone industry is predicting, the majority of Internet access will soon be through handheld devices, then how relevant will be all the generalizations about EMC character that have hitherto been based only on an analysis of large-screen displays?

Finally, this paper has largely focused on written language. The main issue for the future will be how to deal with the increased presence of spoken outputs, as a result of growth in Voice over Internet and mobile communication. There are several new kinds of speech situation here, such as the modifications which are introduced into conversation to compensate for the inevitable lag between participants, automatic speech-to-text translation (as when voicemail is turned into text messages), text-to-speech translation (as when a web page is read aloud), voice recognition interaction (as when we tell the washing machine what to do), and voice synthesis (as when we listen to GPS driving instructions). Each of these domains is going to introduce us to new kinds of output over the next twenty years. Evidently, we ain't seen nothin' yet.

References

Ad Pepper Media.
http://www.adpepper.com/advertiser/overview (accessed March 18, 2013).

British Library.
UK Web Archive. 2008. http://www.webarchive.org.uk/ukwa/

Crystal, David.
Txtng: The Gr8 Db8. Oxford: Oxford University Press, 2008.

Dürscheid, Christa, and Andreas H. Jucker.
"Text As Utterance: Communication in the Electronic Media." Paper presented at the conference "Language As a Social and Cultural Practice: Advances in Linguistics," University of Basel, 2011.

Forsyth, Neil [also known as Bob Servant].
Delete This at Your Peril. Edinburgh: Birlinn, 2010.

Grice, H. Paul.
"Logic and Conversation." In Peter Cole and Jerry L. Morgan, eds. *Syntax and Semantics 3: Speech Acts*. New York: Academic Press, 1975. 41–58.

Leech, Geoffrey.
Principles of Pragmatics. London: Longman, 1983.

Nielsen Company.
"The Ageing UK Internet Population." Nielsen Online News Release, December 18, 2007. http://www.netratings.com/pr/pr_071218_UK.pdf

Pingdom.
"Internet 2012 in Numbers." *Pingdom*, January 16, 2013. http://royal.pingdom.com/2013/01/16/internet-2012-in-numbers

The Internet's Influence on the Production and Consumption of Culture: Creative Destruction and New Opportunities

Paul DiMaggio

A. Barton Hepburn Professor of Sociology and Public Affairs, Princeton University

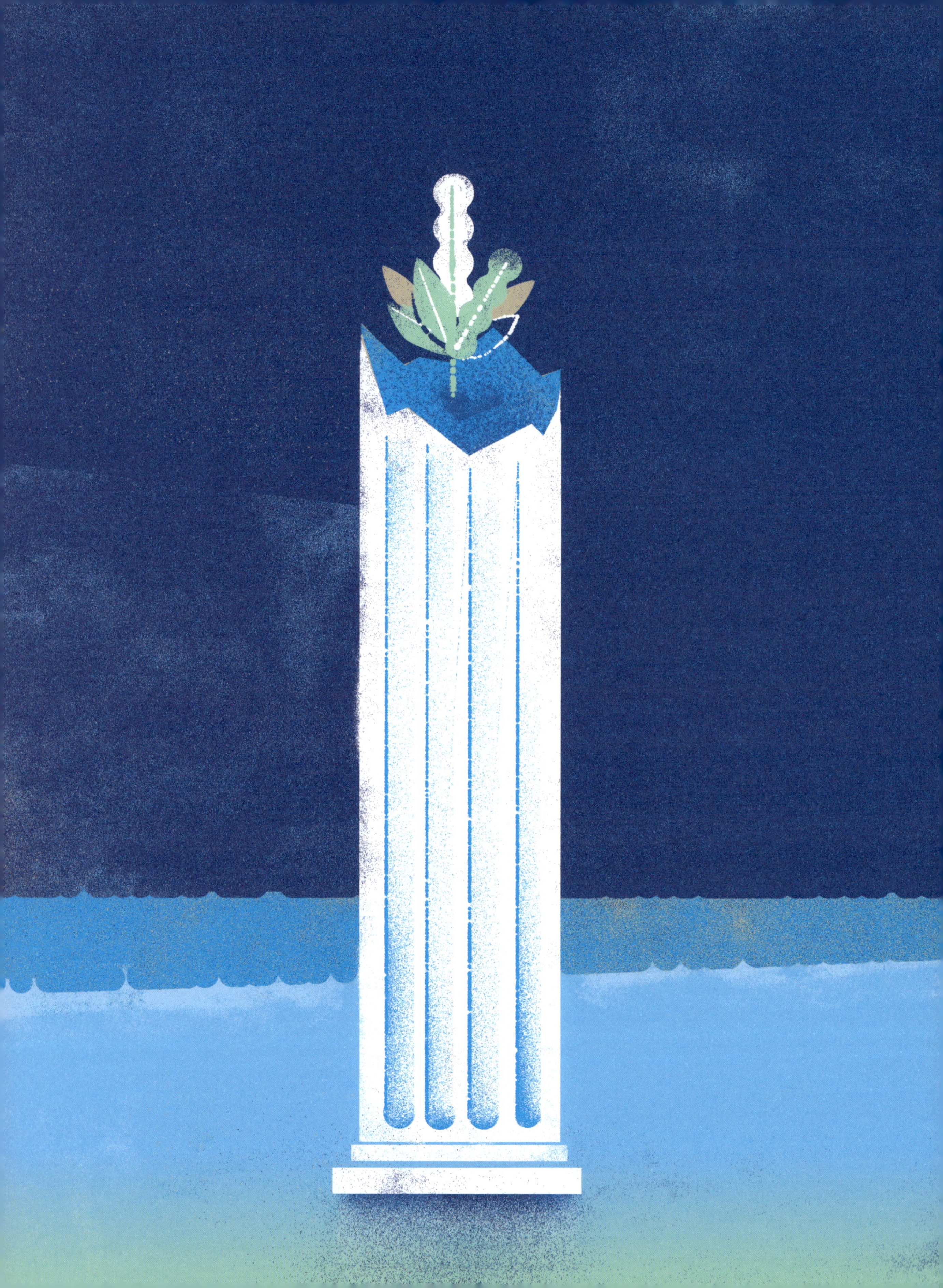

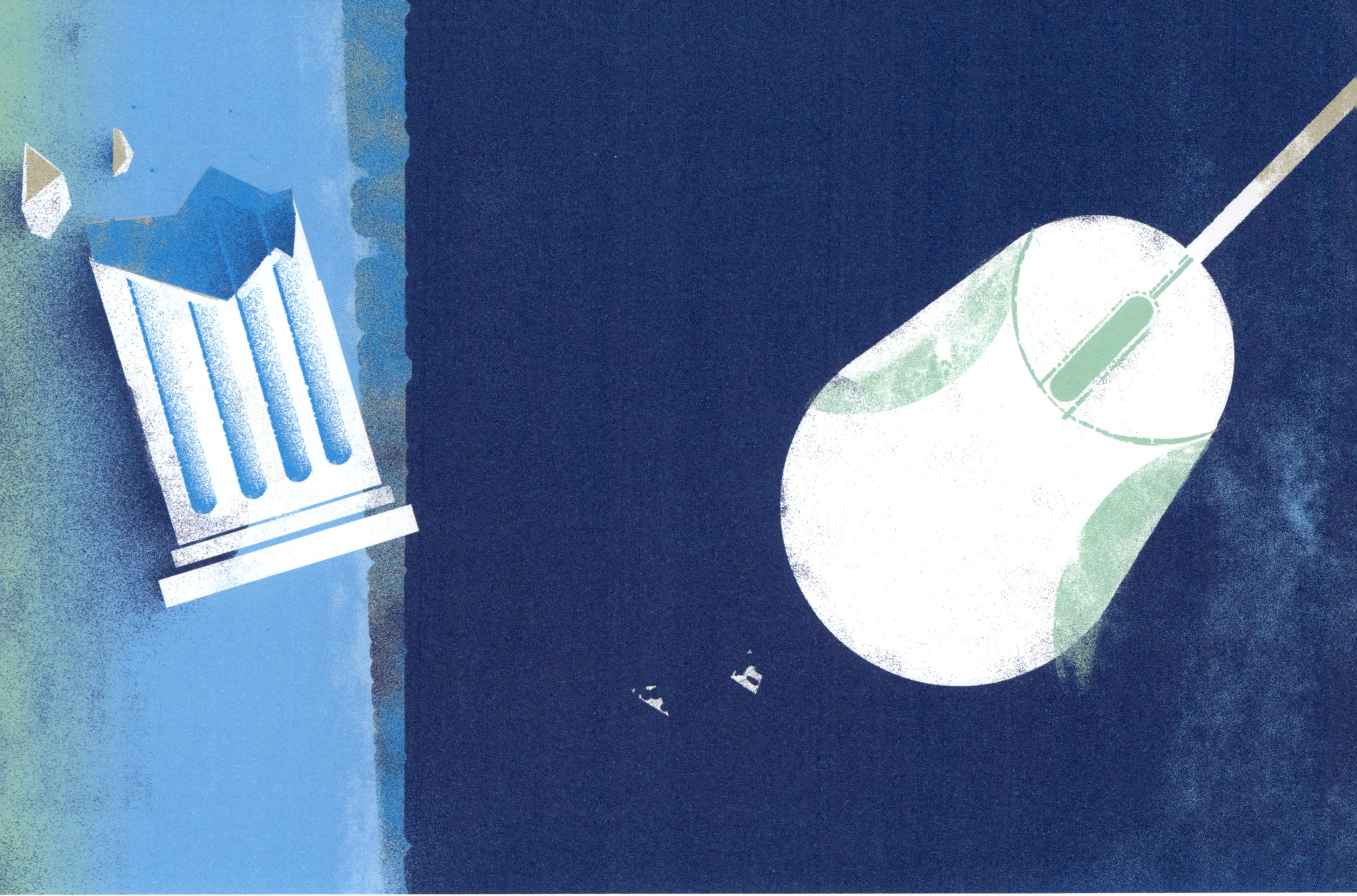

The Internet's Influence on the Production and Consumption of Culture

Paul DiMaggio

Paul DiMaggio

princeton.edu/~artspol/pd_prof.html

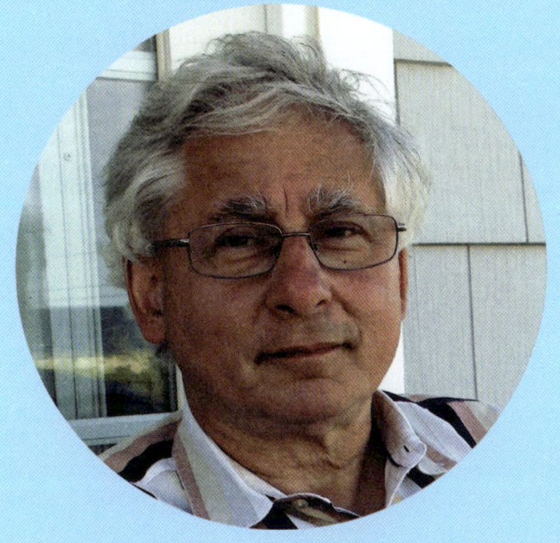

Paul DiMaggio is A. Barton Hepburn Professor of Sociology and Public Affairs at Princeton University, where he also serves as Director of Graduate Studies in the Department of Sociology, Director of the Center for the Study of Social Organization, and is a member of the Executive Committee of the Center for Information Technology Policy. A graduate of Swarthmore College, he earned his PhD in Sociology at Harvard University in 1979. Over the course of his career, he has undertaken research and published papers about such topics as arts institutions, culture and inequality, political polarization, economic networks, and information technology. He has written about the relationship between Internet use and social inequality, and teaches a regular course with a computer science colleague on information and public policy at Princeton's Woodrow Wilson School of International and Public Affairs. DiMaggio is a member of the American Academy of Arts and Sciences and the American Academy of Political and Social Science.

Sites and services that have changed my life
spotify.com
scholar.google.com
amazon.com

The Internet's Influence on the Production and Consumption of Culture: Creative Destruction and New Opportunities

In this essay, I consider the impact of the Internet on the arts and media, focusing, though not exclusively, on film, journalism, and, especially, popular music, which serves as an extended case study. For many of these creative fields, the Internet has been "a disruptive technology" (Christensen 1997), reshaping industries and rendering long-established business strategies unsupportable, while introducing new ways to organize production and distribution. I will consider these economic changes, but also discuss the implications for creative workers and for the public at large.

At certain points, I may use language that implies that the Internet has had an effect on the world or on its users. The reader should be aware that talk about the *Internet effect*, although at times a useful shorthand, should never be taken too seriously, for at least three reasons.

First, technologies don't change us. They provide affordances (Gibson 1977) that allow us to be ourselves, to do the things we like or need to do, more easily. The availability of these affordances may change behavior by reducing the cost (in time or money) of certain activities (e.g., watching excerpts from movies or comedy shows) relative to other activities (watching network television). But the Internet will not make the politically apathetic vote, or the atheist go to church.

Second, when we talk about the role of the Internet in the lives of individuals, we must not forget that the technology is still absent from or only marginally part of the lives of many persons, even in the economically advanced societies, where between 10 and 30 percent of the public lack broadband access (Miniwatt 2013), many of those who have access fail to reap its benefits (Van Deursen and Van Dijk 2013) and far fewer actually produce online content (Schradie 2011). For those on the wrong side of the *digital divide*, the main impact of the Internet may be reduced access to public and commercial services that have migrated online. Participation is even lower, of course, in much of the Global South.

Finally, what we call *the Internet* is a moving target, a product not only of technological ingenuity but of economic strategy and political struggle. What we think of as *the Internet* in the advanced industrial democracies reflects a particular regulatory regime through which states allocate rights to intellectual property and, through regulation, influence the cost and potential profitability of investments in different kinds of networking technologies (Benkler 2006; Crawford 2013). Technological change, inflected by economic incentives and regulatory constraint, guarantees that today's Internet will be as remote by 2025 as the Internet of 2000 seems today.

The Internet is a technology that unleashes powerful opportunities. But the realization of these opportunities is dependent, first, on the inclination of humans to exploit them in creative ways; and, second, on the capacity of entrenched stakeholders in both the private sector and the state to use such tools as copyright, regulation, surveillance, and censorship to stand in the way. Where the Internet's effect on culture lies on the continuum between dystopic and euphoric—to what extent it ripens into a sphere of unbridled creativity and communication, to what extent it develops into some combination of conventional entertainment medium and instrument of political domination—will depend on both economic incentives and public policies that structure the way those incentives operate. In this sense, then, the Internet's future cultural impact is both uncertain and ours to make.

The Internet and Cultural Production

By cultural production, I refer to the performing and visual arts, literature, and the media industries. A key distinction is between artistic activities that require the co-presence of artistic workers (or of artworks) and consumers (live theater and dance, musical performance, art museums and galleries) on the one hand; and artistic activities that produce artifacts subject to digital distribution (recorded music, film and video). The Internet, thus far, has had the most marked effects on the latter.

Art with the Personal Touch

The performing arts, museums, and restaurants are perhaps least vulnerable to the Internet's impact for two reasons. First, their appeal is sensual: no digital facsimile satisfies our desire to see a dancer perform, hear music in a live setting, stand before a great work of art, or eat a freshly prepared meal. Second, because it is difficult to make live performances and exhibitions highly profitable, in most of the world these activities have been left to public or nonprofit institutions that are ordinarily less dynamic in their response to environmental change (DiMaggio 2006). Indeed, in the U.S., at least, theaters, orchestras, and museums have been tentative in their embrace of the new technology. Almost all respondents to a recent study of 1,200 organizations that had received grants from the U.S.'s federal arts agency reported that their organizations maintained websites, used the Internet to sell tickets and post videos, and maintained a Facebook site. Yet just one third employ a full-time staff member primarily responsible for their online presence, suggesting a somewhat restrained engagement with social media (Thomas and Purcell 2013).[1] In sum, then, it appears that, in the U.S. at least, conventional noncommercial cultural organizations have adopted the Internet, but only at the margins.

Yet it is the outliers who are more interesting if we think about the *potential* influence of the Internet on the arts. Consider, for example, MUVA (Museo Virtual de Artes), a virtual museum of contemporary art hosted in Uruguay and devoted to work by Uruguayan artists. This architecturally impressive building (which exists only online) offers several exhibits simultaneously. The visitor uses a mouse to move about the exhibit (hold the cursor to the far right or left to move quickly, closer to the center to stroll more slowly, click to zoom onto an image and view documentation), much as one would a physical gallery. (The site also has affordances that physical galleries do not offer, such as the opportunity to change the color of the wall on which the work is *hung*.)[2] To be sure, this is not yet a true

1. Just one-third of the organizations surveyed responded; if, as seems likely, organizations with a web presence and dedicated employees were more likely to respond to a survey about this topic than others, the results almost certainly overestimate arts organizations' web activities.

2. Museo Virtual de Artes, http://muva.elpais.com.uy/

museum experience—one has little control over one's distance from the work, latencies are high, and navigation is at times clunky—but it provides both an opportunity to see fascinating art that is otherwise inaccessible, and technological advances will almost certainly make such experiences even more compelling within a few years. Such developments, which could vastly increase the currently tiny proportion of museums' holdings on public view (as opposed to in storage), will be important to people who visit museums and care about art. But their cultural impact will be modest because people who regularly visit museums and attend performing-arts events constitute a relatively small and, at least in some countries, declining share of the population. Such declines, one should note, began in the pre-Internet era and cannot be attributed to the technology's growth (DiMaggio and Mukhtar 2004; Schuster 2007; Shekova 2012).

Creative Destruction in the Cultural Industries

The Internet has had a deeper impact on those cultural industries where the product can be digitized—i.e., converted into bits and reassembled at an end user's computer, tablet, or cell phone. This happened quickly with photographs and text; and then, as bandwidth and transmission speeds expanded, music and film. And as it occurred, dominant business models fell, leaving some industries in disarray. The Austrian economist Joseph Schumpeter (1942) referred to this process as "creative destruction"—destructive because of its harsh impact on existing firms, but creative because of the economic vitality it unleashed.

Analytically, we must distinguish two effects of digitization, one on cultural production and one on distribution. In traditional industries, production and distribution were largely, although not completely, unified, and, outside the fine-arts field, creators eager to reach a market were typically employed by or under contract to content-producing firms that also promoted and distributed their creations.

Digitization both reduced the cost of distribution and made it much simpler: I can post a photo, MP3, or video to Facebook in just a moment, and my *friends* can distribute it to their friends ad infinitum. Were incumbent firms able to capture such efficiencies, this would have expanded their bottom lines; but, of course, they have often been reluctant and slow to do so, at times with dramatic results. To cite the two most notable examples of creative destruction, since 1999, when Internet use began to take off in the U.S., sales of recorded music as a share of GDP have declined by 80 percent, and newspaper revenues have fallen by 60 percent (Waterman and Li 2011).

But the affordances of digitization for production has been just as important, if often overlooked, perhaps because they are connected to user-owned devices (computers, soundboards and mixers, cameras and video editors) rather than to the Internet itself. In many creative fields—photography, digital art, recorded music, radio programming (podcasting), journalism (blogging)—the cost of production has declined markedly, opening the fields to many more players. While the percentage of people who are *culture producers* remains small—remember that technologies provide affordances but do not change what people *want* to do—these numbers have grown and barriers to entry have declined, at least for creative workers who have no illusions about supporting themselves financially. The result, for people who are sufficiently engaged in both technology and the arts to care, is a far less centralized, more democratic, system in which specialized fan networks replace mass-mediated cultural markets.

A second result is the elision, in some fields (like photography) of the distinction between professional and amateur (Lessig 2009). In fields with strong business models, amateurs are practitioners who do not care to make art for profit, or are not accomplished enough to do so. In an increasing number of fields, *amateurs* are accomplished practitioners for whom the returns offer, at best, a partial livelihood. Thus far, the democratizing impact of technological change seems to have drawn people into cultural production more quickly than declining returns have driven them out. In many fields, we are seeing a regime in which small groups of artists interact intensely with one another and with sophisticated and committed publics, reviving (as Henry Jenkins [2006] has noted) the intimacy of *folk cultures*, but in genres in which innovation is prized. This combination may produce a golden age of artistic innovation and achievement (although it is also possible that, due to this decentralization of production and consumption, relatively few people will be aware of it).

In some industries, creative workers have succeeded in establishing new kinds of firms for which the Internet is central.

Difficult conditions often root out more vulnerable mid-sized firms (or, as in the case of the book and record industries, lead the incumbent firms to concentrate on large projects and neglect niche markets).

When this occurs, a process called "resource partitioning" (Carroll, Dobrev, and Swaminathan 2002) may lead to an increase in the number of small firms, producing specialized products for specialized markets. Such newcomers are often sole proprietorships, which gives them much flexibility. Whereas large media firms must net high profit margins to survive because they compete for investment with firms in every sector, private firms need earn only enough to motivate the proprietor to keep them in business. Thus podcasters, independent record labels, and community media outlets can survive by producing products for which no radio network, music conglomerate, or newspaper chain will compete.

In other words, we must question the widely held belief that the Internet has marched through the creative industries laying waste on all sides on two counts. First, if we look at statistics on the creative industries in the U.S. (which is the largest producer and where statistics are most accessible), we see, first, that not all industries have suffered marked declines; and some that have were doing badly before the Internet's arrival. Movie theater revenues accounted for about the same proportion of GDP in 2009 as in 1999; and cable television revenues rose dramatically, more than making up for declining broadcast television and home video revenues. Book sales declined between 1999 and 2009, but not much more than they had during the previous decade (Waterman and Ji 2011).

Second, when one speaks of *destruction*, one must distinguish between the Internet's impact on incumbent firms—the oligopolists who controlled most of the market for film, recorded music, and books in 2000—and its impact on the entertainment industries defined more broadly to include all of the creative workers and distributions channels that bring their work to consumers (Masnick and Ho 2012). The creative system as a whole might flourish, even as historically dominant firms and business models face grave challenges.

Let us consider three of the industries that have been affected. Film is an outlier in that it has weathered the storm especially well. The newspaper industry has been especially hard hit, with potentially significant consequences for democratic societies that rely on a vigorous press. And the recorded music industry has experienced the greatest disruption, and has adapted in the most interesting and perhaps promising ways.

Film

As we have seen, the film industry has survived the Internet's arrival with relatively little damage, especially compared to the newspaper and re-cording industries (BLS 2013). And this was the case despite the industry's complaints about illegal downloads and despite the massive volume of BitTorrent traffic, much of which entails the illegal transfer of film and video. The number of establishments showing motion pictures and videos and the number of persons they employ both declined in the U.S. more than 10 percent between 2001 and 2011 (in part due to consolidation, and an increase in the number of screens per theater) (BLS 2013). Similarly, between 2003 and 2012, in the U.S. and Canada, the number of tickets sold, and the value of these tickets in real dollars, both declined about 10 percent. But sharply rising box office in the Asia Pacific region and Latin America more than made up for this decline. Moreover, outside of film exhibition, the film and video industries have held their own since 2000, both in terms of number of establishments and number of employees (BLS 2013). Other sources of revenue have supplemented theater admissions. And technological change has dramatically lowered the cost of film pro-duction, bringing more independents into the industry and increasing the number of films. During the first decade of the twentieth century, the num-ber of films released to theaters grew by nearly 50 percent. Significantly, growth occurred outside of the major firms, which focused their energies on blockbusters, releasing many fewer movies at the same time that the number of films released by independents doubled in number (MPAA 2012). Moreover, the decade witnessed an equally dramatic increase in films produced outside of Europe and North America (Masnick and Ho 2012, 10). Between 2005 and 2009, India, which produces the largest number of feature films globally, increased production (i.e., number of films) by almost 25 percent. Nigeria, which is second, rose by more than 10 percent. China passed Japan to move into fourth place, behind the U.S., increasing from 260 films in 2006 to 448 in 2009 (Acland 2012).

Remarkably enough, prosperity has occurred even as film piracy—the massive transmission of product across BitTorrent P2P (peer-to-peer) networks—has remained substantial and, thus far at least, largely impervious to copyright-enforcement efforts (Safner 2013). Research suggests that film downloading may only minimally influence box office receipts. Using information on release date variations, BitTorrent use, and box office across countries, Danaher and Waldfogel (2013) conclude that downloading depresses box-office receipts for U.S. movies by about 7 percent—but that this cost is not intrinsic but rather reflects delays in international release dates (since they find no such effect in the domestic market). Presumably theater admissions would be even higher were it not for the increased availability of films through other channels, like cable television, subscription sites (e.g., Netflix), rentals (e.g., Amazon), and online sales (e.g., Amazon, iTunes). A quasi-experimental study of downloads concludes that the availability of legal film downloads (through iPods) depresses by about 5 to 10 percent, but does not affect sales of physical DVDs. (Whether this will continue to be the case as consumers who prefer DVDs age out of the population remains to be seen.) (Danaher et al. 2010)

Why has the film industry been relatively immune to the ravages experienced by the recording industry? There are probably five reasons. First, film companies had become proficient at new forms of distribution—licensing their product to cable stations, selling and renting physical media through video stores and other outlets—well before rise of the Internet, and therefore gaining experience that made digital transmission less disruptive than it might otherwise have been.

Second, greater bandwidth requirements for film piracy gave them a few more years to adjust to the new world, enabling them to avoid the antagonistic posture that the record industry took toward many of its customers. Observing the feckless response of the music industry may well have given the film companies a second-mover advantage.

Third, related to the first two points, the film industry was more effective in reaching agreements with online distributors who licensed their wares for distribution. Before the rise of the Internet the film companies had already changed their business models from one that depended almost exclusively on revenues from rentals to theatrical outlets to a mix of theatrical release, sale and rental of tapes and CDs to individuals through retail establishments, and sale of rights to broadcasters. When it came time to move to sale by download, or rental of streaming media, they had plenty of experience negotiating deals.

Fourth, since the end of the studio system, major film companies have organized movie production on a project basis—with each film, in effect, its own small organization. This mode or organization both reduces risk through cost sharing and, at the same time, reduces the ratio of fixed to variable costs, making it easier to adapt to changing economic conditions.

Fifth, because their core expertise is in marketing and distributing films, film companies can also serve as distributors for independent filmmakers. Even when their share of production declined, they could benefit from the expansion of the independent studios.

Finally, whereas consumers listen to pirated versions of music tracks the same way that they use copies they purchase legally, the movie companies' major distribution channel, theatrical release, offers an experience that is quite different from watching a film at home. Many consumers who could download a film for free or rent it from Amazon or their cable provider for less than the cost of two tickets are still willing to pay for the experience of spending a night out at a movie theater, a complement to the film itself that cannot be downloaded.

Newspapers

Few industries have declined more dramatically since the rise of the Internet than the newspaper industry. Two events in the U.S. in summer

2013 are emblematic of this trend: Amazon founder Jeff Bezos purchased the *Washington Post* for a modest sum, while the company that owned it retained other holdings, including an online education firm; and the *New York Times* sold the *Boston Globe* to local interests for just 6 percent of what it had paid for it two decades earlier. Overall, aggregate U.S. newspaper ad receipts (print and online) had toppled by more than half during the period the *Times* owned the *Globe*, and in 2010 were at about the same levels (in real dollars) as in 1960.[3] Moreover, ad revenues increased more or less steadily during the postwar era until 2000 (around the time that the Internet became mainstreamed), and then began a steep and uninterrupted decline. Since 2001, newspaper employment has fallen by almost 50 percent (BLS 2013).

In the U.S., at least, newspapers have depended upon an advertising-driven model, which the Internet has devastated in two ways. First, it almost immediately destroyed the demand for *classified advertising* which had accounted for a large part of most newspapers' revenues. When one wishes to sell a used end table, book, or article of clothing, eBay and Craig's List—searchable sites that reach an international market—are simply more efficient media for anyone operating online. (Here the affordances of the Internet for consumers interacted with those of high-speed computing and wireless communication for firms like FedEx and DHL, rendering the Internet's global reach more valuable by making long-haul shipping more reliable and more affordable.) Similarly, the market for *want ads*, another staple newspaper revenue source, dried up as newspapers were displaced by online companies like Monster.com and more specialized employment listings. Newspapers in the U.S. have also suffered collateral damage from the Internet, as online shopping and auction sites have largely eliminated the generalist department stores that had for decades been major purchasers of newspaper advertising space.

Second, newspapers lost the ability to sell their reader's attention to large-scale advertisers as more and more readers accessed their content through third-party links, most notably those provided by Google News.

3. To calculate these figures I downloaded ad data in spreadsheet form from the Newspaper Association of America (NAA 2013) and GDP deflator data from the website of the St. Louis Fed (FRED 2013), using the latter to deflate the former.

Those links went back to the newspapers themselves, so the problem was not lost readership so much as lost ad revenue.

Newspapers were vulnerable because they had long used attractive content—headlines, national politics, local coverage, and sports—to cross-subsidize the less popular content, like financial or science reporting, that appeared in the same document.

Moreover, both kinds of content were nestled amongst print advertisements that the reader skimming through could hardly avoid. The Internet eliminated this fixed proximity, enabling readers to cherry-pick the content in which they were most interested and to avoid advertisements as they did. By decoupling more popular from less attractive content, including ads, the online model made journalism far more difficult to monetize.

Because of this problem, newspapers have found it difficult to respond to the Internet's challenge. Although major newspapers have sporadically attempted to require consumers to pay for website access, these efforts have failed. In response, publishers have laid off reporters, set their employees to reporting for multiple platforms (Boczkowski 2010), and slashed budgets for investigative reporting. Sober observers have suggested that the industry will require philanthropic or government support to survive (Downie and Schudson 2009).

Major online news sites like Google News or *The Huffington Post* still rely mostly on the reporting of others. Thus we face the ironic possibility that just as online distribution has made news more readily available than ever, the supply of news will decline, both in quantity (fewer newspapers generating fewer stories) and quality (as papers pull away from in-depth reporting and rely more on wire services). There is some evidence of resource partitioning in the industry, as laid-off journalists and graduates of journalism schools have created new entities—some businesses, some nonprofit organizations, some websites sponsored by larger nonprofit entities—devoted to community journalism and investigative reporting (Nee 2013). One report identified 172 nonprofit outlets doing original reporting,

71 percent of which had been established since 2008. Most of these focused on local (rather than national or international) news, and about one in five emphasized investigative reporting. And most were staffed sparely, relying on part-time workers and, in many cases, volunteers, and very lightly capitalized (Mitchell et al. 2013). A directory of citizen and community news sites in the U.S. lists more than one thousand, most of which are noncommercial (Knight Community News Network 2013). Lacking a revenue model other than self-exploitation, the prospects of such entities are highly uncertain. Patch.com emerged in 2007 as an effort to provide news online to underserved suburban communities in the U.S, and was acquired by media firm AOL two years later. Like its noncommercial counterparts it appears to have suffered from undercapitalization and difficulty in monetizing its project. In August 2013, the parent company eliminated 300 of its 900 community sites and laid off many of its paid employees. Until journalist-run news sites find a way to produce serious news that is self-sustaining, the great promise of the Internet as a platform for democratic and commercially unconstrained journalism will be overshadowed by the technology's threat to the sources of news and information on which citizens had previously relied.

The Music Industry: A Case Study

The recording industry has suffered the most at the hands of technological change, especially if we define *recording industry* in terms of unit sales of recorded music by integrated multinational recording and distribution firms, of whom five dominated most music sales (90 percent in the U.S. and approximately 75 percent globally [Hracs 2012]) by the late 1990s. Until 2012, the industry marked a steady decline in sales, employment, and establishments. According to the Bureau of Labor Statistics, which includes not just record labels but agents, music studios, and other intermediaries in its counts, employment in the U.S. sound recording industries has declined steadily since 2001, falling by about 40 percent by 2012. Over that same period, the number of establishments in the industry fell by more than 25 percent (BLS 2013). The majors signed fewer artists and released fewer albums in 2009 than they had even five years earlier (IFPI 2010). Globally, the revenues from recorded music in all its forms fell by more than

40 percent between 1999 (its peak) and its nadir in 2011 (Smirke 2013). Particular subsectors like retail record stores (which suffered both from illegal and, later, legal downloading) and recording studios (which were harmed by the growth of better software and cheaper hardware available to independent musicians) declined even more sharply (Leyshon 2008).

Recording industry trade associations blamed the decline on illegal P2P file sharing—Napster, Grokster, and a range of successor technologies. File sharing did cut into record sales, but this occurred in the context of a broader failure on the part of the industry to adjust to technological change. Economists who study file sharing have, with some exceptions, found moderate negative effects of file sharing on music purchases, though a few have found no effects or very weak negative effects (Waldfogel 2012b; Tschmuck 2010). File sharing almost certainly *has* harmed music sales, but does not account for the entire decline, some portion of which likely reflects a combination of the end of the CD product cycle, the absence of a new hot genre (like rock or rap) to boost sales, negative consumer reaction to high prices and industry lawsuits against student downloaders, and the emergence of new legal, but less lucrative, modes of music access, such as Pandora (a San Francisco-based *freemium* service that provides personalized radio streams based on user-provided information) and Spotify (a Swedish-based freemium streaming site with [as of late summer 2013] a worldwide catalogue of more than 20 million tracks that permits users to create and share playlists).[4] In so far as the latter depress sales (by producing less revenue than equivalent distribution using the physical-album model), their impact can be credited to the Internet; but most of the drop in sales occurred before these services became popular and, indeed, digital sales and licensing appear to have revived the industry and now account for about 40 percent of the industry's global revenues.

Indeed, developments in the music field remind us that technological destruction is creative, in two senses. First, file sharing produces winners as well as losers. The big losers, of course, are the integrated multinational record companies and the small percentage of artists who are fortunate enough to get recording contracts with them. But such artists, although

4. The number of tracks comes from Spotify, which notes that not all tracks are licensed for all countries in which it operates. http:// press.spotify.com/us/information/ (accessed August 29, 2013).

they account for a large share of economic activity, are a small minority. Other losers may be artists at the margins of commercial success, who might have received contracts in an earlier time; and organizational forms that relied on physical record sales or on business from the integrated producers.

For most musicians, however, file sharing is part of a complex of technological career-building tools that create or expand opportunities to obtain at least some income from one's musical work.

Relatively few musicians have been able to support themselves through income attributable to copyright. More commonly, they knit together earnings from combinations of such activities as live performance, sale of merchandise, teaching, music production, and session work (DiCola 2013). In many cases the Internet has improved opportunities for non-copyright linked earnings. Musicians use their websites, for example, to market sweatshirts, recordings, and other merchandise. Whereas musicians once gave concerts to promote album sales, today many give the music away (e.g., by posting videos on YouTube or offering free downloads from their websites or Facebook pages), viewing the music as a means of increasing performance revenues. Research suggests that although file sharing reduces album sales, it actually increases the demand for live concerts, especially for artists who have not reached (and perhaps will never reach) stardom (Mortimer, Nosko, and Sorensen 2012). Not surprisingly, then, surveys indicate that while the most commercially successful artists decry file sharing, many musicians who record their own music are either indifferent to or supportive of the practice (Madden 2004; DiCola 2013).

The shift away from integrated music companies has created opportunities for small firms so that, although revenues for the industry are down, the music field's artistic vitality is robust. Just as indie film production has more than made up for declining releases by major film studios, indie record companies have more than made up the slack in album production caused by the major recording companies malaise. Between 1998 and 2010, album releases by major labels declined by about 40 percent. During that time, releases by independent record companies increased dramatically, passing the majors in 2001 and peaking in 2005. Between 2005, their numbers declined, as the number of self-released albums (of which there were just a handful in 1998) has rocketed to fill in the gap (Waldfogel 2012a). Despite the decline in revenues, the overall number of releases grew steadily from 1998 through 2009, as artists have used the Internet to take control of their fates. During the process, the percentage of all sales accounted for by top-selling albums has declined, and the percentage of best sellers produced by the independents has risen, increasing the diversity of the music available for purchase and streaming (Waldfogel 2012a).

Furthermore, there is evidence from the U.S., Spain, and Sweden that, as record sales fell, musicians' concert revenues increased steadily. Just as theater distribution, and the non-downloadable social element in movie-going, protected film revenues, so the concert market, which offers an experience that cannot be downloaded, has sustained the earnings of many musicians (Albinsson 2013; Krueger 2005; Montoro-Pons and Cuadrado-Garcia 2011).

To be sure, we ought not to romanticize the shift: many of the musicians signing with independent labels or producing their own albums might prefer to have contracts with the majors; and many who write their own tunes resent the low royalty payments they receive from streaming services. The streaming services themselves have yet to find a profitable business model, and time will tell whether they survive in their current form. Moreover, in one sense, the industry has shifted to an economy of self-exploitation, whereby educated creative workers labor for far less financial return than they might receive in another line of work. Nonetheless we are witnessing a sea change within the music industry that would have been impossible without the affordances the Internet offers.

What are these affordances?

1. *Digital recording technology and the capacity to make and mix masters at a small fraction of the cost required in the analog era.* Although these technologies are technically independent from the Internet, their development has been vastly accelerated by the rise of the MP3 as a means of moving music from one place to another.

The decline in production costs, coupled with the virtually zero marginal cost of online distribution, dramatically lowered barriers to entry, so that every artist can, in effect, create his or her own record company.

2. *The Internet has become a powerful means of marketing new music.* Not all artists do create their own companies, of course, for three reasons. First, most artists still want some number of physical records (CDs or, increasingly, vinyl) and it is convenient to pool the skills required to contract with manufacturers and distribute physical units. Second, contracting with digital intermediaries like LastFM, Spotify, Deezer, or Saavn is also subject to skill efficiencies. Third, and most important, the Internet has done less to reduce the cost of marketing, and arguably has made it more difficult to gain attention in a more densely populated musical marketplace. The major firms still can invest in media ad campaigns, outreach to radio stations, and major promotional tie-ins, albeit for many fewer albums.

   Most recording artists, however, rely on the Internet—Facebook, Twitter, and similar sites—to announce new products, sell merchandise (which may be more lucrative than the music), set up tours and other events, and communicate with fans. This approach seems rational as by 2010 more than 50 percent of American consumers used the Internet to learn about new music, while only 32 percent primarily encountered new music on radio (Waldfogel 2012b).

3. *The Internet is itself a platform for the publication of albums, many of which may exist primarily in digital form.* Galuszka (2012) identified more than 569 online record companies (or *netlabels*) that employ Creative Commons licenses in lieu of copyright, ceding users a wide range of rights contingent upon their crediting the authors for the works in question. Promotion is almost entirely through websites, blogs, and social media. Most of these labels were relatively young, three-quarters were managed by one or two people, and just 13 percent of the owners viewed them as potential sources of income. Yet most of them had released 16 or more albums and the top 10 percent had more than 50 releases.

4. *New forms of technology enable new forms of sociability, built around the technologies they employ.*

Whereas the music that most people listened to was for many years produced and distributed by large corporations, increasingly music is created and distributed in diffuse networks connected by a combination of face-to-face relations and social media.

As Manuel *Castells* (1996) noted at the dawn of the Internet age (1996), the increasing importance of networks as opposed to formal organization is a feature of contemporary societies in many fields. In the most vital music scenes, dense local networks employ social media both to intensify local participation *and* to reach audiences around the nation or the world.

Barry Wellman (Wellman et al. 2003), writing of the Internet's impact on social relations more generally, has called this combination of local and global impact *glocalization*. Contemporary pop acts, except for the most commercially successful, are rooted in place: bands and singer-songwriters establish close relations with one another and with local club owners, playing in one another's bands, sharing information and cooperating to produce shows (Pacey, Borgatti, and Jones 2011; Cummins-Russell and Rantisi 2012). With the emergence of ubiquitous portable wireless devices, messaging becomes a central means of communication *within* these densely connected groups: an artist may text a club to check on sound equipment, text other musicians to put together a show, promote it to his fans on Facebook and Twitter (counting on the most ardent followers to retweet it to their networks), and count on fans to take videos of the performance and post them on YouTube or circulate them as Instagrams.

These dense networks provide basic support, opportunities for artists to try out new songs and develop their crafts, and to build connections they may use throughout their careers (Lena 2012). In that sense, this is nothing new. Dynamic musical movements often experienced gestation in densely connected networks of interacting artists and fans: take, for example, the rise of the bebop style in jazz in New York in the 1950s (DeVeaux 1999), of political folk music in Greenwich Village in the early 1960s (Van Ronk and Wald 2006), of acid rock in San Francisco a few years later (Gleason 1969), or of punk music in London in the 1970s (Crossley 2008). Each of these movements exemplified *glocalization*, in the sense that it drew on and maintained deep local roots while using technology (the vinyl record or analog tape) to reach a global audience. Artists found ingenious technological ways to build community and fan loyalty before the Internet, as well: as early as 1983 and through the early 2000s, the Brooklyn band They Might Be Giants used a home telephone answering machine to offer a "Dial a Song" service to fans who called a special phone number. At its peak in the 1980s, the band added a new song every few days, publicizing the service through classified ads in youth-oriented papers and the distribution of cards and stickers in New York City's proto-hipster neighborhoods.[5]

Yet the situation today is different; first, because technology enables the community to scale upward and outward, and, second, because the endgame is no longer a contract with a major record company. In the old model, the artist could build a local following. But such a following could only grow nationally (or, more rarely, globally) if she or he was taken under a major company's wing and promoted heavily to such intermediaries as record stores and radio stations. Today, the artist may use social media to build out a base, releasing a tune on SoundCloud or a record on Spotify and LastFM. Radio stations are broadcasters, seeking the single stream of programming that will yield the largest audience and constrained by the limits of time to play only a limited number of tunes. Online streaming services, by contrast, compete to offer the greatest number of selections, with playlists tailored to each listener's tastes.

Getting onto an Internet music provider's *playlist* is simple; getting played once you are on it is much more difficult.

5. Documented at "This Might be a Wiki: The They Might Be Giants Knowledge Base," http://tmbw.net/wiki/ Dial-A-Song (accessed August 28, 2013).

Gaining attention from the multitude of music blogs, some local and many national or global in focus, is one strategy for building a reputation. Competition is stiff, but the Internet enables the performer to build on positive press. If, in 1990, I (as a consumer) read about a new band in *Rolling Stone*, I could only have heard that band's music if my local radio station happened to play it or if I chose to buy the album. In 2013, if I read about a new band at *Pitchfork.com*, I can go to its website, listen to (or perhaps download) some of its songs, listen to more tunes on Spotify or a similar service, and watch it play on YouTube. If I like the music enough, I can follow the band (and get links to new downloads) on one of countless specialized pop-music blog sites, put some songs on a Deezer or Spotify playlist, download them from iTunes, or even purchase a CD on Amazon.

Artists themselves build ties across space that scale outward. Some connections are still face to face. Performers in a local community share resources and information, and the more entrepreneurial may create small record labels that record the others' albums or work with venues to organize performances, asking affiliated bands to join the bill. In some cases, the activity may scale up to larger labels or, in the case of groups like the Disco Biscuits or Insane Clown Posse, to annual musical festivals that draw a national or international audience. Artists who tour through the indie club scene may help performers they meet organize tours to other regions or countries.

Still other connections are digitally mediated through artists' community sites, one of the most interesting which is Soundcloud.com, a rapidly growing German-based service with 40 million users as of fall 2013 (Pham 2013). In addition to making new files available to their fans, participating artists post their compositions as waveforms and listeners can post comments linked to particular moments in the piece. Especially in the case of electronic compositions (e.g., DJ mixes), interaction can be both enthusiastic and technical, sometimes ripening into transnational computer-mediated collaborations. Such interactions, or other long-distance social-media encounters, may lead to tours, with artists using their Facebook or Twitter accounts to announce their intentions, arrange gigs, and, once gigs are arranged, securing lodging from local fans. Indeed, in some cases, the tours themselves are organized by fan bases that mobilize through the Internet (Baym 2011).

This case study has described the emergence of a web-enabled, popular-music industry, organized around social networks that, at once, are intensely local yet also global in scope, combining face-to-face and digital relationships in new ways. This part of the industry, network based and organized less by the market than by self-exploitation and mutual assistance (what Baym [2011] refers to as a "gift economy") produce countless musical tracks, innumerable concerts, and much musical innovation. The Internet did not create this segment of the music industry, which has existed to varying degrees from time immemorial. But it has fortified it, enabled it, and enhanced its role in the overall ecology of contemporary culture.

Concluding Observations

In closing, I address two themes. First, to what extent can we generalize about the Internet's influence on the cultural industries and how likely are the developments I have described to persist into the future. Second, how do the changes I have described map onto larger trends in contemporary culture.

The Internet and the Cultural Industries

Here I will make three points. First, the Internet's influence varies from industry to industry, so that facile generalizations must be avoided. Second, there are reasons to believe that current adjustments in some fields at least may be unstable. Third, the way that creative workers and cultural industries use the Internet will depend on public policies.

We have seen that the Internet's influence depends, first, on the extent to which digital substitutes for analog experience are likely to satisfy consumers; second, on the extent to which producers compete for financial investments (and must thus maintain competitive profits), as opposed to needing only enough funding to persist; and, third, on the ability of incumbent firms to exploit changes inherent in digital production and distribution. The Internet has had relatively little impact on traditional theaters, ballet companies, and orchestras, because such organizations provide a service that requires physical presence in an actual audience. The same is true, *a fortiori*, for cuisine, the value of which emerges out of the sensual engagement of the consumer and the product. Institutions that exhibit the visual arts have also been affected only marginally, although it is possible that virtual museums may develop a more substantial presence. Workers in these sectors are keenly aware of the Internet, of course, and websites and social media play an important role in marketing, sales, and fundraising in all of them. But the Internet has not challenged the basic business models.

It is in those industries where the core product—a movie, news story, or musical track—can be downloaded and enjoyed in private that the Internet has been an agent of creative destruction.

Yet, as we have seen, each industry is somewhat different. The film industry, with its project-based production regime and a product that (as long as people value the theater experience and theaters must rent their product from studios) retains strong social externalities, has made the transition somewhat gracefully, becoming less centralized but no less profitable. Although film distribution will change, the position of filmmakers—both conglomerates and independents—appears relatively stable.

The rise of illegal downloading and the reluctance of many consumers to purchase music; the shift in the legal market from the sale of packaged albums (in which strong tracks induced consumers to, in effect, purchase weaker ones) to consumer choice and track-based online sales; and, finally, the rise of streaming services and licensing as a source of revenue, have together upended the business models of the major integrated music production companies that dominated the industry in the 1990s. Note, however, that pain has been felt most keenly by the major companies and their shareholders. By contrast, the Internet appears to have increased the availability of live music (returns from which, unlike returns from real-time film exhibition, are in most cases not appropriable by the majors) and produced a more vigorous set of popular-music institutions organized around a combination of local and technology-assisted networks in which online services and face-to-face relationships interact.

At the same time, it is somewhat unclear where this new regime is headed. Although revenues for the major companies are beginning to turn up after their steep decline, the new business model is far from certain. Streaming services, despite immense growth and consumer acceptance, have trouble converting free-service users to paid subscribers, and, as a result, provide only relatively modest revenues to record companies and vanishingly small royalties to composers. For its part, the networked musical economy that has emerged in the vacuum left by the majors' retrenchment depends heavily on a kind of economic self-exploitation: contributed effort or acceptance of below-market incomes by the musicians, micro-label owners, bloggers, promoters, and fans (some of whom play all these roles) whose efforts make the system work. If, as seems likely, people's tolerance for self-exploitation declines as their family obligations grow, time will tell if the supply of participants will sustain itself sufficiently to maintain the vitality that we now observe.

Finally, the newspapers industry, and the field of journalism, faces a particularly difficult future, given the reluctance of readers to pay for its product (especially when they can obtain much of it legally from newspaper and magazine websites) and given the rise of online advertising media that have made newspaper advertising less attractive to traditional purchases. (And, of course, as paid circulation declines, so do advertising rates for physical media.) Displaced journalists have produced an efflorescence of journalistic blogging, and some have combined forces to produce successful web-based publications and even to undertake serious investigative journalism. But how long such efforts can survive, and how widely they can scale, remains uncertain. The issue is less whether newspapers will survive than whether they will be willing and able to pay for the quality of reporting—especially local and international news and investigative reporting—that healthy democracies require.

These developments will, of course, be affected by public policy. Government subsidies for the press, for example, would change the economics of journalism, both by providing support directly and by freeing newspapers from capital markets' demands for competitive returns on investment. Similarly, government support for local media centers with high-speed Internet and media production equipment—a program pioneered by Brazilian Minister of Culture Gilberto Gil in his Pontos de Cultura program—could sustain the vitality of independent journalists, musicians, filmmakers, and other creative persons working outside the framework of the major media industries (Rogério 2011).

Intellectual property policy has been an especially highly contested field of struggle. Confronted by downloading, media firms have fought back in country after country, succeeding in tightening restrictions on downloading and increasing penalties in France, Sweden, the United States, and many other nations. Whether such legal changes will be effective, however, is questionable, and, of course, they only address one part of the media companies' troubles. And all too often, media companies have sought copyright expansion that has endangered traditional notions of fair use (including secondary uses by artists and educators), without solving the underlying problem of illegal digital distribution (Lessig 2004).

In the longer run, the structure of the Internet itself may change depending on the outcome of debates over the relative rights and obligations of content providers, online businesses, cable television companies, and other Internet service providers, as well as regulation of the flow of information and the openness of systems in mobile devices. The issues involved are technical, and they will be critically important in determining whether the Internet will continue to be as open and useful to creative workers and their publics as it is today (Benkler 2006; Crawford 2013).

The Internet, the Arts, Information, and Cultural Change

Ultimately, the Internet's influence on the production and use of culture is conditioned by broader trends that shape the way that people choose to use the affordances that technology offers. Here I consider just a few of these broader possibilities.

Can the Internet cultivate an expansion of creativity?

In much of the world, the rise of the Internet appears to have come at a time of increased interest in many forms of cultural expression, including the arts, political debate, and religion.

Although some have argued that this is a consequence of the emergence of the Internet as a public forum, it is far more likely that, as Castells (1996) anticipated, changes in the organization of human societies have produced cultural effects—including greater fluidity and salience of individual identity—that have enhanced many people's appetite for culture. Indeed there is some evidence that the Internet's rise has coincided with a period of artistic democratization. In the field of music, for example, one indicator is retail activity in musical instrument and supply stores: if more people are playing music, these stores should thrive. Indeed, in the U.S., sales of musical instruments and accessories boomed, rising almost 50 percent between 1997 and 2007.[6] It is possible that the increased availability of diverse forms of music online as well as increased vitality of local music scenes accounts for some of this change.

Will we benefit from increased cultural diversity? The rise of music streaming services with many millions of subscribers, the increased tendency of art museums to display some of their holdings online, the ability to view images and performances of the past on YouTube, or to easily stream films from many cultures and eras, have all increased dramatically the availability of what Chris Anderson (2006) called the "long tail" of market demand. Technology has reduced the cost of storing inventory— which now requires space on a server rather than a warehouse—making it easier for firms to profit from supplying artifacts for which there is relatively little demand. That this has occurred is indisputable. The effect on taste is less certain, for two reasons. First, culture is an experience good: how much one gets out of listening to music or viewing a museum exhibit depends, in part, on how much experience one has with this kind of art beforehand. (This is even more true for artistic styles or genres that are intellectually challenging or based on novel or unfamiliar aesthetic conventions [Caves 2000].) Second, psychologists recognize that most people respond poorly to choice, especially if it is in a field in which they are not already well versed: after a fairly low threshold their subjective utility declines as the number of options amongst which they must choose rises (Schwartz 2008). For those who are passionate about music, art, or film, the enhanced availability that the Internet provides is a tremendous boon. For those who are indifferent it is a matter of no concern. But for those in between, who enjoy the arts but are disinclined to invest much of their time in learning about them, expanded choice may be more irksome than beneficial.

A world of omnivores? Sociologists have argued that people's relationship to culture has changed, so that educated and sophisticated culture consumers no longer specialize in traditional works of high culture (if they ever did) but instead distinguish themselves through easy familiarity with a wide range of aesthetic genres and styles (Peterson and Kern 1996). This development antedated the Internet, but the technology provides extensive affordances for its growth. To be sure, research in France, Spain, and the U.S. suggests that some high-status people, at least, still embrace the conventional divide between high and popular culture (Bourdieu 1984; Coulangeon and Lemel 2007; Goldberg 2011; Lizardo 2005). And we have little sense of with just *how many* styles it pays to be familiar. But certainly in so far as social changes have increased the tendency of educated people to explore and become familiar with a wide range of cultural forms, the Internet makes that much easier.

Or will the Internet lead to cultural balkanization? At the onset of the Internet, legal scholar Cass Sunstein (2001) predicted that the vast array of views and information on the Internet would lead to cultural and political balkanization, as consumers exposed themselves only to views that were congenial. It turned out that Americans, at least, did not need the Internet to accomplish that: the emergence of politically polarized networks on cable news effectively accomplished the same thing. But the underlying concern remains and, indeed, has grown stronger, especially in the U.S., where privacy is less protected than in the EU. The cause of this concern is the proliferation of technologies like third-party cookies and browser fingerprinters that track one's behavior across multiple websites, the rise of information-aggregation companies that produce extensive profiles of

Internet users by combining information from many sources, and the use of this information by online retailers and content providers to decorate users' web pages with personalized content that reflects the tastes and interests they have already acquired (Turow 2011). In other words, the Internet lays a table before us of unprecedented abundance, and then tries to keep us from that table by constantly showing us reflections of ourselves. Clearly, the effect of these technologies will depend on the proclivities of users: the path of least resistance will be to use the Internet in ways that constantly reinforce one's prior views and tastes. What we do not yet know is to what extent people will choose to overcome these tendencies and explore the wider range of ideas and styles that the Internet can provide.

A new form of cultural inequality? For many years, political scientists have explored what they call the "knowledge gap hypothesis"—the paradoxical notion that if good information becomes cheaper, better-informed members of the public will become even *more* well informed, and less-informed citizens will fall even further behind. The assumption behind this expectation is that well-informed people value information more highly than people with little information, so that they will acquire more of it if the price goes down. Markus Prior's research (2005) indicates that, as far as political information is concerned, this is true of the Internet as it has been of other media. Another study (Tepper and Hargittai 2009) demonstrated similar dynamics in the field of music: students from higher social class backgrounds used a broader range of websites and P2P sources to explore new kinds of music, developing greater expertise and getting more out of their online experience than students from more humble backgrounds.

The implications of this research are sobering. The Internet provides a remarkably rich supply of art, music, and information, enabling citizens to dig deeper into the policy issues before them, to learn more about their worlds, and to enjoy an unprecedented wealth of aesthetic experience. But it is unclear just how many people this potential will benefit. Indeed, it seems that this expanded supply may be welcomed by a relatively small group of highly educated people, those who are already engaged in politics, involved in the arts, and conversant with the Internet's affordances. Other users may be unaware of the possibilities or unwilling to take the time to explore a range of new ideas and unfamiliar options. And the significant minorities who still lack meaningful Internet access will, of course, have no choice. The possibility that the Internet may usher us into a world of even greater cultural and informational inequality—one in which an educated elite gets its information and entertainment online from a vast range of diverse sources, while the majority settle for the offerings of chastened and diminished giant media firms—poses a challenge to both cultural and political democracy.

References

Acland, Charles.
"From International Blockbusters to National Hits: Analysis of the 2010 UIS Survey on Feature Film Statistics." UNESCO Institute of Statistics, Bulletin No. 8. February 2012. http://www.uis.unesco.org/culture/Documents/ib8-analysis-cinema-production-2012-en2.pdf

Albinsson, Staffan.
"Swings and Roundabouts: Swedish Music Copyrights 1980–2009." *Journal of Cultural Economics* 37 (2013): 175–84.

Anderson, Chris.
The Long Tail: Why the Future of Business is Selling Less of More. New York: Hyperion, 2006.

Baym, Nancy K.
"The Swedish Model: Balancing Markets and Gifts in the Music Industry. *Popular Communication* 14 (2011): 22–38.

Benkler, Yochai.
The Wealth of Networks: How Social Production Transforms Markets and Freedom. New Haven: Yale University Press, 2006.

BLS (U.S. Bureau of Labor Statistics).
"Spotlight on Statistics: Media and Information." 2013. U.S. Bureau of Labor Statistics, http://www.bls.gov/spotlight/2013/media/ (accessed August 26, 2013).

Boczkowski, Pablo.
News at Work: Imitation in an Age of Information Abundance. Chicago: University of Chicago Press, 2010.

Bourdieu, Pierre.
Distinction: A Social Critique of the Judgment of Taste. Cambridge, MA: Harvard University Press, 1984.

Carroll, Glenn R., Stanislav Dobrev, and Anand Swaminathan.
"Organizational Processes of Resource Partitioning." *Research in Organizational Behavior* 24 (2002): 1–40.

Castells, Manuel.
The Rise of the Network Society. London: Blackwell, 1996.

Caves, Richard E.
Creative Industries. Cambridge, MA: Harvard University Press, 2000.

Christensen, Clayton.
The Innovator's Dilemma: When New Technologies Cause Great Firms to Fail. Boston: Harvard Business Press, 1977.

Coulangeon, Philippe, and Yannick Lemel.
"Is 'Distinction' Really Outdated? Questioning the Meaning of the Omnivorization of Taste in Contemporary France." *Poetics* 35 (2007): 93–111.

Crawford, Susan.
Captive Audience: The Telecom Industry and Monopoly Power in the New Gilded Age. New Haven: Yale University Press, 2013.

Crossley, Nick.
"Pretty Connected: The Social Network of the Early UK Punk Movement." *Theory, Culture and Society* 25 (2008): 89–116.

Cummins-Russell, Thomas, and Norma M. Rantisi.
"Networks and Place in Montreal's Independent Music Industry." *Canadian Geographer* 56 (2012): 80–97.

Danaher, Brett, Samita Dhanasobhon, Michael D. Smith, and Rahul Telang.
"Converting Pirates without Cannibalizing Purchasers: The Impact of Digital Distribution on Physical Sales and Internet Privacy." Social Science Research Network (SSRN), March 3, 2010. http://ssrn.com/abstract=1381827

Danaher, Brett, Michael D. Smith, Rahul Telang, and Siwen Chen. 2012.
"The Effect of Graduated Response Anti-Piracy Laws on Music Sales: Evidence from an Event Study in France." Social Science Research Network (SSRN), January 21, 2012. http://ssrn.com/abstract=1989240

Danaher, Brett, and Joel Waldfogel.
"Reel Piracy: The Effect of Online Film Piracy on International Box Office Sales." Social Science Research Network, January 16, 2012. http://ssrn.com/abstract=1986299

DeVeaux, Scott.
The Birth of Bebop: A Social and Musical History. New York: Picador, 1999.

DiCola, Peter.
"Money From Music: Survey Evidence on Musicians' Revenue and Lessons About Copyright Incentives." *Arizona Law Review* (forthcoming). Social Science Research Network (SSRN), January 9, 2013. http://ssrn.com/abstract=2199058

DiMaggio, Paul.
"Nonprofit Organizations and the Intersectoral Division of Labor in the Arts." In Walter Powell and Richard Steinberg, eds. *The Nonprofit Sector: A Research Handbook*. 2nd ed. New Haven: Yale University Press, 2006.

DiMaggio, Paul, and Toqir Mukhtar.
"Arts Participation as Cultural Capital in the United States, 1982–2002: Signs of Decline?" *Poetics* 32 (2004): 169–94.

Downie, Leonard, Jr., and Michael Schudson.
"The Reconstruction of American Journalism." *Columbia Journalism Review*, October 19, 2009. http://www.cjr.org/reconstruction/the_reconstruction_of_american.php?page=all

Foster, Pacey, Stephen P. Borgatti, and Candace Jones.
"Gatekeeper Search and Selection Strategies: Relational and Network Governance in a Cultural Market." *Poetics* 39 (2011): 247–65.

FRED (Federal Reserve Bank of St. Louis).
"Gross Domestic Product (Implicit Price Deflator)." Federal Reserve Bank of St. Louis, July 31, 2013 (updated). http://research.stlouisfed.org/fred2/series/A191RD3A086NBEA/downloaddata?cid=21

Gibson, James J.
"The Theory of Affordances." In Robert Shaw and James Bradford, eds. *Perceiving, Acting, and Knowing*. Hillsdale, New Jersey: Lawrence J. Erlbaum, 1977. 67–82.

Gleason, Ralph.
The Jefferson Airplane and the San Francisco Sound. New York: Ballantine, 1969.

Goldberg, Amir.
"Mapping Shared Understandings Using Relational Class Analysis: The Case of the Cultural Omnivore Reexamined." *American Journal of Sociology* 116 (2011): 1397–1436.

Hracs, Brian J.
"A Creative Industry in Transition: The Rise of Digitally Driven Independent Music Production." *Growth and Change: A Journal of Urban and Regional Policy* 43 (2012): 442–61.

(IFDI) International Federation of the Phonographic Industry.
"IFPI Digital Music Report 2010: Music How, Where and When You Want It." International Federation of the Phonographic Industry, 2010. http://www.ifpi.org/content/library/dmr2010.pdf

Jenkins, Henry.
Convergence Culture: Where Old and New Media Collide. New York: NYU Press, 2006.

Knight Community News Network.
"Directory of Community News Sites." Knight Community News Network, 2013. http://www.kcnn.org/citmedia_sites/ (accessed August 24, 2013).

Krueger, Alan B.
"The Economics of Real Superstars: The Market for Rock Concerts in the Material World." *Journal of Labor Economics* 23 (2005): 1–30.

Lena, Jennifer.
Banding Together: How Communities Create Genres in Popular Music. Princeton: Princeton University Press, 2012.

Lessig, Lawrence.
Free Culture: How Big Media Uses Technology and the Law to Lock Down Culture and Control Creativity. New York: The Penguin Press, 2004.
———. *Remix: Making Art and Commerce Thrive in the Hybrid Economy*. New York: Penguin Press. 2009.

Leyshon, Andrew.
"The Software Slump?: Digital Music, the Democratisation of Technology, and the Decline of the Recording Studio Sector within the Musical Economy." *Environment and Planning* 41 (2009): 1309–31.

Lizardo, Omar.
"Can Cultural Capital Theory
    Be Reconsidered in the
    Light of World Polity
    Institutionalism? Evidence
    from Spain." *Poetics* 33
    (2005): 81–110.

Madden, Mary.
"Artists, Musicians and the
    Internet." Pew Internet
    and American Life Project,
    December 5, 2004. http://
    www.pewinternet.org/~/
    media//Files/Reports/2004/
    PIP_Artists.Musicians_
    Report.pdf.pdf

Masnick, Michael, and Michael Ho.
"The Sky is Falling: A Detailed
    Look at the State of the
    Entertainment Industry."
    TechDirt, 2012a. http://www.
    techdirt.com/skyisrising/
———. "The Sky is Falling:
    Regional Study—Germany,
    France, UK, Italy, Russia,
    Spain." Computer &
    Communications Industry
    Association, 2012b. http://
    www.ccianet.org/CCIA/
    files/ccLibraryFiles/
    Filename/000000000733/
    Sky%20is%20Rising%20
    2013.pdf

Miniwatt Marketing Group.
"Internet World Stats:
    Usage and Population
    Statistics." Internet World
    Stats, 2013. http://www.
    internetworldstats.com/
    (accessed August 20, 2013).

McLuhan, Marshall.
*Understanding Media: The
    Extensions of Man*. New York:
    New American Library, 1964.

Mitchell, Amy, Mark Jurkowitz,
Jesse Holcomb, Jodi Enda, and
Monica Anderson.
"Nonprofit Journalism: A
    Growing But Fragile Part of
    the Nonprofit News System."
    Project for Excellence in
    Journalism, Pew Research
    Center, Washington, D.C.,
    2013. http://www.journalism.
    org/analysis_report/
    nonprofit_journalism

Montoro-Pons, Juan D., and
Manuel Cuadrado-García.
"Live and Prerecorded Popular
    Music Consumption." *Journal
    of Cultural Economics* 35
    (2011): 19–48.

Mortimer, Julie Holland, Chris
Nosko, and Alan Sorensen.
"Supply Responses to Digital
    Distribution: Recorded Music
    and Live Performances."
    *Information Economics and
    Policy* 24 (2012): 3–14.

MPAA (Motion Picture
Association of American).
"Theatrical Market Statistics
    2012." Motion Picture
    Association of American,
    2012. http://www.mpaa.org/
    Resources /3037b7a4-58a2-
    4109-8012-58fca3abdf1b.pdf

NAA (Newspaper Association of
America.
"Annual Newspaper Ad
    Revenue." Newspaper
    Association of America, April
    2013. http://www.naa.org/~/
    media/NAACorp/Public%20
    Files/TrendsAndNumbers/
    Newspaper-Revenue/
    Annual-Newspaper-Ad-
    Revenue.ashx

Nee, Rebecca Coates.
"Creative Destruction: An
    Exploratory Study of How
    Digitally Native News
    Nonprofits Are Innovating
    Online Journalism Practices."
    *International Journal on Media
    Management* 15 (2013): 3–22.

Peterson, Richard A., and Roger
M. Kern.
"Changing Highbrow Taste: From
    Snob to Omnivore." *American
    Sociological Review* 61
    (1996): 900–7.

Pham, Alex.
"Google+ Plus in SoundCloud
    for Its 343 Million Users
    (Exclusive)." *Billboard*,
    August 12, 2013. http://
    www.billboard.com/biz/
    articles/news/digital-
    and-mobile/5645566/
    google-plugs-in-soundcloud-
    for-its-343-million-users

Prior, Markus.
"News vs. Entertainment: How
    Increasing Media Choice
    Widens Gaps in Political
    Knowledge and Turnout."
    *American Journal of Political
    Science* 49 (2005): 577–92.

Rogério, Paulo.
"Learning From Gilberto Gil's
    Efforts to Promote Digital
    Culture for All." *Americas
    Quarterly*, November 7, 2011.
    http://americasquarterly.org/
    node/3077

Romanesko, Jim.
"Patch is Laying Off Hundreds
    of Employees on Friday." *Jim
    Romenesko.com* (blog), August
    8, 2013. http://jimromenesko.
    com/2013/08/08/patch-is-
    laying- off-hundreds-of-
    employees-on-friday/

Safner, Ryan.
"Steal This Film, Get Taken
     Down? A New Dataset
     on DMCA Takedown and
     Movie Piracy." RyanSafner.
     com, May 2, 2013. http://
     ryansafner.com/papers/
     dmcatakedowns.pdf

Schradie, Jen.
"The Digital Production Gap: The
     Digital Divide and Web 2.0
     Collide." *Poetics* 39 (2011):
     145–68.

Schumpeter, Joseph A.
*Capitalism, Socialism, and
     Democracy*. New York:
     Harper and Bros., 1942. Repr.
     London: Routledge, 1994.

Schuster, J. Mark.
"Participation Studies and
     Cross-National Comparison:
     Proliferation, Prudence and
     Possibility." *Cultural Trends*
     16 (2007): 99–196.

Schwartz, Barry.
"Can There Ever Be Too Many
     Flowers Blooming?" In Steven
     J. Tepper and Bill Ivey, eds.
     *Engaging Art: The Next Great
     Transformation of America's
     Cultural Life*. New York:
     Routledge, 2008. 239–56.

Shekova, Ekaterina.
"Changes in Russian Museum
     Attendance: 1980–2008."
     *Museum Management
     and Curatorship* 27 (2012):
     149–59.

Smirke, Richard.
"IFPI Digital Music Report 2013:
     Recorded Music Revenues
     Climb for First Time Since
     1999." *Billboard*, February 26,
     2013. http://www.billboard.
     com/biz/articles/news/

digital-and-mobile/1549915/
ifpi-digital-music-report-
2013-global-recorded-music

Sunstein, Cass.
Republic 2.0. Princeton: Princeton
     University Press, 2001.

Thomson, Kristin, and Kristen
Purcell.
"Arts Organizations and Digital
     Technologies." Report of Pew
     Internet and American Life
     Project, Washington, D.C.,
     January 13, 2013.

Tepper, Steven J., and Eszter
Hargittai.
"Pathways to Music Exploration
     in the Digital Age." *Poetics 37*
     (2009): 227–49.

Tschmuck, Peter.
*Creativity and Innovation in the
     Music Industry*. Dordrecht:
     Springer, 2006.
———. "The Economics of Music
     File Sharing—A Literature
     Overview." Paper delivered
     at Vienna Music Business
     Research Days, University of
     Music and Performing Arts,
     Vienna, June 9–10, 2010.

Turow, Joseph.
*The Daily You: How the New
     Advertising Industry is
     Defining Your Identity and
     Your Worth*. New Haven: Yale
     University Press, 2011.

Van Deursen, Alexander, and Jan
Van Dijk.
"The Digital Divide Shifts to
     Differences in Usage."
     New Media and Society,
     June 7, 2013. http://nms.
     sagepub.com/content/
     early/2013/06/05
     /1461444813487959.full.
     pdf+html

Van Ronk, Dave, and Elijah Wald.
The Mayor of MacDougal Street.
     New York: Da Capo, 2006.

Waldfogel, Joel.
"And the Bands Played On:
     Digital Disintermediation and
     the Quality of New Recorded
     Music." Social Science
     Research Network (SSRN),
     July 25, 2012a. http://ssrn.
     com/abstract=2117372.
———. "Music Piracy and Its
     Effects on Demand, Supply
     and Welfare." *Innovation
     Policy and the Economy* 12
     (2012b): 91–110.

Waterman, David, and Sung
Wook Ji.
"Online and Offline in the U.S.:
     Are the Media Shrinking."
     Paper presented at the
     39th TRPC Conference,
     Washington, D.C., September
     2011. Social Science
     Research Network (SSRN),
     September 24, 2011. http://
     ssrn.com/abstract=1979916

Wellman, Barry, Anabel Quan-
Haase, Jeffrey Boase, Wenhong
Chen, Keith Hampton, Isabel
Diaz de Isla, and Kakuko Miyata.
"The Social Affordances of the
     Internet for Networked
     Individualism." *Journal
     of Computer Mediated
     Communication* 8, no. 3
     (2003). http://onlinelibrary.
     wiley.com/doi/10. 1111/
     j.1083-6101.2003. tb00216.x/
     full

First the Media, Then Us: How the Internet Changed the Fundamental Nature of the Communication and Its Relationship with the Audience

Peter Hirshberg

Executive, entrepreneur, and marketing specialist, Silicon Valley

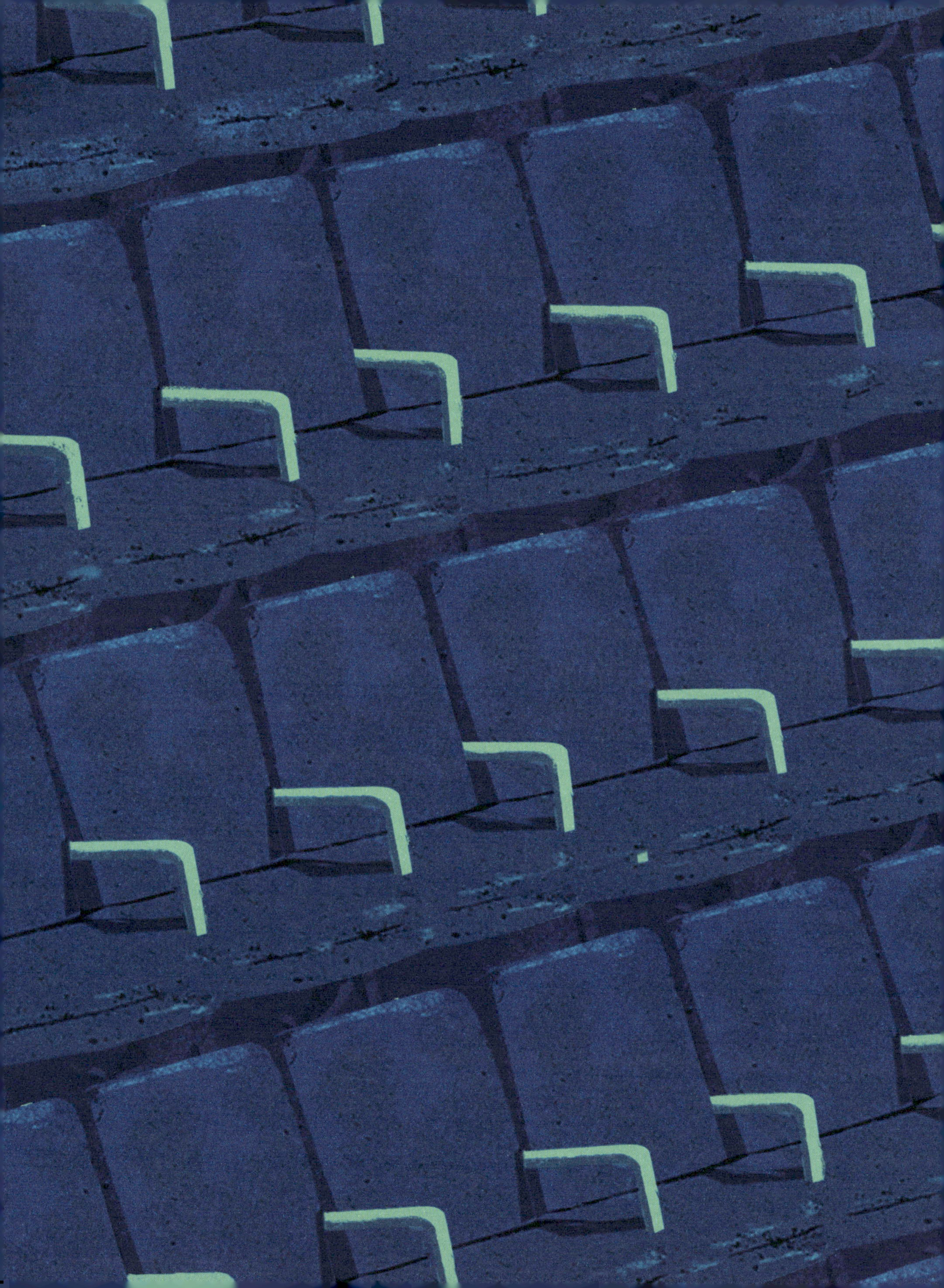

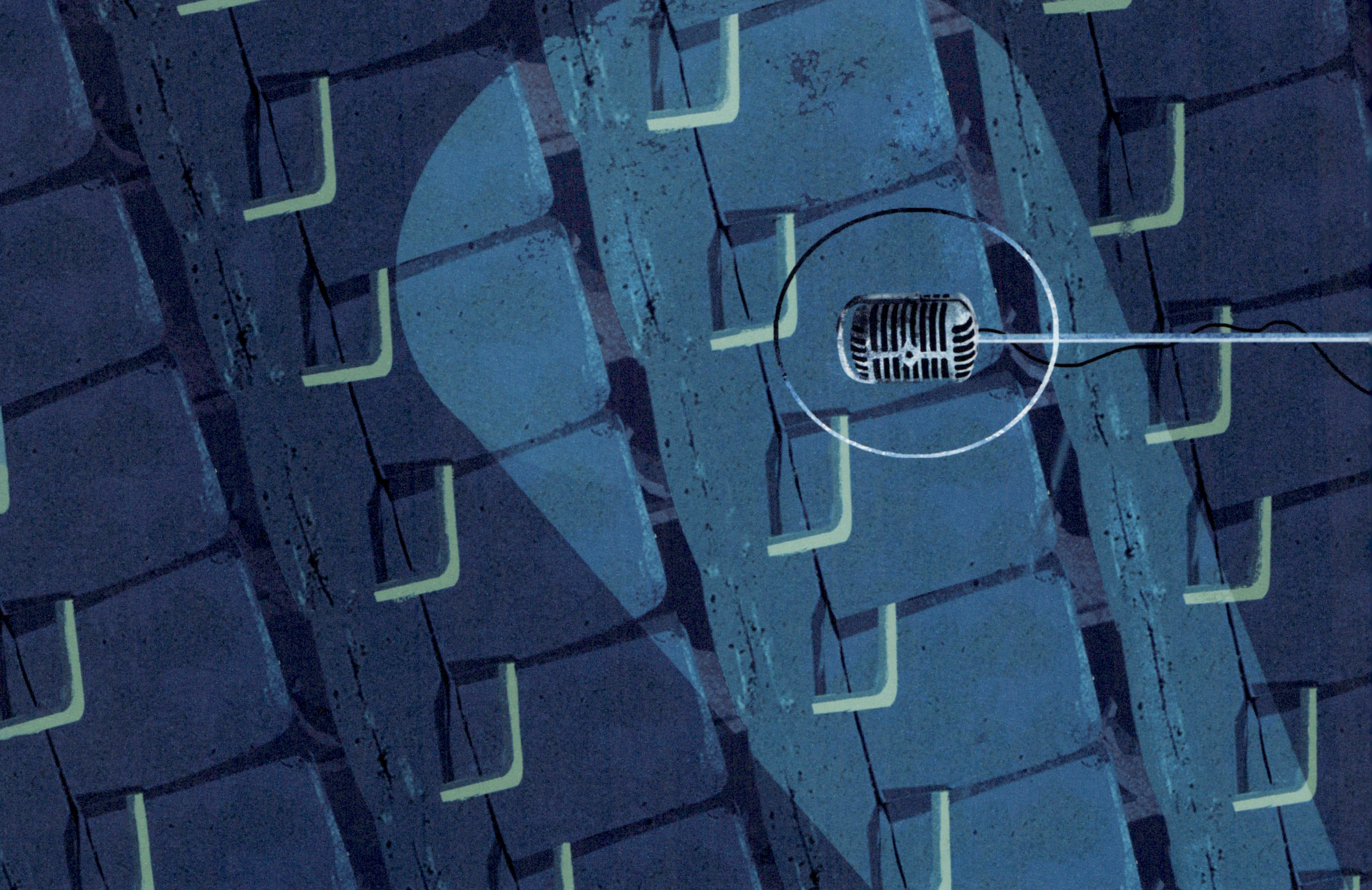

Peter Hirshberg

reimaginegroup.com/peter-hirshberg.html

Illustration
Eva Vázquez

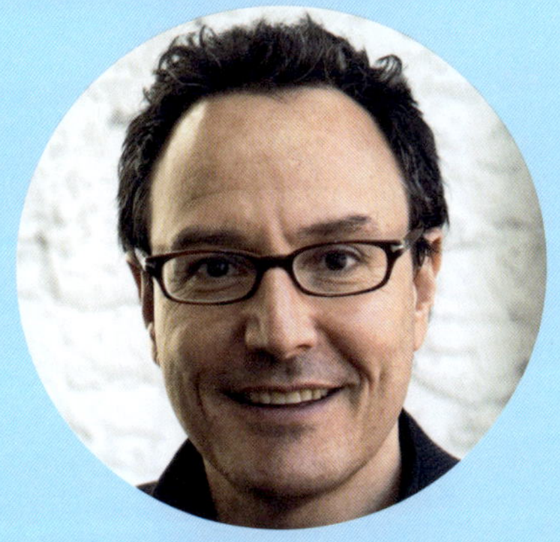

Peter Hirshberg has led emerging media and technology companies for more than 25 years. As Chairman of Re: Imagine Group, he shapes strategies at the confluence of people, places, brands, and cities. He has worked with executive teams at Time Warner, Sony, Unilever, IBM, Telefónica, and many others on digital and growth strategies. He is Chairman of San Francisco's Gray Area Foundation for the Arts, where he has developed initiatives such as San Francisco's Summer of Smart with 16 mayoral candidates and Urban Prototyping in Singapore, London, San Francisco, Geneva, and Zurich. As an advisor to United Nations Global Pulse, he's addressed the General Assembly on real-time data for international development and is editor of "Taking the Global Pulse." He was founder and CEO of Elemental Software, served as President and CEO of Gloss.com, and is former Chairman of Technorati. He headed Enterprise Marketing at Apple Computer for nine years, and is a Senior Fellow at the USC Annenberg Center on Communication Leadership and a Henry Crown Fellow of the Aspen Institute. He is a frequent technology and media industry speaker, having presented at TED and the World Economic Forum, among many others. He earned his bachelor's degree at Dartmouth College and his MBA at the Wharton School.

Sites and services that have changed my life

twitter.com
archive.org
Heard
NextBus
Flipboard

First the Media, Then Us: How the Internet Changed the Fundamental Nature of the Communication and Its Relationship with the Audience

In just one generation the Internet changed the way we make and experience nearly all of media. Today the very act of consuming media creates an entirely new form of it: the social data layer that tells the story of what we like, what we watch, who and what we pay attention to, and our location when doing so.

The audience, once passive, is now cast in a more central and influential role than ever before. And like anyone suddenly thrust in the spotlight, we've been learning a lot, and fast.

This social data layer reveals so much about our behavior that it programs programmers as much as they program us. Writers for the blog website *Gawker* watch real-time web consumption statistics on all of their posts—and they instantly learn how to craft content to best command an audience. The head programmer for Fox Television Network similarly has a readout that gives an in-depth analysis of audience behavior, interest, and sentiment. In the run-up to the final episode of the American television drama *Breaking Bad*, the series was drawing up to 100,000 tweets a day, a clear indication that the audience was as interested in what it had to say as what the producers were creating.

All this connected conversation is changing audiences as well. Like Narcissus, we are drawn to ourselves online and to the siren of ever-more social connections. In her book *Alone Together*, Sherry Turkle (2011) points out that at this time of maximum social connection, we may be experiencing fewer genuine connections than ever before. The renowned media theorist Marshall McLuhan (1968, 73) saw the potential for this more than 40 years ago when he observed that *augmentation leads to amputation*. In other words, in a car we don't use our feet—we hit the road and our limbs go into limbo. With cell phones and social devices, we are connected to screens and virtually to friends worldwide, but we may forfeit an authentic connection to the world. Essentially, we arrive at Turkle's "alone together" state.

In the past, one could turn the media off—put it down, go offline. Now that's becoming the exception, and for many, an uncomfortable one. Suggest to a young person today that she go offline and she'll ask, "Offline, what's that?" or "Why am I being punished?" We are almost always connected to an Internet-enabled device, whether in the form of a smartphone, fitness monitor, car, or screen. We are augmented by sensors, signals, and servers that record vast amounts of data about how we lead our everyday lives, the people we know, the media we consume, and the information we seek. The media, in effect, follows us everywhere, and we're becoming anesthetized to its presence.

It is jarring to realize that the implication of this total media environment was also anticipated more than 40 years ago by McLuhan. When he spoke of the "global village," his point was not just that we'd be connected to one another. He was concerned that we'd all know each other's business, that we'd lose a measure of privacy as a result of living in a world of such intimate awareness. McLuhan (1969) called this "retribalizing," in the sense that modern media would lead us to mimic the behavior of tribal villages. Today, the effects of this phenomenon help define the media environment: we consciously manage ourselves as brands online; we are more concerned than ever with each other's business; and we are more easily called out or shamed than in the bygone (and more anonymous) mass communication era.

We maintain deeply intimate relationships with our connected devices. Within minutes of waking up, most of us reach for a smartphone. We go on to check them 150 or more times throughout the day, spending all but two waking hours with a mobile device nearby (IDC 2013). As these devices become omnipresent, more and more data about our lives is nearly permanently stored on servers and made searchable by others (including private corporations and government agencies).

This idea that everything we do can be measured, quantified, and stored is a fundamental shift in the human condition. For thousands of years we've had the notion of accountability to an all-seeing, all-knowing God. He kept tabs on us, for our own salvation. It's one of the things that made religion effective. Now, in just a few thousand days, we've deployed the actual all-seeing, all-knowing network here on earth—for purposes less lofty than His, and perhaps even more effective.

We are also in the midst of an unprecedented era of media invention. We've passed from the first web-based Internet to the always-connected post-PC world. We will soon find ourselves in an age of pervasive computing, where all devices and things in our built world will be connected and responsive, with the ability to collect and emit data. This has been called the *Internet of Things*.

In the recent past, the pace of technological change has been rapid—but it is accelerating quickly. One set of numbers tells the story. In 1995, the Internet connected together about 50 million devices. In 2011, the number of connections exceeded 4.3 billion (at the time roughly half of these were people and half were machines). We ran out of Internet addresses that year and are now adopting a new address mechanism called IPv6. This scheme will allow for about 340 billion billion billion billion unique IP addresses. That's probably the largest number ever seriously used by mankind in the design of anything. (The universe has roughly 40 orders of magnitude more atoms than we have Internet addresses, but man didn't invent the universe and for the purpose of this chapter it is not a communication medium, so we'll move on.)

Here is a big number we will contend with, and soon: there will likely be one trillion Internet-connected devices in about 15 years. Nothing on earth will grow faster than this medium or the number of connected devices and the data they emit. Most of these devices will not be people, of course, but the impact of a trillion devices emitting signals and telling stories on our mediated world cannot be overstated.

To visualize the size of all this, imagine the volume of Internet connections in 1995 as the size of the Moon. The Internet of today would be the size of Earth. And the Internet in 15 years the size of giant Jupiter!

Exponential change like this matters because it points out how unreliable it is to predict how media will be used tomorrow. Examining the spotty record of past predictions is humbling and helps open our minds to the future.

In 1878, the year after he invented the phonograph, Thomas Edison had no idea how it would be used; or rather, he had scores of ideas—but he could not come up a priori with the killer application of his hardware. Edison was a shrewd inventor who kept meticulous notes. Here were his top 10 ideas for the use of the phonograph:

1. Letter writing, and all kinds of dictation without the aid of a stenographer.
2. Photographic books, which will speak to blind people without effort on their part.
3. The teaching of elocution.
4. Music—the phonograph will undoubtedly be liberally devoted to music.
5. The family record; preserving the sayings, the voices, and the last words of the dying members of the family, as of great men.
6. Music boxes, toys, etc.—A doll which may speak, sing, cry or laugh may be promised our children for the Christmas holidays ensuing.
7. Clocks, that should announce in speech the hour of the day, call you to lunch, send your lover home at ten, etc.
8. The preservation of language by reproduction of our Washingtons, our Lincolns, our Gladstones.
9. Educational purposes; such as preserving the instructions of a teacher so that the pupil can refer to them at any moment; or learn spelling lessons.
10. The perfection or advancement of the telephone's art by the phonograph, making that instrument an auxiliary in the transmission of permanent records.

He first attempted a business centered on stenographer-free letter writing. That failed, largely because it was a big threat to the incumbent player—stenographers. It would be years (and a few recapitalizations) later that music would emerge as the business of phonographs. And this was a business that survived for well over 100 years before cratering.

When I reflect on my own career, I see this pattern of trying to understand—"Exactly what is this anyway?"—constantly repeat itself. In 1993, I collaborated with Bill Gates (1995) as he wrote *The Road Ahead*. The book outlined what Gates believed would be implications of the personal computing revolution and envisioned a future profoundly impacted by the advent of what would become the Internet. At the time, we called this a "global information superhighway."

I was working with Gates on envisioning the future of television. This was one year before the launch of the Netscape (then Mosaic) browser brought the World Wide Web to the masses. In 1993, we knew that in the coming years there would be broadband and new distribution channels to connected homes. But the idea that this would all be based on an open Internet eluded us completely. We understood what technology was coming down the pike. But we could not predict how it would be used, or that it would look so different from what we had grown accustomed to, which was centralized media companies delivering mass media content from the top down. In 1993 what we (and Al Gore) imagined was an "information superhighway"—Gates and I believed that this would be a means to deliver Hollywood content to the homes of connected people.

We understood that the Internet would be a means to pipe content to connected homes and to share information. But here's what we missed:

- *User-Generated Anything*. The idea that the audience, who we treated as mere consumers, would make their own content and fascinate one another with their own ideas, pictures, videos, *feeds*, and taste preferences (*Likes*) was fantastical. We knew people would publish content—this had been taking place on online bulletin boards and other services for years. But the idea that the public would be such a big part of the media equation simply did not make sense.

- *The Audience As Distributor, Curator, Arbiter*. We'd all be able to find content, because someone big like Microsoft would publish it. The idea that what the audience liked or paid attention to would itself be a key factor in distribution was similarly unfathomable. It would take the invention of Google and its PageRank algorithm to make clear that what everyone was paying attention to was one of the most important (and disruptive) tools in all of media. In the early 2000s, the rise of social media and then social networks would make this idea central.

- *The Long Tail*. In retrospect, it seems obvious: in a world of record shops and video rental stores it cost money to stock physical merchandise.

Those economics meant stocking hits was more cost-effective than keeping less popular content on the shelves. But online, where the entire world's content can be kept on servers, the economics flip: unpopular content is no more expensive to provision that a blockbuster move. As a result, audiences would fracture and find even the most obscure content online more easily than they could at Blockbuster or Borders. This idea was first floated by Clay Shirky in 2003, and then popularized by *Wired*'s Chris Anderson in 2004. That was also the year Amazon was founded, which is arguably the company that has capitalized on this trend most. It has been one of the most pervasive and disruptive impacts of the Internet. For not only has the long tail made anything available, but in disintermediating traditional distribution channels it has concentrated power in the hands of the new media giants of today: Apple, Amazon, Google, and Facebook. (And Microsoft is still struggling to be a relevant actor in this arena.)

- *The Open Internet*. We missed that the architecture of the Internet would be open and power would be distributed. That any one node could be a server or a directory was not how industry or the media business, both hierarchal, had worked. The Internet was crafted for military and academic purposes, and coded into it was a very specific value set about openness with no central point of control. This openness has been central to the rapid growth of all forms of new media. Both diversity and openness have defined the media environment for the last generation. This was no accident—it was an act of willful design, not technological determinism. Bob Khan at DARPA and the team at BBN that crafted the Internet had in mind a specific and radical design. In fact, they first approached AT&T to help create the precursor of the Internet and the American communication giant refused—they wanted no part in building a massive network that they couldn't control. They were right: not only was it nearly impossible to control, but it devoured the telephony business. But as today's net neutrality battles point out, the effort to reassert control on the Internet is very real. For 50 years the Cold War was the major ideological battle between the free world and the totalitarian world. Today, it's a battle for openness on the Internet. The issues—political and economic at their core—continue to underpin the nature of media on the Internet.

The Internet Gives Television a Second Act

New media always change the media that came before it, though often in unexpected ways. When television was born, pundits predicted it would be the death of the book. (It wasn't.) The death of television was a widely predicted outcome of Internet distribution, the long tail, new content creators, and user-generated media. This caused fear in Hollywood and a certain delight, even schadenfreude in Silicon Valley. At conferences, technology executives took great pleasure in taunting *old media* with its novel forms and reminding the establishment that "it is only a matter of time." New media would fracture audiences, and social media would hijack the public's attention. The Internet was set to unleash an attention-deficit-disorder epidemic, leading viewers away from traditional television programming en masse. Yet television is doing better than ever. What happened?

As it turns out, the most widely discussed topic on social media is television. One third of Twitter users in the United States post about television (Bauder 2012), and more than 10 percent of all tweets are directly related to television programming (Thornton 2013). New forms of content (as well as new distribution methods) have increased the primacy of great programming, not diminished it. Competing platforms from Google, Apple, Amazon, Netflix, and others have meant more competition for both network and cable television networks—and more power for program creators over whose content all the new distributors are fighting.

Despite the volume of content accessible via online platforms—100 minutes of video is uploaded to YouTube every minute—people still spend much of their time watching television, and television programming continues to reach a large majority of the population in developed countries. In the United States, people consume an average of 4 hours and 39 minutes of television every day (Selter 2012). In the United Kingdom, nearly 54.2 million people (or about 95 percent of the population above the age of four) watch television in a given week (Deloitte 2012). Thus, it appears that the "demise of television" is far from imminent (Khurana 2012).

In fact, television is better than it has ever been. Few predicted, even five years ago, that we would find ourselves in the middle of a new golden age in television. There is more content vying for our attention than ever before, and yet a number of rich, complex, and critically-acclaimed series have emerged. Shows like *Heroes*, *Mad Men*, *Breaking Bad*, *Game of Thrones*, and *Homeland* are a testament to the success with which television has adapted to a new and challenging climate.

Networks are now developing niche shows for smaller audiences, and thrive on distribution and redistribution through new platforms. Hulu, Netflix, YouTube, and HBO GO have pioneered new forms of viewing and served as the catalyst for innovative business deals. The practice of *binge viewing*, in which we watch an entire season (or more) of a program in a short amount of time, is a product of on-demand streaming sites and social media. Before, viewers would have to consume episodes of televisions as they were aired or wait for syndication. Boxed DVD seasons were another way that audiences could consume many episodes at once, but this often meant waiting for networks to trickle out seasons spaced over time. Now, networks are pushing whole seasons to platforms such as Netflix at once. With enough spare time, one can now digest a whole series in an extremely condensed time frame.

This has changed not only our viewing habits, but also the nature of television content. Screenwriters are now able to develop deeper and more complex storylines than they ever had before. Where once lengthy, complex, and involved storylines were the domain of video games, we see this type of storytelling in drama series with some regularity. In addition, television shows are now constructed differently. As audiences become more conscious of the media and media creators, we find that programming is much more self-referential. Jokes on shows like *The Simpsons*, *Family Guy*, *30 Rock*, and *The Daily Show* are often jokes about the media.

The consumption of television via on-demand streaming sites is not the only significant change to how we consume television content. There has been a tremendous shift in how we engage with television programming and how we interact with one another around television.

During the early decades of television, television viewing was a scheduled activity that drew groups of people together in both private homes and public spaces. The programming served as the impetus for such gatherings, and television watching was the primary activity of those who were seated in living rooms or stood before television sets in department stores or bars. Television continued to serve as a group medium through the 1960s and 1970s, but technological innovations ultimately transformed viewer behavior. The remote control, the videotape, the DVR, and mobile devices have led people to consume television content in greater quantities, but they do so increasingly in isolation. Once a highly anticipated social event, television programming is now an omnipresent environmental factor.

As television moved from a communal appointment medium to an individual activity initiated on demand, the community aspect of television has moved to the Internet. We have recreated the social function of television, which was once confined to living rooms, online—the conversation about television has expanded to a global level on social networking sites.

The sharp rise in multiscreen consumption is perhaps one of the most significant changes in modern media consumption, and has been a source of both excitement and concern among television network and technology executives alike. This form of media multitasking, in which a viewer engages with two or more screened devices at once, now accounts for 41 percent of time spent in front of television screens (Moses 2012). More than 60 percent of tablet users (Johnson 2012) and nearly 90 percent of smartphone users (Nielsen 2012) report watching television while using their devices.

Currently, television viewers are more likely to engage with content about television programming (such as Tweets or Facebook status updates) on complementary devices than they are to consume supplementary programming (such as simulcast sports footage) on a second screen. What is clear is that even if we are watching television in isolation, we are not watching alone.

Even when we're alone, we often watch television with friends. Some 60 percent of viewers watch TV while also using a social network. Of this group, 40 percent discuss what they are currently watching on television via social networks (Ericsson 2012). More than half of 16 to 24-year-olds regularly use complementary devices to communicate with others via messaging, e-mail, Facebook, or Twitter about programs being watched on television (Ericsson 2012).

With all of this online communication, of course, comes data. With exacting precision, Twitter can monitor what causes viewers to post about a given program. During the 2011 MTV Video Music Awards, a performance by Jay-Z and Kanye West generated approximately 70,000 tweets per minute (Twitter 2013). Later in the program, the beginning of a performance by Beyoncé generated more than 90,000 tweets per minute. Before she exited the stage, the superstar revealed her pregnancy by unbuttoning her costume. Tweets spiked at 8,868 per second, shattering records set on the social network shortly after such significant events as the resignation of Steve Jobs and the death of Osama Bin Laden (Hernandez 2011).

It is clear that television programming drives social media interaction. But do tweets drive consumers to tune in to a particular program? A report by Nielsen (2013) suggests that there is a two-way causal relationship between tuning in for a broadcast program and the Twitter conversation about that particular program. In nearly half of 221 primetime episodes analyzed in the study, higher levels of tweeting corresponded with additional viewers tuning in to the programming. The report also showed that the volume of tweets sent about a particular program caused significant changes in ratings among nearly 30 percent of the episodes.

The second-screen conversation about television programming is not limited to Twitter. Trendrr (2013), a social networking data analysis platform, recorded five times as much second-screen Facebook activity during one week in May 2013 than on all other social networks combined. Facebook recently released tools that will allow partner networks, including CNN and NBC, to better understand second-screen conversation taking place on the social network as it happens (Gross 2013). Using these tools, it is now possible to break down the number of Facebook posts that mention a certain term during a given time frame.

This real-time data—about who is watching television, where they are watching it from, and what they are saying about it—is of interest not just to television executives and advertisers, but the audience, too. There are several drivers for social television watching behavior, including not wanting to watch alone and the desire to connect with others (Ericsson 2012). Beyond connecting with the audience at large, dual-screen television viewers report using social networks to seek additional information about the program they are watching and to validate their opinions against a public sample.

I've witnessed times in my own life where watching TV alone became unacceptable. In order to make my viewing experience tolerable, I needed to lean on the rest of the viewing audience's sensibility. Moments like these changed my relationship to the medium of television forever.

In January 2009, I watched the inauguration of President Barack Obama on television along with 37.8 million other Americans. As Chief Justice John Roberts administered the oath of office, he strayed from the wording specified in the United States Constitution. I recognized that something had gone wrong—the president and the chief justice flubbed the oath? How could that be? What happened? I immediately turned to Twitter—and watched as everyone else was having the same instantaneous reaction. The audience provided context. I knew what was going on.

Twitter was equally useful to me during Super Bowl XLV when the Black Eyed Peas performed at the halftime show. The pop stars descended from the rafters of Cowboys Stadium and launched into a rendition of their hit song "I Gotta Feeling." It sounded awful. I turned to my girlfriend in dismay: "There is something wrong with the television. My speakers must have blown! There is no way that a performance during the most-watched television event of all time sounds this horrible." After tinkering with my sound system to no avail, I thought, "Maybe it's not me. Could it be? Do they really sound this bad?" A quick check of Twitter allayed my fears of technical difficulties—yes, the Black Eyed Peas sounded terrible. My sound system was fine.

As the level of comfort with and reliance upon multiscreen media consumption grows among audiences, content producers are developing rich second-screen experiences for audiences that enhance the viewing experience.

For example, the Lifetime channel launched a substantial second-screen engagement for the 12th season of reality fashion competition *Project*

Runway (Kondolojy 2013). By visiting playrunway.com during live broadcasts of the show, fans could vote in opinion polls and see results displayed instantly on their television screens. In addition to interactive voting, fans could access short-form video, blogs, and photo galleries via mobile, tablet, and desktop devices.

There are indications that second-screen consumption will move beyond the living room and into venues like movie theaters and sports stadiums. In connection with the theatrical rerelease of the 1989 classic *The Little Mermaid*, Disney has created an iPad app called "Second Screen Live" that will allow moviegoers to play games, compete with fellow audience members, and sing along with the film's score from their theater seats (Stedman 2013). In 2014, Major League Baseball will launch an application for wearable computing device Google Glass that will display real-time statistics to fans at baseball stadiums (Thornburgh 2013).

Music: Reworked, Redistributed, and Re-Experienced Courtesy of the Internet

The Internet has also completely transformed the way music is distributed and experienced. In less than a decade physical media (the LP and the CD) gave way to the MP3. Less than a decade after that, cloud-based music services and social sharing have become the norm. These shifts took place despite a music industry that did all it could to resist the digital revolution—until after it had already happened! The shareable, downloadable MP3 surfaced on the early web of the mid-1990s, and the music industry largely failed to recognize its potential. By the early 2000s, the Recording Industry Association of America had filed high-profile lawsuits against peer-to-peer file sharing services like Napster and Limewire (as well as private persons caught downloading music via their networks). Total revenue from music sales in the United States plummeted from $14.6 billion in 1999 to $6.3 billion in just ten years (Goldman 2010).

The truth was inescapable: its unwillingness to adopt new distribution platforms had badly hurt the music industry's bottom line. Television (having watched the music debacle) adjusted far better to the realities of the content business in the digital age. But the recording industry was forced to catch up to its audience, which was already getting much of its music online (legally or otherwise). Only in recent years did major labels agree to distribution deals with cloud-streaming services including Spotify, Rdio, iHeartRadio, and MOG. The music industry has experienced a slight increase in revenues in the past year, which can be attributed to both digital music sales and streaming royalties (Faughnder 2013).

Ironically, what the music industry fought so hard to prevent (free music and sharing) in the early days of the web is exactly what they ended up with today. There is more music available online now than ever before, and much of it is available for free.

Applications like Spotify and Pandora give users access to vast catalogs of recorded music, and sites like SoundCloud and YouTube have enabled a new generation of artists to distribute their music with ease. There is also a social layer to many music services. Their sites and applications are designed to allow users to share their favorite songs, albums, and artists with one another. Spotify, SoundCloud, and YouTube (among others) enable playlist sharing.

The rapid evolution of online music platforms has led to fundamental changes in the way we interact with music. The process of discovering and digesting music has become an almost frictionless process. Being able to tell Pandora what you like and have it invoke a personalized radio station tailored to your tastes is not only more convenient that what came before it, it's a qualitatively different medium. Gone are the days when learning about a new artist required flipping through the pages of a magazine (not to mention through stacks of albums at the record store).

As a kid I didn't have much of a popular music collection, which was somewhat traumatic whenever it came to throwing a party or having friends over. The cool kids had collections; the rest didn't. Telling friends to bring all their LPs over for the night didn't make a lot of sense growing up in New York City, where they'd have to drag them along in a taxi or public bus. Fast forward to 2011. I was hosting a cocktail party at my home in San Francisco, which became an experiment in observing the effect of different kinds of Internet music services. In the kitchen, I played music via an iPod that contained songs and albums I had purchased over the years. (And my collection still was not as good as my cool friends.) In the living room, I streamed music via the Pandora app on my iPhone. Guests would pick stations, skip songs, or add variety as the night went on. Upstairs, I ran Spotify from my laptop. I had followed, as the service allows you to do, two friends whose taste I really admired—a DJ from New York, and a young woman from the Bay Area who frequently posted pictures of herself at music festivals to Facebook. In playing a few of their playlists, I had created the ultimate party soundtrack. I came across as a supremely hip host, without having to curate the music myself. Ultimately, everyone gravitated upstairs to dance to *my* Spotify soundtrack.

The iPod, Pandora, and Spotify all allowed me to digitally deliver music to my guests. However, each delivery device is fundamentally different. Adding music to an iPod is far from a frictionless process. I had purchased the songs on my iPod over the course of several years, and to discover this music I depended on word of mouth of friends or the once-rudimentary recommendations of the iTunes store. Before the introduction of iCloud in 2011, users had to upload songs from their iTunes library to an iPod or iPhone, a process that took time (and depending on the size of a user's library, required consideration of storage constraints).

With Pandora came access to a huge volume of music. The Internet radio station boasts a catalog of more than 800,000 tracks from 80,000 artists. And it is a learning system that becomes educated about users' tastes over time. The Music Genome Project is at the core of Pandora technology. What was once a graduate student research project became an effort to "capture the essence of music at the fundamental level." Using almost 400 attributes to describe and code songs, and a complex mathematical algorithm to organize them, Pandora sought to generate stations that could respond to a listener's taste and other indicators (such as the "thumbs down," which would prevent a song from being played on a particular station again).

Spotify has a catalog of nearly 20 million songs. While the size of the service's catalog is one of its major strengths, so too are its social features. The service, which launched in the United States in 2011 after lengthy negotiations with the major record labels, allowed users to publish their listening activity to Facebook and Twitter. The desktop player enabled users to follow one another, and make public playlists to which others could subscribe. In addition, users could *message* each other playlists. The sharing of Spotify playlists between connected users mimicked the swapping of mixtape cassettes in the late eighties and early nineties.

All of these are examples of how what the audience creates is a growing part of the creative process.

In the heyday of the album, the exact flow of one song to another and the overall effect was the supreme expression of overall artistic design and control. It wasn't only the songs—the album represented 144 square inches of cover art and often many interior pages of liner notes in which to build a strong experience and relationship and story for your fans. It was a major advance over the 45, which provided a much smaller opportunity for a relationship with the band. With the arrival of MP3s, all of this was undone. Because we bought only the songs we were interested in, not only was the artist making less money, but he had lost control of what we were listening to and in what order. It didn't much matter, because we were busy putting together playlists and mixtapes where we (the audience) were in charge of the listening experience.

The Internet has given us many tools that allow us to personalize the listening experience. More than that, listening to music has increasingly become a personal activity, one that is done in isolation. The simplicity with which music can be consumed online has changed music from an immersive media to a more ambient media, one that is easily taken for granted.

Interestingly, the rise in personal consumption of music (via MP3 and the cloud) has coincided with a sharp rise in festival culture. Now more than ever, audiences seek to be together—whether in Indio, California for Coachella; Black Rock City, Nevada for Burning Man; Chicago, Illinois for Lollapalooza; or Miami, Florida for the Ultra Music Festival—to experience music as a collective group.

At a time where we collectively listen to billions of hours of streamed music each month, nothing compels us in a stronger fashion than the opportunity to come together, outdoors, often outside of cell phone range, to bask in performances by our favorite artist. Festival lineups are stacked with independent artists and superstars alike. Interestingly, a lineup is not unlike a long playlist on iTunes. There is no way to catch every performance at South by Southwest or Electric Daisy Carnival—but there is comfort in knowing that many of your favorite artists are there in one place.

This has also proven out economically. At a time when selling recorded music had become ever-more challenging, the business of live music is experiencing a renaissance. In 2013, both weekend-long installments of the Coachella festivals sold out in less than 20 minutes and raked in $47.3 million in revenue (Shoup 2013). The rise of festivals (now one in every state of the U.S.) is a response to the Internet having made the act of consuming recorded music more ambient and banal than ever before while creating the need for greater social and immersive experiences.

At the core of going to a music festival or listening to *The White Album* with a group of friends is the need to experience music collectively. It is a realization that beyond even the song itself, perhaps the most inspiring and rousing element of music is not just the music itself, but our collective human experience of it.

Today, as the audience is restlessly making its own media, it is also learning fast that with new media come new rules and new exceptions. Media confer power on the formerly passive audience, and with that comes new responsibilities.

This was made startlingly evident in the wake of the April 15, 2013 Boston Marathon bombings. At five o'clock in the evening on April 18, the FBI released a photo one of the suspects and asked the public for help in identifying him. Hours later, the Facebook page of Sunil Tripathi, a student who bore a resemblance to the suspect and was reported missing, was posted to the social news site Reddit. Word spread that this was the bomber. Within hours the story was amplified by the Internet news site BuzzFeed and tweeted to its 100,000 followers. Only, Tripathi had nothing to do with the crime. His worried family had created a Facebook page to help find their missing son. Over the next few hours Tripathi's family received hundreds of death threats and anti-Islamic messages until the Facebook page was shut down.

The audience was making media, and spontaneously turning rumors into what appeared to be facts but weren't, and with such velocity that facts were knocked out of the news cycle for hours that day (Kang 2013).

Four days later, an editor of Reddit posted to the blog a fundamental self-examination about crowd-sourced investigations and a reflection of the power of new media:

This crisis has reminded all of us of the fragility of people's lives and the importance of our communities, online as well as offline. These communities and lives are now interconnected in an unprecedented way. Especially when the stakes are high we must strive to show good judgement and solidarity. One of the greatest strengths of decentralized, self-organizing groups is the ability to quickly incorporate feedback and adapt. reddit was born in the Boston area (Medford, MA to be precise). After this week, which showed the best and worst of reddit's potential, we hope that Boston will also be where reddit learns to be sensitive of its own power.

(erik [hueypriest] 2013)

We are now able to surround ourselves with news that conforms to our views. We collect friends whose tastes and opinions are our own tastes and opinions. The diversity of the Internet can ironically make us less diverse. Our new media are immersive, seductive, and addictive. We need only turn to today's headlines to see how this plays out.

On October 8, 2013, a gunman entered a crowded San Francisco commuter train and drew a .45-caliber pistol. He raised his weapon, put it down to wipe his nose, and then took aim at the passengers.

None of the passengers noticed because they were attending to something far more interesting than present reality. They were subsumed by their smartphones and by the network beyond. These were among the most connected commuters in all of history. On the other side of their little screens, passengers had access to much of the world's media and many of the planet's people. They were not especially connected to the moment or to one another. They were somewhere else.

Only when the gunman opened fire did anyone look up. By then, 20-year-old Justin Valdez was mortally wounded. The only witness to this event, which took place on a public train, in front of dozens of people, was a security camera, which captured the scene of connected bliss interrupted. The *San Francisco Chronicle* reported the district attorney's stunned reaction:

> *"These weren't concealed movements—the gun is very clear," said District Attorney George Gascón. "These people are in very close proximity with him, and nobody sees this. They're just so engrossed, texting and reading and whatnot. They're completely oblivious of their surroundings."*
>
> (Ho 2013)

Gascón said that what happened on the light-rail car speaks to a larger dilemma of the digital age. As glowing screens dominate the public sphere, people seem more and more inclined to become engrossed, whether they are in a car or a train or are strolling through an intersection.

In 1968, Marshall McLuhan observed how completely new media work us over. In *War and Peace in the Global Village* he wrote, "Every new technological innovation is a literal amputation of ourselves in order that it may be amplified and manipulated for social power and action." (73)

We've arrived in full at an always-on, hyper-connected world. A network that connects us together yet can disconnect us from our present reality. An Internet that grants us the ability to create and remix and express ourselves as never before. One that has conferred on us responsibilities and implications we are only beginning to understand. The most powerful tools in media history are not the province of gods, or moguls, but available to practically all mankind. *The media* has become a two-way contact sport that all of us play. And because the media is *us*, we share a vital interest and responsibility in the world we create with this, our extraordinary Internet.

References

Anderson, Chris.
"The Long Tail." *Wired*, 12.10 (October 2004). http://www.wired.com/wired/archive/12.10/tail.html

Bauder, David.
"Study Shows Growth in Second Screen Users." Associated Press, December 3, 2012. http://bigstory.ap.org/article/study-shows-growth-second-screen-users

Deloitte.
"TV: Why? Perspectives on TV: Dual-Screen, Catch-Up, Connected TV, Advertising, and Why People Watch TV." MediaGuardian Edinburgh International Television Festival, 2012. http://www.deloitte.com/assets/Dcom-UnitedKingdom/Local%20Assets/Documents/Industries/TMT/uk-tmt-tv-why-perspectives-on-uk-tv.pdf

Edison, Thomas.
"The Phonograph and its Future." *North American Review*, no. 126 (May–June 1878).

Ericsson.
"TV and Video: An Analysis of Evolving Consumer Habits." An Ericsson Consumer Insight Summary Report, August 2012. http://www.ericsson.com/res/docs/2012/consumerlab/tv_video_consumerlab_report.pdf

Erik [hueypriest].
"Reflections on the Recent Boston Crisis." *Reddit*, April 22, 2013. http://blog.reddit.com/2013/04/reflections-on-recent-boston-crisis.html

Faughnder, Ryan.
"Global Digital Music Revenue To Reach $11.6 Billion in 2016." *Los Angeles Times*, July 24, 2013. http://articles.latimes.com/2013/jul/24/entertainment/la-et-ct-digital-global-music-industry-20130724

Gates, Bill, with Nathan Myhrvold and Peter Reinearson. *The Road Ahead*. New York: Viking Penguin, 1995.

Goldman, David.
"Music's Lost Decade: Sales Cut in Half." *CNN Money*, February 3, 2010. http://money.cnn.com/2010/02/02/news/companies/napster_music_industry/

Gross, Doug.
"CNN Among First with New Facebook Data-Sharing Tools." *CNN.com*, September 9, 2013. http://www.cnn.com/2013/09/09/tech/social-media/facebook-media-data/index.html

Hernandez, Brian Anthony.
"Beyonce's Baby Inspired More Tweets Per Second Than Steve Jobs' Passing." *Mashable*, December 6, 2011. http://mashable.com/2011/12/06/tweets-per-second-2011/

Ho, Vivian.
"Absorbed Device Users Oblivious to Danger." *San Francisco Gate*, October 7, 2013. http://www.sfgate.com/crime/article/Absorbed-device-users-oblivious-to-danger-4876709.php?cmpid=twitter

IDC (International Data Corporation).
"Always Connected: How Smartphones and Social Keep Us Engaged." An IDC Research Report, Sponsored by Facebook. 2013. https://fb-public.app.box.com/s/3iq5x6uwnqtq7ki4q8wk

Johnson, Lauren.
"63pc of Tablet Owners Use Device while Watching TV: Study." *Mobile Marketer*, September 17, 2012. http://www.mobilemarketer.com/cms/news/research/13781.html

Kang, Jay Caspian.
"Should Reddit Be Blamed for the Spreading of a Smear?" *New York Times*, July 25, 2013. http://www.nytimes.com/2013/07/28/magazine/should-reddit-be-blamed-for-the-spreading-of-a-smear.html?pagewanted=1&_r=1

Khurana, Ajeet.
"The End of the Television." *Technorati*, February 11, 2012. http://technorati.com/entertainment/tv/article/the-end-of-the-television/

Kondolojy, Amanda.
"Project Runway To Reveal Biggest Second-Screen Interactivity in Its History for Launch of Season 12." TV by the Numbers, July 17, 2013. http://tvbythenumbers.zap2it.com/2013/07/17/project-runway-to-reveal-biggest-second-screen-interactivity-in-its-history-for-launch-of-season-12/192387/

McLuhan, Marshall.
"The Playboy Interview." *Playboy Magazine*, March 1969.
———. *War and Peace in the Global Village*. New York: McGraw-Hill, 1968.

Moses, Lucia.
"Data Points: Two-Screen Viewing." *AdWeek*. November 7, 2012. http://www.adweek.com/news/technology/data-points-two-screen-viewing-145014

Nielsen Company.
"Double Vision: Global Trends in Tablet and Smartphone Use while Watching TV." Nielsen Newswire, April 5, 2012. http://www.nielsen.com/us/en/newswire/2012/double-vision-global-trends-in-tablet-and-smartphone-use-while-watching-tv.html
———. "The Follow-Back: Understanding the Two-Way Causal Influence Between Twitter Activity and TV Viewership." Nielsen Newswire, August 6, 2013. http://www.nielsen.com/us/en/newswire/2013/the-follow-back--understanding-the-two-way-causal-influence-betw.html

Selter, Brian.
"Youths Are Watching, but Less Often on TV." *New York Times*, February 8, 2012. http://www.nytimes.com/2012/02/09/business/media/young-people-are-watching-but-less-often-on-tv.html?_r=2&ref=technology&

Shirky, Clay.
"Power Laws, Weblogs, and Inequality." First published on the "Networks, Economics, and Culture" mailing list, February 8, 2003. http://shirky.com/writings/powerlaw_weblog.html

Shoup, Brad.
"Deconstructing: Coachella and the Music Festival Industry." *Stereogum*, January 28, 2013. http://www.stereogum.com/1245041/deconstructing-coachella-and-the-music-festival-industry/top-stories/lead-story/

Stedman, Alex.
"Disney Invites Kids to Bring iPads to Theaters for 'The Little Mermaid' Re-Release." *Variety*, September 11, 2013. http://variety.com/2013/digital/news/disney-invites-kids-to-bring-ipads-to-theaters-for-the-little-mermaid-re-release-1200608309/

Thornburgh, Tristan.
"Blue from Google Glass Allows You to Get Real-Time Info at Baseball Games." *Bleacher Report*, September 12, 2013. http://bleacherreport.com/articles/1771741-blue-from-google-glass-allows-you-to-get-real-time-info-at-baseball-games

Thornton, Kirby.
"Nielsen Engages Twitter for TV Insights." Media Is Power, March 21, 2013. http://www.mediaispower.com/nielsen-engages-twitter-for-tv-insights/

Trendrr.
"New Facebook Data Strengthens Tools for Measuring Second-Screen Activity." *Trendrr* (blog), July 23, 2013. https://blog.trendrr.com/2013/07/23/new-facebook-data-strengthens-tools-for-measuring-second-screen-activity/

Turkle, Sherry.
Alone Together: Why We Expect More from Technology and Less from Each Other. New York: Basic Books, 2011.

Twitter.
"Twitter on TV: A Producer's Guide." Twitter. https://dev.twitter.com/media/twitter-tv (accessed October 9, 2013).

YouTube.
"Press: Statistics." YouTube. http://www.youtube.com/yt/press/statistics.html (accessed October 9, 2013).

The Music Industry in an Age of Digital Distribution

Patrik Wikström

Principal Research Fellow at the ARC Centre of Excellence of Creative Industries and Innovation,
Queensland University of Technology

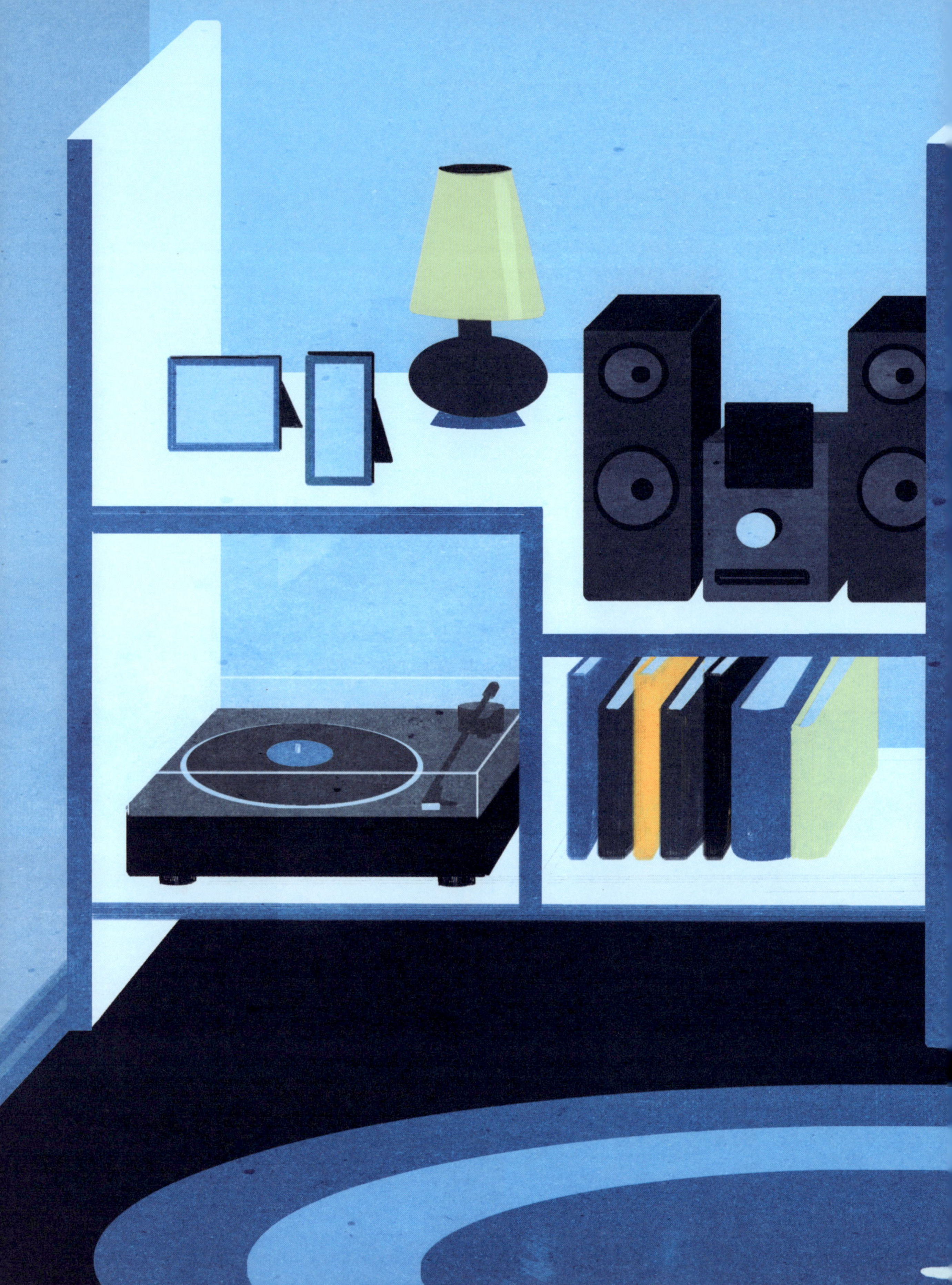

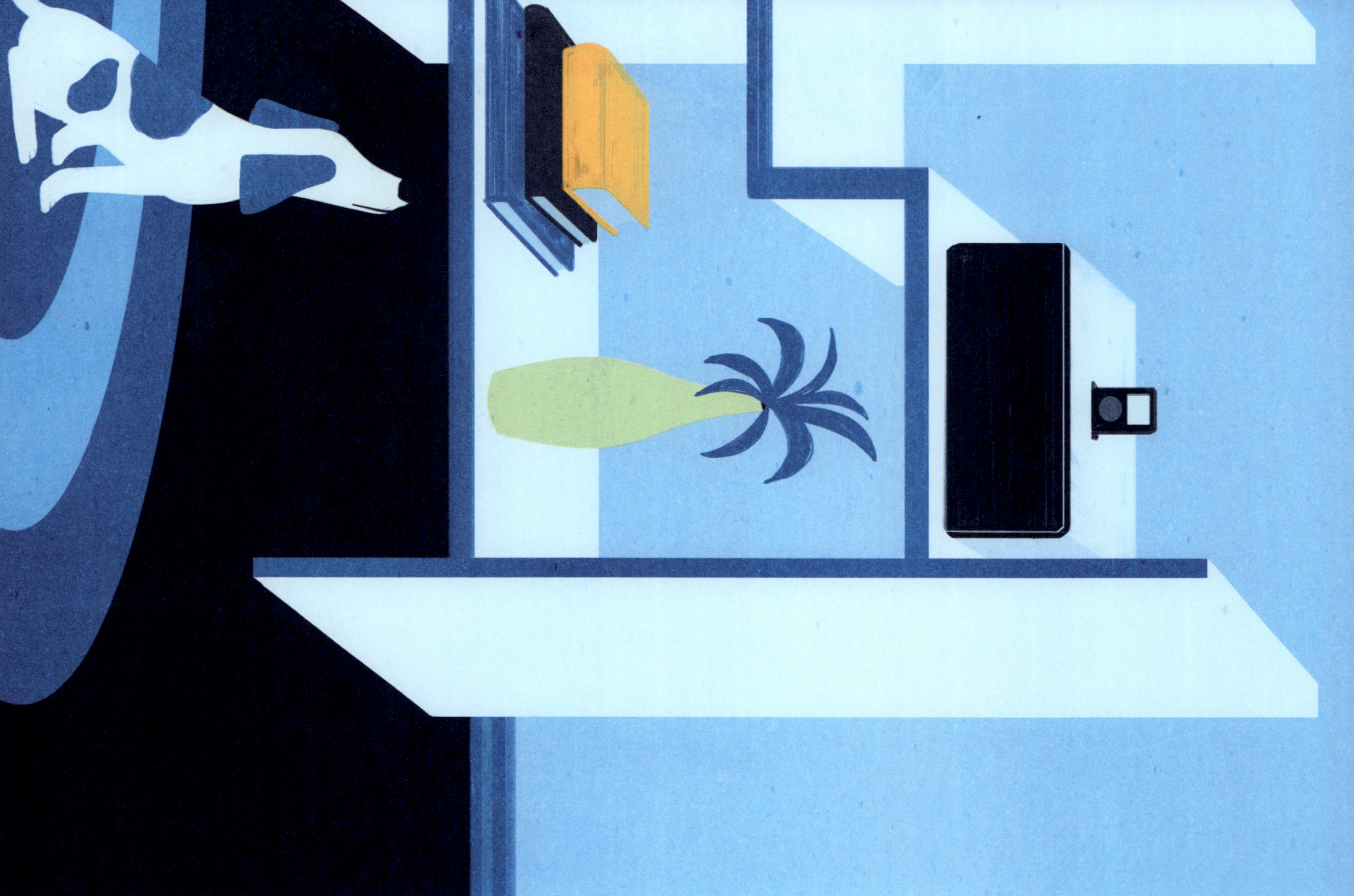

Patrik Wikström

patrikwikstrom.com

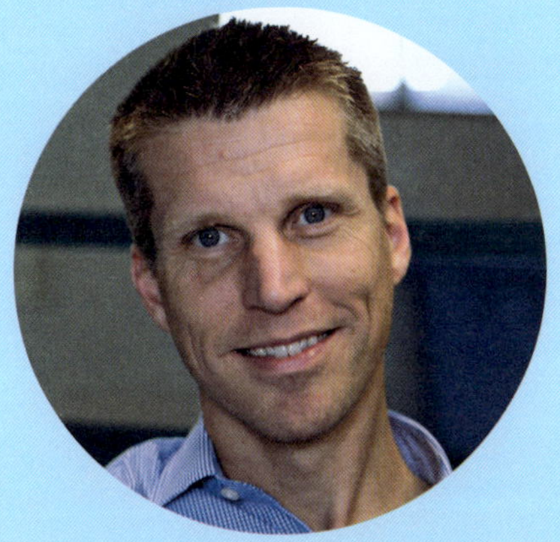

Patrik Wikström is Principal Research Fellow at the ARC
Centre of Excellence of Creative Industries and Innovation,
Queensland University of Technology, Australia. Dr. Wikström's
research is primarily focused on innovation and learning
in the creative industries. He is the author of *The Music
Industry: Music in the Cloud* (Polity Press, 2009) and has
published his research in journals such as *Technovation*,
International Journal of Media Management, *Journal of
Media Business Studies*, *Journal of Music Business Studies*,
and *Popular Music and Society*. Dr. Wikström has served as
a faculty member at Northeastern University in Boston and
at Jönköping International Business School and Karlstad
University in Sweden. Dr. Wikström received his PhD in Media
and Communication Studies from Karlstad University and
he is a graduate from Chalmers University of Technology,
Gothenburg, where he received a master's degree from the
School of Technology Management and Economics. Before his
academic career, Dr. Wikström worked in the European media
and telecom industry where he held positions as business
development manager and strategy consultant.

Sites and services that have changed my life
wikipedia.org
amazon.com
google.com
coursera.org
napster.com

The Music Industry in an Age of Digital Distribution

In 1999 the global recorded music industry had experienced a period of growth that had lasted for almost a quarter of a century. Approximately one billion records were sold worldwide in 1974, and by the end of the century, the number of records sold was more than three times as high. At the end of the nineties, spirits among record label executives were high and few music industry executives at this time expected that a team of teenage Internet hackers, led by Shawn Fanning (at the time a student at Northeastern University in Boston) would ignite the turbulent process that eventually would undermine the foundations of the industry.

Shawn Fanning created and launched a file sharing service called Napster that allowed users to download and share music without compensating the recognized rights holders. Napster was fairly quickly sued by the music industry establishment and was eventually forced to shut down the service. However, a string of other, increasingly sophisticated services immediately followed suit. Even though the traditional music industry used very aggressive methods, both legal and technical, to stop the explosion of online-piracy services such as Napster, Kazaa, Limewire, Grokster, DC++, and The Pirate Bay, it was to no avail. As soon as one file sharing service was brought to justice and required to cease its operations, new services emerged and took its place. By the end of 2013, the sales of physically distributed recorded music (e.g., cassettes, CD, vinyl) measured in unit sales, were back at the same relatively low levels of the early 1970s.

During the 15 years that has passed since Napster was launched, the music industry has been completely transformed and the model that ruled the industry during most of the past century has been largely abandoned.

This rapid transformation of the music industry is a classic example of how an innovation is able to disrupt an entire industry and make existing industry competencies obsolete. The power and influence of the pre-Internet music industry was largely based on the ability to control physical distribution. Internet makes physical music distribution increasingly irrelevant and the incumbent major music companies have been required to redefine themselves in order to survive. This chapter will examine the impact of the Internet on the music industry and present the state of the music industry in an age of digital distribution.

Three Music Industries

In order to understand the dynamics of the music industry, it is first of all necessary to recognize that the music industry is not one, but a number of different industries that are all closely related but which at the same time are based on different logics and structures. The overall music industry is based on the creation and exploitation of music-based intellectual properties. Composers and songwriters create songs, lyrics, and arrangements that are performed live on stage; recorded and distributed to consumers; or licensed for some other kind of use, for instance sheet music or as background music for other media (advertising, television, etc.). This basic structure has given rise to three core music industries: the recorded music industry—focused on recording and distribution of music to consumers; the music licensing industry—primarily licensing compositions and arrangements to businesses; and live music—focused on producing and promoting live entertainment, such as concerts, tours, etc. There are other companies that sometimes are recognized as members of the music industrial family, such as makers of music instruments, software, stage equipment, music merchandise, etc. However, while these are important industry sectors they are traditionally not considered to be integral parts of the industry's core.

In the pre-Internet music industry, recorded music was the biggest of the three and the one that generated the most revenues. Most aspiring artists and bands in the traditional music industry dreamed about being able to sign a contract with a record label. A contract meant that the record label bankrolled a professional studio recording and allowed the artist entry into the record labels' international distribution system, something which otherwise was beyond reach of most unsigned bands. The second music industry sector—music licensing—was much smaller and more mundane than the recorded music industry sector. Music publishers, who were operating in this business, were largely a business-to-business industry without any direct interaction with the audience. Their main responsibility was to ensure that license fees were collected when a song was used in whatever context and that these fees subsequently were fairly distributed among the composers and lyricists. The third music industry sector—live music—generated its revenues from sales of concert tickets. Although live music has a long and proud history, it came to play second fiddle to the recording industry during the twentieth century. Record sales was undoubtedly the most important revenue stream and record labels generally considered concert tours as a way to promote a studio album, and were not really concerned whether the tour was profitable or not. Sometimes the record label even paid *tour support*, which would enable bands to go on tour and promote the album even though the actual tour was running with a loss.

This music industry structure, including the relationships between the three industries, was developed during the mid-twentieth century and was deeply cemented when the Internet emerged to challenge the entire system. The short-term impact of the Internet on the music industries primarily concerned the distribution of recorded music to consumers. This means that while the recorded music industry was severely affected by the loss of distribution control and rampant online piracy, the other two music industry sectors were initially left more or less unaffected. As a matter of fact, while the recorded music industry has suffered during the past 15 years, the other two industries have gained in strength and prominence. There are several reasons why this shift in balance has happened.

One of the primarily reasons is simply that as one revenue stream is diminishing, the music industry is required to reevaluate its other businesses and try to compensate for the lost revenues from recorded music by increasing revenues from music licensing and live music.

For instance, revenues from music licensing have more than doubled during the past 15 years due to new and more active licensing practices, but also due to the fact that the media industries have changed in a similar way as the music industry. There are now considerably more television channels, radio channels, videogames, Internet websites, and other outlets than only two decades ago, and most of these outlets need music as their primary or secondary content. Music publishers have also in general been more nimble than the record labels to address the demand from new media outlets. A clear example of how music publishers changed their business practices is how they strive to establish themselves as a one-stop shop for musical intellectual properties, where media outlets can clear all their music licenses with a single contract. That may sound like an obvious service, but in the traditional music industry it was not always the case. Rather, there was one legal entity holding the rights to the composition and another legal entity controlling the rights of the recording of the musical work (the *master*). Music publishers in the age of digital distribution increasingly control both the master and the composition, which makes the licensing process more efficient. The music licensing industry has during the past 15 years evolved into the most profitable music industry sector and is often also considered as the most innovative and agile sector of the three.

While music licensing is the most profitable music industry sector, live music has developed into the largest music sector. There is a fairly straightforward explanation why live music has experienced a surge during the past 15 years. Live music is simply easier to control than recorded music. A musical band that is in demand can grow their revenues from live music by increasing the number of concerts and raising the ticket prices. Even though the financial crisis of 2007–08 put a dent in the growth of the live music industry, it has nevertheless surpassed the recorded music industry in size. During most of the second half of the previous century, the largest music company was a record company, but after the Internet transformation of the music industry the world's largest music company is Live Nation, a U.S.-based live music company spun off from Clear Channel in 2005. This is a further marker of the changing power relationships in the music industry. It should be noted, though, that the boundaries between the three industries are not as clear as they were during the pre-Internet era. Music companies, including Live Nation, serve as a general business partner to artists and composers and support their activities regardless of whether they concern live concerts, merchandise, licensing, or distribution and promotion of recorded music to consumers. This means that it is no longer entirely easy to categorize a music company into one of the three industries, but, nevertheless, in the case of

Live Nation its revenues are still mainly generated via live concerts, which still makes it relevant to refer to them as primarily a live music company.

This section has presented how the three main music industry sectors have been affected by the introduction of the Internet and how the size, strength, routines, and relationships between the industry sectors have been transformed. The next section will turn its attention specifically to recorded music and examine how new business models for music distribution may be able to lead the recorded music industry on a path toward recovery.

A Growing Digital Music Market

The music industry went to great lengths at the beginning of the century to put a stop to online piracy; however, they were not equally ambitious and innovative in developing new models for legal online distribution. Certainly, there were a few feeble attempts from the major record labels at the time, but the most important criterion in the development of these services seemed to be that they should not in any way threaten the existing revenue streams but should only add additional revenue to the companies. The majors did succeed with one of their goals, which is that the new services should not compete with the existing physical sales. However, unfortunately the services could not compete with anything, especially not with online piracy.

The first company that was able to create a successful online service for legal sales and distribution of music was not a music industry player at all—it was Apple Computer (as it was called at the time). In 2003, Apple was able to convince the major labels that music consumers would buy music legally if they were offered an extremely simple service that allowed them to buy and download music for less than a dollar per track. The service was called iTunes Music Store. In one sense,

iTunes was a radical change for the music industry. It was the first online retailer that was able to offer the music catalogs from all the major music companies, it used an entirely novel pricing model, and it allowed consumers to de-bundle the music album and only buy the tracks that they actually liked.

On the other hand, iTunes can also be considered as a very careful and incremental innovation, as the major labels' positions and power structures remained largely unscathed. The rights holders still controlled their properties and the structures that guided the royalties paid per every track that was sold was predictable and transparent. Apple were correct in their prediction of consumer behavior and the iTunes Music Store can not be considered as anything but an enormous success. In 2013, iTunes Music Store is the world's largest music retailer (offline and online) and it has sold more than 25 billion songs since its launch in 2003. The service has evolved substantially during its decade-long existence, and a

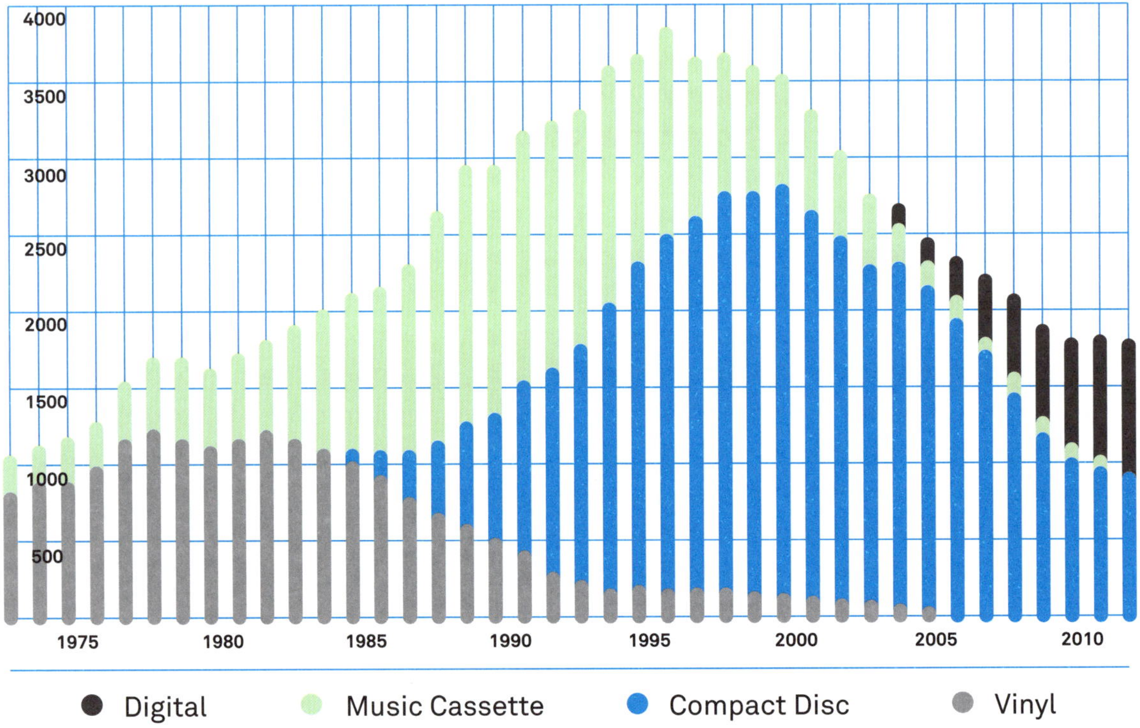

Fig. 1
Recorded Music Volume, 1973–2012.
Note: Digital includes full-length albums and singles split by 4. Vinyl includes LPs and EPs split by 4. Music DVDs are not included.
Source: IFPI 2013

number of competitors using more or less the same business model have entered the digital download music market. Even though the competition has increased, iTunes remains on top with a market share of more than 50 percent of the global digital music market. Figure 1 indicates how the global recorded music market has evolved since 1973, and shows that while the digital music market has been able to partially compensate for the decline of physical sales, the total recorded music market still has lost more than 50 percent of its sales since the peak in 1999.

While digital download services, such as iTunes Music Store, introduce a gradual change to the music business logic, there are other legal music services that are far more radical and thereby also far more controversial. These services do not offer individual tracks for purchase at a set price— they rather offer the users *access* to a large music library that they are able to listen to at their leisure. The users normally pay a monthly subscription fee that allows them to listen to as many songs in the library as they want, how often as they want.

This may sound like an appealing proposition, but these legal *access-based* music services have struggled both to convince record labels to license their catalogs to the services as well as to convince users that it is possible to enjoy music without actually buying and owning a copy of the track or album.

There is a considerable entrepreneurial activity in this segment of the music business, and services go live and bust on a weekly basis. Many service providers are still desperately looking for the business model that can attract music listeners and satisfy rights holders. The challenges are certainly considerable but the music service that so far has received the most attention of the international music industry and the one that could possibly have found the right path is a service called Spotify. Spotify is a useful vehicle for explaining the logic of the music industry in the age of digital distribution, and this section will present how service drives the music industrial transformation forward. Even if it eventually turns out that Spotify is unable to create a business model that is sustainable in the long term, it has already been able to transform the mindsets of both users and rights holders and will most likely be a music technological milestone on the magnitude of the Walkman, the Compact Disc, and Apple iTunes.

Spotify was founded in 2006 by Daniel Ek and Martin Lorentzon with the ambition to create a legal ad-supported music service that was free for the music listener but that generated licensing revenues to copyright holders.

Spotify was by no means the first attempt to create a legal service that could compete with illegal file sharing. Most predecessors had for various reasons failed miserably with their projects, which may be one reasonable explanation why the rights holders that Spotify was negotiating with were not particularly enthusiastic about engaging in another risky online music project. Despite all their initial skepticism, on October 7, 2008, the company announced that after two years of discussions and negotiations, they had signed agreements with the music industry's leading rights holders to distribute their music to audiences in a handful of European countries. In order to succeed where many others had failed, Spotify had been forced to make a number of concessions. In addition to offering the major rights holders shares in the company, they were also required to implement a fundamental change in their business model. Instead of offering a service that was solely funded by ads, they also developed a more advanced version of the service, which was funded by subscription fees.

Spotify's model with two or more different service versions where the most basic version is free and the more advanced versions are offered on a subscription basis is usually called *freemium*—a play on the words *free* and *premium*. Often, the profit margin for the free version is very low, or even negative, and it is expected that it is the subscription fees that will generate enough revenues to make the service profitable. The logic behind a freemium service model is that users shall be willing to use the service for free and that they while using the service gradually will make behavioral and emotional investments in the service that will increase the costs and efforts to switch to another service. The goal is to make as many of the users of the free version to convert to the subscription version. In order to achieve that goal, the free version has to have a number of increasingly annoying features (such as advertising) or lack a few key features (such as the ability to use the service on certain devices) that are removed/available on the premium versions of the service. The challenge for Spotify and other freemium services is to balance the different versions in a way that stimulates the *right* customer behavior and entices users to become paying subscribers. To date, few music services manage this feat. Either the free version has been too good to motivate customers to upgrade their service or it has been too deprived of features to attract customers at all. In Spotify's case they have achieved a *conversion rate* of approximately 20 percent, which means that 20 percent of the total user base is using the premium version and pay a monthly subscription fee.

Spotify has received a considerable amount of attention from the music industry across the world, but some of this attention has been largely based on suspicion and criticism toward their business model and methods. The criticism has to some extent focused on whether the freemium model presented above is long-term sustainable or not, but even stronger criticism has been focused on how the revenues have been shared with rights holders on different levels in the value chain. There are at least two reasons why this criticism has emerged. First of all, music companies have since decades back been used to a royalty model where a licensee pays a fixed amount per song sold, played, or used in whatever way. That model is very difficult to apply to an access-based service since the revenues that are generated by the service is not based on songs sold, played, or used, but based on the number of users of the service. Providers of access-based music services—regardless if the services are funded by subscriptions or advertising—have argued that rather than paying a fixed amount per track that is listened to, they should simply share whatever revenues are generated with the rights holders. Without getting too deep into the accounting detail, such a scheme is very beneficial to the service provider but transfer a considerable part of the business risk to rights holders.

Rights holders argue that their revenues should not depend on the skills of the service's advertising sales team, but they should simply get paid for the music distributed to customers. In the past, a number of access-based service providers have been required to sign contracts that have generated fixed royalties per track to rights holders. However, such agreements make it very difficult to get an access-based music service off the ground, and several pioneers in the access-based music service market have not been able to survive for very long. One of the reasons why Spotify is considered as a milestone in the shaping of the new music economy is that the company seems to have successfully convinced the major music companies in certain markets that they should indeed share Spotify's business risk and instead of taking a fixed license fee per track, they should take a share of Spotify's revenue, regardless of how high or low it is. Spotify succeeded by making a number of concessions in their negotiations, for instance by offering the major music companies the opportunity to buy a minority share of Spotify's shares.

Spotify has reported that 70 percent of their revenues from ads and subscriptions has been paid in royalties to rights holders. At the end of 2013, the company has generated more than a billion dollars for rights holders around the world, which according to Spotify is proof that their model does work.

However, even though it seems possible to generate revenues from access-based music services, the new contract structure is a radical change in the music business attitude toward distributors, and it is by no means uncontroversial. Some of the criticisms expressed by artists and composers are caused by the fact that the royalties are primarily paid by the service providers to music companies and not directly to the composers, musicians, or artists. The creatives argue that they are not given a fair share of the revenues and some of them even actively choose not to license their music to the services such as Spotify because the revenues that end up in their pockets is almost ridiculously low and that they do not want to support a corrupt and unsustainable system.

One reason why this problem has occurred is a debate about the classification of the royalties generated by access-based music services. Music companies (i.e., in this case the old record companies) claim that the royalties shall be considered as unit-based music sales, which in that case would mean that the musicians receive between 10 and 20 percent of the royalties paid by Spotify to the music companies. The musicians claim on the other hand that Spotify cannot be compared to traditional record sales at all but should rather be categorized as a performance, which in that case would mean that the musicians are entitled to 50 percent of the revenues rather than 20. The conflict concerns to a great extent the interpretation of agreements between record companies and artists that were established before Spotify and even the Internet existed. The debate about what type of royalty a particular Internet-based music service should generate may seem like a legal issue with minor real-world implication, but it is an absolutely crucial question that will determine the structure of the future of the music industry. Much is at stake and it is unlikely that the music industry players will easily agree on a model that is perceived as fair to all parties.

This section has discussed the emergence of access-based music services and the challenges they have encountered as they try to enter the digital music economy. The next section takes this discussion one step forward by reflecting on how these services change the audiences' relationships with music. The section argues that access-based music is merely a transitional phase in the evolution of a new music economy and points at indications of how the industry increases its reliance on so-called context-based features and services.

The Real-Time Listening Experience

While revenues from recorded music have fallen dramatically during the past 15 years, people across the world do not listen less to music—rather they listen to more recorded music than ever before.

Recorded music permeates every aspect of our daily lives and legal access-based music services combined with illegal online file sharing services means that more or less every song is available everywhere, all the time. This *access explosion* transforms the way people use and relate to recorded music.

For instance, in the pre-Internet days recorded music was expensive and scarce. Music listeners chose what record to buy with care and the growing record collection in their living room cabinets served as a diary of their lives told via a number of record purchases. Music listeners *owned* their physical records in the same way as they had a strong sense of ownership about other physical objects, such as books, souvenirs, or furniture, and these objects served as tools for both identity formation and communication.

Institutions, such as *collection* and *ownership*, become increasingly irrelevant in the age of digital distribution and ubiquitous access to music. In the light of this observation, a relevant question is what the new role of recorded music as an identity marker in the age of digital distribution may be. The retrospective record collection served as such an identity marker in the pre-Internet age, but as music listeners abandon their physical collections they are required to search for new ways to use recorded music as a tool for communication of their identities to their friends and the world. The scenes that are increasingly used for that purpose are online-based social networks such as Facebook, Twitter, etc. Access-based music services are commonly interconnected with such social network services, and thereby allow music listeners to constantly announce to the world what track they are currently listening to. This stream of information is primarily of interest to advertising platforms and their clients since it allows them to profile the audience based on their listening habits and send them advertising messages that are adapted to their demographics and interests.

The shift from the *retrospective collection* to the *real-time listening experience* is a radical shift in music listeners' relationship to music. It diminishes the significance of the memory of past music experiences and moves the focus to the here and the now. It is interesting to note the kind of structures and behaviors that emerge as music consumption shifts from *ownership* to *access* and from *the collection* to the *now playing*. Amaral et al. (2009) have, for instance, shown that music listeners actively curate their music-listening feed in order to make sure that it does not reveal a track that does not fit with the image they want to exhibit. Some access-based music services have even created a "private-listening feature" in order to enable users to listen to music without sharing the experience with the world.

The access-based services are still in their early days and they still actively search for the optimal service and pricing structure that will allow them to compete and survive. Currently, the competition between the services is largely based on the size of their music catalogs, availability in different territories and different mobile platforms, etc. However, it is reasonable to assume that eventually all these services will asymptotically converge toward a similar music offering and will be available on all platforms and include more or less every song that has ever been recorded.

According to basic economic theory, the competition between similar services or products will be based on price, profit margins will eventually shrink, and a few large players will eventually survive and compete in an oligopolistic market. Access-based music services will in other words become a commodity market and behave in a similar way as the markets for sugar or oil.

When the market has reached this gloomy state and the room for innovation and differentiation based on the pure access model is more or less exhausted, online music service providers will most likely look for other ways to differentiate their services and to keep up their profitability. One way of doing this is to go beyond the pure access model and to create services and features that provide a *context* to the songs in their catalog. The context may for instance enable music listeners a way to search and easily find the song they are looking for at a particular moment, it may allow users to share their music experiences with their friends, to organize their favorite music experiences in convenient ways, etc. Such context-based services provide a less deterministic and far more expansive space for innovation than those services that are based on a pure access model. While innovation within the access-model framework leads toward the same ultimate goal (universal access to all songs ever recorded), innovation within the context-model framework lacks such a knowable outcome. A provider of a context-based music service has a greater possibility to create a competitive advantage based on unique, innovative features than what is possible within the access-model framework.

Today the number of context-based services grows alongside access-based music services and most often a music service offers both access to music as well as a range of features that allow users to *do things* with music. The customer problem that needs to be solved is not that the customer needs access to music but rather how to navigate and *do things* with that music. In other words, customer value is increasingly created by providing the audience with tools that allow them to *do things* with music rather than by providing the audience with basic access to music. This shift from providing access to music to providing services and features that are based on the assumption that access to music is already provided is part of a similar general transformation of the music industry. The discussion has up until now been focused on the distribution of music, but the shift *from content to context* can be also observed in other segments of the music industry value chain.

A number of artists and composers have during recent years implemented the context-focused model in the creative production of their musical works. Rather than only making polished recordings for the audience to experience and enjoy, they have created services and practices that involve the audience in the creative process and allow the fans to *do things* with music. The British singer-songwriter Imogen Heap is one example of this trend. Heap actively encouraged her fans to upload sounds, images, and videos during the production of her latest album. She used this material in her work both as inspiration and as actual building blocks to her songs. As a consequence, Heap's fans felt they were collaborating with their idol and were part of a communal, creative experience. Billy Bragg is also a singer-songwriter from Britain, but from a different generation and in a different genre than Heap. Bragg has also established a context-oriented experience for his fans, albeit perhaps primarily driven by his fans than by Bragg himself. Bragg reflects on his relationship with his fans and explains that he provides a "social framework" for his fans and that some of his fans don't even like his music but they enjoy being part of a social community (Baym 2012).

Other musical artists and producers go way beyond the traditional format of the song and create mobile applications that allow the users to play with music in different ways. London-based RjDj and San Francisco-based Smule are two examples of organizations that have developed such applications that challenge the boundaries between music and interactive videogames. These tendencies raise fundamental questions about the definitions of the music industry and music organizations. Will tools and software for playing with music become recognized as a vital part of the music industry and a fourth core sector of the industry, next to live music, music licensing. and recorded music? If so, what will this mean for established music companies, artists, and composers? When live music and music publishing became increasingly important industry sectors in the first years of this millennium, traditional record labels reinvented themselves, built new capabilities that allowed them to serve as record labels, music publishers, management companies, live music companies, etc. They turned into *360-degree music companies*, which placed equal emphasis on all three music industry segments. If context-based services and software will continue to grow in importance, music companies will need to add yet another new competency and perhaps new business areas to their organizations that will enable them to capture the increasing value created by context-based music services.

The Music Industrial Transformation Continues

The recorded music industry has been radically transformed during the past 15 years, but much remains before the industry takes the definitive step and leaves the physical world behind. This chapter has discussed some aspects of how this transformation continues, and how access-based music services play a substantial role in this process. The chapter has also touched upon how the recorded music becomes increasingly marginalized as a revenue source and how other industry segments such as live music and music licensing become increasingly significant. Finally, it has also presented how the audiences' relationships with music change as a part of this transformation and how services and features that allow users to play *with* music rather than merely to play music move into center stage of the music industry in the digital age.

References

Amaral, Adriana, Simone Pereira
de Sá, and Marjorie Kibby.
"Friendship, Recommendation
    and Consumption on a
    Music-Based Social Network
    Site." Presented at the AOIR
    Conference, Milwaukee,
    Wisconsin, 2009.

Baym, Nancy K.
"Friends or Fans?: Seeing
    Social Media Audiences as
    Musicians Do." *Participations*
    9, no. 2 (2012): 286–316.

Wikström, Patrik.
*The Music Industry: Music in the
    Cloud*. 2nd ed. Cambridge,
    UK: Polity Press, 2013.

Games and the Internet:
Fertile Ground for Cultural Change

Edward Castronova

Professor of Telecommunications, Indiana University

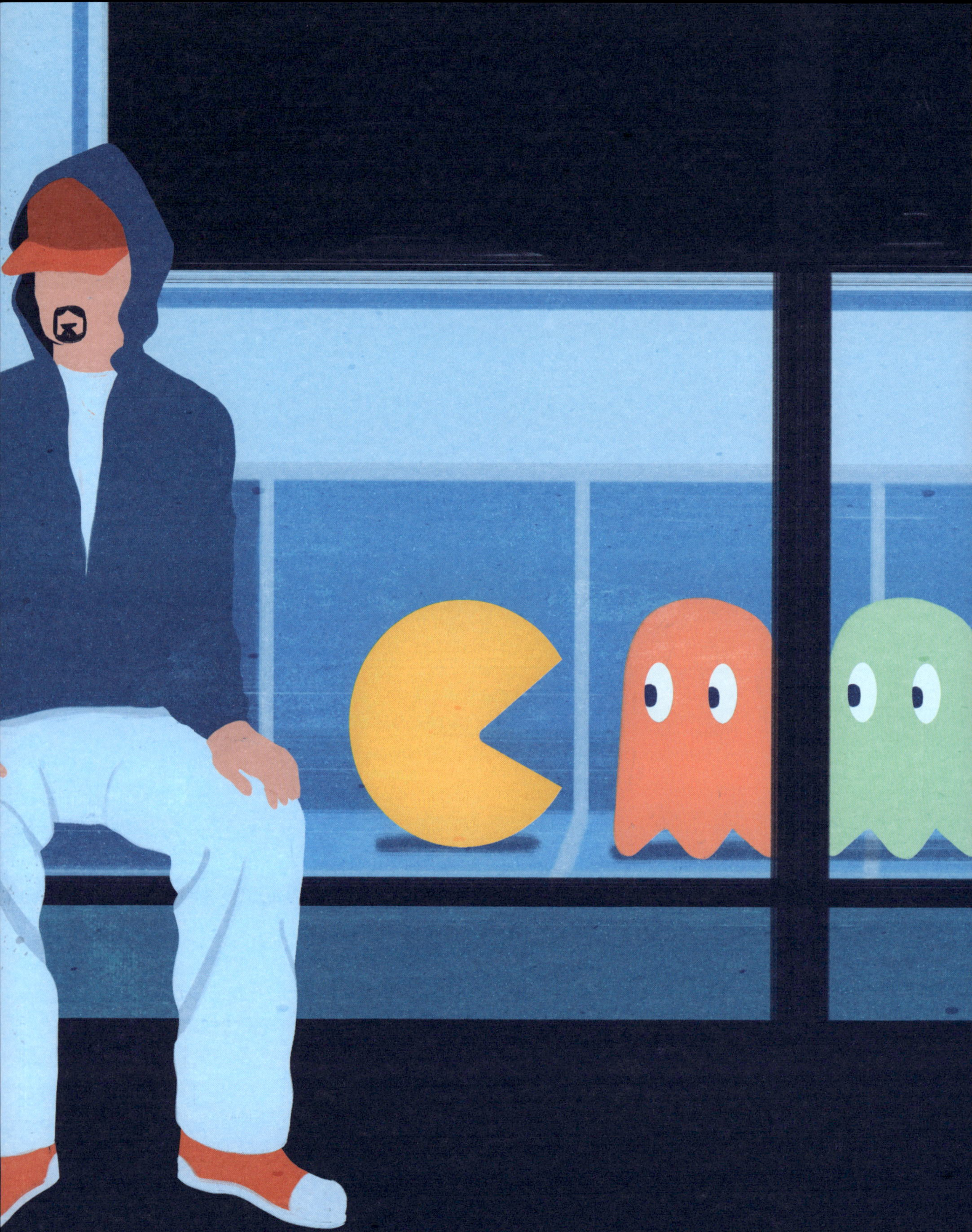

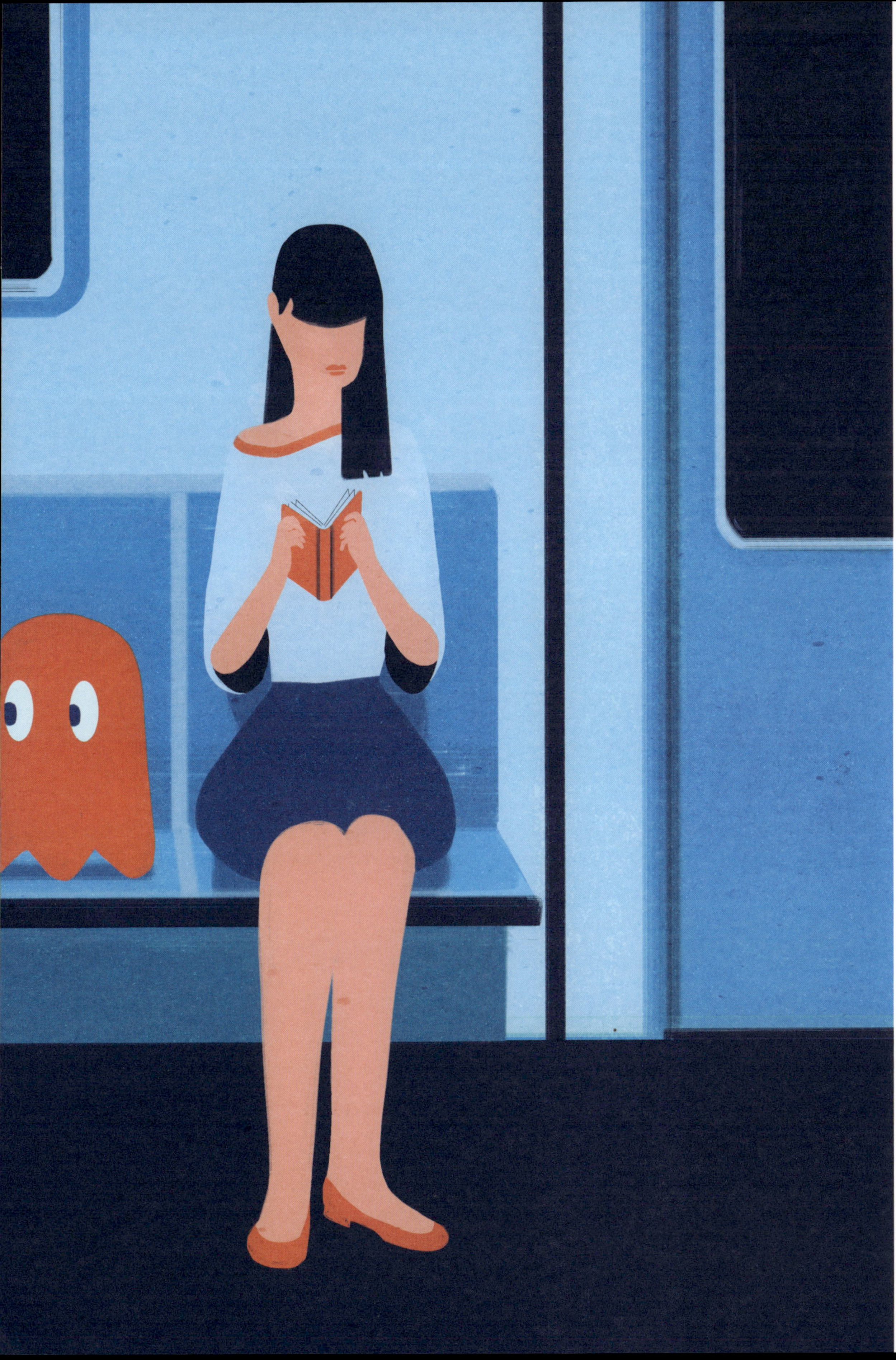

Edward Castronova

Games and the Internet: Fertile Ground for
Cultural Change

Edward Castronova
mypage.iu.edu/~castro/home.html

Illustration
Emiliano Ponzi

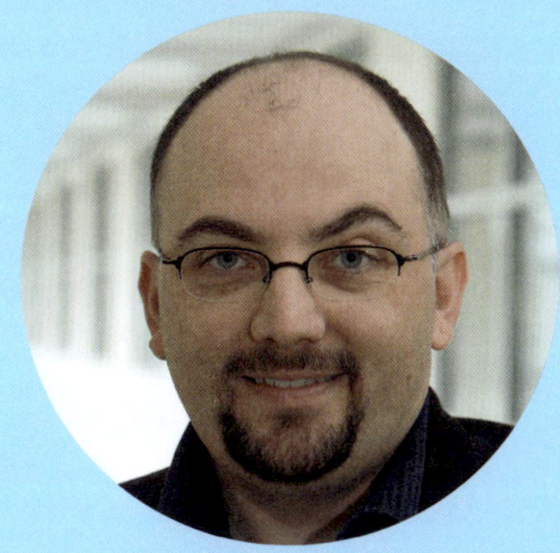

Edward Castronova is Professor of Telecommunications at Indiana University and holds a PhD in Economics from the University of Wisconsin-Madison. Professor Castronova specializes in the study of games, technology, and society. Notable works include *Synthetic Worlds: The Business and Culture of Online Games* (University of Chicago Press, 2005), *Exodus to the Virtual World* (Palgrave Macmillan, 2007), *Virtual Economies: Analysis and Design* (with Vili Lehdonvirta, MIT Press, forthcoming), and *Wildcat Currency: The Virtual Transformation of the Economy* (Yale University Press, forthcoming).

Sites and services that have changed my life
everquest.com
ssrn.com
google.com

Games and the Internet: Fertile Ground for Cultural Change

Introduction

There has been much interest in recent years in online games as an economic and social force. Virtual currencies such as Bitcoin were first created inside online games, and have been the focus of a significant study by the ECB (2012). Many researchers and policy analysts are interested in using games for serious purposes. There are games for education, games for science, games for health, and games for public policy.[1] Meanwhile, the commercial digital game sector remains very strong, even as other media industries suffer decline.[2]

All of this activity suggests that many observers believe that games represent a powerful cultural force. Games are not like previous media, which were largely passive. Games entertain people by allowing them to act. People watching TV may change their minds, but people playing games change their minds while doing something. Often, the things gamers are doing are not very significant. What if the game design allows their actions to be significant? We live in an age in which a large number of simple clicks can change the world. Can games generate such a world-changing wave action?

I will address this question first by considering the nature of cultural change. Then I will discuss recent research into the cultural impact of games. Finally I will place games in the context of the Internet. I conclude

1.   For example, *Darfur is Dying* puts players in the role of a person in the suffering Darfur region in Africa; *Foldit* lets players fold proteins to minimize energy use; *PlayMoolah* teaches you how to manage money; *SmartDiet* helps people manage weight.

2.   U.S. music industry revenue was $38b in 2000 and has fallen to $16b. U.S. movie revenues have remained between $10b and $11b since 2009. Global TV ad spending was up 4.3 percent in 2012–13 while newspaper ad revenue is off more than 80 percent since 2000. Game-related sales topped $21b in 2012 and are growing at 10 percent per year (Blodget 2012; Nielsen 2013; Pfanner 2013; Smith 2012; ESA 2013).

by suggesting that, now that games have been unleashed on the Internet, they have great potential to create vast cultural change.

Cultural Change

I will adopt a game-theoretic approach to culture (Boyd and Richerson 1988). Culture, in game-theoretic terms, is a state of social equilibrium regarding symbols (Schelling 1960). The symbol + has meaning only insofar as all users of the symbol agree on the meaning. In our world and our time, + refers to the additive operation in mathematics. It has this meaning only because everyone agrees on this meaning. There is however no necessary connection between the symbol and the meaning. The same process that makes + a sign for addition could just as easily make it into a sign for a sound. We could write the letter *a* as + and, so long as everyone understood the underlying meaning, no meaning would be lost. There is no theoretical difference between "The man sat on his chair" and "The m+n s+t on his ch+ir." There is an immense cultural difference between the two sentences, however. One culture refers to the letter *a* with "a" and the other refers to it with "+."

Cultural differences have large practical effects. Two people who do not share the same understanding of symbols must spend time negotiating the meaning of terms. There may be misunderstandings, which may lead to mistrust or even war.

In game-theoretic terms, culture is the result of a large interlocking set of coordination games. In a coordination game, people do best by doing what others do. Driving is a good example. In most countries, you drive on the right side of the road. This makes sense because everyone else drives on the right side of the road. If you chose to drive on the left, you would get into a terrible accident. Nobody likes accidents, therefore everybody conforms to the simple rule "Drive on the right." However, there is no theo-retical difference between this rule and the opposite rule, "Drive on the left." In some countries, "Drive on the left" operates with all the force and power as "Drive on the right" does in most countries. These two rules are exactly the same in their power and expression, but radically different in their effect on behavior. Driving is a coordination game with two outcomes,

Left and Right. Neither outcome is *better* than the other. Each is equal. They just require coordination on different behavior.

Cultural change is the process by which a culture coordinates on a new set of behavior. This has two aspects, innovation and adoption.

Innovation

In order for a culture to change, someone in the culture must conceive of a new point of cultural equilibrium. This is not mere fantasizing. Cultural forms that cannot happen are not credible. Dreams about cultural forms that are not feasible are the bugbear of many idealists, but there is a difference between idealists and innovators.

A cultural innovation is a cultural equilibrium that is not in force now but could be. In a right-driving country, left-driving would be such an innovation. Innovations can emerge in several ways. They may spontaneously come to the minds of several or many people at once. It has been said that most people in Eastern Europe in the 1970s and 1980s were aware that a quasi-capitalist society would probably be better than communism. It was not a movement so much as a general awareness.

Innovations may spring from the mind of an inspired theorist or an inspired intellectual tradition. This seems to have been the case with the notion of elected representative democracy, which had its roots in Europe as far back as ancient Greece but was driven along by such people as the nobles who wrote the Magna Carta, the Protestant reformers, and the Enlightenment philosophers.

Innovations may occur when a group of people establish their culture in a way that the rest of society does not. At times this is explicit, as when Amish folk in the United States purposefully keep themselves apart from the broader culture. At other times it is accidental. Christianity somehow came to Ireland in the third and fourth centuries AD and developed an ecclesial organization based on monastic houses rather than the system of bishoprics which was the norm everywhere else. When the Celtic Christians encountered the Roman Orthodox Christians in northern Britain in the sixth century, the Synod of Whitby was called to bring the two practices into conformity.

Finally, cultural innovations may be explicitly designed as such. Religious reformers designed ideal communities—most failures—with the explicit goal of showing the rest of the world how living is to be done.

The advent of advanced communications made possible strategies of *propaganda* and *tactical media* with the explicit intent to change how a culture thinks, works, and judges.

Adoption

Cultural change occurs when a cultural innovation is adopted by society at large. It becomes the new equilibrium. In order for that to happen, people must change their behavior. And in order for behavior to change, people must first change their minds.

The role of expectations

In game theory, expectations of behavior have a critical effect on which of a number of possible equilibria actually occurs. If a person expects that everyone else will drive on the right, she will drive on the right also. If she expects everyone else to drive on the left, she will drive on the left. Everyone thinks this way. The right-driving equilibrium occurs because of the universal expectation that it will occur. If the universal expectation were left-driving, then left-driving would occur. In cultural affairs, expectations create the conditions for their own fulfillment.

Gradual change

Cultural change then involves changing expectations. Some times this happens gradually. Consider inflation. Inflation is a process whereby the common understanding of how much a piece of currency is worth changes over time. It is, today, a purely cultural affair. Money is no longer backed by a specific real item, such as gold or silver.[3] Money has value simply

3. Or beaver pelts, as once was
the case in Finland.

because we all expect it to have value. Because of that expectation, we accept money in exchange for real goods and services. We do this only because we expect other people to accept our money in turn. However, every year, the money loses a little bit of value. Most advanced forms of money experience inflation of 1 to 5 percent every year. It is too small for most people to notice. Yet over the course of several decades, the change in the value of money appears quite substantial. In America, a pound of hamburger cost $1.39 in 1981; today it costs more than $3.00.[4] There has been no major change in the economics of cow-making or the demand for beef. The price change is largely the change in the value of money.

Cultures can change slowly and gradually. Everyone shares the same understanding of a concept, and everyone has similar expectations about the behavior of others, but, these understandings and expectations shift slowly over time.

Certain innovations can spread this way. Fashion is an example. It was once the case that every professional person had to wear uncomfortable clothing. Anyone who did not was treated with disrespect. Fashion is like that. Any thinking person is aware that clothing is meaningless, yet it is understood that clothing choices express a certain stance about clothing. As a result, clothes are taken to be a measure of how well the wearer understands social affairs. Attire may make one out to be a rebel, or strange person, a conformist, a professional, a leader, or simply an idiot. Just what kind of clothing is required to trigger these judgments, however, changes gradually every year. Fashion innovators are acutely aware of their role in generating new standards and propagating them.

Abrupt change: revolution and policy

Culture can change rapidly as well. This can come from the ground up as in the East European revolutions of 1989. It can also happen as a result of policy. In 1967, Sweden changed from driving on the left to driving on the right. It was done all at once. At 4:50 a.m. on September 3, 1967, all

4.   A Thanksgiving brunch at a Hilton Hotel was $11.95 per person in 1981. In 2013, it cost $32.95. Compare http://www. gti.net/mocolib1//prices/1981. html#thanksgiving and http:// www.sandestinbeachhilton.com/ events

Swedes stopped driving on the left. For the next ten minutes, they were not allowed to drive at all. Then at 5:00 a.m., the Swedes all began driving on the right.

Underlying conditions largely determine whether cultural change is gradual or abrupt. When culture can change gradually, it generally does so. In a few cases, however, gradual change is not possible, and in these cases only abrupt change can happen.

When is gradual change impossible? It is impossible when it is strictly disadvantageous or even dangerous for one person or a small group of people to change their behavior. This is clearly the case with driving. Any one person or small group of people living in a right-driving society that suddenly decided to drive on the left would soon be injured or killed by car accidents. It was also the case in Eastern Europe in the 1970s and 1980s. Although everyone knew that the current system was not very good, any one person who said something would be sent off to jail. So no one spoke. This continued until Gorbachev started speaking openly of *glasnost* and *perestroika*, signaling that those who proposed change would not be hustled away. At that point, everyone began speaking; everyone became aware that everyone felt communism was doomed; therefore everyone's expectations of the future of communism changed from *perpetual* to *doomed*; therefore, everyone's behavior shifted from "Accept things as they are" to "prepare for the end of communism"; therefore communism was doomed. It went away very quickly.

In circumstances where it is impossible or dangerous for one person to make a change, the possibility of change is still there but it remains latent.

Change requires some common signal, indicating to the whole society that it is now time to jump into a new world. Such times are called revolutions.

Those who live through revolutions often remark on their sense of amazement, how things that seemed so impossible only days before should suddenly become not only possible but completely normal. And vice versa:

they also express amazement that omnipresent behaviors were suddenly banished from the world overnight, as if by magic.[5]

Of course cultural change is not magic. It proceeds according to known forces involving expectations and behavior. How are these things affected by games?

Games and Culture

Games are powerful cultural artifacts. Games instantiate play. Play can occur without a game, but when you put a game in action, play will generally occur. Games are a tool by which to bring play to bear on a situation, and play is believed by many scholars to be a critical driving force in social and cultural affairs.

Play and the origins of culture

Robert Bellah has recently written an exhaustive study of the origins of religion prior to the rise of modern civilization. Bellah's theoretical framework places play at the center of culture. In so doing, he continues a line of thought that goes back as least as far as Johan Huizinga (1938) and includes many astute critics and commenters (Borges 1941; Caillois 1958; Baudrillard 1981; Eco 1988; Sutton-Smith 1997).

The essence of this reasoning is this: when people play, they step formally into a world of make believe. In this make-believe world, anything is possible. Unlike fantasy, which is a mental place inhabited only by the person doing the fantasizing, play is inhabited by many people at once.

5.   I once spoke to a German woman who was 12 when World War II ended. "We started school every day with 'Heil Hitler.' Then one day it was just 'Guten Morgen, Herr Professor.' And that was it!"

It is therefore a site of collective fantasy. In these collective fantasies, people can become aware of new possibilities for the culture of the real world.

In America, for many years of the twentieth century and perhaps earlier there was a tradition called the Sadie Hawkins Dance. For a Sadie Hawkins Dance, the girls invited the boys. This reversed the usual social role. In so doing, the Sadie Hawkins Dance exposed all members of society to the simple idea that there is actually no good reason at all why a girl could not ask a boy to attend a dance. After a Sadie Hawkins Dance, the boys and girls could see that it was not the end of the world for the sexes to be equal. Suggested and implemented as a moment of harmless play, the Sadie Hawkins Dance enabled a large-scale awareness of the possibility of a different equilibrium, one that is certainly no worse than the current one and perhaps even better. It was a site of cultural innovation.

Another way to see the cultural importance of play is to recognize that most of serious society involves some sort of coordination. We are all danc-ing with one another, attempting to operate under shared principles, or, if in an innovative mode, we are attempting to influence how others will dance. All the social world bears a veneer of imaginary significance, a fact that has been highlighted by writers from Shakespeare to Borges. Even the serious parts of culture are infused with the same sort of coordination problems as are made explicit when we play. The rules of the game are *everywhere*.

The shift from emergent games to designed games

Through most of human history, play was an informal emergent property of human social behavior. When embodied in ritual and protocol, play become more formal but was still emergent. There is no identifiable moment in human history when a known person announced that worship of the gods will involve a public sacrifice. The innovation is buried in the mists of time.[6]

6. My sons play a game called Four Square at their school. One day they asked me who invented it. My reply was, "Nobody. Four Square just lives there." Cultural equilibria are similar to living organisms in which we humans are the component parts. As the children come and go, Four Square molds them into a recognizable pattern. Four Square also induces them to copy its rules and transmit them to new children. Thus the form of Four Square is passed on from year to year. The game rules are like DNA, the children are like proteins, and the playground during a Four Square game is like a cell.

With advanced civilization, however, the design of play opportunities became like everything else: a formal and conscious affair. While no one knows who designed chess, we do know who designed Monopoly, and when. Objects intended to facilitate play, such as balls, came to be explicitly and evenly scientifically designed in pursuit of a formal performance expectation.

Today, the share of all play that stems from emergent practice as opposed to designed games is quite small. When people play, they are following rules conceived by someone in recent history.

Those rules, as before, structure their behavior. But now there is a consciousness behind the manipulation. If play is now designed, then behavior is now being manipulated by a designer.

The personality and intentions of game designers have come into high relief. Distinctions are made between commercial designers, who generally just want to make an honest living, and serious game designers, who are trying to make the world a better place. There are also the *indie* designers who make games for the sake of the art. All of these designers compete with one another for the play time of the people, which in our age is increasingly gladly given.

Games and the Internet

The Internet does not change what games are but it makes them vastly more effective at what they do.

Persistence and scale

With computers and the Internet, a game can now be kept going on a persistent basis for all time among millions of people. It used to be that only the *real* world had that property. You used to be able to identify games by their short time frame, limited geographic area, and small number of players. No more.

Computer games already exist that cover many thousands of square miles; that continue for more than a decade; and that involve more than 10 million players at a time.

This is just for *existing* games. Current technology would allow much bigger achievements. The commercial game industry has every incentive to push outward on all these dimensions, and it certainly will.

What happens when a game gets so big it is indistinguishable from real life? Borges (1941) speculated about this quite a bit. The core mechanics of society and games are the same; both involve a certain kind of dance or coordination among all the people. The only real difference used to be that games were small, local, and limited. Since they are no longer restricted in this way, there is no reason why games could not grow to such a scale that they replace important aspects of the real world. At sufficient scale, a game could *become* the real world.

This may be going too far, of course. Leaving this gargantuan possibility aside, then, we will focus below on games as a site of innovation. The point to take away here is simply that very big, very long, very populous games can look an awful lot like a real social world, a real culture.

The maker revolution

The Internet has also introduced a further development in the production of games. I said above that play was once emergent and is now largely designed. The profession *game designer* has come into being. But already things are changing again. New software products are emerging that allow anybody to make games for anyone else.[7] This development seems to parallel developments in music and film, whereby just about anybody can make a music video or a short film. This kind of creativity will not be the exclusive domain of professionals. Lots of people will get into the act.

7. Construct 2 for example costs only $60 and can be used to make an incredibly wide variety of games.

When millions and millions of people make small things on the Internet, one of them eventually blows up and makes a difference. The explosion is completely unpredictable, except in the sense that we know an explosion will happen.

Where, who, when, of what content—no one can tell. Thus we cannot begin to predict what kind of huge and hugely popular games may be invented in the near future.

How Game Designers Will Change the World

If we put these strands together, a picture emerges in which culture changes dramatically as a result of Internet games.

Games as sites of innovation

A large, persistent game is a very good site for cultural innovation. A game is generally a safe space; all agree that the game is just a game, and that nothing in the game really matters. Therefore people feel more free to experiment and express themselves in new ways.

If individuals feel a sense of freedom in games, so do groups of people. If one person innovates a practice, other people are more likely to assess it fairly and perhaps even adopt it—simply because it does not matter. If a group of *different* people emerges, there is no particular reason for them to fear persecution as a result of their behavior. It is just a game, after all.

With an Internet game, the scope of such innovation groups is very large. They could acquire thousands and thousands of people from around the globe, and they could persist safely for many years. In a large game, such a group could expose many millions of others to its behavior. All of this makes adoption by the real world more likely.

Adoption could follow one of two paths.

Gradual

Some in-game behaviors may involve subtle changes in behavioral expectation outside of the game. For example, it is common in games for men to use female characters and women to use male characters. It is therefore not strange to encounter a female character who uses male language patterns, and vice versa. A person who spends much time in games where this is true may gradually change his expectations of language outside the game, and not be particularly shocked by a woman who happens to talk like a man.

This seems to be the case with virtual currencies. In games it became common over the years to trade real money for virtual money that was valid only in a certain game. Despite its virtual character, people came to expect that game gold would have a persistent value. As a result of this shift in expectations, people are more willing to trade in virtual currencies like Bitcoin and the Amazon Coin.

In such cases, practices spawned in games may spread slowly into the outside world.

Abrupt

Conversely, there may be a great leap. A designer may produce a superior way of life that is quite feasible for people today yet utterly incompatible with current culture. In this case we would expect the game population to grow and grow, while the outside world does not change. Then at some tipping point, the outside world would leap with both feet into the new way of living.

Thus games may be seen as incubators of major cultural change.

Conclusion

The role of designer comes into high relief indeed. People who make Internet games today have the power to change our cultural world. Perhaps they will create a small change that seeps into our daily lives, changes our expectations slowly and subtly until one day, decades later, we suddenly realize that our culture has changed forever. Or perhaps a designer may invent a very new and very wonderful world that solves many of our problems and helps us to live as people ought to live. A tension will arise between the in-worlders and the out-worlders; it will be resolved in favor of the in-worlders eventually, but not without a great deal of stress.

Who will make these wonderful new worlds? Perhaps game designers; perhaps elite creators in other fields. But we can expect ordinary people to come to the fore eventually. An isolated genius, probably already alive today, will design the game that changes our lives forever.

As empowered by the Internet, games today are a demonstration infrastructure for that new City on a Hill. Many such Cities will be built, and some will directly point the way to our future.

References

Baudrillard, Jean.
Simulacres et simulation. Paris: Galilée, 1981. English: *Simulacra and Simulation*, 1994.

Blodget, Henry.
"For Whom the Bell Tolls? It Tolls for TV." *Business Insider*, October 19, 2012. http://www.businessinsider.com/for-whom-the-bell-tolls-it-tolls-for-tv-2012-10

Borges, Jorge Luis.
"La lotería en Babilonia." *Sur*, January 1941. English: "The Lottery in Babylon," 1962.

Boyd, Robert, and Peter J. Richerson.
Culture and the Evolutionary Process. Chicago: University of Chicago Press, 1988.

Caillois, Roger.
Les jeux et les hommes. Paris: Gallimard: 1958. English: *Man, Play, and Games*, 1961.

ECB (European Central Bank).
"Virtual Currency Schemes." European Central Bank, October 2012. http://www.ecb.europa.eu/pub/pdf/other/virtualcurrencyschemes201210en.pdf

Eco, Umberto.
Il pendolo di Foucault. Milan: Bompiani, 1988. English: *Foucault's Pendulum*, 1989.

ESA (Entertainment Software Association).
"Industry Facts: Economic Data." Entertainment Software Association. http://www.theesa.com/facts/econdata.asp (accessed September 9, 2013).

Huizinga, Johan.
Homo Ludens. Proeve eener bepaling van het spel-element der cultuur. Haarlem: Tjeenk Willink, 1938. English: *Homo Ludens: A Study of the Play-Element in Culture*, 1949.

Nielsen Company.
"Newswire: The Small Screen Captured Big Ad Revenue in 2012." Nielsen Newswire, April 18, 2013. http://www.nielsen.com/us/en/newswire/2013/the-small-screen-captured-big-ad-revenue-in-2012.html

Pfanner, Eric.
"Music Industry Sales Rise, and Digital Revenue Gets the Credit." *New York Times*, February 26, 2013. http://www.nytimes.com/2013/02/27/technology/music-industry-records-first-revenue-increase-since-1999.html?_r=0

Schelling, Thomas C.
The Strategy of Conflict. Cambridge, MA: Harvard University Press, 1960.

Smith, Grady.
"Box Office Report 2012: Film Industry Climbs to Record-Breaking $10.8 Billion." *Entertainment Weekly*, December 31, 2012. http://insidemovies.ew.com/2012/12/31/box-office-report-2012/

Sutton-Smith, Brian.
The Ambiguity of Play. Cambridge, MA: Harvard University Press, 1997.

Appendix

Publisher
BBVA

Project direction and coordination
Chairman's Advisory, BBVA

Texts
Yochai Benkler, Federico Casalegno, Manuel Castells, Edward Castronova, David Crystal, Zaryn Dentzel, Paul DiMaggio, Lucien Engelen, David Gelertner, Peter Hirshberg, Mikko Hypponen, Thomas Malone, Evgeny Morozov, Michael Nielsen, Dan Schiller, Neil Selwyn, Juan Ignacio Vázquez, Patrik Wikström

Illustrations
Ignacio Molano, Emiliano Ponzi, Catell Ronca, Pieter van Eonoge, and Eva Vázquez

Publishing coordination
Turner

Graphic design
David Cano

Layout
Myriam López Consalvi

Translations
Mike Escarzaga (F. González and J. I. Vázquez)

Copyediting
Jonathan Fox

Printing
Artes Gráficas Palermo

Binding
Ramos

© of the publication, BBVA, 2013
© of the texts, their respective authors, 2013
© of the illustrations, their respective authors, 2013

ISBN: 978-84-15832-45-4
DL: M-30728-2013
Printed in Spain

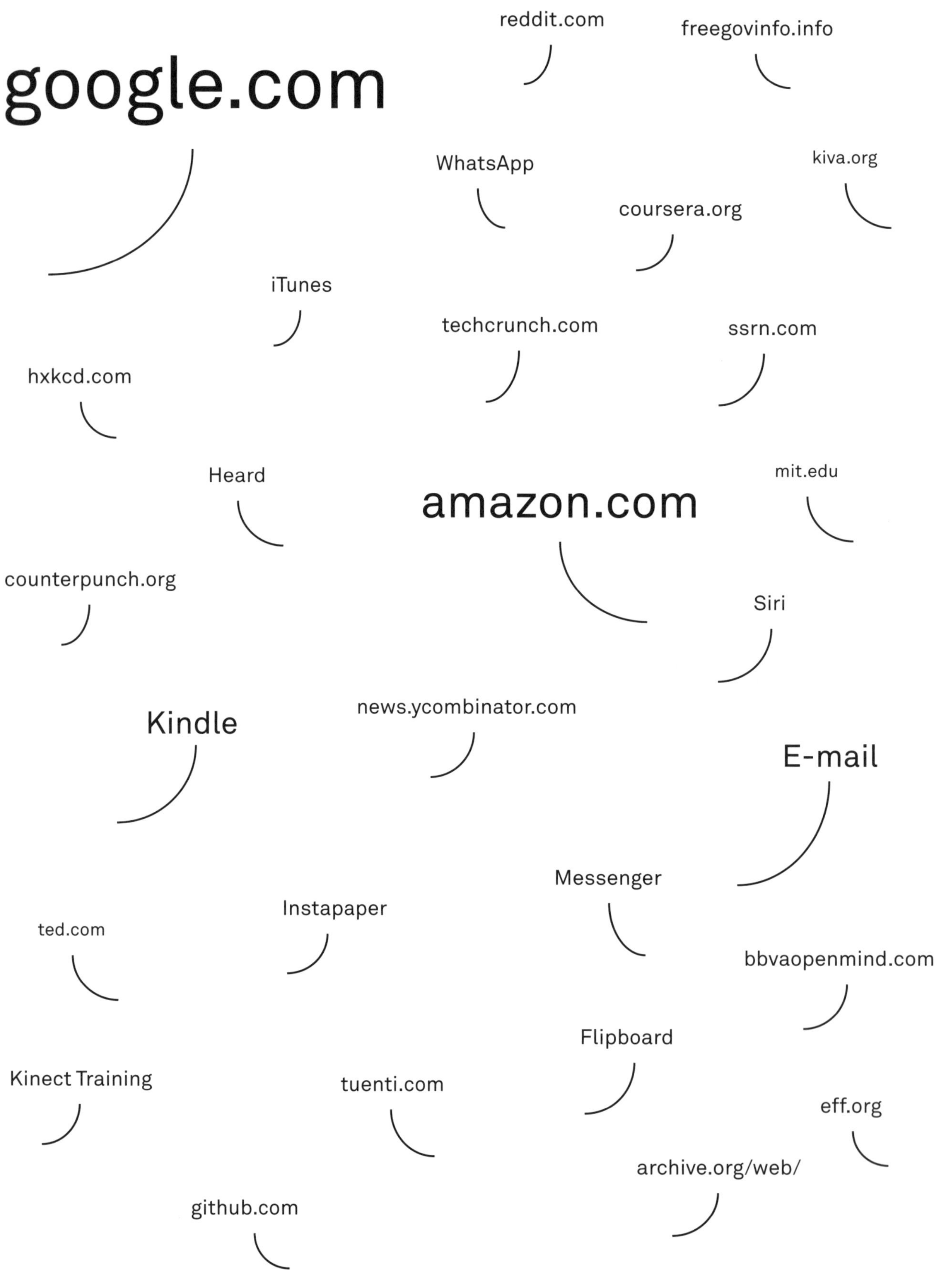

reddit.com
freegovinfo.info
google.com
WhatsApp
kiva.org
coursera.org
iTunes
techcrunch.com
ssrn.com
hxkcd.com
Heard
amazon.com
mit.edu
counterpunch.org
Siri
Kindle
news.ycombinator.com
E-mail
Messenger
ted.com
Instapaper
bbvaopenmind.com
Kinect Training
Flipboard
tuenti.com
eff.org
archive.org/web/
github.com

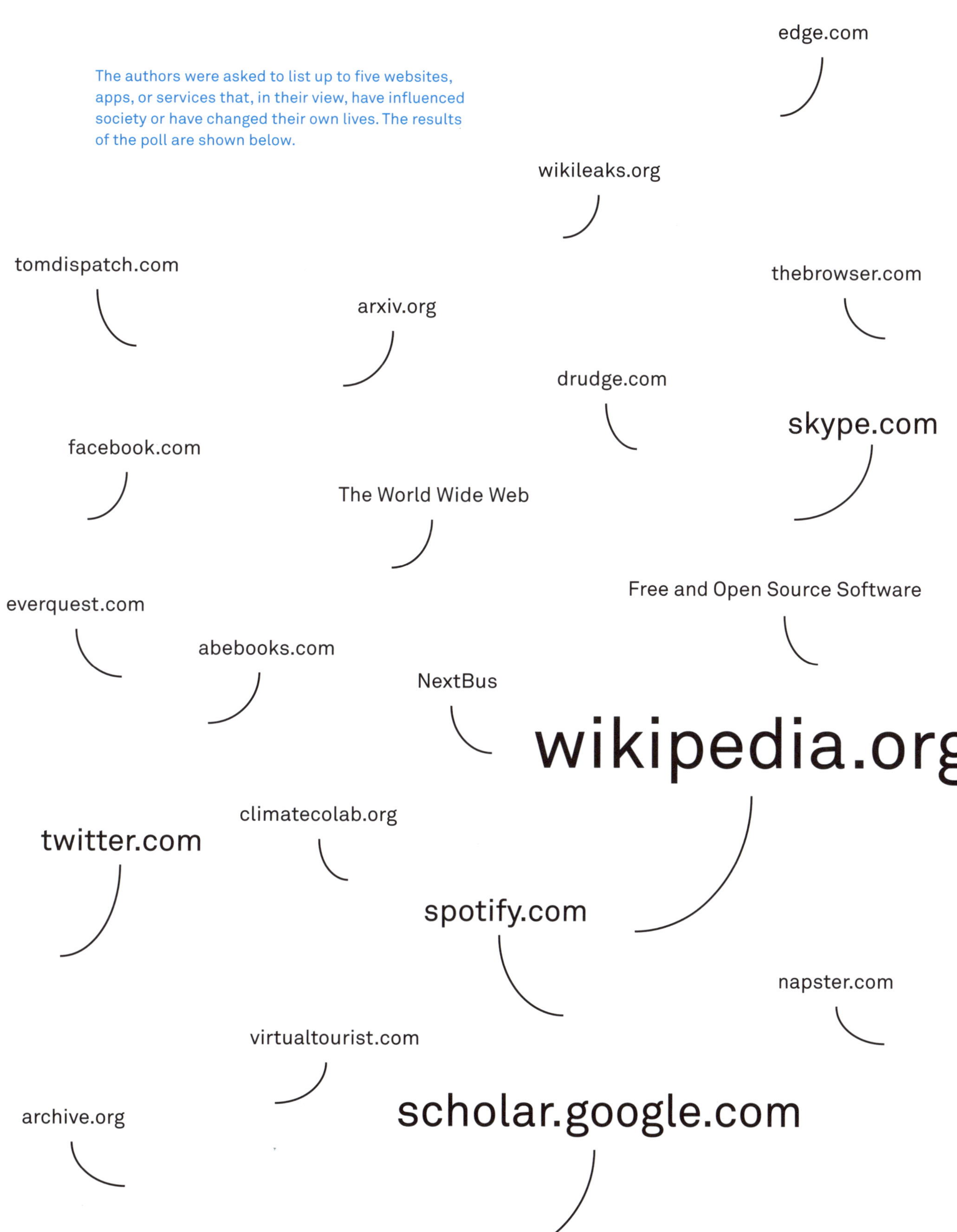

The authors were asked to list up to five websites, apps, or services that, in their view, have influenced society or have changed their own lives. The results of the poll are shown below.
edge.com
wikileaks.org
tomdispatch.com
thebrowser.com
arxiv.org
drudge.com
skype.com
facebook.com
The World Wide Web
Free and Open Source Software
everquest.com
abebooks.com
NextBus
wikipedia.org
twitter.com
climatecolab.org
spotify.com
napster.com
virtualtourist.com
archive.org
scholar.google.com

468

Sites and Services That Have Changed our Lives